D1789531

SCOTT.

1995 U.S. FIRST DAY COVER CATALOGUE and CHECKLIST

by Michael A. Mellone

Complete Up-to-date Catalogue

VICE PRESIDENT/PUBLISHER ....Stuart J. Morrissey
EDITOR ....William W. Cummings
ASSISTANT EDITOR ....James E. Kloetzel
VALUING EDITOR ....Martin J. Frankevicz
NEW ISSUES EDITOR...David C. Akin
COMPUTER CONTROL COORDINATOR ....Denise Oder
VALUING ANALYST ....Jose R. Capote
EDITORIAL ASSISTANTS...................Judith E. Bertrand, Beth Brown
CONTRIBUTING EDITOR..Joyce Nelson
ART/PRODUCTION DIRECTOR.............................Janine C. S. Apple
PRODUCTION COORDINATOR .... Meg Schultz
PRODUCTION ARTIST...Cinda McAlexander
SALES MANAGER ....Bill Fay
ADVERTISING ....David Lodge
CIRCULATION/PRODUCT PROMOTION MANAGER ....Tim Wagner

CONTENTS

ACKNOWLEDGEMENTS

Appreciation and gratitude go to the following individuals who have assisted us in preparing information included in this catalogue. These individuals have generously shared their knowledge with others through the medium of this work. Those whose names follow have provided information that is in addition to the many dealer price lists and advertisements, as well as auction results, which were used in producing the 1995 Scott U.S. First Day Catalogue. Support from these people goes beyond data leading to catalogue values, for they also are key to editorial changes: Gil Celli, Larry Graf, Steve Levine, Scott Pelcyger, Alan Piscina, William Geijsbeek and Edward Siskin.

THE "COVERS" ON THE "COVER"

The front cover shows three winners in the 1993 American First Day Cover Society Cachetmakers Contest. This contest judges first day cover and event cachets in eleven categories, and has been held annually since 1991.

The Elvis first day cover in the center is the "Best Cachet of 1993." The cachet was completely handdrawn and handpainted by Elain Thompson. The clown bursting through the envelope by Gary Koter is a winner in Category 1, which judged handdrawn and handpainted cachets. The 1993 Michigan State Duck Cover by Fred Collins is a winner in Category 7, for the Best Duck Cover.

The American First Day Cover Society is a non-profit organization of collectors who just "love" FDCs. Membership includes a subscription to the award winning journal *First Days*. For more information on all of the services offered to first day cover collectors, send a SASE to Mrs. M.S. Eiserman, 14359 Chadbourne, Houston, TX 77079.

7A

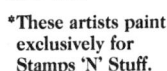

HOW TO USE THIS CATALOGUE

Sample Listing

SCOTT NUMBER	DESCRIPTION	UNCACHETED SGL	BLK	CACHETED SGL	BLK
	1923				
☐☐ 610	**2c Warren G. Harding,** 9/1/23, DC	30.00	35.00		
☐☐	Marion, OH (5,000)	20.00	22.50		
☐☐	Brooklyn, NY; Mt. Rainier, MD; Caledonia, OH (Unofficial cities)	37.50			
☐☐	**Pre-date,** 8/31/23, DC, (1 known)	250.00			
☐☐	1st George W. Linn cachet (1st modern cachet)			800.00	

The first number is the Scott catalogue number. This is followed by the denomination and subject. Next is the official first day (FD) date, 9/1/23, and the official FD city, Washington, D.C. which normally is listed only as "DC."

Marion, Ohio is another official FD city. Some issues have more than one official FD city. The number after Marion, Ohio, is the approximate number of covers canceled there on the FD. There's no number after the Washington, D.C. listing because it is not known.

Listed next is "Caledonia, Ohio, unofficial." This listing is for a cover postmarked on the first day of issue in Caledonia, Ohio, which was not an official FD city. Often collectors have purchased stamps in the official FD city and taken them to other cities to create "unofficial" FDCs.

Unofficial cities from which cancellations are obtained on the FD normally add to the value of the FDC, when the value is compared to that of the official city. Often a special slogan cancel, related to the new stamp, will be available on the FD. Even when these are from the official city, they are valued as unofficials on FDCs since 1940.

A **Pre-dated FDC** or Pre-FDC is a stamp or stamps on cover with a postmark before the official first day of issue.

A **1st Cachet** is simply the first cachet that a particular cachet maker has produced. Only the most prominent are listed in this catalogue. The total number could exceed 2,000.

CATALOGUE VALUES

Catalogue Values shown in this book are retail prices. A value represents what you could expect to pay for the cover. The values listed are a reference which reflects recent actual dealer selling prices drawn from retail lists and auction realizations.

A catalogue value in italics suggests that not enough information was available to establish a firm value, and the italicized number is as close an estimate as we could ascertain.

Use this catalogue as a guide in your own buying and selling. The actual price you pay for a cover may be higher or lower than the catalogue value because of one or more of the following: the amount of personal service a dealer offers, increased interest in the cachet maker or time period when the stamp was issued, whether an item is a "loss leader," part of a special sale, or otherwise is being sold for a short period of time at a lower price, or if at a public auction you are able to obtain a cover inexpensively because of little interest in the cover at that time.

Minimum catalogue value

The minimum value for an item in this catalogue is one dollar. For items where the stamp or item of postal stationery has a face value of 25 cents or more, the minimum value is $1.25. In all cases, the minimum value is designed to reflect the cost of purchasing a single item from a dealer.

Values by year range

Values for pre-1920 first day covers (FDCs) are for uncacheted FDCs with single stamps, unless otherwise stated. Many early FDCs or earliest known use (EKU or eku) covers are unique. A dash in the value column means that FDCs are seldom found in these categories, or that no market value has been determined through recent sales of the covers.

Before 1920, stamps were not regularly released with an official first day of issue observance. In many of these cases, the catalogue shows the earliest known postal use of the stamp.

Regular issues of 1922-26, Scott 551-600, are valued as uncacheted FDCs with singles and blocks of four stamps or as singles and pairs of stamps.

During the issues of 1923-35, Scott 610-771, cachets on FDCs first appeared. Values are arranged in four columns, giving values for singles and blocks both as uncacheted and cacheted FDCs. FDCs with plate blocks from this period sell for two to three times the price for singles.

From 1935 to date, values are given for common cacheted FDCs with singles, blocks, and plate blocks. Coils are valued as common cacheted FDCs with singles, and pairs (Pr), line pairs (Lp), and plate number coils (PNCs) where appropriate. **Uncacheted covers sell for about 10-15 percent of the catalogue value of common cacheted covers.**

Cacheted FDCs, 1950 (Scott 987) to date values, are for clean unaddressed FDCs with printed cachets. **Addressed FDCs usually sell for about 50-75 percent of catalogue value.**

Values for Cacheted FDCs in this catalogue are for common mass-produced commercial cachets. Specific cachets may sell for several times catalogue value. Values for many various cachets can be found in our Cachet Valuing Calculator section of this book.

EXPLANATION OF ABBREVIATIONS

BLK.........Block of 4 stamps on FDC
DC...........Washington, DC
eku ....earliest known use
FD...........First Day
FDC.........First Day Cover
ln ....line
lp ....Line pair of coil stamps on FDC
PL BLK ...Plate Block on FDC
PNC.........Plate number coil
PR...........Pair of coil stamps on FDC
SGL.........Single stamp on FDC
USPS.......U.S. Postal Service
wmk........watermark

16A

INTRODUCTION TO FDC COLLECTING

WHAT IS A FIRST DAY COVER?

When a new stamp is issued by the U.S. Postal Service (USPS), it is offered for sale in (usually) only a single city on one day and then throughout the country on the second day and thereafter. That date of sale in a single city is designated as the "official" First Day of Issue. It is permissible to purchase stamps at that official city and have the stamps canceled elsewhere on that day, which lead to "unofficial" first day cancellations.

The USPS requires that cancellations may be applied only to those covers which contain enough postage to at least meet the current First Class Mail rate. For newly issued stamps which individually do not meet that rate, multiples of that stamp to "make rate" or that stamp coupled with other stamps to reach the minimum are required.

A special cancel is applied to the new stamp in the official city. These cancellations can never again be duplicated after the grace period allowed by the USPS to secure such postal markrags.

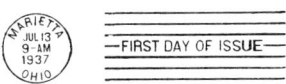

Figure 1. The first official First Day of Issue machine cancel used for the Ordinance of 1787 commemorative (Scott 795) issue July 13, 1937, in Marietta, Ohio, and New York, New York.

In the 1920's and 1930's, FDCs were canceled with everyday working postmarks. The post office first used an official FD postmark with the words "First Day of Issue," in killer bars, for the 1937 Ordinance of 1787 Commemorative (Scott 795). An official "First Day of Issue" machine cancel has been supplied for almost every new issue since.

An official "First Day of Issue" hand cancel was first

used for the first stamps released in the Famous
Americans Series, the 1-cent and 2-cent Authors,
Washington Irving and James Fenimore Cooper (Scott
859-860), both issued January 29, 1940.

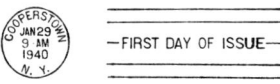

*Figure 2. The first official First Day of Issue hand cancel used
for the 1-cent and 2-cent Famous Americans Authors
(Scott 859-860), issued in Cooperstown or Tarrytown, New York,
on January 29, 1940.*

*Figure 3. The first official pictorial First Day of Issue cancel used
for the Horticulture commemorative (Scott 1100) issued on March
15, 1958, in Ithaca, New York.*

A third type of official FD cancel has been available for
many U.S. new issues. In the 1940's and 1950's this third
type of cancel was a short-bar hand cancel. Now it is a
bull's eye, which is usually identical to the town machine
cancel, without the killer bars or "First Day of Issue" slogan.

Sometimes the stamp with FD postmark can be found on
some other object: postcard, souvenir, piece of wood, bark,
or cloth, or anything that will accept a stamp and postmark.

Most often an FDC is an envelope. Some are just plain
white envelopes. Some bear elaborate and attractive cachets.

WHAT IS A CACHET?
(pronounced ka-SHAY)
A cachet is a design of words and/or pictures which
refers specifically to the new stamp on the FDC. Designs

are usually found on the front, left side of the envelope. They can be printed, rubber stamped, individually hand created, or pasted-on. The purpose of a cachet is to enhance the meaning and appearance of the cover.

WHY COLLECT CACHETED FDCs?

For a long time, collectors wanted an example of every stamp issue on an FDC. They did not really care if the FDC was uncacheted or cacheted, or who made the cachet. If they could find one with an attractive cachet, all the better, but any FDC to fill the space in the collection would do.

Today, many (if not most) collectors don't want just any FDC. They are looking for cacheted FDCs. There are several reasons for this.

Information about cachet collecting has been published and promoted in many places and in many ways. The American First Day Cover Society has promoted FDCs through its magazine First Days for more than 25 years. More recently, several cover-oriented columns have appeared in the philatelic press, helping to generate additional interest. And, there has been a steady upsurge in mass-produced FDCs offered on a subscription basis, each with its own cachet series.

The real reason for the great increase in interest is the collector himself. Collectors have become much more knowledgeable about FDC cachets. They have been captured by the quest for new cachets and information about them.

WHAT TO SEEK WHEN BUYING FDCs

When you are buying an FDC, look at the whole cover. It should be in good condition, without tears, wrinkles, stains, or wear. The stamp should not be torn or damaged. The postmark should be legible and it should have the correct FD date.

Many collectors prefer unaddressed FDCs because they are perceived as neater and more attractive. Often the specialist will want to see an address on a cover because it can sometimes help identify the cachet or the servicer of the cover. Occasionally collectors put their own name on previously unaddressed FDCs.

Just because this book emphasizes cacheted FDCs does not mean that uncacheted FDCs are not collectible. A number of the important early FDC servicers, — Adam Bert, C.E. Nickles, and Edward Worden — made many uncacheted FDCs which remain valuable.

Only a small percentage of all pre-1930 FDCs that exist are cacheted, because most collectors and dealers of that period were happy enough to have an uncacheted FDC. Some collectors today prefer uncacheted FDCs because they look more like legitimate pieces of mail than elaborately cacheted covers. Thus, the choice is left to the collector.

When buying cacheted FDCs, seek unusual looking cachets when you can. You will always be able to find the mass-produced commercial cachets for your collection. If you bypass an unusual cachet, however, you may not ever see that cachet offered for sale again.

If you generally collect one of the mass-produced commercial cachets, the same rule applies. Keep your eyes open for unusual color or text varieties.

WHAT ARE THE SPECIALISTS COLLECTING?

Specialists collect in many ways: by cachet maker, by issue, by set, by years or periods of years, and by topic. They collect first cachets, combination FDCs, unofficial FDCs, and hand painted cachets.

If you find a cachet maker whose work you particularly like, you can try to put together an entire run of FDCs. For example, Anderson, Artcraft, and House of Farnam all started producing cachets before 1940. While you may not have too much trouble finding most of the cachets, it will be a challenge to fill in some of the early cachets of any of these three makers. It will be particularly hard to find some of the early cachet color varieties of Anderson and Artcraft.

Some specialists pick out a particular issue or set that they like and try to make a complete collection of cachet varieties. This can be a modern issue, such as a space issue, a Kennedy issue, or an older issue that is of special interest to you. Pick out a stamp issued in your home state, or issued for your profession, or one that is related to one of your other hobbies.

Check the new issue information in any of the stamp periodicals. If there is a new stamp for which the first day of issue is near your home, you might enjoy going to a FD ceremony, collecting all the cachets you can find on that issue, and perhaps producing a cachet for that stamp that you design yourself.

Figure 4. An example of a combination FDC.

Collectors sometimes seek groupings: all FDC cachets of the 3-cent purple-colored stamps of the late 1930's, all cachets of the 28 stamps issued in 1948, and so on. Some specialists collect early uncacheted regular issues or commemoratives by set or for FD postmark varieties.

People also collect by topic - masonic, military, or

professional topics, women's history, national or local history, sesquicentennials, bicentennials, or just about anything else that interests them.

First Cachet collecting has become very popular with FDC specialists. A "first cachet" is simply the initial effort a particular cachet maker has produced. First cachets have been researched, documented, and firmly established for hundreds of cachet makers.

For other cachet makers, the search for the first cachet is still going on. First-cachet collecting is just one of many areas in FDC collecting where the knowledgeable collector can find desirable cachets in dealers' boxes. Very often first cachets are priced the same as the more common mass-produced commercial cachets because the former are not recognized for what they are.

Listings for many first cachets appear under the appropriate Scott number in this catalogue.

A combination FDC is one which has other stamps or labels along with the new stamp. Together the stamps help to tell a more complete story about the new issue.

The stamps or labels should be related thematically, usually by the history or topic of the stamp. For example, a stamp with a bird on it could be accompanied by other U.S. or foreign stamps with birds, or perhaps a wildlife conservation label.

A new stamp issued for an anniversary of statehood could be used in combination with older issues related to the state's history, or other stamps that had FDs in the state. The possibilities are only limited by imagination.

An unofficial FDC is one canceled on the official FD date, but not in the official FD city. An unofficial FDC can be canceled in any city as long as it has a postmark showing the FD date. An unofficial FDC is more meaningful when the city is related to the new issue. These relationships may be historically significant or by name only.

In 1926, Edward Worden prepared a truly classic unofficial FDC for the 13-cent Harrison stamp (Scott 622). He took 500 stamps from Indianapolis, Indiana, one of the official FD cities, to North Bend, Ohio, Harrison's home town.

On the Battle of Fallen Timbers stamp of 1929 (Scott 680), unofficial FDCs are known postmarked in Fallen Timbers, Pennsylvania. The only connection here between the stamp and the unofficial FDC is the town name. There are a number of issues from the 1920's and 1930's which have 50 or more unofficial FDCs known. While all of these unofficials are not related to the new issue, they are still eagerly collected.

A semi-official FDC is canceled in the official city, but with something other than the usual first-day-of-issue slogan or bull's eye cancels. Often these are pictorial cancels, perhaps from a stamp show where the show cancel is used rather than the FD cancel.

Hand-painted cachets are collected because they often have attractive and colorful original artwork. Each FDC represents a lot of time, effort and talent on the part of the cachet maker. Hand-painted FDCs are often difficult to find in dealers' boxes, because they are usually produced in limited quantities. Some of the well-known commercial cachet designers also make handpainted cachets. Ralph Dyer, who designed cachets for Artcraft during the 1930's, produced hand-painted cachets for several decades after that.

HOW TO LEARN MORE ABOUT FDCs

The best way to learn about FDCs is to be in touch with other FDC collectors. Visit them or write to them to exchange information and opinions on covers.

Join the American First Day Cover Society (AFDCS), which publishes the journal First Days eight times per year. The journal contains new issue information, free cover exchange ads, several columns on modern FDCs, and detailed research articles on cachet makers.

The AFDCS also has regular FDC auctions, an annual convention, periodic regional get-togethers, an FDC Expertizing Committee and numerous slide shows on FDCs available on loan. For additional information write AFDCS, c/o M. Eiserman, 14359 Chadbourne, Houston, TX 77079.

HOW TO ACQUIRE CURRENT FDCs

There are several ways that a collector can obtain current FDCs. The collector may service his own FDCs by sending envelopes to the FD city postmaster as new stamps are released. Different unserviced cacheted envelopes can be purchased from local or mail order cover dealers. Or the collector may choose to join a cover club or service offered by many cover dealers, and automatically receive each new FDC.

HOW TO SERVICE YOUR OWN FDCs

Many collectors believe that servicing their own FDCs is what FDC collecting is all about. There is a tremendous feeling of involvement and accomplishment. You may service your own FDCs by purchasing the new stamp when it is available at your local post office, affixing the stamp to your envelope and forwarding the envelope for servicing to the FD post office within 30 days of the issue date.

Your local post office has bulletins on upcoming stamps, their date of issue, and FD city, along with an illustration of the new stamp.

A detailed procedure for servicing your FDCs is outlined below:

Method 1: You affixing your stamps

1. Purchase the new stamp at your local post office as soon as it becomes available, which usually will be one or two days after the FD date. If you cannot obtain the

stamp at your local post office, you may need to visit your nearest post office with a Philatelic Center.

2. Affix the stamp(s) to the upper right corner of the envelope, 1/4-inch from the top and 1/4-inch from the right edge. Pencil address your cover or affix an addressed peelable label near the bottom of the envelope.

3. Send your cover(s) in an outer envelope to the FD city within 30 days after the first day of issue. No payment is necessary.

Method 2: How to join an FDC service

A more convenient method of obtaining current FDCs is to join an FDC new issue service, usually that of a cachet maker, or purchase the FDCs separately from dealers. By subscribing to a service, there is no chance of missing upcoming issues due to oversight. Uncacheted First Day Covers are now available through the USPS Philatelic Fulfillment Service Center.

The postal service will no longer affix stamps to envelopes sent in to FC cities.

There are over 200 different cachet makers who sell their cacheted FDCs for current issues. Some cachet makers produce individually hand-painted cachets in very limited quantities. Also, there are "comic" cachets, "silks" and many others. Some collectors purchase current FDCs from several different cachet makers, adding variety to their collections.

Most cachet makers stock FDCs of past issues, allowing you to add to your collection.

HOW TO MAKE YOUR OWN FIRST DAY COVERS
by B. Wayne Caldwell

A great deal of the fun I have with First Day Covers is making my own limited edition FDCs. While this information is presented to help you prepare your own cachets for the first day of issue of a stamp, the process also is valid for any event for which you would like a postal cancellation as a commemoration. Two of my favorite FDCs are the Barrymores (Scott 2012), issued June 8, 1982, and the Knoxville World's Fair (Scott 2006-2009), issued April 29, 1982.

Here are the steps I follow:

1. First decide how many FDCs you want to make. I prefer to make 100. You may want to do more or less. There are no requirements here. I have chosen 100 as a base because at that level I have found average cost per cover to be reasonable.

The USPS charges for canceling more than 50 covers at a time with handstamp cancels. You may wish to investigate this charge if you choose to prepare covers in such a quantity.

2. Buy a box of No. 6 3/4 envelopes. A nice quality envelope can be purchased reasonably at a paper company or an office supply store.

3. When you purchase the stamps you will be using on the envelopes, be sure to buy a few more than you will need. You may not want to break up the plate number block or any of the other marginal blocks.

4. Make arrangements to have the envelope stamped (you can request this) on the day and in the city where the event took place. If you are not able to attend the event personally, you can provide a return envelope for all the covers you are having canceled. Explain that you want to print on them and do not want any smudges or stains on them.

If you are not able to have the covers returned in a single package, you will need to use a peel off label on each prepared cover with your return address on it. These can be purchased from a stamp shop or office supply store or ordered through the classified ads of the philatelic newspapers.

5. While you are waiting for the envelopes to be returned, decide what you want as the envelope cachet. You are free to use whatever means you want, q.v., commercial printing, hand drawing (color if you want), collage, or even a computer-generated piece of art or art and text. I recommend that you number your "limited-edition" covers, which adds to the later appeal.

6. If you choose to go with a commercial printer, or

even a hobbyist with a printing press, you will need to make your arrangements while the envelopes are being canceled. (Of course, if you prefer, you may wish to have the cachet prepared far enough in advance to send the finished envelope for cancellation. Before committing to a commercial printer, be certain he is able to print on the canceled envelopes. Most of the printers I talked to assure me they can.

When you have completed all of these steps, you will have a group of cachets for your own collection, to trade with others, or to sell. An increasing number of FDC collectors are choosing this route to having an enjoyable time with First Day Covers.

INTRODUCTION TO CACHET COLLECTING

As more and more FDC collectors turn to collecting FDCs by cachet varieties, the question is asked, "Who makes this cachet?" Included in this introduction to cachet collecting is a mini-identifier, with several popular cachet makers of the past 40 years.

Sixty cachet makers are identified and priced in *The Cachet Identifier,* available for $7.95 from FDC Publishing, Box 206D, Stewartsville, NJ 08886, or from your local dealer.

C. Stephen Anderson

C. Stephen Anderson produced cachets for every issue between 1933 and 1979. Anderson cachets are easy to identify. They usually are signed "C. Stephen Anderson" or "CSA" and contain an illustration and some historical information in the text. His cachets are usually one color, with the earliest ones printed in black. Later purple, and then other color varieties, were printed. Many cachets were printed in several different colors.

Figure AND-1
THE FIRST ANDERSON CACHET was prepared for the Oglethorpe Issue of 1933. Anderson cachets can usually be identified by the lettering style and use of scrolls. Most are signed "C. Stephen Anderson" or "CSA."

Artcraft Leo August - Washington Stamp Exchange

Leo August of Washington Stamp Exchange traces the history of Artcraft cachets back to the World's Fair Issue of 1939. The earliest Artcraft cachets were not signed, but can be identified by their usual high quality engraving. Some early Artcraft cachets exist both unsigned and signed with the familiar Artcraft pallet with brush trademark. Most Artcraft FDC cachets since 1940 are signed.

The first Artcraft cachet is not the first cachet produced by Leo August. August started to service FDCs in the late 1920's, and he started producing cachets in the early 1930's. Washington Stamp Exchange cachets of the 1930's were designed by J.W. Clifford, John Coulthard and Ralph Dyer. Many of these cachets are signed by the cachet artist, and occasionally with "WSE."

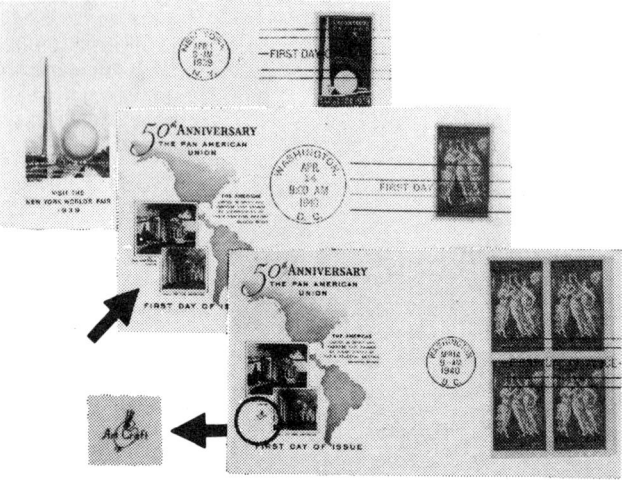

Figure ARC-1
THE FIRST ARTCRAFT CACHET was prepared for the New York World's Fair commemorative issue. This is an engraved cachet, printed in blue. Also shown are two Artcraft varieties for the 1940 Pan American Union commemorative. As with a number of early Artcraft FDCs, the cachet exists both with and without the Artcraft trademark.

Artmaster

Artmaster cachets have been created by Robert Schmidt of Louisville, Kentucky, since 1946. The firm is currently owned and operated by his nephew, Mike Zoeller. The first Artmaster cachet was prepared for the Honorable Discharge Emblem commemorative.

Artmaster cachets can be easily identified because they are high quality engravings signed "Artmaster."

Figure ARM-1
The first Artmaster cachet

W.G. Crosby

A typical Crosby cachet has a small photo pasted on the cover. Crosby thermographed the text and frames found around the photos, which resulted in an unmistakably heavy raised printing. Crosby often produced several cachets for each issue, and occasionally produced cachets without a photo. Crosby cachets without photos can be identified by a similarity in text and cachet design. Crosby cachet photos are not to be confused with Ioor's, since Crosby's are actual photos that have been pasted onto the envelopes after the cachet was printed, and Ioor's are printed on the envelopes.

A few of Crosby's covers are signed. The trick is to see his name, which he had printed in the upper right-hand corner, right where the stamp is affixed. To see his name, one must hold the cover up to a bright light.

Crosby made cachets for ship covers in the early 1930's. He died in 1947, but his wife continued to make the Crosby covers through the Annapolis Tercentenary issue of 1949.

Figure WC-1
Most Crosby covers contain a pasted-on photo, making them easy to identify.

It was not uncommon for Crosby to have more than one cachet for a stamp issue. There are some issues where he created as many as 20 different designs.

Notice that one of the cachets for this issue does not contain a photo. However, the cachet does contain the same familiar raised print.

Figure WC-2
A few Crosby cachets are signed with a fine-line Crosby advertising imprint. This imprint is found in the upper right-hand corner of the envelope or, occasionally, on the back.

House of Farnam

House of Farnam cachets have been produced for nearly every issue since the TIPEX Souvenir sheet of 1936. Many Farnam cachets are signed 'HF' or "House of Farnam." The early unsigned Farnams are usually small, simple, one-color designs found in the upper left-hand corner of the envelope. They are printed from steel-die engravings with slightly raised printing.

Figure HF-1
THE FIRST FARNAM CACHET is an unsigned design prepared for the 1936 TIPEX Souvenir sheet. Also shown is a typical unsigned early Farnam and a signed Farnam from the 1980's.

Dr. Harry Ioor (pronounced EYE-or)

Dr. Ioor's cachet career spanned the period from 1929 to 1951. His cachet designs fall into three different patterns.

Figure OR-1
Two early Ioor's, including the first Ioor cachet prepared for the George Rogers Clark commemorative of 1929. Notice that both cachets contain fine line drawings.

Early Ioor cachets (1929-1933) followed no particular pattern except that many are fine line drawings. Several are printed in black and light pink ink. In some cases the covers are addressed to Ioor, which allows for easy identification.

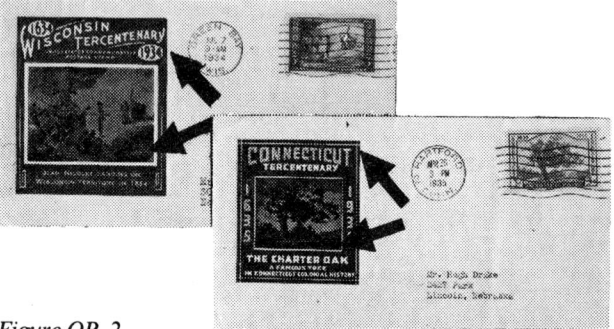

Figure OR-2
From 1934-1940 Ioor's covers followed a definite pattern. Almost all of them contained a printed photo as part of the cachet. These photos are printed on the envelopes and are not to be confused with Crosby's cachets, where the photos are pasted on the envelope. During this period, Ioor often produced several cachet varieties, using different black and white photos, with different colors around them.

34A

Figure OR-3
Harry Ioor died before the completion of the Famous American series of 1940. His sister completed the series and then continued to produce cachets with a different design pattern. This particular period of Ioor is easy to identify since most of the covers are signed.

F.R. Rice

Rice cachets are undoubtedly one of the easiest cachets to identify. Most are signed and have a definite and consistent style. Rice's career spanned from 1932 to 1940.

Figure RI-1
Rice used different illustrations or text inside this common border for about 75 percent of his cachets.

CACHET CALCULATOR

As discussed in the introduction, values in this catalogue are for an average market FDC. Many FDCs, depending on the cachet, sell for many times the catalogue value, while others may sell for much less.

Below is a list of cachet makers, the dates they serviced FDCs and a multiplier. By taking the muliplier range listed below and multiplying it by the catalogue value for a cacheted FDC, you will get the approximate catalogue value of the specific cacheted FDC.

First cachets of all makers are in great demand and usually sell for a substantial premium.

Cachet Maker Dates	Pricing Multiplier	Cachet Maker Dates	Pricing Multiplier
Adelphia Stamp Shop		**Andrews**	
1932-1939	2 times	1978	6 times
Aero Print		1979-1982	2 times
1931-1932	2 to 3 times	**Animated (Ellis) Covers**	
1933-1934	1 to 2 times	1968-1969	6 times
Apage Cachets		1970-date	3 to 4 times
1984-date	7 times	**Annis, D. R.**	
Albers Cache		1938-1939	2 to 4 times
1966-1974	2 to 3 times	**Ardee Covers**	
Alexander, George A.		1975-date	3 to 4 times
1981-1984	6 to 12 times	**Aristocrat**	
America		1936-1937	4 times
1975-1980	3 times	1938-1940	1 to 2 times
1981-1988	2 to 3 times	1941-date	1 time
Anagram hand colored Cachets		**Artcraft**	
1987-date	8 to 15 times	1939	4 times
Anderson, C.		1940-1945	1 1/2 times
1933-1934	1 1/2 to 2 times	1946-date	1 time
1935-date	1 time	**Artique**	
		1974-date	3 to 4 times

Cachet Maker Dates	Pricing Multiplier	Cachet Maker Dates	Pricing Multiplier
Artmaster		**Bi-Color Craft**	
1946-1950	...1 to 1 1/2times	1945-1947	.......3 to 4 times
1951-date	................1 time	**Bickford, C.L.**	
Artopages		1931-1932	...............2 times
1962-1969	.... 4 times	**Bill Ressl Cachets**	
1970-date	.........2 to 3 times	1977-date	.........2 to 3 times
Aubry		**Bittings**	
1936-1938	...............2 times	1979-date	.........1 to 2 times
Ayerst Laboratories		**Black Heritage**	
(Artcraft variety)		1978-1984	...............4 times
1965-circa		**Boerger (ABC)**	
1970's	......................5 times	1952-date	.........2 to 3 times
Barcus, Norman		**Border Craft**	
1931-1939	...............5 times	1966-1968	.....8 to 12 times
Baxter, James H.		**Broadway Stamp Co.**	
1929-1932	.......2 to 3 times	(Max Sage)	
Bazaar		1923-1929	...............3 times
1971-1972	...............2 times	1930-1937	.......4 to 5 times
1973-date	..1 to 1 1/2 times	**Brookhaven**	
Beardsley, Waiten S.		1933-1938	.......5 to 6 times
1933-1939	.......4 to 5 times	**Buchanan, Bradie**	
Beazell, R.		1927-1939	.......1 to 2 times
1929-1934	.............10 times	**Burfeind, George H.**	
1935-1937	.............20 times	1928-1934	...............3 times
Beck Printing Co. Inc.		**Burroughs, E.L.**	
1930-1931	.......2 to 3 times	1940-1941	.......2 to 3 times
Bert, Adam		**Cachet Craft**	
1929-1933	.1 1/2 to 2 times	Pre-1950	..........1 to 2 times
Bennett, Ira		1950-1972	.......2 to 3 times
1948-1949	... 10 to 15 times	**Calhoun Collectors Soc.-Gold**	
Bernet Egon & Fred		1978	........................3 times
1929-1941	...............4 times	**Carrollton**	
Bernet-Reid W. Sheetlets		1977-date	................2 times
1938-1939	...............3 times	**Cascade Cachet**	
1940-1945	...............4 times	1958-1968	.......2 to 4 times
Betts W.W.		**Chambers Gold Bond**	
1928-1931	..1 1/2 to 2 times	1935-1953	...............5 times
Beverly Hills		**Clifford, J**	
1933-1937	.......2 to 3 times	1936-1944	...............2 times

Cachet Maker Dates	Pricing Multiplier	Cachet Maker Dates	Pricing Multiplier
Clinton Classics		**DRC hand painted**	
1984-date	2 to 3 times	1979-1984	8 to 15 times
Collins, F., hand painted		**DYS**	
1978-date	10 to 50 times	1978-date	2 to 3 times
Colonial		**David "C" Cachets, hand painted**	
1974	5 times	1966-1980	7 to 8 times
1975-1983	1 to 2 times	1980-date	5 times
Colorano "silks"		**DeRosset hand painted**	
1971-1973	15 to 20 times	1986-date	20 times
1974-1976	4 to 5 times	**Doak Ernest L.**	
1977-date	3 to 4 times	1978-1950	5 to 8 times
Corn Cut		**Dome**	
1932-1939	.1 to 2 1/2 times	1983-date	4 to 7 times
1940-1948	2 to 3 times	**Doris Gold Cachets**	
Combo Cover Co.		1977-date	2 to 4 times
1975-date	2 times	**Double A**	
Comic Cachets		1981-date	2 to 4 times
1977-1982	2 times	**Dragon Card**	
Copecrest Woven Cachets		1983	2 to 3 times
1969-1974	6 to 8 times	**Dyer R.**	
Cos-Art Covers		1928-1938	.1 1/2 to 2 times
1944-1950	1 to 2 times	**Dyer, R hand painted**	
Coulson Cachet		1950-date	60-100 times
1972-1977	2 times	**Dysinger, M.**	
Coulthard, John		1975-1979	2 times
1936-1948	2 to 3 times	**Eagle Cover Service**	
Cover Craft		1933-1936	1 to 2 times
1964-1966	5 times	**Eastern Covers**	
1967-date	1 1/2 to 2 times	1983-date	2 to 5 times
Covered Wagon		**Edgerly, Robert K.**	
1931-1934	3 to 4 times	1932-1948	2 to 4 times
Crosby, W.		**Edken**	
Pre-1939	5 times	1989-date	3 to 6 times
1940-1948	5 to 10 times	**Egolf**	
Cuscaden		1928-1931	2 to 3 times
1978-date	2 times	**Edminston, Florence, hand painted**	
Czubay, W.		1936-1939	10 to 20 times
1936-1954	6 times		

Cachet Maker Dates	Pricing Multiplier	Cachet Maker Dates	Pricing Multiplier
Elliott		**Gamm**	
1929-1931	.......1 to 2 times	1977	..............8 to 10 times
Emblem Cachet		1978-date...	2 to 3 times
1982-date	.........2 to 3 times	**Geerling hand painted**	
Emeigh		1984-date	......25 to 40 times
1929-1930	.......1 to 3 times	**George, C. W.**	
Emerson		1927-1931	.......3 to 4 times
1925-1932	.......2 to 4 times	1931-1950	.......2 to 3 times
Espenshade		**Gilbert, John C.**	
1935-1942	..............2 times	1937-1939	.......2 to 3 times
Evans, C. M.		**Gill John**	
1929-1932	.......2 to 3 times	1932-1933	...............2 times
Evans, Glen L.		**Gill Craft**	
1935-1942	.......3 to 4 times	1980	.....................10 times
Fairway		1981-date	.........2 to 5 times
1931-1940	.......1 to 2 times	**Glen**	
Fawcett, James W.		1974	.......................3 times
1934-1936	.......2 to 4 times	1975-date	..........1 1/2 times
Ferryman F.R.		**Glory**	
1938-1940	...............4 times	1962-1963	.......3 to 4 times
Fidelity Stamp Co.		**Gold Bond**	
1937-1950	..1 to 1 1/2 times	1935-1950	.......3 to 5 times
First Rank First Day Covers		**Goldcraft**	
1979-date	.........2 to 3 times	1959-date	....1 1/2 to 2 times
Fleetwood		**Gorham, A.**	
1941-1947	.......3 to 5 times	1932-1938	.......2 to 3 times
1948-1960	.......2 to 3 times	**Grandy, W.**	
1961-date	.........2 to 4 times	1935-date	.........2 to 4 times
Flok		**Griffin, H. H.**	
1954-1955	.....6 to 10 times	1926-1933	.......3 to 4 times
Fluegel, I.		**Grimsland, H.**	
1945-1959	.......6 to 8 times	1932-1934	.1 1/2 to 2 times
1960-1964	...10 to 15 times	1935-1952	.......1 to 2 times
Folio-Print	........3 to 4 times	**Gundel, T.**	
Fox Jack		1929-1941	.......6 to 7 times
1928-1930	.......2 to 4 times	**HM Cachets**	
Fulton Stamp Co.		1977-date	.........4 to 7 times
1947-1949	.1 1/2 to 2 times		

Cachet Maker Dates	Pricing Multiplier	Cachet Maker Dates	Pricing Multiplier
HS Color Tint 1954-circa 1960's	2 to 4 times	**Intercity Stamp Co.** 1939-1948	3 to 5 times
Habbert, George Lewis 1927-1929	5 times	**Ioor, H.** 1929-1931	3 to 4 times
Hacker, E. 1931-1938	4 to 5 times	1932-1939	1/2 to 1 time
Halvorsen, Ejgil J. S. 1926-1930	2 to 4 times	1940 & later	1 to 2 times
Hammond Maxi 1957-1972	2 to 4 times	**Jackson, Gladys** 1948-date	2 to 3 times
HAM hand painted Cachets 1977-1978	80 times	**Janis, C. W.** 1935-1936	3 to 4 times
1979-date	15 to 50 times	**Jeweled Envelopes** 1935-1939	2 to 3 times
Heartland FDC 1984-date	2 times	1940-1948	4 to 6 times
Hist-O-Card 1952-circa 1970's	2 to 4 times	**Joseph, N.** 1929-1933	4 to 6 times
Hobby Cover Service 1932-1933	2 to 3 times	**Judith Fogt hand painted** 1982- date	15 to 40 times
Hobby Life-WCO 1945-1950	2 to 3 times	**Justice Covers** 1979-date	1 1/2 times
House of Farnam 1946-1960	.1 to 1 1/2 times	**Kapner** 1934-1937	.1 to 1 1/2 times
1960-date	1 time	**Kee Ed** 1933-1935	1 to 2 times
Horseshoe hand painted 1983-1987	3 to 6 times	**Kirk Kover** 1947-1949	4 to 7 times
Hubbard 1935-1937	2 to 3 times	**Klotzbach** 1929-1935	2 to 3 times
Hunt Harris R. 1927-1930	3 to 4 times	**KMC Venture** 1978	10 times
HUX 1928-1950	.1 1/2 to 2 times	1979-date	2 1/2 times
Imperial 1934-1940	4 to 5 times	**Knapp, Dorothy, hand painted** 1941-1945	200 to 300 times
Info Cachets 1992-date	2 to 6 times	1945-1952	.150 to 300 times
		Knoble, Dr. Ross M. hand painted 1952-circa 1960's	15 to 25 times

Cachet Maker Dates	Pricing Multiplier	Cachet Maker Dates	Pricing Multiplier
Kolor Kover		**Orbit Covers**	
1948	10 times	1962-1967	3 to 10 times
1949-1960	8 times	**Overseas Mailers**	
1960-1973	5 times	1953-1977	6 to 10 times
Kraft B, hand painted		**Panda Cachets**	
1982-date	4 times	1982-date	5 to 10 times
Kribb's Kovers		**Parsons, Albert B.**	
1978	10 times	1933-1936	2 to 4 times
1979-date	2-4 times	**Paslay Classic hand painted**	
Kurkjian, S.S.		1982-date	10 to 50 times
1927-1929	3 to 4 times	**Pavois**	
LEB Cachets		1937-1940	1 time
1981-date	3 to 6 times	**Pent Arts**	
Laird		1943-1958	1 to 11/2 times
1935-1937	1 to 2 times	**Phoenix Insurance Overprint**	
Linprint		1937-1956	2 to 8 times
1932-1941	1 time	**Pilgrim**	
Linto, Williams S.		1937-1941	6 to 10 times
1937-1940	8 to 10 times	**Plimpton**	
1940-1959	10 to 15 times	1936-1939	1 time
Ludwig, Oswald A.		**Plotz David O.**	
1937-1949	2 to 3 times	1926-1927	2 to 3 times
Marg		**Pontiac Press**	
1962-1964	6 times	1944-circa	
1965-date	2 times	1960's	3 to 10 times
Mauck		**Post/Art Engraved**	
1927-1930	1 to 2 times	1980-1981	5 times
Minkus, J.		1982-1986	2 times
1940-date	1 time	**Post/Art hand painted**	
Munprint		1983-1985	10 to 20 times
1936-1941	2 to 4 times	**Postmasters of America**	
Nickles, C. E.		1976	3 times
1925-1929	1 time	1977-date	1 time
Nix		**Pugh hand painted Cachets**	
1934-1958	3 to 5 times	1979-date	15 to 30 times
Nu-art			
1945-1946	3 to 5 times		

Cachet Maker Dates	Pricing Multiplier	Cachet Maker Dates	Pricing Multiplier
Quadracolorplus		Smartcraft	
1977-1987	3 to 5 times	1942-1952	.1 to 1 1/2 times
Raley		Softones	
1932-1938	2 to 3 times	1978-1980	2 to 3 times
Rank II (flocked)		Spartan	
1955-1959	3 to 8 times	1948-1950	2 to 3 times
Rice, F. R.		Spectrum	
1932-1941	1 to 3 times	1977	6 times
Risko Art		1978-1983	2 to 3 times
1935-1938	10 to 15 times	Steelcraft	
Roessler, A. C.		1952-1953	2 times
1925-1931	2 times	Sudduth	
1932-1938	2 to 3 times	1936-1937	.1 to 1 1/2 times
Ross Foil		Sun Craft	
1971-date	2 to 3 times	1947-1948	2 times
Rothblum		Texture Craft	
1929-1934	2 to 3 times	1955-1957	4 to 6 times
Roy J.A.		Top Notch	
1934-1937	2 to 3 times	1934-1937	.1 1/2 to 2 times
Sadworth G.V.		Tri-Color	
1940-1952	2 to 8 times	1958-1960	2 to 4 times
Sanders, Michael		Truby	
1933-1939	2 to 3 times	1931-1934	5 to 6 times
1940-1952	2 to 5 times	Tudor House	
Sarzin Metallic		1977	3 times
1964-1970	3 to 6 times	1978-date	11/2 to 2 times
1970-1977	3 to 4 times	Uladh Covers	
Scatchard, Norwood B.		1977-date	2 to 3 times
1935-1938	3 to 6 times	Ulrich Frank J., hand painted	
Scenic Craft		1960-1968	15 to 50 times
1940-1948	3 to 6 times	Urie, C. W.	
Serug Cachet		1926-1929	2 to 3 times
1944	2 to 3 times	Vaughn Hord hand painted Cachets	
Shockley		1983-date	30 to 60 times
1929-1930	1 time	Velvatone	
Sidenius		1951-1970	3 to 5 times
1932-1939	2 to 3 times		

Cachet Maker Dates	Pricing Multiplier	Cachet Maker Dates	Pricing Multiplier
Von Ohlen, William J.		**Weddle, T. M.**	
1937-1945	3 times	1977-1981	15 to 25 times
1945-1969	5 to 8 times	1981-date	10 to 20 times
WCO		**Western Silk Cachets**	
1946-1949	3 to 8 times	1978	4 times
Wanstead & Co.		1979-1983	2 to 3 times
1935-1937	2 to 4 times	**Wright, William N. hand**	
Warneford		**painted**	
1937-1940	2 to 3 times	1945-1950	40 to 75 times
Washington Stamp		1951-1959	40 to 50 times
Exchange		**Zaso**	
1931-1939	2 to 5 times	1977	6 times
Weaver, Howard M.		1978-1983	.1 1/2 to 2 times
1928-1934	2 to 3 times		

COMMEMORATIVES AND REGULAR ISSUES

Editors Note:

All listings prior to Sc 551 are considered 'Earliest Known Uses' (EKUs), unless otherwise specified as a 'First Day Cover'. An EKU is defined as a cover that has either received a valid certificate of authenticity from a recognized expertizing service, or has been examined by acknowledged experts in the field.

The editor wishes to thank Edward J. Siskin for his help in compiling the earliest-known use (EKU) dates.

Since EKUs can change as new discoveries are made, with a few exceptions, no prices are given for these covers. As a general rule, an EKU is worth a premium over the 'on cover' price found in the 'Scott Specialized Catalogue of United States Stamps', published by Scott Publishing Company. Collectors are urged to document covers with earlier dates than those listed here, and share their discoveries with the editors, so that we may update future listings.

| | 1 | 2 | 230 | 231 |

SCOTT NUMBER	DESCRIPTION	UNCACHETED SINGLE

1847

| | 1 | 5c Benjamin Franklin, 7/7/1847, New York, NY, eku...................... | — |
| | 2 | 10c George Washington, 7/2/1847, New York, NY, eku .... | 130,000 |

1851-57

	5	1c Benjamin Franklin, 7/5/1851, eku...	—
	5A	1c Benjamin Franklin, 7/1/1851, First Day Cover (1 known).........	20,000
	6	1c Benjamin Franklin, 4/19/1857, eku...	—
	7	1c Benjamin Franklin, 7/1/1851, First Day Cover (1 known).........	13,000
		on printed circular dated 7/1/1851 without postmark...............	2,500
	9	1c Benjamin Franklin, 6/18/1852, eku..	—
	10	3c George Washington, 7/1/1851, First Day Cover, any city (40-50 known)	7,500
	11	3c George Washington, 10/4/1851, eku...	—
	12	5c Thomas Jefferson Ty I, 3/24/1856, eku......................................	—
	14	10c George Washington Ty II, 5/12/1855, eku................................	—
	15	10c George Washington Ty III, 5/23/1855, eku..............................	—
	17	12c George Washington, 8/4/1851, eku...	—

The 4 varieties of the 10c 1855, Sc 13-16, all came from one plate, but to date, only Scott 14-15 are known used in May, 1855.

1857-61

	18	1c Benjamin Franklin, 1/25/1861, eku..	—
	19	1c Benjamin Franklin, 4/2/1857, eku..	—
	20	1c Benjamin Franklin, 7/26/1857, eku..	—
	21	1c Benjamin Franklin, 11/20/1857, eku..	—

1

SCOTT NUMBER	DESCRIPTION	UNCACHETED SINGLE

	22	1c Benjamin Franklin, 7/26/1857, eku.....................................	—
	23	1c Benjamin Franklin, 7/25/1857, eku.....................................	—
	24	1c Benjamin Franklin, 11/17/1857, eku....................................	—

Listed above are the earliest-known uses for the 1c 1857 varieties. These varieties are found on a number of plates, hence the different earliest-known use dates.

	25	3c George Washington, 2/28/1857, eku..................................	—
	26	3c George Washington, 9/15/1857, eku..................................	—
	26a	3c George Washington, 7/11/1857, eku..................................	—
	27	5c Thomas Jefferson Ty I, 10/6/1858, eku	—
	28	5c Thomas Jefferson Ty I, 8/22/1857, eku	—
	28A	5c Thomas Jefferson Ty I, 3/31/1858, eku	—
	29	5c Thomas Jefferson Ty I, 4/4/1859, eku	—
	30	5c Thomas Jefferson Ty II,5/8/1861, eku	—
	30A	5c Thomas Jefferson Ty II, 5/14/1860, eku...........................	—
	32	10c George Washington, 7/27/1857, eku................................	—

The four varieties of the 10c 1857, Scott 31-34, all come from one plate, but to date, only Scott 32 is known postmarked July 27, 1857.

	35	10c George Washington, 4/29/1859, eku..............................	—
	36	12c George Washington, 7/30/1857, eku..............................	—
	36b	12c George Washington, 12/9/1859, eku..............................	—
	37	24c Benjamin Franklin, 7/7/1860, eku..................................	—
	38	30c Benjamin Franklin, 8/8/1860, eku..................................	—
	39	90c Benjamin Franklin, 9/11/1860, eku................................	—

1861-66

	62B	10c George Washington, 9/17/1861, New York, NY, eku	—
	63	1c Benjamin Franklin, 8/17/1861, First Day Cover......................	15,000
	64b	3c George Washington, 8/17/1861, First Day Cover	15,000
	65	3c George Washington, 8/19/1861, eku..................................	—
	67	5c Thomas Jefferson, 8/19/1861, eku	—
	68	10c George Washington, 8/20/1861, eku................................	—
	69	12c George Washington, 8/20/1861, eku................................	—
	70	24c George Washington, 1/7/1862, eku..................................	—
	70c	4c George Washington, 8/20/1861, eku..................................	—
	71	30c Benjamin Franklin, 8/20/1861, eku..................................	—
	72	90c George Washington, 11/27/1861, eku...............................	—
	73	2c Andrew Jackson, 7/6/1863, eku..	—
	75	5c Thomas Jefferson, 1/2/1862, eku	—
	76	5c Thomas Jefferson, 2/3/1863, eku	—
	77	15c Abraham Lincoln, 4/14/1866, eku	—
	78	24c George Washington, 2/20/1863, eku................................	—

1867 Grilled Issue

| | 79 | 3c George Washington, 8/13/1867, eku................................... | — |

1869

	112	1c Benjamin Franklin, 5/2/1869, eku.....................................	—
	113	2c Post Horse & Rider, 3/26/1869, eku	—
	114	3c Locomotive, 3/27/1869, eku	—
	115	6c Washington, 4/26/1869, eku	—
	116	10c Shield & Eagle, 4/1/1869, eku	—

☐ 117	12c S.S. Adriatic, 4/1/1869, eku	—
☐ 118	15c Landing of Columbus Ty I, 4/2/1869, eku	—
☐ 119	15c Landing of Columbus Ty II, 5/23/1869, eku	—
☐ 120	24c Declaration of Independence, 4/7/1869, eku	—
☐ 121	30c Shield, Eagle & Flags, 5/22/1869, eku	—

1870-71

☐ 134	1c Franklin, 4/9/1870, eku	—
☐ 135	2c Jackson, 9/1/1870, eku	—
☐ 136	3c Washington, 3/25/1870, eku	—
☐ 137	6c Lincoln, 7/31/1870, eku	—
☐ 138	7c Stanton, 2/12/1871, eku	—
☐ 139	10c Jefferson, 6/11/1870, eku	—
☐ 140	12c Clay, 2/9/1872, eku	—
☐ 141	15c Webster, 10/29/1870, eku	—
☐ 143	30 Hamilton, 8/?/70, eku	—
☐ 145	1c Franklin, 7/18/1870, eku	—
☐ 146	2c Jackson, 6/11/1870, eku	—
☐ 147	3c Washington, 3/13/1870, eku	—
☐ 148	6c Lincoln, 3/28/1870, eku	—
☐ 149	7c Stanton, 5/11/1871, eku	—
☐ 150	10c Jefferson, 5/29/1870, eku	—
☐ 151	12c Clay, 7/9/1870, eku	—
☐ 152	15c Webster, 9/24/1870, eku	—
☐ 153	24c Scott, 11/18/1870, eku	—
☐ 154	30c Hamilton, 1/31/1871, eku	—
☐ 155	90c Perry, 9/1/1872, eku	—

1873

☐ 156	1c Franklin, 8/22/1873, eku	—
☐ 157	2c Jackson, 7/12/1873, eku	—
☐ 158	3c Washington, 7/17/1873, eku	—
☐ 159	6c Lincoln, 7/24/1873, eku	—
☐ 160	7c Stanton, 10/5/1873, eku	—
☐ 161	10c Jefferson, 8/2/1873, eku	—
☐ 162	12c Clay, 1/3/1874, eku	—
☐ 163	15c Webster, 7/22/1873, eku	—
☐ 165	30c Hamilton, 10/30/1874, eku	—
☐ 166	90c Perry, ?/?/1875, eku	—

1875

☐ 178	2c Jackson, 7/17/1875, eku	—
☐ 179	5c Taylor, 7/12/1875, eku	—

1879

☐ 182	1c Franklin, 4/25/1879, eku	—
☐ 183	2c Jackson, 2/4/1879, eku	—
☐ 184	3c Washington, 2/7/1879, eku	—
☐ 185	5c Taylor, 5/12/1879, eku	—
☐ 186	6c Lincoln, 7/1/1879, eku	—
☐ 187	10c Jefferson, 9/5/1879, eku	—
☐ 188	10c Jefferson (w/secret mark), 2/21/1879, eku	—
☐ 189	15c Webster, 1/20/1879, eku	—

☐	190	30c Hamilton, 11/13/1882, eku..	—
☐	191	90c Perry, 6/17/1880, eku	—

1881-88

☐	205	5c Garfield, 2/18/82, eku	—

The designated first day for Scott 205 was 4/10/1882, but stamps
were legitimately sold as early as 2/18. Curiously, no 4/10 covers
are currently known.

☐	206	1c Franklin, 12/5/1881, eku..	—
☐	207	3c Washington, 7/16/1881, eku	—
☐	208	6c Lincoln, 9/27/1882, eku..	—
☐	209	10c Thomas Jefferson, 5/11/1882, eku	—
☐	210	2c Washington, 10/1/1883, any city, First Day Cover	
		(30-40 known)	2,000
☐	211	4c Andrew Jackson, 10/1/1883, First Day Cover, no solo usage known	—
		Scott 210 & 211 on one cover (1 known)	10,000
☐	212	1c Franklin, 7/28/1887, eku...	—
☐	213	3c Washington, 9/21/1887, eku	—
☐	214	3c Washington, 10/3/1887, eku	—
☐	215	4c Jackson, 7/11/1889, eku..	—
☐	216	5c Garfield, 4/7/1888, eku	—
☐	217	30c Andrew Jackson, 9/22/1888, eku.............................	—

1890

☐	219	1c Franklin, 4/19/1890, eku..	—
☐	219D	2c Washington, 2/22/1890, First Day Cover (1 known)	14,500
☐	220	2c Washington, 5/31/1890, eku	—
☐	221	3c Jackson, 7/1/1890, eku..	—
☐	222	4c Lincoln, 10/22/1890, eku..	—
☐	223	5c Grant, 6/14/1890, Haddonfield NJ, eku.....................	—
☐	224	6c Garfield, 5/30/1890, eku	—
☐	225	8c Sherman, 5/21/1893, eku	—
☐	226	10c Webster, 4/30/1890, eku...	—
☐	227	15c Clay, 7/21/1891, eku	—
☐	228	30c Jefferson, 7/30/1892, eku...	—
☐	229	90c Perry, 6/10/1892, eku	—

1893

☐	230	1c Columbian, 1/1/1893, First Day Cover	4,000
☐	231	2c Columbian, 1/1/1893, First Day Cover	4,000
☐	232	3c Columbian, 1/1/1893, First Day Cover	6,000
☐	233	4c Columbian, 1/1/1893, First Day Cover	6,000
☐	234	5c Columbian, 1/1/1893, First Day Cover	6,000
☐	235	6c Columbian, 1/2/1893, First Day Cover	6,000
☐	236	8c Columbian, 4/17/1893, eku	—
☐	237	10c Columbian, 1/1/1893, First Day Cover	7,500
☐	238	15c Columbian, 2/8/1893, eku	—
☐	239	30c Columbian, 2/8/1893, eku	—
☐	240	50c Columbian, 2/8/1893, eku	—
☐	241	$1 Columbian, 1/21/1893, eku..	—
☐	242	$2 Columbian, 1/2/1893, First Day Cover	18,000
☐	243	$3 Columbian, 4/4/1893, eku..	—
☐	244	$4 Columbian, 7/14/1893, eku..	—

| ☐ | 245 | **$5 Columbian, 1/6/1893, eku** .... | — |

Since Jan. 1, 1893 was a Sunday, few post offices were open. January 1st and January 2nd are both collected as First Day Covers. Several values are known with Dec. 30 or Dec. 31, 1892 pre-dates.

1894-95

☐	246	**1c Franklin (ultramarine), 10/24/1894, eku**	—
☐	247	**1c Franklin (blue), 11/11/1894, eku**	—
☐	248	**2c Washington, 10/20/1894, eku**	—
☐	249	**2c Washington, 10/11/1894, eku**	—
☐	250	**2c Washington, 10/19/1894, eku**	—
☐	251	**2c Washington, 2/18/1895, eku**	—
☐	252	**2c Washington, 10/11/1894, eku**	—
☐	253	**3c Jackson, 1/5/1895, eku**	—
☐	254	**4c Lincoln, 1/5/1895, eku**	—
☐	255	**5c Grant, 11/22/1894, eku**	—
☐	256	**6c Garfield, 8/11/1894, eku**	—
☐	257	**8c Sherman, 9/15/1895, eku**	—
☐	258	**10c Webster, 11/19/1894, eku**	—
☐	259	**15c Clay, 2/20/1895, eku**	—
☐	260	**50c Jefferson, 1/15/1895, eku**	—
☐	261A	**$1 Perry (Ty II), 3/22/1895, eku**	—
☐	262	**$2 Madison, 7/6/1896, eku**	—

1897-98

☐	279	**1c Franklin, 2/2/1898, eku**	—
☐	279B	**2c Washington (Ty III), 1/16/1898, eku**	—
☐	280	**4c Lincoln, 12/12/1898, eku**	—
☐	281	**5c Grant, 3/19/1898, eku**	—
☐	282	**6c Garfield, 5/30/1899, eku**	—
☐	282C	**10c Webster (Ty I), 3/24/1899, eku**	—
☐	283	**10c Webster (Ty II), 3/13/1899, eku**	—
☐	284	**15c Clay, 5/1/1899, eku**	—
☐	285	1c Marquette on the Mississippi, 6/17/1898, First Day Cover, DC, NY	7,000
☐	286	2c Farming in the West, 6/17/1898, First Day Cover, DC, Pittsburgh, PA	7,000
☐	287	4c Indian Hunting Buffalo, 6/17/1898, First Day Cover, DC	7,000
☐	288	5c Fremont on the Rocky Mountains, 6/17/1898, First Day Cover, DC	7,000
☐	289	8c Troops Guarding Trains, 6/17/1898, First Day Cover, DC........	7,500
☐	290	10c Hardships of Emigration, 6/17/1898, First Day Cover	8,000
☐		Sc 285-290 on one cover , 6/17/1898...	20,000
☐	291	50c Western Mining Prospector, 6/17/1898, First Day Cover	10,000
☐	292	$1 Western Cattle in a Storm, 6/17/1898, First Day Cover...........	12,500
☐	293	**$2 Mississippi River Bridge, 6/24/1898, eku**................................	—

1901

☐	294	1c Fast Lake Navigation, 5/1/1901, First Day Cover (10 known)...	4,800
☐	295	2c "Empire State Express", 5/1/1901, First Day Cover (30-40 known)	2,500
☐	296	**4c Electric Automobile, 5/1/1901, First Day Cover**	5,000
☐	297	**5c Bridge at Niagara Falls, 5/1/1901, First Day Cover**	5,000
☐	298	**8c Soo Locks, 5/1/1901, First Day Cover**	9,000

| ☐ | 299 | 10c Fast Ocean Navigation, 5/1/1901, First Day Cover.................. | 10,000 |
| ☐ | | Scott 294-299, complete set of 6 on one cover, 5/1/01 (6 known).. | 12,500 |

1902-08 (Regular Issue)

☐	300	1c Franklin, 2/8/03, eku...	—
☐	301	2c Washington, 1/17/03, eku	—
☐	302	3c Jackson, 3/21/03, eku	—
☐	303	4c Grant, 4/13/03, eku	—
☐	304	5c Lincoln, 1/28/03, eku	—
☐	305	6c Garfield, 5/8/03, eku	—
☐	306	8c Martha Washington, 12/27/02, eku	—
☐	307	10c Webster, 4/24/03, eku	—
☐	308	13c Harrison, 12/22/02, eku	—
☐	309	15c Clay, 9/24/03, eku	—
☐	310	50c Jefferson, 11/2/03, eku...	—
☐	311	$1 Farragut, 11/2/03, eku...	—
☐	312	$2 Madison, 11/2/03, eku..	—
☐	313	$5 Marshall, 11/2/03, eku...	—
☐	314	1c Franklin (imperf), 2/12/07, eku...	—
☐	315	5c Lincoln (imperf), 9/15/08, eku	—
☐	319	2c Washington, 11/19/03, eku	—
☐	320	2c Washington (imperf), 1/28/07, eku..	—

1904

☐	323	1c Livingston, 4/30/04, First Day Cover (6 known)	5,000
☐	324	2c Jefferson, 4/30/04, First Day Cover (10-15 known)..................	6,000
		pre-dates exist as early as 4/25	
☐	325	3c Monroe, 4/30/04, First Day Cover (5 known)	6,000
☐	326	5c McKinley, 4/30/04, First Day Cover (5 known)...........................	6,000
☐	327	10c Map of Louisiana Purchase, 4/30/04, First Day Cover (2 known)	9,000
		Scott 323-327 on one cover, 4/30/04 (1 known)	25,000

Notice was sent to postmasters that this set was being shipped from Washington on Apr. 21, but could not be sold to the public before Apr. 30, 1904. Because of these instructions, any cover dated before Apr. 30, 1904, is considered a pre-dated cover.

1907

☐	328	1c Capt. John Smith, 4/26/07, First Day Cover (6 known)	6,000
☐	329	2c Founding of Jamestown, 4/26/07, First Day Cover .. (2 known)	9,000
☐	330	5c Pocahontas, 5/10/07, Norfolk VA, eku (3 known)	10,000

1908-09 (Regular Issue)

☐	331	1c Franklin, 12/1/08, eku...	—
☐	331a	1c Franklin (booklet single), 12/2/08, First Day Cover (1 known).	18,000
☐	332	2c Washington, 12/4/08, eku	—
☐	332a	2c Washington (booklet single), 11/16/08, First Day Cover	
		(1 known)...	35,000
☐	333	3c Washington (Ty I), 1/12/09, eku...	—
☐	334	4c Washington, 1/12/09, eku	—
☐	335	5c Washington, 1/12/09, eku	—
☐	336	6c Washington, 1/6/09, eku	—
☐	337	8c Washington, 1/9/09, eku	—
☐	338	10c Washington, 2/1/09, eku	—
☐	339	13c Washington, 3/5/09, eku	—

340	15c Washington, 3/12/09, eku	—
341	50c Washington, 10/23/09, eku	—
343	1c Franklin (imperf), 2/11/09, eku	—
344	2c Washington (imperf), 2/1/09, eku	—
345	3c Washington (Ty I, imperf), 2/13/09, eku	—
346	4c Washington (imperf), 3/13/09, eku	—
347	5c Washington (imperf), 3/4/09, eku	—
348	1c Franklin (coil), 1/25/09, eku	—
349	2c Washington (coil), 5/16/09, eku	—
351	5c Washington (coil), 9/21/09, eku	—
352	1c Franklin (coil), 3/30/09, eku	—
353	2c Washington (coil), 10/6/09, eku	—
354	4c Washington (coil), 6/9/09, eku	—
355	5c Washington (coil), 10/25/09, eku	—
356	10c Washington (coil), 3/9/09, eku	—
357	1c Franklin (blue paper), 2/22/09, eku	—
358	2c Washington (blue paper), 3/25/09, eku	—

1909

367	2c Lincoln, 2/12/09, any city, First Day Cover (600-800 known)	500
	on Lincoln-related post-card	600
	pre-dated covers exist as early as 2/10/09	600
368	2c Lincoln (imperf), 2/12/09, First Day Cover (7 known)	7,500
369	2c Lincoln (blue paper), 3/27/09, eku	—

Feb. 12, 1909 was designated as the official First Day of the Lincoln stamp. Nine pre-dated covers are known postmarked on Feb. 10, from Boston MA (5), Olivet KS & Brooklyn NY; and on Feb. 11 from Mechanicsburg PA & Superior WI. A total of 149 different cities are known on Scott 367 FDCs, with Boston MA and Canton OH being the most common.

370	2c Alaska-Yukon, 5/29/09, First Day Cover	5,000
	on expo-related post-card	7,500
	covers dated 6/1/09,	2000
371	2c Alaska-Yukon (imperf), 6/7/09, Richmond, VA, eku	—
372	2c Hudson-Fulton, 9/25/09, and city, First Day Cover	
	(100-200 known)	1,000
	9/25/09, Lancaster PA, on 2-part Hudson-Fulton post-card	1,500
373	2c Hudson-Fulton (imperf), 9/25/09, First Day Cover	5,000

1911-13

390	1c Franklin (endwise coil), 10/22/11, eku	—
391	2c Washington (endwise coil), 5/3/11, eku	—
392	1c Franklin (sidewise coil), 3/24/11, eku	—
393	2c Washington (sidewise coil), 12/27/10, eku	—
394	3c Washington (sidewise coil), 9/18/11, Orangeburg, NY, eku	—
395	4c Washington (sidewise coil), 6/21/12, eku	—
396	5c Washington (sidewise coil), 5/20/13, eku	—

1913-15

397	1c Balboa (perf 12), 1/1/13, First Day Cover .... (10-15 known)	4,000
398	2c Pedro Miguel Locks (perf 12), 1/17/13, eku	—
399	5c Golden Gate (perf 12), 1/1/13, First Day Cover (1 known)	8,000
400	10c San Fran Bay (perf 12, orange-yellow), 1/1/13, First Day Cover	
	(2 known)	7,000
	Scott 397, 399 & 400 on one cover, 1/1/13, San Fran CA	9,000

☐ 400A	10c San Fran Bay (perf 12, orange), 12/18/13, eku	—
☐ 401	1c Balboa (perf 10), 12/21/14, eku	—
☐ 402	2c Pedro Miguel Locks (perf 10), 1/13/15, eku	—
☐ 403	5c Golden Gate (perf 10), 2/6/15, eku	—
☐ 404	10c San Fran Bay (perf 10), 8/27/15, eku	—

1912-15 (Regular Issue)

☐ 405	1c Washington, 2/23/12, eku	—
☐ 405b	1c Washington (booklet), 4/1/12, eku	—
☐ 406	2c Washington, 2/23/12, eku	—
☐ 406a	2c Washington (booklet), 6/6/12, eku	—
☐ 407	7c Washington, 5/1/14, eku (probably a first day cover)	—
	Scott 407, 415, 419, 420 & 421 on one cover, 5/1/14	15,000
☐ 408	1c Washington (imperf), 3/27/12, eku	—
☐ 408	1c Washington (Kansas City Roulette perfs), 11/25/14, eku	—
☐ 409	2c Washington (imperf), 4/15/12, eku	—
☐ 409	2c Washington (w/Schermack III perfs), 5/14/12, eku	—
☐ 409	2c Washington (Kansas City Roulette perfs), 12/10/14, eku	—
☐ 410	1c Washington (endwise coil), 7/5/12, eku	—
☐ 411	2c Washington (endwise coil), 5/31/12, eku	—
☐ 412	1c Washington (sidewise coil), 5/31/12, eku	—
☐ 413	2c Washington (sidewise coil), 5/13/12, eku	—
☐ 414	8c Franklin, 4/20/12, eku	—
☐ 415	9c Franklin, 5/1/14, eku (probably a first day cover)	—
☐ 416	10c Franklin, 5/11/12, eku	—
☐ 417	12c Franklin, 6/2/14, eku	—
☐ 418	15c Franklin, 5/17/13, eku	—
☐ 419	20c Franklin, 5/1/14, eku (probably a first day cover)	—
☐ 420	30c Franklin, 5/1/14, eku (probably a first day cover)	—
☐ 421	50c Franklin (sng line wmrk), 5/1/14, eku (probably a first day cover)	—
☐ 422	50c Franklin (dbl line wmrk), 7/15/15, eku	—
☐ 423	$1 Franklin (dbl line wmrk), 7/15/15, eku	—
☐ 424	1c Washington, 11/30/14, eku	—
☐ 424a	1c Washington (perf 12x10), 1/8/14, eku	—
☐ 424	1c Washington (coil waste), 8/2/15, First Day Cover	5,000
☐ 424d	1c Washington (booklet single), 12/20/13, eku	—
☐ 425	2c Washington, 12/2/14, eku	—
☐ 425e	2c Washington (booklet single), 1/6/14, eku	—
☐ 426	3c Washington, 11/26/14, eku	—
☐ 427	4c Washington, 1/19/15, eku	—
☐ 428	5c Washington, 1/29/15, eku	—
☐ 428a	5c Washington (perf 12x10), 4/14/15, eku	—
☐ 429	6c Washington, 2/6/15, eku	—
☐ 431	8c Franklin, 7/15/15, eku	—
☐ 433	10c Franklin, 11/13/14, eku	—
☐ 434	11c Franklin, 10/8/15, eku	—
☐ 435	12c Franklin, 4/24/15, eku	—
☐ 438	20c Franklin, 11/28/14, eku	—
☐ 439	30c Franklin, 2/13/15, eku	—
☐ 441	1c Washington (endwise coil), 2/16/15, eku	—
☐ 442	2c Washington (endwise coil), 7/22/14, eku	—
☐ 443	1c Washington (sidewise coil), 6/24/14, eku	—
☐ 444	2c Washington (sidewise coil), 5/28/14, eku	—
☐ 445	3c Washington (sidewise coil), 7/1/16, eku	—

9

	SCOTT NUMBER	DESCRIPTION	UNCACHETED SINGLE
☐	446	4c Washington (sidewise coil), 8/4/15, eku	—
☐	448	1c Washington (endwise coil), 4/30/16, eku	—
☐	449	2c Washington Ty I (endwise coil), 10/29/15, eku	—
☐	450	2c Washington Ty III (endwise coil), 12/21/15, eku	—
☐	452	1c Washington (sidewise coil), 3/22/15, eku	—
☐	453	2c Washington Ty I (sidewise coil), 11/14/14, eku	—
☐	454	2c Washington Ty II (sidewise coil), 7/7/15, eku	—
☐	455	2c Washington Ty III (sidewise coil), 2/4/16, eku	—
☐	456	3c Washington (sidewise coil), 4/13/16, eku	—
☐	457	4c Washington (sidewise coil), 11/5/15, eku	—
☐	458	5c Washington (sidewise coil), 5/15/17, eku	—
☐	460	$1 Franklin, 5/25/16, eku	—
☐	461	2c Washington (perf 11), 7/19/15, eku	—

1916-17

☐	462	1c Washington, 10/25/16, eku	—
☐	463	2c Washington, 11/1/16, eku	—
☐	464	3c Washington, 6/6/17, eku	—
☐	465	4c Washington, 2/18/17, eku	—
☐	466	5c Washington, 12/18/16, eku	—
☐	467	5c Washington carmine (color error), 5/25/17, eku	—
☐	470	8c Franklin, 10/17/17, eku	—
☐	472	10c Franklin, 12/29/16, eku.......................................	—
☐	473	11c Franklin, 4/13/17, eku	—
☐	474	12c Franklin, 10/13/16, eku	—
☐	475	15c Franklin, 3/2/17, eku	—
☐	477	50c Franklin, 8/31/17, eku	—
☐	478	$1 Franklin, 11/9/17, eku	—
☐	479	$2 Madison, 8/31/17, eku	—
☐	480	$5 Marshall, 8/31/17, eku	—
☐	481	1c Washington (imperf), 11/17/16, eku	—
☐	482	2c Washington (imperf), 1/9/17, eku	—
☐	482A	2c Washington (Ty Ia, imperf w/Schermack III perfs), 2/17/20, eku	20,000
☐	483	3c Washington (Ty I, imperf), 11/8/17, eku	—
☐	484	3c Washington (Ty II, imperf), 4/30/18, eku.................	—

1916-22

☐	486	1c Washington (endwise coil), 6/30/18, eku	—
☐	489	3c Washington Ty I (endwise coil), 2/16/17, eku	—
☐	490	1c Washington (sidewise coil), 3/30/17, eku................	—
☐	491	2c Washington Ty II (sidewise coil), 2/2/17, eku	—
☐	492	2c Washington Ty III (sidewise coil), 2/17/17, eku........	—
☐	493	3c Washington Ty I (sidewise coil), 11/2/17, eku	—
☐	494	3c Washington Ty II (sidewise coil), 5/29/18, eku	—
☐	497	10c Washington (sidewise coil), 1/31/22, First Day Cover, DC	2,500
		Only seen serviced by Henry Hammelman	

1917-19

☐	498	1c Washington, 4/19/17, eku	—
☐	498e	1c Washington (booklet), 6/22/17, eku........................	—
☐	498f	1c Washington (AEF booklet single), 9/10/17, eku........	—
☐	499	2c Washington, 3/27/17, eku	—
☐	499e	2c Washington (booklet), 10/30/17, eku.......................	—

SCOTT NUMBER	DESCRIPTION	UNCACHETED SINGLE
☐ 499f	2c Washington (AEF booklet single), 8/12/17, eku (probably a first day cover)	8,000
☐ 500	2c Washington Ty Ia, 12/22/19, eku	—
☐ 501	3c Washington Ty I, 7/3/17, eku...	—
☐ 501b	3c Washington Ty I (booklet), 2/8/18, eku	—
☐ 502c	3c Washington Ty II (imperf between), 5/7/22, eku	—
☐ 510	10c Franklin, 3/27/17, eku..	—
☐ 513	13c Franklin, 2/4/19, eku..	—
☐ 518	$1 Franklin, 12/13/17, eku	—

1918-20

☐ 523	$2 Franklin, 12/17/18, eku	—
☐ 525	1c Washington, 12/24/18, eku	—
☐ 526	2c Washington Ty IV, 3/15/20, First Day Cover (50-75 exist)........	900
☐ 527	2c Washington Ty V, 4/20/20, eku	—
☐ 528A	2c Washington Ty VI, 7/30/20, eku	—
☐ 528B	2c Washington Ty VII, 11/10/20, eku	—
☐ 529	3c Washington Ty III, 4/24/18, eku..	—
☐ 530	3c Washington Ty IV, 6./30/18, eku..	—
☐ 533	2c Washington Ty V (imperf), 6/30/20, eku	—
☐ 534B	2c Washington Ty VII (imperf), 11/3/20, eku, probably a first day cover	4,000
☐ 535	3c Washington Ty IV (imperf), 10/5/18, eku	—

1919

☐ 536	1c Washington, 8/15/19, First Day Cover (2 known)	4,000
☐ 537	3c Victory Issue, 3/3/19, First Day Cover (75-100 known)............	800
☐ 541	3c Washington, 6/14/19, eku	—

1920

☐ 542	1c Washington, 5/26/20, First Day Cover (40-50 known)..............	1000
☐ 543	1c Washington, 5/26/21, eku	—
☐ 548	1c The Mayflower, 12/21/20, First Day Cover (30-50 exist)	900
☐ 549	2c Landing of the Pilgrims, 12/20/20, First Day Cover (3 known).	5000
☐	covers dated 12/21/20 (50-75 exist)..	750
☐ 550	5c Signing the Compact, 12/21/20, First Day Cover (5-10 known)	2,500
☐	full set of three on one cover, 12/21/20 (15-20 known)..............	3,500

SCOTT NUMBER	DESCRIPTION	UNCACHETED SGL	BLK

1922-26

☐☐ 551	1/2c Nathan Hale, 4/4/25, DC...15.00		
☐☐	New Haven, CT 20.00		
☐☐	Unofficial city 40.00		
☐☐	Scott 551 & 576 (1/2c Hale & 1 1/2c Harding imperf.) on one cover, DC...125.00		
☐☐ 552	1c Benjamin Franklin, 1/17/23, DC, pair..............................25.00		30.00
☐☐	Philadelphia, PA 45.00		60.00
☐☐	Norristown, PA 50.00		
☐☐	Unofficial city 50.00		
☐☐ 553	1 1/2c Warren G. Harding, 3/19/25, DC, pair.......................25.00		35.00
☐☐ 554	2c George Washington, 1/15/23, DC.....................................35.00		50.00

| 551 | 552, 581,
597, 604 | 553, 576, 582,
598, 605, 631 | 557 | 562 |

| 565 | 567 | 571 | 572 | 573 |

1st George W. Linn cachet

610, 611, 612

614

615

616

617

1st Guy Atwood Jackson cachet

618

619

1st Ernest J. Weschcke cachet

1st Albert C. Roessler cachet

| 620 | 621 | 622 | 623 |

☐☐ 555	3c Abraham Lincoln, 2/12/23, DC 30.00		50.00
☐☐	Hodgenville, KY 250.00		375.00
☐☐	Unofficial city 150.00		—
☐☐ 556	4c Martha Washington, 1/15/23, DC 50.00		100.00
☐☐ 557	5c Theodore Roosevelt, 10/27/22, DC 125.00		175.00
☐☐	New York, NY 200.00		300.00
☐☐	Oyster Bay, NY 800.00		950.00
☐☐ 558	6c James A. Garfield, 11/20/22, DC.........................225.00		300.00
☐☐ 559	7c William McKinley, 5/1/23, DC.............................140.00		200.00
☐☐	Niles, OH..200.00		300.00
☐☐ 560	8c U.S. Grant, 5/1/23, DC 175.00		200.00
☐☐ 561	9c Thomas Jefferson, 1/15/23, DC...........................175.00		200.00
☐☐ 562	10c James Monroe, 1/15/23, DC 160.00		200.00
☐☐	Scott 554, 556, 561,562 on one cover.....................2500.		
☐☐ 563	11c Rutherford B. Hayes, 10/4/22, DC 600.00		775.00
☐☐	Fremont, OH...1200.		
☐☐ 564	12c Grover Cleveland, 3/20/23, DC..........................175.00		200.00
☐☐	Boston, MA (Philatelic Exhibition)........................175.00		200.00
☐☐	Caldwell, NJ...200.00		225.00
☐☐ 565	14c American Indian, 5/1/23, DC 375.00		475.00
☐☐	Muskogee, OK...1000.		
☐☐	Scott 565 and 560 on one cover, DC.......................1500.		
☐☐ 566	15c Statue of Liberty, 11/11/22, DC..........................500.00		
☐☐ 567	20c Golden Gate, 5/1/23, DC....................................500.00		
☐☐	San Francisco, CA..1200.		
☐☐	Oakland, CA, unofficial city ....1500.		
☐☐ 568	25c Niagara Falls, 11/11/22, DC...............................675.00		1000.
☐☐ 569	30c Buffalo, 3/20/23, DC...825.00		1350.
☐☐	Scott 569 and 564 on one cover, DC (1 known) ....2500.		
☐☐ 570	50c Arlington Amphitheater, 11/11/22, DC.............1200.		1650.
☐☐	Scott 566, 568, 570 on one cover ....4000.		
☐☐ 571	$1 Lincoln Memorial, 2/12/23, DC..........................5500.		
☐☐	Springfield, IL..5500.		
☐☐	Scott 571,555 on one cover, DC.............................7000.		
	1 exists - legal size		
☐☐ 572	$2 U.S. Capitol, 3/20/23, DC...............................11,000.		
☐☐ 573	$5 Head of Freedom Statue, 3/20/23, DC.............16,000.		
☐☐ 576	1 1/2c Warren G. Harding, 4/4/25, DC 45.00		60.00
☐☐ 581	1c Benjamin Franklin, unprecanceled 10/17/23, DC (1		
	known)..2000.		
☐☐ 582	1 1/2c Warren G. Harding, 3/19/25, DC 50.00		65.00
☐☐ 583	2c George Washington, 4/14/24, New York, NY, earliest		
	known use ....—		—
☐☐ 583a	George Washington, booklet pane of 6, 8/27/26, DC.............1500.		
☐☐ 584	3c Abraham Lincoln, 8/1/25, DC 55.00		90.00
☐☐ 585	4c Martha Washington, 4/4/25, DC 55.00		90.00
☐☐ 586	5c Theodore Roosevelt, 4/4/25, DC 57.50		90.00
☐☐ 587	6c James A. Garfield, 4/4/25, DC 60.00		110.00
☐☐ 588	7c William McKinley, 5/29/26, DC 70.00		120.00
☐☐ 589	8c U.S. Grant, 5/29/26, DC.......................................72.50		135.00
☐☐ 590	9c Thomas Jefferson,5/29/26, DC.............................72.50		135.00
☐☐	Scott 588, 589, 590 on one cover 300.00		
☐☐ 591	10c James Monroe, 6/8/25, DC.................................95.00		170.00

1923-29 Coils

Scott #	Description	PR	L PR
597	1c Benjamin Franklin, 7/18/23, DC	550.00	650.00
598	1 1/2c Warren G. Harding, 3/19/25, DC	50.00	70.00
599	2c George Washington, Type I, 1/15/23, DC (37 known)	1000.	
	Lancaster, PA, 1/10/23 (1 known)	1200.	
	South Bend, IN, 1/11/23 (1 known)	1400.	
	St. Louis, MO, 1/13/23 (1 known)	1400.	

Note: January 10, 1923 is the earliest known use of Scott 599. Philip Ward prepared 37 covers on January 15, 1923, the earliest known use in Washington, DC.

Scott #	Description	PR	L PR
599A	2c George Washington, Type II, 3/29/29, earliest known use	—	—
600	3c Abraham Lincoln, 5/10/24, DC	80.00	100.00
602	5c Theodore Roosevelt, 3/5/24, DC	82.50	125.00
603	10c James Monroe, 12/1/24, DC	100.00	150.00
604	1c Benjamin Franklin, 7/19/24, DC	90.00	
605	1 1/2c Warren G. Harding, 5/9/25, DC	70.00	
606	2c George Washington, 12/31/23, DC	100.00	

1923

Scott #	Description	SGL	BLK	SGL	BLK
610	2c Warren G. Harding, 9/1/23, DC	30.00	35.00		
	Marion, OH (5,000)	20.00	22.50		
	Brooklyn, NY; Mt. Rainier, MD; Caledonia, OH (Unofficial cities)	37.50			
	Pre-date, 8/31/23, DC, (1 known)	250.00			
	1st George W. Linn cachet (1st modern cachet)				800.00
611	2c Warren G. Harding, imperf. 11/15/23, DC	90.00	110.00		
	Pair	100.00			
	Pair or Block with line	110.00	160.00		
	Center line block	165.00			
	Unofficial city	100.00	110.00		
612	2c Warren G. Harding, perf 10, 9/12/23, DC	100.00	110.00		

1924

Scott #	Description	SGL	BLK	SGL	BLK
614	1c Huguenot-Walloon Tercentenary, 5/1/24, pair, DC	30.00	35.00		
	Albany, NY	30.00	35.00		
	Allentown, PA	30.00	35.00		
	Charleston, SC	30.00	35.00		
	Jacksonville, FL	30.00	35.00		
	Lancaster, PA	30.00	35.00		
	Mayport, FL	30.00	35.00		
	New Rochelle, NY	30.00	35.00		
	New York, NY	30.00	35.00		
	Philadelphia, PA	30.00	35.00		
	Reading, PA	30.00	35.00		
	Unofficial city	60.00			

1st Charles E. Nickles cachet

627

628

1st Herbert H. Griffin cachet

1st James H. Baxter cachet

1st Scott Stamp & Coin Co. cachet

629, 630

643

1st Joshua R. Gerow Jr. cachet

1st Haris R. Hunt cachet

1st Bradie Buchanan cachet

644

645

18

SCOTT NUMBER	DESCRIPTION	UNCACHETED SGL	UNCACHETED BLK	CACHETED SGL	CACHETED BLK
☐☐ 615	**2c Huguenot-Walloon Tercentenary, 5/1/24, DC.**	40.00	45.00		
☐☐	Albany, NY	40.00	45.00		
☐☐	Allentown, PA	40.00	45.00		
☐☐	Charleston, SC	40.00	45.00		
☐☐	Jacksonville, FL	40.00	45.00		
☐☐	Lancaster, PA	40.00	45.00		
☐☐	Mayport, FL	40.00	45.00		
☐☐	New Rochelle, NY	40.00	45.00		
☐☐	New York, NY	40.00	45.00		
☐☐	Philadelphia, PA	40.00	45.00		
☐☐	Reading, PA	40.00	45.00		
☐☐	Unofficial city	80.00			
☐☐ 616	**5c Huguenot-Walloon Tercentenary, 5/1/24, DC.**	50.00	55.00		
☐☐	Albany, NY	50.00	55.00		
☐☐	Allentown, PA	50.00	55.00		
☐☐	Charlestown, SC	50.00	55.00		
☐☐	Jacksonville, FL	50.00	55.00		
☐☐	Lancaster, PA	50.00	55.00		
☐☐	Mayport, FL	50.00	55.00		
☐☐	New Rochelle, NY	50.00	55.00		
☐☐	New York, NY	50.00	55.00		
☐☐	Philadelphia, PA	50.00	55.00		
☐☐	Reading, PA	50.00	55.00		
☐☐	Unofficial city	100.00			
☐☐	Scott 614-616, set of three on one cover, any official city	125.00	300.00		
	Values are for neat, clean covers.				

1925

SCOTT NUMBER	DESCRIPTION	UNCACHETED SGL	UNCACHETED BLK	CACHETED SGL	CACHETED BLK
☐☐ 617	**1c Lexington-Concord, 4/4/25, pair, DC**	27.50	35.00		
☐☐	Boston, MA	27.50	35.00	100.00	
☐☐	Cambridge, MA	25.00	35.00	100.00	
☐☐	Concord, MA	27.50	35.00	100.00	
☐☐	Concord Junction, MA	30.00	37.50		
☐☐	Lexington, MA	30.00	37.50	115.00	
☐☐	Unofficial city	45.00			
☐☐	1st Guy Atwood Jackson cachet (on any value)			150.00	
☐☐ 618	**2c Lexington-Concord, 4/4/25, DC**	30.00	35.00		
☐☐	Boston, MA	30.00	35.00	110.00	
☐☐	Cambridge, MA	30.00	35.00	110.00	
☐☐	Concord, MA	30.00	35.00	110.00	
☐☐	Concord Junction, MA	30.00	35.00		
☐☐	Lexington, MA	45.00	7500	110.00	
☐☐	Unofficial city	50.00			
☐☐ 619	**5c Lexington-Concord, 4/4/25, DC**	65.00	110.00		
☐☐	Boston, MA	65.00	110.00	125.00	
☐☐	Cambridge, MA	65.00	110.00	125.00	
☐☐	Concord, MA	65.00	110.00	125.00	
☐☐	Concord Junction, MA	65.00	110.00	125.00	
☐☐	Lexington, MA	65.00	110.00	125.00	
☐☐	Unofficial city	80.00			

Values for various cachet makers can be determined by using the Cachet Calculator which begins on page 40A.

SCOTT NUMBER	DESCRIPTION	UNCACHETED SGL	BLK	CACHETED SGL	BLK
☐☐	Scott 617-619 Set on one cover, Concord Junction or Lexington	140.00	250.00		
☐☐	Scott 617-619 Set on one cover, any other official city	110.00	250.00		
☐☐	Scott 617-619 Set on one cover, unofficial city	175.00	300.00		
☐☐	Scott 551,576, 585-587, 617-619 on one cover	*2500*			
	Values are for neat, clean covers.				
☐☐ 620	2c None-American, 5/18/25, DC	20.00	22.50		
☐☐	Algona, IA	20.00	22.50		
☐☐	Benson, MN	20.00	22.50		
☐☐	Decorah, IA	20.00	22.50		
☐☐	Minneapolis, MN	20.00	22.50		
☐☐	Northfield, MN	20.00	22.50		
☐☐	St.Paul, MN	20.00	22.50		
☐☐	Unofficial city	50.00			
☐☐ 621	5c Norse-American, 5/18/25, DC	30.00	45.00		
☐☐	Algona, IA	30.00	45.00		
☐☐	Benson, MN	30.00	45.00		
☐☐	Decorah, IA	30.00	45.00		
☐☐	Minneapolis, MN	30.00	45.00		
☐☐	Northfield, MN	30.00	45.00		
☐☐	St.Paul, MN	30.00	45.00		
☐☐	Unofficial city	65.00			
☐☐	Scott 620-621 Set on one cover, any city	50.00	70.00	250.00	
☐☐	1st Ernest J.Weschcke cachet			300.00	—
☐☐	1st Albert C. Roessler cachet			250.00	—

1925-26

☐☐ 622	13c Benjamin Harrison, 1/11/26, DC	20.00	30.00	—	—
☐☐	Indianapolis, IN	30.00	50.00	—	—
☐☐	North Bend, OH, unofficial city (500)	175.00	325.00	—	—
☐☐	Other unofficial cities	200.00	—	—	—
	Plate blocks, from this period, sell for two to three times the price of singles.				
☐☐ 623	17c Woodrow Wilson, 12/28/25, DC	25.00	27.50	250.00	—
☐☐	New York, NY	25.00	27.50	250.00	—
☐☐	Princeton, NJ	25.00	27.50	250.00	—
☐☐	Staunton, VA	25.00	27.50	250.00	—
☐☐	Bellefonte, PA, AMF, unofficial city	—	—	250.00	—
☐☐	Other unofficial cities	30.00	—	—	—
☐☐	1st Charles E. Nickles cachet			400.00	—

1926

☐☐ 627	2c Sesquicentennial Exposition, 5/10/26, DC	10.00	12.00	70.00	—
☐☐	Boston, MA	10.00	12.00	70.00	—
☐☐	Philadelphia, PA	10.00	12.00	70.00	—
☐☐	Chester, PA, unofficial city	—	—	60.00	—
☐☐	Valley Forge, PA, unofficial city	15.00	—	70.00	—
☐☐	Other unofficial cities	18.00	—	55.00	—
☐☐	1st Herbert H. Griffin cachet	—	—	150.00	—

SCOTT NUMBER	DESCRIPTION	UNCACHETED SGL	BLK	CACHETED SGL	BLK
☐☐	1st James H. Baxter cachet......................................			100.00	

Cacheted Sesquicentennial FDC's are most often found with Chester or Valley Forge, PA, unofficial cancels. Cacheted FDC's on this issue from official FDC cities are worth more than those from most unofficial cities.

☐☐	628 **5c Ericsson Memorial,** 5/29/26, DC 30.00	30.00	32.00	400.00	—
☐☐	Chicago, IL..30.00	30.00	32.00	400.00	—
☐☐	Minneapolis, MN.....................................30.00	30.00	32.00	400.00	—
☐☐	New York, NY...30.00	30.00	32.00	400.00	—
☐☐	Unofficial city..35.00	35.00	—	—	—

The cacheted value given above is for a cachet of two crossed gold bars on a blue envelope. Any other cachet sells for one quarter of the value listed.

☐☐	629 **2c Battle of White Plains,** New York, NY,				
☐☐	10/18/26..6.25	6.25	8.50	55.00	—
☐☐	New York, NY, International Philatelic				
	Exhibition Agency cancellation 6.25	6.25	8.50	55.00	—
☐☐	White Plains, NY (24,830) 6.25	6.25	8.50	55.00	—
☐☐	DC, 10/28/26 ....3.50	3.50	5.00	55.00	—
☐☐	Unofficial city..3.50	3.50	5.00	—	—
☐☐	**10/16/26,** pre-date 15.00	15.00	30.00	—	—
	1st Scott Stamp & Coin Co. cachet			75.00	—
☐☐	630 **2c Battle of White Plains,** souvenir sheet,				
	single or block identifiably from				
	souvenir sheet 7.00	7.00	10.00	50.00	75.00
☐☐	Imprint strip of 10 (top or bottom)......................		50.00	—	—
☐☐	Full sheet, 10/18/26 ....1,500.	1,500.	—	—	—
☐☐	Full sheet, official city, 10/18/26.................2,000.	2,000.	—	—	—
☐☐	Full sheet, 10/28/26 ....800.00	800.00	—	—	—
☐☐	Unofficial city, single 60.00	60.00	—	—	—

Values for various cachet makers can be determined by using the Cachet Calculator found on pages 32 to 38.

1926-34

☐☐	631 **1 1/2c Warren G. Harding,** imperf,8/27/26,				
	DC, pair 35.00	35.00	40.00		
☐☐	632 **1c Benjamin Franklin,** 6/10/27, DC, pair 45.00	45.00	55.00	165.00	—
☐☐	632a **Benjamin Franklin,** booklet pane of 6,				
	11/2/27 ....3500.	3500.	—	—	—
☐☐	633 **1 1/2c Warren G. Harding,** 5/17/27, DC,				
	pair 45.00	45.00	55.00	175.00	—
☐☐	634 **2c George Washington,** 12/10/26, DC.............47.50	47.50	57.50	175.00	—
	Experimental Electric Eye, 3/28/35 ....—	—	—	800.00	—
☐☐	634A **2c George Washington,** Type 2, 12/20/28,				
	Chicago, IL...775.00	775.00	—	—	—
☐☐	635 **3c Abraham Lincoln,** violet, 2/3/27, DC..........47.50	47.50	57.50	165.00	—
☐☐	635a **3c Abraham Lincoln,** bright violet, 2/7/34,				
	DC 25.00	25.00	38.00	38.00	—
☐☐	636 **4c Martha Washington,** 5/17/27, DC 50.00	50.00	57.50	200.00	—
☐☐	637 **5c Theodore Roosevelt,** 3/24/27, DC.............50.00	50.00	57.50	200.00	—
☐☐	638 **6c James A. Garfield,** 7/27/27, DC................57.50	57.50	110.00	200.00	—
☐☐	639 **7c William McKinley,** 3/24/27, DC 57.50	57.50	110.00	200.00	—
☐☐	Scott 637, 639 on one cover......................200.00	200.00	—	—	—

SCOTT NUMBER	DESCRIPTION	UNCACHETED SGL	BLK	CACHETED SGL	BLK
640	8c U.S. Grant, 6/10/27, DC	62.50	120.00	225.00	—
	Scott 632, 640 on one cover	200.00	—	—	—
641	9c Thomas Jefferson,5/17/27, DC	72.50	150.00	225.00	—
	Scott 633, 636, 641on one cover	250.00	—	—	—
642	10c James Monroe, 2/3/27, DC	90.00	155.00	225.00	—

1927

643	2c Vermont Sesquicentennial, 8/3/27, DC	5.00	6.00	50.00	55.00
	Bennington, VT (50,000)	5.00	50.00	55.00	
	Unofficial city	7.50	—	55.00	—
	1st Joshua R. Gerow Jr. cachet	175.00	—		
	1st Haris R. Hunt cachet (Scott 643 or 644)	—	—	90.00	
	1st Bradie Buchanan cachet	—	—	50.00	—
	1st S.S. Kurkjian cachet	—	—	125.00	
644	2c Burgoyne Campaign, 8/3/27, DC	12.50	15.00	55.00	60.00
	Albany, NY	12.50	15.00	55.00	60.00
	Rome, NY	12.50	15.00	55.00	60.00
	Syracuse, NY	12.50	15.00	55.00	60.00
	Utica, NY	12.50	15.00	55.00	60.00
	Oriskany, NY, unofficial city	35.00	—	—	—
	Schuylerville, NY, unofficial city	—	—	125.00	—
	Other unofficial city	20.00	—	—	—

1928

645	2c Valley Forge, 5/26/28, DC	4.00	15.00	45.00	50.00
	Cleveland, OH (town cancel)65.00	85.00	165.00	—	
	Lancaster, PA	4.00	15.00	45.00	50.00
	Norristown, PA (25,000)	4.00	15.00	45.00	50.00
	Philadelphia, PA	4.00	15.00	45.00	50.00
	Valley Forge, PA (70,000)	4.00	15.00	45.00	50.00
	West Chester, PA (15,000)	4.00	15.00	45.00	50.00
	Cleveland Midwestern Philatelic Sta. cancel	4.00	15.00	45.00	50.00
	Other unofficial city	7.50	—	45.00	—
	1st Joseph W. Stoutzenberg cachet			175.00	—
	1st Howard Davis Egolf cachet			100.00	—
	1st Adam K. Bert cachet			75.00	—
	1st Howard W. Weaver cachet			80.00	
646	2c "Molly Pitcher", 10/20/28, DC	15.00	20.00	80.00	—
	Freehold, NJ (25,000)	15.00	20.00	80.00	—
	Red Bank, NJ	15.00	20.00	80.00	—
	Unofficial city	15.00	—	90.00	—
647	2c Hawaii Sesquicentennial, 8/13/28, DC	15.00	17.50	75.00	77.50
	Honolulu, HI	17.50	20.00	75.00	77.50
	Unofficial city	20.00	—	85.00	—
648	5c Hawaii Sesquicentennial, 8/13/28, DC	22.50	25.00	75.00	77.50
	Honolulu, HI	25.00	28.00	75.00	77.50
	Unofficial city	30.00	—	—	—
	Scott 647, 648 on one cover	40.00	45.00	150.00	—
649	2c Aeronautics Conference, 12/12/28,				
	Green International Civil Aeronautic				
	Conference slogan	7.00	9.00	40.00	45.00
	Black, DC, town cancel	9.00	11.00	40.00	45.00
	Unofficial city	15.00	—	—	—

1st Joseph W. Stoutzenberg cachet

1st Howard Davis Egolf cachet

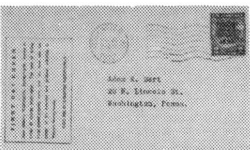

1st Adam K. Bert cachet

646

647

648

649

650

651

1st Floyd D. Shockley cachet

1st Harry C. loor cachet

1st Harry E. Klotzbach cachet

653

654, 655, 656

657

24

SCOTT NUMBER	DESCRIPTION	UNCACHETED SGL	UNCACHETED BLK	CACHETED SGL	CACHETED BLK
☐☐ 650	5c **Aeronautics Conference**, 12/12/28, Green International Civil Aeronautic Conference slogan	10.00	12.50	50.00	55.00
☐☐	Black, DC, town cancel	13.50	16.00	50.00	55.00
☐☐	Unofficial city	20.00	—	—	—
☐☐	Scott 649-650 on one cover, DC	15.00	—	70.00	—

Cacheted values are for covers with printed cachets. Covers with general purpose rubber stamp cachets sell at the uncacheted value. Rubber stamped Chamber of Commerce cachets sell for 1 1/2 to 2 times the uncacheted value.

1929

SCOTT NUMBER	DESCRIPTION	UNCACHETED SGL	UNCACHETED BLK	CACHETED SGL	CACHETED BLK
☐☐ 651	2c **George Rogers Clark**, Vincennes, IN, 2/25/29	6.00	7.50	30.00	32.50
☐☐	Unofficial city	10.00	—	35.00	—
☐☐	DC, 2/26/29, first day of sale by Philatelic Agency	3.00	4.00	22.50	32.50
☐☐	Charlottesville, VA, 2/26/29	7.00	—	30.00	—
☐☐	1st Floyd D. Shockley cachet	—	—	25.00	—
☐☐	1st Harry C. Ioor cachet	—	—	150.00	—
☐☐ 653	1/2c **Nathan Hale**, 5/25/29, DC	—	25.00	—	85.00
☐☐ 654	2c **Electric Light Jubilee**, 6/5/29, Menlo Park, NJ (77,000)	10.00	12.00	40.00	45.00
☐☐	Orange, NJ, unofficial	—	—	35.00	—
☐☐	Other unofficial city	—	—	35.00	40.00
☐☐	DC, 6/6/29, first day of sale by Philatelic Agency	4.00	5.00	16.50	22.50
☐☐	1st Harry E. Klotzbach cachet	—	—	100.00	—
☐☐ 655	2c **Electric Light Jubilee**, 6/11/29, DC	80.00	95.00	175.00	225.00
☐☐ 656	2c **Electric Light Jubilee**, coil, 6/11/29, DC	90.00	110.00	175.00	200.00
☐☐	Line Pair	—	150.00	—	300.00
☐☐	Scott 655-656 on one cover	150.00	—	400.00	—
☐☐ 657	2c **Sullivan Expedition**, Auburn, NY, 6/17/29 (5,000)	4.00	5.00	30.00	32.00
☐☐	Binghamton, NY (50,000)	4.00	5.00	30.00	32.00
☐☐	Canajoharie, NY (12,000)	4.00	5.00	30.00	32.00
☐☐	Canandaigua, NY	4.00	5.00	30.00	32.00
☐☐	Elmira, NY (11,000)	4.00	5.00	30.00	32.00
☐☐	Geneseo, NY	4.00	5.00	30.00	32.00
☐☐	Geneva, NY	4.00	5.00	30.00	32.00
☐☐	Horseheads, NY	4.00	5.00	30.00	32.00
☐☐	Owego, NY	4.00	5.00	30.00	32.00
☐☐	Penn Yan, NY	4.00	5.00	30.00	32.00
☐☐	Perry, NY	4.00	5.00	30.00	32.00
☐☐	Seneca Falls, NY (8,500)	4.00	5.00	30.00	32.00
☐☐	Waterloo, NY	4.00	5.00	30.00	32.00
☐☐	Watkins Glen, NY (6,500)	4.00	5.00	30.00	32.00
☐☐	Waverly, NY	4.00	5.00	30.00	32.00
☐☐	Loman, NY, unofficial city	40.00			
☐☐	Other Unofficial city	6.50	10.00	50.00	55.00
☐☐	DC, 6/18/29	2.00	3.00	20.00	25.00
☐☐	1st Robert C. Beazell cachet			300.00	
☐☐	1st A.C. Elliot cachet			65.00	
☐☐	1st R. Roscher cachet			60.00	

1st Robert C. Beazell cachet

1st A.C. Elliott cachet

1st Delf Norona cachet

680

681

682

683

684, 686

685, 687

688

689

1st Denys J. Truby cachet

690

**Values for various cachet makers can be determined
by using the Cachet Calculator which begins on page 40A.**

658, 668   669, 679

Kansas and Nebraska Overprints

The first day of sale for the complete series of 22 Kansas-Nebraska overprints, Scott 658 through 679, was May 1, 1929, at the Philatelic Agency in Washington, D.C.

Stamps of that series also are known canceled in April 1929 from 27 Kansas and 28 Nebraska towns. These are relatively scarce and command a price greater than the May 1, 1929, Washington, D.C., cancels.

Listed below are the earliest known cancels of these stamps at Kansas and Nebraska post offices in April 1929. Only a few of each are known to exist.

☐☐	658	1c **Kansas**, 5/1/29, DC, pair	35.00
☐☐		Newton, KS, 4/15/29	325.00
☐☐	659	1 1/2c **Kansas**, 5/1/29, DC, pair	35.00
☐☐		Colby, KS, 4/16/29	—
☐☐	660	2c **Kansas**, 5/1/29, DC	35.00
☐☐		Colby, KS, 4/16/29	—
☐☐		Dodge City, KS 4/16/29	—
☐☐		Liberal, KS 4/16/29	—
☐☐	661	3c **Kansas**, 5/1/29, DC	40.00
☐☐		Colby, KS, 4/16/29	—
☐☐	662	4c **Kansas**, 5/1/29, DC	45.00
☐☐		Colby, KS, 4/16/29	—

Plate blocks, from this period, sell for two to three times the price of singles.

☐☐	663	5c **Kansas**, 5/1/29, DC	45.00
☐☐		Colby, KS, 4/16/29	—
☐☐	664	6c **Kansas**, 5/1/29, DC	60.00
☐☐		Newton, KS, 4/15/29	400.00
☐☐	665	7c **Kansas**, 5/1/29, DC	70.00
☐☐		Colby, KS, 4/16/29	—
☐☐	666	8c **Kansas**, 5/1/29, DC	95.00
☐☐		Newton, KS, 4/15/29	400.00
☐☐	667	9c **Kansas**, 5/1/29, DC	95.00
☐☐		Colby, KS, 4/16/29	—
☐☐	668	10c **Kansas**, 5/1/29, DC 125.00	
☐☐		Colby, KS, 4/16/29	—
☐☐		Scott 658-668 on one cover, DC, 5/1/29	1200.00
☐☐		Scott 658, 664, 666, 4/15/29 Newton,KS	700.00

April canceled covers with Kansas overprint stamps are also known from Cape Henry, VA; Denver and Pueblo, CO; Kansas City, MO, and Waynesboro, PA.

☐☐	669	1c **Nebraska**, 5/1/29, DC, pair	35.00
☐☐		Beatrice, NE, 4/15/29	250.00
☐☐	670	1 1/2c **Nebraska**, 5/1/29, DC, pair	35.00
☐☐		Hartington, NE, 4/15/29	250.00
☐☐	671	2c **Nebraska**, 5/1/29, DC	40.00
☐☐		Auburn, NE, 4/15/29	—

SCOTT NUMBER	DESCRIPTION	UNCACHETED SGL	BLK	CACHETED SGL	BLK
☐☐	Beatrice, NE, 4/15/29 ....—				
☐☐	Hartington, NE, 4/15/29............................250.00				
☐☐ 672	3c **Nebraska**, 5/1/29, DC 40.00				
☐☐	Beatrice, NE, 4/15/29................................250.00				
☐☐	Hartington, NE, 4/15/29............................250.00				
☐☐ 673	4c **Nebraska**, 5/1/29, DC 47.50				
☐☐	Beatrice, NE, 4/15/29................................250.00				
☐☐	Hartington, 4/15/29...................................250.00				
☐☐ 674	5c **Nebraska**, 5/1/29, DC 47.50			90.00	
☐☐	Beatrice, NE, 4/15/29................................250.00				
☐☐	Hartington, NE, 4/15/29............................250.00				
☐☐ 675	6c **Nebraska**, 5/1/29, DC 70.00				
☐☐	Auburn, NE, 4/16/29..................................250.00				
☐☐ 676	7c **Nebraska**, 5/1/29, DC 75.00				
☐☐	Auburn, NE, 4/17/29..................................250.00				
☐☐ 677	8c **Nebraska**, 5/1/29, DC 75.00				
☐☐	Humbolt, NE, 4/17/29................................250.00				
☐☐	Pawnee City, NE, 4/17/29...........................250.00				
☐☐ 678	9c **Nebraska**, 5/1/29, DC 85.00				
☐☐	Cambridge, NE, 4/17/29.............................250.00				
☐☐ 679	10c **Nebraska**, 5/1/29, DC 95.00				
☐☐	Tecumseh, NE, 4/18/29................................—				
	Scott 669-679 on one cover, DC, 5/1/29.......1200.				

April canceled covers with Nebraska Overprint stamps are also known from Cleveland, OH, Kansas City, MO; and Washington, DC. There also are 1c and 2c Nebraska overprints canceled April 6, 1929 (pre-date), from Syracuse, NE, known and confirmed genuine by The Philatelic Foundation.

SCOTT NUMBER	DESCRIPTION	UNCACHETED SGL	BLK	CACHETED SGL	BLK
☐☐ 680	2c **Battle of Fallen Timbers**, Erie, PA, 9/14/29 ....3.50		4.00	30.00	32.00
☐☐	Maumee, OH 3.50		4.00	30.00	32.00
☐☐	Perrysburg OH 3.50		4.00	30.00	32.00
☐☐	Toledo, OH 3.50		4.00	30.00	32.00
☐☐	Waterville, OH (18,000) 3.50		4.00	30.00	32.00
☐☐	Fallen Timbers, PA...................7.00				
☐☐	Unofficial city 5.00	35.00			
☐☐	DC, 9/16/29...................2.00		3.00	20.00	22.00
☐☐ 681	2c **Ohio River**, Cairo, IL, 10/19/29 ....3.50		4.00	30.00	32.00
☐☐	Cincinnati, OH...................3.50		4.00	30.00	32.00
☐☐	Evansville, IN (30,000)...................3.50		4.00	30.00	32.00
☐☐	Homestead, PA (55,000)...................3.50		4.00	30.00	32.00
☐☐	Louisville, KY 3.50		4.00	30.00	32.00
☐☐	Pittsburgh, PA (50,000)...................3.50		4.00	30.00	32.00
☐☐	Wheeling, WV 3.50		4.00	30.00	32.00
☐☐	Unofficial city R.P.O....................7.50	40.00			
☐☐	R.P.O.10/18/29, pre-date 50.00				
☐☐	Other unofficial city 45.00				
☐☐	DC, 10/21/29...................2.00		2.50	20.00	22.00
☐☐	1st Delf Norona cachet			60.00	

**Uncacheted covers, from this period,
sell for about 20% that of cacheted covers.**

SCOTT NUMBER	DESCRIPTION	UNCACHETED SGL	UNCACHETED BLK	CACHETED SGL	CACHETED BLK

1930

☐☐ 682	2c Massachusettes Bay Colony, Boston,				
	MA 4/8/30 (60,000)	3.50	4.00	30.00	32.00
☐☐	Salem, MA	3.50	4.00	30.00	32.00
☐☐	Unofficial city	6.50		45.00	47.00
☐☐	DC, 4/11/30	2.00	2.50	20.00	22.00
☐☐ 683	2c Carolina-Charleston, Charleston, SC,				
	4/10/30 (100,000)	3.50	4.00	30.00	32.00
☐☐	Unofficial city	6.00			
☐☐	DC, 4/11/30	2.00	1.50	20.00	25.00
☐☐ 682-683	on one cover, DC, 4/11/30	4.00		35.00	
☐☐ 684	1 1/2c Warren G. Harding, pair, Marion,				
	OH, 12/1/30	4.50	5.00	35.00	37.00
☐☐	DC, 12/2/30	2.50	3.00	25.00	30.00
☐☐ 685	4c William H. Taft, Cincinnati, OH, 6/4/30	6.00	7.50	35.00	37.00
☐☐	DC, 6/5/30	3.00	3.50	25.00	30.00
☐☐ 686	1 1/2c Warren G. Harding, coil, Marion,				
	OH, 12/1/30	5.00	6.00	35.00	37.00
☐☐	DC, 12/2/30	3.00	3.50	25.00	30.00
☐☐	Scott 684, 686 on one cover, Marion,				
	OH, 12/1/30	7.50		45.00	
☐☐	Scott 684, 686, DC, 12/2/30	3.00		40.00	
☐☐ 687	4c William H. Taft, coil 9/18/30, DC	20.00	25.00	45.00	50.00
☐☐ 688	2c Braddock's Field, Braddock PA, 7/9/30				
	(50,000)	4.00	4.50	30.00	32.00
☐☐	Unofficial city	7.00		50.00	
☐☐	DC, 7/10/30	2.00	2.50	20.00	21.00
☐☐ 689	2c Von Steuben, New York, NY, 9/17/30	4.00	4.50	30.00	32.00
☐☐	Unofficial city			50.00	
☐☐	DC, 9/18/30	2.00	2.50	20.00	21.00
☐☐	Scott 687, 689 on one cover, DC	25.00		75.00	

1931

☐☐ 690	2c Pulaski, Brooklyn, NY, 1/16/31	4.00	4.50	30.00	32.00
☐☐	Buffalo, NY	4.00	4.50	30.00	32.00
☐☐	Chicago, IL	4.00	4.50	30.00	32.00
☐☐	Cleveland, OH	4.00	4.50	30.00	32.00
☐☐	Detroit, MI	4.00	4.50	30.00	32.00
☐☐	Gary, IN	4.00	4.50	30.00	32.00
☐☐	Milwaukee, WI	4.00	4.50	30.00	32.00
☐☐	New York, NY	4.00	4.50	30.00	32.00
☐☐	Pittsburgh, PA	4.00	4.50	30.00	32.00
☐☐	Savannah, GA	4.00	4.50	30.00	32.00
☐☐	South Bend, IN	4.00	4.50	30.00	32.00
☐☐	Toledo, OH	4.00	4.50	30.00	32.00
☐☐	Unofficial city	8.50		35.00	
☐☐	DC, 1/17/31	2.00			
☐☐	1st Denys J. Truby cachet			75.00	
☐☐ 692	11c Rutherford B. Hayes, 9/4/31, DC	100.00	135.00		
☐☐ 693	12c Grover Cleveland, 8/25/31, DC	100.00	135.00		
☐☐ 694	13c Benjamin Harrison, 9/4/31, DC	100.00	135.00		
☐☐	Woolrich, PA 9/4/31	500.00			
☐☐ 695	14c American Indian, 9/8/31, DC	100.00	135.00		

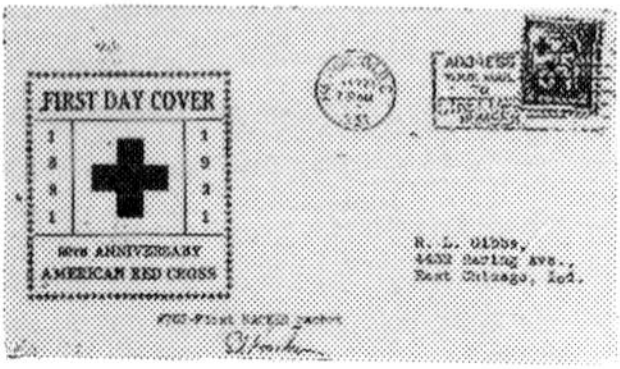

1st Edward G. Hacker cachet

1st Aero Print cachet

1st Covered Wagon cachet

702

703

704

705

706

707

708

709

710

711

712

713

714

715

1st Frederick R. Rice cachet

1st Beverly Hills cachet

1st Linprint cachet

716

717

718

SCOTT NUMBER	DESCRIPTION	UNCACHETED SGL	BLK	CACHETED SGL	BLK
696	15c Statue of Liberty, 8/27/31, DC...............125.00		225.00		
697	17c Woodrow Wilson, 7/25/31, Brooklyn,NY .1400.				
	DC, 7/27/31...400.00		725.00		
698	20c Golden Gate, 9/8/31, DC 325.00		650.00		
	Woolrich, PA, 9/4/31..................................500.00				
699	25c Niagara Falls, 7/25/31, Brooklyn, NY. ......1250.				
	DC, 7/27/31...400.00		800.00		
	Scott 697 and 699 on one cover,				
	Brooklyn, NY...2000.				
700	30c Bison, 9/8/31, DC 325.00		550.00		
701	50c Arlington Amphitheater, 9/4/31, DC.....450.00		875.00		
	Woolrich, PA, 9/4/31..................................700.00				
702	2c Red Cross, 5/21/31, DC...............................3.00		3.50	30.00	32.00
	Dansville, NY...3.00		3.50	30.00	32.00
	Unofficial city 6.00			45.00	
	1st Edward G. Hacker cachet			150.00	
703	2c Yorktown, 10/19/31, Wethersfield, CT.........3.50		4.00	40.00	42.00
	Yorktown, VA 3.50		40.00	40.00	42.00
	Unofficial city 7.00			55.00	
	1st Aero Print cachet			75.00	
	1st Walter G. Crosby cachet................................			200.00	
	1st Covered Wagon cachet...................................			75.00	
	Washington, DC, 10/20/31................................2.00		2.50	20.00	21.00
	10/5/31 pre-date Wenatchee, WA (75)				
	(AAMS #1146) 400.00				
	Any pre-date 10/6/31 through 10/18/31. .....25.00			80.00	

The Post Office Department experimented with a new stamp distribution method with the Yorktown stamp. This resulted in a number of pre-dates on this issue. FDC's postmarked in unofficial cities sell for 50 percent to 100 percent more than catalogue value.

1932 Washington Bicentennial

Scott	Description	SGL	BLK	SGL	BLK
704	1/2c olive brown, 1/1/32, DC ....—		5.00	—	20.00
705	1c green, pair, 1/1/32, DC....................................4.00		5.00	18.00	20.00
706	1 1/2c brown, pair, 1/1/32, DC 4.00		5.00	18.00	20.00
707	2c carmine rose, 1/1/32, DC................................4.00		5.00	18.00	20.00
708	3c deep violet, 1/1/32, DC 4.00		5.00	18.00	20.00
709	4c light brown, 1/1/32, DC 4.00		5.00	18.00	20.00
710	5c blue, 1/1/32, DC 4.00		5.00	18.00	20.00
711	6c red orange, 1/1/32, DC....................................4.00		5.00	18.00	20.00
712	7c black, 1/1/32, DC..4.00		5.00	18.00	20.00
713	8c olive bister, 1/1/32, DC..................................4.50		5.75	18.00	20.00
714	9c pale red, 1/1/32, DC.......................................4.50		5.75	18.00	20.00
715	10c orange yellow, 1/1/32, DC.........................4.50		5.75	18.00	20.00
	Scott 704-715 on one cover, DC................60.00			200.00	
	1st Plimpton cachet (on any single)......................			30.00	
	1st William T. Raley cachet (on any single)..........			40.00	
	1st Frederick R. Rice cachet (on any single			25.00	

Add 100 percent for unofficial first day cancel on this issue.

716	2c Olympic Winter Games, 1/25/32, Lake				
	Placid, NY...6.00		6.50	25.00	30.00
	Unofficial city			30.00	
	DC, 1/26/32..1.50		2.00	10.00	15.00
	1st Beverly Hills cachet			75.00	

719

720, 720b,
721, 722

723

724

725

1st Anderson cachet

1st Henry Grimsland cachet

1st Brookhaven cachet

726

727, 752

728, 730, 766a

729, 731, 767a

733, 735,
753, 768a

734

732

1st Albert B. Parsons cachet

**Values for various cachet makers can be determined
by using the Cachet Calculator which begins on page 40A.**

32

SCOTT NUMBER	DESCRIPTION	UNCACHETED SGL	UNCACHETED BLK	CACHETED SGL	CACHETED BLK
☐☐ 717	2c Arbor Day, 4/22/32, Nebraska City, NE. 4.00		4.50	15.00	18.00
☐☐	DC, 4/23/32..1.50		2.00	5.00	6.00
☐☐	Adams, NY, 4/23/32...6.50			18.00	20.00
☐☐	1st Linprint cachet..			15.00	
☐☐ 718	3c 10th Olympic Games, 6/15/32, Los Angeles, CA..6.00		6.50	25.00	30.00
☐☐	Unofficial..			35.00	
☐☐	DC, 6/16/32...2.75		3.00	8.00	9.00
☐☐ 719	5c 10th Olympic Games, 6/15/32, Los Angeles, CA..8.00		8.50	25.00	30.00
☐☐	Unofficial..			35.00	
☐☐	DC, 6/16/32...2.75		3.00	8.00	9.00
☐☐	Scott 718-719 on one cover, Los Angeles, CA..10.00		13.50	35.00	45.00
☐☐	Scott 718-719 on one cover, DC....................4.50				
☐☐	Scott 718-719 on one cover, unofficial			50.00	
☐☐ 720	3c George Washington, 6/16/32, DC................7.50		8.50	40.00	45.00
☐☐ 720b	George Washington, booklet pane of 6,				
	7/25/32, DC..100.00			200.00	
☐☐ 720b	George Washington, booklet single 20.00			60.00	

SCOTT NUMBER	DESCRIPTION	UNCACHETED SGL	UNCACHETED PR	CACHETED SGL	CACHETED PR
☐☐ 721	3c George Washington, coil, sideways,				
	6/24/32 ....15.00		20.00	50.00	60.00
☐☐ 722	3c George Washington, coil, endways,				
	10/12/32..15.00		20.00	50.00	60.00
☐☐ 723	6c James A. Garfield, coil, 8/18/32, Los				
	Angeles, CA..15.00		20.00	50.00	60.00
☐☐	DC, 8/19/32...4.00		6.00	30.00	35.00

SCOTT NUMBER	DESCRIPTION	UNCACHETED SGL	UNCACHETED BLK	CACHETED SGL	CACHETED BLK
☐☐ 724	3c William Penn, 10/24/32, New Castle, DE 3.25		4.00	15.00	18.00
☐☐	Chester, PA...3.25		4.00	15.00	18.00
☐☐	Philadelphia, PA...3.25		4.00	15.00	18.00
☐☐	Unofficial city..			30.00	
☐☐	DC, 10/25/32..1.25		1.50	9.00	10.00
☐☐ 725	3c Daniel Webster, 10/24/32, Franklin, NH 3.25		4.00	15.00	18.00
☐☐	Exeter, NH..3.25		4.00	15.00	18.00
☐☐	Hanover, NH (70,000) 3.25		4.00	15.00	18.00
☐☐	Marshfield, MA, unofficial............................35.00			37.00	
☐☐	Webster, MA, unofficial..................................			40.00	
☐☐	Any other unofficial city.................................			30.00	
☐☐	DC, 10/25/32..1.25		1.50	9.00	12.00
☐☐	Scott 724-725 on one cover 5.00		6.00	30.00	

1933

☐☐ 726	3c Georgia Bicentennial, 2/12/33,				
	Savannah, GA (200,000) 3.25		4.00	15.00	18.00
☐☐	Any Georgia town, 2/13/33 ....3.25			9.00	12.00
☐☐	DC, 2/13/33..1.50		2.50	8.00	9.00
☐☐	1st Anderson cachet			150.00	
	Because 2/12/33 was a Sunday, second-day covers for				
	Scott 726 were serviced.				
☐☐ 727	3c Peace of 1783, 4/19/33, Newburgh, NY				
	(349,571)...3.50		4.00	15.00	18.00
☐☐	Unofficial city..			30.00	

1st Torkel Gundel cachet

1st Top-Notch cachet

1st Donald Kapner cachet

1st Louis G. Nix cachet

736

737, 738, 754

739, 755

740, 751,
756, 769a

741, 757

742, 750, 758, 770a

743, 759

745, 761

747, 763

744, 760

1st Imperial cachet

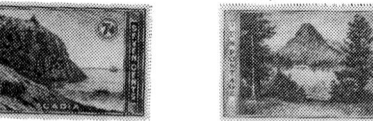

746, 762

748, 764

749, 765

34

SCOTT NUMBER	DESCRIPTION	UNCACHETED SGL	BLK	CACHETED SGL	BLK
☐☐	DC, 4/20/33......1.25	1.25	2.00	8.00	9.00
☐☐	1st Henry Grimsland cachet...............			350.00	
☐☐	1st Brookhaven cachet...............			85.00	
☐☐	1st Eagle Cover Service cachet...............			75.00	
☐☐	1st Newburgh Chamber of Commerce...............			65.00	
☐☐ 728	1c Century of progress, 5/25/33, strip of 3, Chicago, IL......3.00	3.00	3.50	15.00	18.00
☐☐	Unofficial city...............			20.00	
☐☐	DC, 5/26/33......1.00	1.00	2.00	9.00	12.00
☐☐ 729	3c Century of Progress, 5/25/33, Chicago,IL ...3.00	3.00	3.50	15.00	18.00
☐☐	Chicago Ridge fancy cancel 10.00	10.00	12.00	40.00	50.00
☐☐	Any other unofficial city...............			20.00	
☐☐	DC, 5/26/33......1.00	1.00	2.00	9.00	12.00
☐☐	Scott 728-729 on one cover 5.00	5.00	6.00	25.00	30.00
☐☐	1st Lan W. Kreicker cachet...............			40.00	
	Total FDC's mailed May 25: 232,251.				
☐☐ 730	1c American Philatelic Society, imperf. pane of 25, 8/25/33, Chicago, IL......100.00	100.00		200.00	
☐☐ 730a	American Philatelic Society, strip of 3 ......3.25	3.25	4.00	15.00	18.00
☐☐	DC, 8/28/33......1.25	1.25	2.00	9.00	12.00
	Values for various cachet makers can be determined by using the Cachet Calculator found on pages 32 to 38.				
☐☐ 731	3c American Philatelic Society, imperf. pane of 25, 8/25/33, Chicago, IL......100.00	100.00		200.00	
☐☐ 731a	American Philatelic Society, single 3.25	3.25	4.00	15.00	18.00
☐☐	DC, 8/28/33......1.25	1.25	2.00	9.00	12.00
☐☐	Scott 730a, 731a on one cover 5.50	5.50	6.50	20.00	22.00
	Total FDC's mailed Aug. 25: 65,218.				
☐☐ 732	3c National Recovery Act, 8/15/33, DC (65,000)......3.25	3.25	4.00	15.00	18.00
☐☐	Nira, IA, 8/17/33 unofficial 2.50	2.50	5.00	20.00	22.00
☐☐ 733	3c Byrd Antarctic, 10/9/33, DC......7.00	7.00	9.00	20.00	22.50
☐☐	1st Albert B. Parsons cachet...............			75.00	
☐☐ 734	5c Kosciuszko, 10/13/33, Boston, MA (23,025)......4.50	4.50	6.00	15.00	18.00
☐☐	Buffalo, NY (14,981) 5.50	5.50	7.00	15.00	18.00
☐☐	Chicago, IL (26,306)......4.50	4.50	6.00	15.00	18.00
☐☐	Detroit, MI (17,792) 5.25	5.25	6.00	15.00	18.00
☐☐	Pittsburgh, PA (6,282)......32.50	32.50	37.50	50.00	70.00
☐☐	Kosciuszko, MS (27,093)......5.25	5.25	6.00	15.00	18.00
☐☐	St. Louis, MO (17,872) 5.25	5.25	6.00	15.00	18.00
☐☐	DC, 10/14/33......1.60	1.60	2.00	15.00	18.00
☐☐	Unofficial city......10.00	10.00	12.00	40.00	50.00

1934

SCOTT NUMBER	DESCRIPTION	UNCACHETED SGL	BLK	CACHETED SGL	BLK
☐☐ 735	3c National Stamp Exhibition, imperf. pane of 6, 2/10/34, New York, NY 40.00	40.00		75.00	
☐☐	DC, 2/19/34......27.50	27.50			
☐☐ 735a	National Stamp Exhibition, single (450,715)......5.00	5.00	6.00	15.00	18.00
☐☐	DC, 2/19/34......2.75	2.75	3.50	10.00	12.00
☐☐ 736	3c Maryland Tercentenary, 3/23/34, St. Mary's City, MD (148,785)......1.60	1.60	2.00	10.00	12.00
☐☐	DC, 3/24/34......1.00	1.00	1.00	6.00	7.00

772

774

1st Winfred Milton Grandy cachet

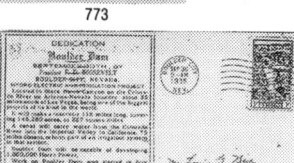

773

1st William H. Espenshade cachet

1st Norwood B. Scatchard cachet

775

776

777

778

1st John C. Sidenius cachet

1st Walter Czubay cachet

1st J. W. Clifford cachet

1st House of Farnam cachet

36

SCOTT NUMBER	DESCRIPTION	UNCACHETED SGL	BLK	CACHETED SGL	BLK
☐☐	1st Torkel Gundel cachet			350.00	
☐☐	1st Top-Notch cachet			30.00	
☐☐	1st Donald Kapner cachet			30.00	
☐☐	1st Louis G. Nix cachet			125.00	
☐☐ 737	3c Mothers of America, perf. 11x10 1/2,				
	5/2/34, any city...1.60	2.00	10.00	12.00	
☐☐ 738	3c Mothers of America, perf 11, 5/2/34,				
☐☐	any city..1.60	2.00	10.00	12.00	
☐☐	Scott 737-738 on one cover 4.00	5.00	25.00		
	FDC's mailed at Washington May 2: 183,359.				
☐☐ 739	3c Wisconsin Tercentenary, 7/7/34, Green				
	Bay, WI (130,000) 1.10	1.65	15.00	18.00	
☐☐	DC, 7/9/34...1.00	1.10	5.75	9.50	

National Parks Issue

SCOTT NUMBER	DESCRIPTION	UNCACHETED SGL	BLK	CACHETED SGL	BLK
☐☐ 740	1c Yosemite, strip of 3, 7/16/34, Yosemite,				
	CA (60,000) 2.75	3.25	10.00	12.00	
☐☐	DC, (26,219) 2.25	2.75	7.00	8.00	
☐☐ 741	2c Grand Canyon, pair, 7/24/34, Grand				
	Canyon, AZ (75,000) 2.75	3.25	10.00	12.00	
☐☐	DC, (30,080) 2.25	2.75	7.00	8.00	
☐☐ 742	3c Mt. Rainier, 8/3/34, Longmire, WA				
	(64,500)..3.00	3.50	10.00	12.00	
☐☐	DC, (30,114) 2.50	3.00	7.00	8.00	
☐☐ 743	4c Mesa Verde, 9/25/34, Mesa Verde, CO				
	(51,882)..2.75	3.25	10.00	12.00	
☐☐	DC, (21,729) 2.25	2.75	7.00	8.00	
☐☐ 744	5c Yellowstone, 7/30/34, Yellowstone, WY				
	(87,000)..2.50	3.00	10.00	12.00	
☐☐	DC (32,150) 2.25	2.75	7.00	8.00	
☐☐ 745	6c Crater Lake, 9/5/34, Crater Lake, OR				
	(45,282)..3.25	3.75	10.00	12.00	
☐☐	DC (19,161) 3.00	3.50	7.00	8.00	
☐☐ 746	7c Acadia, 10/2/34, Bar Harbor, ME (51,312)..3.25	3.75	10.00	12.00	
☐☐	DC, (20,163) 3.00	3.50	7.00	8.00	
☐☐ 747	8c Zion, 9/18/34, Zion, UT (43,650) 3.75	4.25	10.00	12.00	
☐☐	DC (19,001) 3.25	3.75	7.00	8.00	
☐☐ 748	9c Glacier Park 8/27/34, Glacier Park, MT				
	(52,626)..3.75	4.00	10.00	12.00	
☐☐	1st Imperial cachet		60.00		
☐☐	DC (16,250) 3.50	4.00	7.00	8.00	
☐☐ 749	10c Smoky Mountains, 10/8/34,				
	Sevierville, TN (39,000) 7.50	8.50	12.50	14.00	
☐☐	DC (18,368) 6.00	7.00	10.00	12.50	
☐☐	Smokemont, TN, unofficial		25.00		
☐☐	Scott 740-749 with park cancels		115.00	130.00	
☐☐ 750	3c American Philatelic Society, imperf.				
	pane of 6, 8/28/34, Atlantic City, NJ 40.00		65.00		
☐☐ 750a	American Philatelic Society, single (40,000)...3.25	4.25	10.00	12.00	
☐☐	DC, 9/4/34...2.00	2.50	8.00	10.00	
☐☐ 751	1c Trans-Mississippi Philatelic Exposition,				
	imperf. pane of 6, 10/10/34, Omaha, NE 35.00		65.00		

Plate blocks, from this period, sell for two to three times the price of singles.

782   783   784

1st Historic Art cachet

785

786   787   788

789   790   791

792   793   794

Values for various cachet makers can be determined by using the Cachet Calculator which begins on page 40A.

SCOTT NUMBER	DESCRIPTION	UNCACHETED SGL	BLK	CACHETED SGL	BLK
☐☐ 751a	**Trans-Mississippi Philatelic Exposition,**				
	strip of 3 (125,000) 3.25		4.25	10.00	—
☐☐	DC, 10/15/34................................2.00		2.50	6.00	—

1934 Special Printing

Nos. 752-771 issued 3/15/35.

☐☐ 752	3c Peace of 1783, DC 5.00		7.50	35.00	40.00
☐☐ 753	3c Byrd Antarctic, DC.........................6.00		7.50	35.00	40.00
☐☐ 754	3c Mothers of America, DC....................6.00		7.50	35.00	40.00
☐☐ 755	3c Wisconsin Tercentenary, DC...............6.00		7.50	35.00	40.00
☐☐ 756	1c Yosemite, strip of 3, DC....................6.00		7.50	35.00	40.00
☐☐ 757	2c Grand Canyon, pair, DC....................6.00		7.50	35.00	40.00
☐☐ 758	3c Mount Rainier, DC..........................6.00		7.50	35.00	40.00
☐☐ 759	4c Mesa Verde, DC............................6.50		7.50	35.00	40.00
☐☐ 760	5c Yellowstone, DC...........................6.50		7.50	35.00	40.00
☐☐ 761	6c Crater Lake, DC............................6.50		7.50	35.00	40.00
☐☐ 762	7c Acadia, DC.................................6.50		7.50	35.00	40.00
☐☐ 763	8c Zion, DC...................................7.50		8.00	35.00	40.00
☐☐ 764	9c Glacier Park, DC...........................7.50		8.00	35.00	40.00
☐☐ 765	10c Smokey Mountains, DC 7.50		8.00	35.00	40.00
☐☐ 766	1c Century of progress, imperf. pane of 25,				
	imperf, DC...................................			250.00	
☐☐ 766a	Century of Progress, strip of 3 ....5.50		7.50	40.00	45.00
☐☐ 767	3c Century of Progress, imperf. pane of 25,				
	DC			250.00	
☐☐ 767a	Century of Progress, single....................5.50		7.50	40.00	45.00
☐☐ 768	3c Byrd, imperf. pane of 6, DC................			250.00	
☐☐ 768a	Byrd, single..................................6.50		8.50	40.00	45.00
☐☐ 769	1c Yosemite, imperf. pane of 6, DC............			250.00	
☐☐ 769a	Yosemite, strip of 3 ....4.00		6.00	40.00	45.00
☐☐ 770	3c Mount Rainier, imperf. pane of 6, DC			250.00	
☐☐ 770a	Mount Rainier, single 5.00		7.00	40.00	45.00
☐☐ 771	16c Air Mail Special Delivery, DC.................12.50		16.00	40.00	60.00

SCOTT NUMBER	DESCRIPTION	CACHETED SGL	BLK	PL BLK
☐☐ 772	**3c Connecticut Tercentenary, 4/26/35, Hartford, CT.**			
	(217,800) 8.00		9.00	17.50
☐☐	DC, 4/27/35................................	1.25	1.75	2.75
☐☐	1st Winfred Milton Grandy cachet 40.00			
☐☐ 773	**3c California-Pacific Exposition, 5/29/35,**			
	San Diego, CA (214,042) 8.00		9.00	17.50
☐☐	DC, 5/31/35................................1.25		1.75	2.75
☐☐	1st William H. Espenshade cachet..............	50.00		
☐☐ 774	**3c Boulder Dam, 9/30/35, Boulder City, NV**			
	(166,180) 10.00		11.00	22.50
☐☐	DC, 10/1/35................................	2.00	2.75	3.75
☐☐	1st Norwood B. Scatchard cachet..............	75.00		
☐☐ 775	**3c Michigan Centenary, 11/1/35, Lansing, MI**			
	(176,962) 8.00		9.00	16.00
☐☐	DC, 11/2/35................................	1.25	1.75	2.00
☐☐	1st Risko Art Studio cachet...................	125.00		

1st Cachet Craft cachet

1st Pilgrim cachet

1st Fidelity Stamp Co. cachet

795

796

798

797

799

800

801

802

804, 839, 848

815, 847

HOW TO USE THIS BOOK

The number in the first column is its Scott number or
identifying number. Following that is the denomination
of the stamp, description, date of issue, and the value.

1936

☐☐	776	3c Texas Centennial, 3/2/36, Gonzales, TX			
		(319,150)..20.00	22.00	25.00
☐☐		DC, 3/3/36...1.50	2.00	3.00
☐☐		1st John C. Sidenius cachet 75.00		
☐☐		1st Walter Czubay cachet.........................75.00		
☐☐	777	3c Rhode Island Tercentenary, 5/4/36, Providence,			
		RI (245,400) 8.00	10.00	18.00
☐☐		DC, 5/5/36...1.25	1.75	2.75
☐☐		1st J.W. Clifford cachet 35.00		
☐☐	778	3c TIPEX, souvenir sheet, 5/9/36, New York, NY			
		(297,194) (TIPEX cancellation) 18.00		
☐☐		DC, 5/11/36...3.50		
☐☐		1st House of Farnam cachet 450.00		
		Uncacheted covers, from this period, sell for about 20%			
		that of cacheted covers.			
☐☐	778a-778d	Single from sheet.....................................5.00		
☐☐	782	3c Arkansas Centennial, 6/15/36, Little Rock, AR			
		(376,693)..8.00	10.00	18.00
☐☐		DC, 6/16/36...1.00	1.75	2.75
☐☐	783	3c Oregon Territory, 7/14/36, Astoria, OR (91,110)...8.50	9.50	15.00
☐☐		Daniel, WY (67,013)................................8.50	9.50	15.00
☐☐		Lewiston, ID (86,100)..............................8.00	9.00	15.00
☐☐		Missoula, MT (59,883).............................8.50	9.50	15.00
☐☐		Walla Walla, WA (106,150) 8.00	9.00	15.00
☐☐		DC, 7/15/36...1.25	1.75	2.75
☐☐		1st Whitman Centennial Inc. cachet 35.00		
☐☐	784	3c Susan B. Anthony, 8/26/36 DC (178,500) 7.00	8.00	9.00
☐☐		1st Historic Art cachet 35.00		

1936-37

☐☐	785	1c Army, strip of 3, 12/15/36, DC 5.00	6.00	11.00
☐☐	786	2c Army, pair, 1/15/37 ....5.00	6.00	11.00
☐☐	787	3c Army, 2/18/37, DC..............................5.00	6.00	11.00
☐☐		1st William J. Von Ohlen cachet 60.00		
☐☐	788	4c Army, 3/23/37, DC..............................5.50	6.50	11.00
☐☐	789	5c Army, 5/26/37, West Point, NY (160,000) 5.50	6.50	12.50
☐☐		DC, 5/27/37...1.25	1.75	2.75
☐☐		Scott 785-789 on one cover 40.00		
☐☐	790	1c Navy, strip of 3, 12/15/36, DC 5.00	6.00	11.00
☐☐	791	2c Navy, pair, 1/15/37, DC.......................5.00	6.00	11.00
☐☐	792	3c Navy, 2/18/37, DC..............................5.00	6.00	11.00
☐☐	793	4c Navy, 3/23/37, DC..............................5.50	6.50	11.00
☐☐	794	5c Navy, 5/26/37, Annapolis, MD (202,806)................5.50	6.50	12.50
☐☐		DC, 5/27/37...1.25	1.75	2.75
☐☐		Scott 790-794 on one cover 40.00		
☐☐		Scott 785-794 on one cover 80.00		
		Covers for both 1c values total 390,749; 2c values total			
		292,570; 3c values total 320,888; 4c values total 331,000.			

1937

☐☐	795	3c Northwest Ordinance Centennial, 7/13/37,			
		Marietta, OH (130,531)............................6.00	7.00	12.50
☐☐		New York, NY (125,134) 6.00	7.00	12.50

835

836

837

838

1st Artcraft cachet

852

853

854

855

856

858

857

859

864

869

874

879

884

889

HOW TO USE THIS BOOK
The number in the first column is its Scott number or
identifying number. Following that is the denomination
of the stamp, description, date of issue, and the value.

			CACHETED	
☐☐	DC, 7/14/37...1.20	1.75	2.75
☐☐	1st William S. Linto cachet 100.00		
☐☐	1st Cachet Craft cachet..........................75.00		
☐☐ 796	5c Virginia Dare, 8/18/37, Manteo, NC (226,730)......7.00	9.00	15.00
☐☐	Dare, VA, unofficial 11.00		
☐☐	DC, 8/19/37..1.50	2.50	3.50
☐☐ 797	10c Society of Philatelic Americans, souvenir sheet,		
	8/26/37, Asheville, NC (164,215).............................6.00		
☐☐	DC, 8/28/37..1.50		
☐☐ 798	3c Constitution Sesquicentennial, 9/17/37,		
	Philadelphia, PA (281,478)...............................6.50	7.50	11.00
☐☐	DC, 9/18/37..1.00	1.50	2.50
☐☐	1st Pilgrim cachet 100.00		
☐☐	1st Fidelity Stamp Co. cachet................................15.00		
☐☐ 799	3c Hawaii, 10/18/37, Honolulu, HI (320,334) 7.00	8.00	12.50
☐☐	DC, 10/19/37..1.00	1.50	2.50
☐☐ 800	3c Alaska, 11/12/37, Juneau, AK (230,370)...............7.00	8.00	12.50
☐☐	DC, 11/13/37..1.00	1.50	2.50
☐☐ 801	3c Puerto Rico, 11/25/37, San Juan, PR (244,054) 7.00	8.00	12.50
☐☐	DC, 11/26/37..1.00	1.50	2.50
☐☐ 802	3c Virgin Islands, 12/15/37, Charlotte Amalie, VI		
	(225,469) 7.00	8.00	12.50
☐☐	DC, 12/16/37..1.00	1.50	2.50
☐☐	799-802 Set of 4 on one cover 30.00	—	—

1938-54 Presidential Issue

			CACHETED	
☐☐ 803	1/2c Benjamin Franklin, block of 6, 5/19/38,		
	Philadelphia, PA (224,901)...............................	3.00	3.50
☐☐	DC, 5/20/38..	1.00	1.25
☐☐ 804	1c George Washington, strip of 3, 4/25/38, DC		
	(124,037) 3.00	3.50	6.00
☐☐ 804b	George Washington, booklet pane of 6, 1/27/39,DC 15.00		
☐☐ 805	1 1/2c Martha Washington, pair, 5/5/38, DC		
	(138,339) 3.00	3.50	4.00
☐☐ 806	2c John Adams, pair, 6/3/38, DC (127,806)................2.00	2.50	4.00
☐☐ 806b	John Adams, booklet pane of 6, 1/27/39, DC 15.00		
☐☐ 807	3c ThomnsJefferson,6/16/38,DC(118,097)...............3.00	3.50	4.00
☐☐ 807a	Thomas Jefferson, booklet pane of 6, 1/27/39, DC..18.00		
☐☐	Scott 804b, 806b, 807a on one cover, 1/27/39, DC..60.00		
☐☐ 808	4c James Madison, 7/1/38 (118,765), DC..................3.00	4.00	5.00
☐☐ 809	4 1/2c White House, 7/11/38, DC (115,820)................3.00	4.00	5.00
☐☐ 810	5c James Monroe, 7/21/38, DC (98,282) 3.00	4.00	5.00
☐☐ 811	6c John Q. Adams, 7/28/38, DC (97,428) 3.00	4.00	5.00
☐☐ 812	7c Andrew Jackson, 8/4/38, DC (98,414)..................3.00	4.00	5.00
☐☐ 813	8c Martin Van Buren, 8/11/38, DC (94,857) 3.00	4.00	5.00
☐☐ 814	9c William H. Harrison, 8/18/38, DC (91,229) 3.00	4.00	5.00
☐☐ 815	10c John Tyler, 9/2/38, DC (84,707) 3.00	4.00	5.00
☐☐ 816	11c James K. Polk. 9/8/38, DC(63,966) 3.00	4.00	5.00
☐☐ 817	12c Zachary Taylor, 9/14/38, DC (62,935)..................3.00	4.00	5.00
☐☐ 818	13c Mi!lard Fillmore, 9/22/38, (58,965)..................3.00	4.00	5.00
☐☐ 819	14c Franklin Pierce, 10/6/38, DC (49,819)..................3.00	4.00	5.00
☐☐ 820	15c James Buchanan, 10/13/38, DC (52,209) 3.00	4.00	5.00
☐☐ 821	16c Abraham Lincoln, 10/20/38, DC (59,566)............5.00	6.00	8.00
☐☐ 822	17c Andrew Johnson, 10/27/38, DC (55,024)............5.00	6.00	8.00

SCOTT NUMBER	DESCRIPTION	CACHETED SGL	BLK	PL BLK
823	18c U.S. Grant, 11/3/38, DC(53,124) 5.00		6.00	8.00
824	19c Rutherford B. Hayes, 11/10/38, DC (54,124) 5.00		6.00	8.00
825	20c James A. Garfield, 11/10/38, DC (51,971)...........5.00		6.00	8.00
	Scott 824,825 on one cover...................................25.00			
826	21c Chester A. Arthur, 11/22/38, DC (44,367) 5.00		6.00	8.00
	1st Union College cachet...................................30.00			
827	22c Grover Cleveland, 11/22/38, DC (44,358)............5.00		6.00	8.00
	Scott 826,827 on one cover...................................25.00			
828	24c Benjamin Harrison, 12/2/38, DC (46,592)...........5.00		6.00	8.00
829	25c William McKinley, 12/2/38, DC (45,691)............6.00		7.50	10.00
	Scott 828, 829 on one cover 30.00			
830	30c Theodore Roosevelt, 12/8/38, DC (43,528)..........7.50		9.00	14.00
831	50c William Howard Taft, 12/8/38, DC (41,984)......10.00		12.50	20.00
	Scott 830, 831 on one cover 30.00			
832	$1 Woodrow Wilson, 8/29/38, DC (24,618) 60.00		70.00	80.00
832c	$1 Woodrow Wilson, dry-printed, 8/31/54, DC (20,202)..30.00		40.00	45.00
833	$2 Warren G. Harding, 9/29/38, DC(19,895)..........125.00	175.00		250.00
834	$5 Calvin Coolidge, 11/17/38, DC (15,615).............200.00	300.00		450.00
	803-834 Set of 32 covers, matched cachets.....................550.00	650.00		800.00

1938-42 Presidential Electric Eye Issues

SCOTT NUMBER	DESCRIPTION	CACHETED SGL	BLK	PL BLK
803	1/2c Benjamin Franklin, block of 6, 9/8/41, DC		11.00	13.00
804	1c George Washington, strip of 3, 9/8/41, DC...........7.00		11.00	13.00
	Scott 803, 804, E 15 on one cover 25.00		40.00	
	Total for Scott 803, 804, and El5 Electric Eye is 22,000.			
805	1 1/2c Martha Washington, pair, 1/16/41.................8.00		11.00	13.00
	Total for Scott 805 Electric Eye is less than l0,000.			
806	2c John Adams, pair, 6/3/38, DC, Type I....................8.00		11.00	13.00
806	2c John Adams, pair, 4/5/39, DC, Type II..................8.00		11.00	13.00
807	3c Thomas Jefferson, 4/5/39, DC..............................8.00		11.00	13.00
	Scott 806, 807 on one cover 12.00		20.00	
	Total for Scott 806 and 807 Electric Eye is 28,500.			
808	4c James Madison, 10/28/41, DC...............................8.00	11..30		13.00
809	4 1/2c White House, 10/28/41, DC.............................8.00		11.00	13.00
810	5c James Monroe, 10/28/41, DC.................................8.00		11.00	13.00
811	6c John Q. Adams, 9/25/41, DC..................................8.00		11.00	13.00
812	7c Andrew Jackson, 10/28/41, DC..............................8.00		11.00	13.00
813	8c Martin Van Buren, 10/28/41, DC...........................8.00		11.00	13.00
814	9c William H. Harrison, 10/28/41, DC.......................8.00		11.00	13.00
815	10c John Tyler, 9/25/41, DC 8.00		11.00	13.00
	Scott 811,815 on one cover....................................20.00		30.00	
	Total for Scott 811 and 815 Electric Eye is 7,300.			
816	11c James K. Polk, 10/8/41, DC 15.00		18.00	30.00
817	12c Zachary Taylor, 10/8/41, DC..............................15.00		18.00	30.00
818	13c Millard Fillmore, 10/8/41, DC............................15.00		18.00	30.00
819	14c Franklin Pierce, 10/8/41, DC..............................15.00		18.00	30.00
820	15c James Buchanan, 10/8/41, DC 15.00		18.00	30.00
	Scott 816-820 on one cover 30.00		47.50	
821	16c Abraham Lincoln, 1/7/42, DC............................20.00		25.00	30.00
822	17c Andrew Johnson, 10/28/41, DC..........................20.00		25.00	30.00
	Scott 808-810, 812-814, 822 on one cover............35.00		55.00	
	Total for Scott 808-810 and 812-814, 822 Electric Eye is 16,200.			
823	18c U.S. Grant, 1/7/42, DC.....................................20.00		25.00	30.00

		SGL	BLK	PL BLK
☐☐ 824	19c Rutherford B. Hayes, 1/7/42, DC	20.00	25.00	30.00
☐☐ 825	20c James A. Garfield, 1/7/42, DC	20.00	25.00	30.00
☐☐	Scott 824-825 on one cover	30.00	55.00	
☐☐ 826	21c Chester Arthur, 1/7/42, DC	20.00	25.00	30.00
☐☐	Scott 821,823-826 on one cover	35.00	55.00	
☐☐ 827	22c Grover Cleveland, 1/28/42, DC	20.00	25.00	30.00
☐☐ 828	24c Benjamin H. Harrison, 1/28/42, DC	20.00	25.00	30.00
☐☐ 829	25c William McKinley, 1/28/42, DC	20.00	25.00	30.00
☐☐ 830	30c Theodore Roosevelt, 1/28/42, DC	20.00	25.00	30.00
☐☐ 831	50c William Howard Taft, 1/28/42, DC	20.00	25.00	30.00
☐☐	Scott 827-831 on one cover	35.00	55.00	

Total for Scott 827-831 Electric Eye is 6,700. These covers must have sheet selvage electric eye markings attached to stamps.

1938

☐☐ 835	3c Constitution Ratification, 6/21/38, Philadelphia, PA (232,873)	6.50	7.50	12.50
☐☐	DC, 6/16/38	1.00	1.50	2.50
☐☐ 836	3c Swedish-Finnish Tercentenary, 6/27/38, Wilmington, DE (225,617)	6.00	7.50	12.50
☐☐	DC, 6/28/38	1.00	1.50	2.50
☐☐ 837	3c Northwest Territory, 7/15/38, Marietta, OH (180,170)	6.00	7.50	12.50
☐☐	DC, 7/16/38	1.00	1.50	2.50
☐☐ 838	3c Iowa Territory, 8/24/38, Des Moines, IA (209,860)	6.00	7.50	12.50
☐☐	DC, 8/25/38	1.00	1.50	2.50
☐☐	1st G.S. Purcell cachet	30.00		

Perf. 10 Vertically   1939 Presidential Coils

		SGL	PR	L PR
☐☐ 839	1c George Washington, strip of 3, 1/20/39, DC		5.00	10.00
☐☐ 840	1 1/2c Martha Washington, pair, 1/20/39, DC		5.00	10.00
☐☐ 841	2c John Adams, pair, 1/20/39, DC		5.00	10.00
☐☐ 842	3c Thomas Jefferson, 1/20/39, DC	5.00	7.00	10.00
☐☐ 843	4c James Madison, 1/20/39, DC	5.00	7.00	10.00
☐☐ 844	4 1/2c White House, 1/20/39, DC	5.00	7.00	10.00
☐☐ 845	5c James Monroe, 1/20/39, DC	5.00	7.00	10.00
☐☐ 846	6c John Q. Adams, 1/20/39, DC	7.00	8.00	12.50
☐☐ 847	10c John Tyler, 1/20/39, DC	9.00	12.50	15.00
☐☐	Scott 839-847 set of 9 on one cover, 1/20/39	45.00	75.00	125.00

Perf. 10 Horizontally

		SGL	PR	L PR
☐☐ 848	1c George Washington, strip of 3, 1/27/39, DC		5.00	10.00
☐☐ 849	1 1/2c Martha Washington, pair, 1/27/39, DC		5.00	10.00
☐☐ 850	2c John Adams, pair, 1/27/39, DC		5.00	10.00
☐☐ 851	3c Thomas Jefferson, 1/27/39, DC	6.00	8.00	12.50
☐☐	Scott 848-851 set of 4 on one cover	30.00	40.00	60.00

1939

☐☐ 852	3c Golden Gate International Exposition, 2/18/39, San Francisco, CA (352, 165)	6.00	6.50	11.50

**Uncacheted covers, from this period,
sell for about 10% that of cacheted covers.**

1st Aristocrats cachet

1st Spartan cachet

894

896

895

897

898

899

900

901

903

1st Fleetwood cachet

902

904

905

906

907

908

909

910

☐☐ 873	10c Booker T. Washington, 4/7/40, Tuskegee Institute, AL (163,507) 6.00		7.00	9.00
☐☐ 874	1c John James Audubon, strip of 3, 4/8/40, St. Francisville, LA (144, 123).................2.00		2.50	3.00
☐☐ 875	2c Dr. Crawford W. Long, pair, 4/8/40, Jefferson, GA (158,128) 2.00		2.50	3.00
☐☐ 876	3c Luther Burbank, 4/17/40, Santa Rosa, CA (147,003).................2.00		3.00	4.00
☐☐ 877	5c Dr. Walter Reed, 4/17/40, DC (154,464) 2.50		3.50	5.00
☐☐ 878	10c Jane Addams, 4/26/40, Chicago, IL (132,375).................5.00		6.00	8.00
☐☐ 879	1c Stephen Collins Foster, strip of 3, 5/3/40, Bardstown, KY (183,461).................2.00		2.50	3.00
☐☐	1st Foster Assembly of Bardstown cachet 22.50			
☐☐	1st Bardstown Distillery cachet 22.50			
☐☐ 880	2c John Philip Sousa, pair, 5/3/40, DC (131,422) 2.00		2.50	3.00
☐☐	1st Fifth Battalion Marine Corps Reserve cachet. .22.50			
☐☐ 881	3c Victor Herbert, 5/13/40, New York, NY (168,200).................2.00		2.50	3.00
☐☐ 882	5c Edward A. MacDowell, 5/13/40, Peterborough, NH (135,155).................2.50		3.00	4.00
☐☐ 883	10c Ethelbert Nevin, 6/10/40, Pittsburgh, PA (121,951).................5.00		6.00	8.00
☐☐ 884	1c Gilbert Charles Stuart, strip of 3, 9/5/40, Narragansett, RI (131,965).................2.00		2.50	3.00
☐☐ 885	2c James A. McNeill Whistler, pair, 9/5/40, Lowell, MA (130,962).................2.00		2.50	3.00
☐☐ 886	3c Augustus Saint-Gaudens, 9/16/40, New York, NY (138,200).................2.00		2.50	3.00
☐☐ 887	5c Daniel Chester French, 9/16/40, Stockbridge, MA (124,608).................2.50		3.00	4.00
☐☐ 888	10c Frederic Remington, 9/30/40, Canton, NY (116,219).................5.00		6.00	8.00
☐☐ 889	1c Eli Whitney, strip of 3, 10/7/40, Savannah, GA (140,868) 2.00		2.50	3.50
☐☐ 890	2c Samuel F.B. Morse, pair, 10/7/40, New York, NY (135,388).................2.00		2.50	3.50
☐☐ 891	3c Cyrus Hall McCormick, 10/14/40, Lexington, VA (137,415).................2.00		2.50	3.50
☐☐	1st International Harvester cachet 18.00			
☐☐ 892	5c Elias Howe, 10/14/40, Spencer, MA (126,334) 5.00		6.00	8.00
☐☐ 893	10c Alexander Graham Bell, 10/28/40, Boston, MA (125,372).................7.50		8.50	10.00
☐☐	859-893 Set of 35 covers, matched cachets.................125.		175.	250.

1940

☐☐ 894	3c Pony Express, 4/3/40, St. Joseph, MO (194,589)...5.00		6.00	7.00
☐☐	Sacramento, CA (160,849) 5.00		6.00	7.00
☐☐	1st Aristocrats cachet 25.00			
☐☐ 895	3c Pan American Union, 4/14/40, DC (182,401)........4.50		5.50	7.50
☐☐ 896	3c Idaho Statehood, 7/3/40, Boise, ID (156,429) 4.50		5.50	7.50
☐☐	1st Papercraft Corp. cachet 30.00			
☐☐	1st Scenic Craft cachet.................30.00			

1st Smartcraft cachet

1st Pent Arts cachet

916

921

922

923

924

925

926

927

928

929

930

1st Bi-Color Craft cachet

1st Fluegel Cover cachet

934

937

RKA's

P. O. Box 6508
Lafayette, IN

Cachets

Phone/FAX
317-296-2502

- ★ Classic FDCs
- ★ Modern FDCs
- ★ Hand-Painted FDCs
- ★ First Cachets
- ★ Advertising Covers

C-10A booklet pane

We carry a large inventory. Send us your want lists and we'll send you a photocopy of what we have in stock along with the price.

RKA's Cachets introduced Dynamite Covers in 1994 with the Buffalo Soldier issue. The covers are printed, then hand watercolored and every U. S. stamp and postal stationery issue is offered.

Call or write for free catalog

Dynamite Covers

Subscriptions available • No deposit required

A.S.D.A.   A.F.D.C.S.   A.P.S.

935

936

938

939

940

941

942

1st Artmaster cachet

1st WCO cachet

943

944

946

945

947

948

949

950

951

**Values for various cachet makers can be determined
by using the Cachet Calculator which begins on page 40A.**

☐☐ 897	3c **Wyoming Statehood**, 7/10/40, Cheyenne, WY (156,709) 4.50		5.50	7.50
☐☐	1st Spartan cachet 30.00			
☐☐ 898	3c **Coronado Expedition**, 9/7/40, Albuquerque, NM (161,012) 4.50		5.50	7.50
☐☐	1st Albuquerque Philatelic Society cachet 30.00			
☐☐ 899	1c **Defense**, strip of 3, 10/16/40, DC 4.25		5.50	7.50
☐☐ 900	2c **Defense**, pair, 10/16/40, DC 4.25		5.50	7.50
☐☐ 901	3c **Defense**, 10/16/40, DC 4.25		5.50	7.50
☐☐	Scott 899-901 on one cover (450,083) 10.00		12.00	15.00
☐☐ 902	3c **Thirteenth Amendment**, 10/20/40, World's Fair, NY (156,146) 5.00		6.00	10.00

1941

☐☐ 903	3c **Vermont Statehood**, 3/4/41, Montpelier, VT (182,423) 6.00		7.50	10.00
☐☐	1st Dorothy Knapp cachet ....1000.			
☐☐	1st Fleetwood cachet 80.00			

1942

☐☐ 904	3c **Kentucky Statehood**, 6/1/42, Frankfort, KY (155,730) 4.00		6.00	9.00
☐☐	1st Signed Fleetwood cachet 50.00			
☐☐ 905	3c **"Win the War,"** 7/4/42, DC (191,168) 3.75		5.00	8.00
☐☐ 906	5c **Chinese Commemorative**, 7/7/42, Denver, CO (168,746) 9.00		10.00	14.00

1943

☐☐ 907	2c **Allied Nations**, pair, 1/14/43, DC (178,865) 3.50		5.25	7.00
☐☐ 908	1c **Four Freedoms**, strip of 3, 2/12/43, DC (193,800).3.50		5.25	7.00

1943-44 Overrun Countries

☐☐ 909	5c **Poland**, 6/22/43, Chicago, IL (88, 170) 5.00		6.00	15.00
☐☐	Washington, DC (136,002) 4.00		5.00	15.00
☐☐	1st Smartcraft cachet 20.00			
☐☐	1st Pent Arts cachet 25.00			
☐☐	1st Polonus Philatelic Society cachet 30.00			
☐☐ 910	5c **Czechoslovakia**, 7/12/43, DC (145,112) 4.00		5.00	10.00
☐☐ 911	5c **Norway**, 7/27/43, DC (130,054) 4.00		5.00	10.00
☐☐ 912	5c **Luxembourg**, 8/10/43, DC (166,367) 4.00		5.00	10.00
☐☐ 913	5c **Netherlands**, 8/24/43, DC (148,763) 4.00		5.00	10.00
☐☐ 914	5c **Belgium**, 9/14/43, DC (154,220) 4.00		5.00	10.00
☐☐ 915	5c **France**, 9/28/43, DC (163,478) 4.00		5.00	10.00
☐☐ 916	5c **Greece**, 10/12/43, DC (166,553) 4.00		5.00	10.00
☐☐ 917	5c **Yugoslavia**, 10/26/43, DC (161,835) 4.00		5.00	10.00
☐☐ 918	5c **Albania**, 11/9/43, DC (162,275) 4.00		5.00	10.00
☐☐ 919	5c **Austria**, 11/23/43, DC (172,285) 4.00		5.00	10.00
☐☐ 920	5c **Denmark**, 12/7/43, DC (173,784) 4.00		5.00	10.00
☐☐	Scott 909-920 on one cover 65.00			
☐☐ 921	5c **Korea**, 11/2/44, DC (192,860) 5.00		6.00	11.00
☐☐	Scott 909-921 on one cover 80.00			

1st Fulton cachet

1st C. W. George cachet

953

952

1st Jackson cachet

954

955

956

957

958

959

960

961

962

963

964

965

966

1944

☐☐ 922	3c **Transcontinental Railroad**, 5/10/44, Ogden, UT			
	(151,324)...5.00	6.00	9.00
☐☐	Omaha, NE (171,000)..............................5.00	6.00	9.00
☐☐	San Francisco,CA (125,000)......................5.00	6.00	9.00
☐☐ 923	3c **Steamship**, 5/22/44, Kings Point, NY (152,324) . .4.00	4.50	7.50
☐☐	Savannah, GA (181,472) 4.00	4.50	7.50
☐☐ 924	3c **Telegraph**, 5/24/44, DC (141,907)..........3.50	4.00	7.00
☐☐	Baltimore, MD (136,480)...........................3.50	4.00	7.00
☐☐ 925	3c **Philippines**, 9/27/44 (214,865), DC.............3.50	4.00	7.00
☐☐	1st Hobby Life cachet..............................35.00		
☐☐ 926	3c **Motion Picture**, 10/31/44, Los Angeles,		
	Hollywood Sta., CA (190,660) 3.50	4.00	7.00
☐☐	New York, NY (176,473) 3.50	4.00	7.00

1945

☐☐ 927	3c **Florida Statehood**, 3/3/45, Tallahassee, FL			
	(228,435)...3.50	4.00	7.00
☐☐ 928	5c **United Nations Conference**, 4/25/45, San		
	Francisco, CA (417,450)............................4.00	4.50	8.00
☐☐ 929	3c **Iwo Jima (Marines)**, 7/11/45, DC (391,650) 14.00	15.00	18.00
☐☐	1st Nu-Art cachet....................................30.00		

1945-46

☐☐ 930	1c **Franklin D. Roosevelt**, strip of 3, 7/26/45, Hyde			
	Park, NY (390,219)...................................2.50	3.50	5.50
☐☐	1st Bi-Color Croft cachet.........................25.00		
☐☐ 931	2c **Franklin D. Roosevelt pair**, 8/24/45, Warm		
	Springs, GA (426,142) 2.50	3.50	5.50
☐☐ 932	3c **Franklin D. Roosevelt**, 6/27/45, DC (391,650).......2.50	3.50	5.50
☐☐	1st Fluegel Covers cachet 60.00		
☐☐ 933	5c **Franklin D. Roosevelt**, 1/30/46, DC (466,766) 3.00	3.50	5.00
☐☐	Scott 930-933 on one cover 8.00		
☐☐ 934	3c **Army**, 9/28/45, DC (392,300)....................5.00	6.00	8.00
☐☐	1st R. Lee Southworth cachet 30.00		
☐☐ 935	3c **Navy**, 10/27/45, Annapolis, MD (460,352)..............7.00	8.00	9.00
☐☐ 936	3c **Coast Guard**, 11/10/45, New York, NY		
	(405,280)...7.00	8.00	9.00
☐☐ 937	3c **Alfred E. Smith**, 11/26/45, New York, NY		
	(424,950)...2.50	3.50	6.00
☐☐ 938	3c **Texas Statehood**, 12/29/45, Austin, TX (397,860).4.00	5.00	7.00

1946

☐☐ 939	3c **Merchant Marine**, 2/26/46, DC (432,141)..............7.00	8.00	9.00
☐☐	Scott 929, 934-936, 939 on one cover, 2/26/46 .....20.00		
☐☐ 940	3c **Veterans of World War II**, 5/9/46, DC (492,786). ..7.00	8.00	9.00
☐☐	1st Artmaster cachet...............................20.00		
☐☐	1st WCO cachet......................................30.00		
☐☐	Scott 929, 934-936, 939-940 on one cover, ...30.00		
☐☐ 941	3c **Tennessee Statehood**, 6/1/46, Nashville, TN		
	(463,512)...2.00	2.50	3.50
☐☐ 942	3c **Iowa Statehood**, 8/3/46, Iowa City, IA (517,505)....2.00	2.50	3.50
	1st Iowa City Stamp Club cachet 22.50		

	943	3c Smithsonian Institution, 8/10/46, DC (402,448) ...2.00	2.50	3.50
		1st Z-Special cachet...30.00		
	944	3c Kearny Expedition, 10/16/46, Santa Fe, NM		
		(384,300)..2.00	2.50	3.50

1947

	945	3c Thomas A. Edison, 2/11/47, Milan, OH		
		(632,473)..2.00	2.50	3.50
		1st Dorn's Wines cachet..................................20.00		
	946	3c Joseph Pulitzer, 4/10/47, New York, NY		
		(580,870)..2.00	2.50	3.50
	947	3c Postage Stamp Centenary, 5/17/47, New York,		
		NY (712,873)..2.00	2.50	3.50
		1st Fulton cachet..30.00		
	948	5c & 10c CIPEX, souvenir sheet, 5/19/47, New		
		York, NY (502,175)..3.00		
	949	3c Doctors, 6/9/47, Atlantic City, NJ (508,016)...........5.00	6.00	8.00
	950	3c Utah, 7/24/47, Salt Lake City, UT (456,416) 2.00	2.50	3.50
	951	3c U.S. Frigate Constitution, 10/21/47, Boston,		
		MA (683,416)...2.00	2.50	3.50
		1st C.W. George cachet 60.00		
		1st Sun Craft cachet..25.00		
	952	3c Everglades National Park 12/5/47, Florida		
		City, FL 2.00	2.50	3.50
		1st Artist Craft cachet.....................................20.00		
		1st Miami Philatelic Society cachet.......................20.00		

1948

	953	3c George Washington Carver, 1/5/48, Tuskegee		
		Institute, AL (402,179) 2.00	2.25	3.00
		1st Ira Bennett cachet.....................................50.00		
		1st Jackson cachet 40.00		
	954	3c California Gold Centennial, 1/24/48, Coloma,		
		CA (526,154)...2.00	2.25	3.00
	955	3c Mississippi Territory, 4/7/48, Natchez, MS		
		(434,804)..2.00	2.25	3.00
	956	3c Four Chaplains, 5/28/48, DC (459,070) 2.00	2.25	3.00
	957	3c Wisconsin Statehood, 5/29/48, Madison, WI		
		(470,280)..2.00	2.25	3.00
		1st Halpert cachet...20.00		
		1st Pearson cachet 20.00		
	958	5c Swedish Pioneers, 6/4/48, Chicago, IL (364,318)..2.00	2.25	3.00
		1st American Institute of Swedish Arts,		
		Literature & Science cachet...............................20.00		
	959	3c Progress of Women, 7/19/48, Seneca Falls, NY		
		(401,923)..2.00	2.25	3.00
	960	3c William Allen White, 7/31/48, Emporia, KS		
		(385,648)..2.00	2.25	3.00
	961	3c U.S.-Canada Friendship, 8/2/48, Niagara		
		Falls, NY (406,467)..2.00	2.25	3.00
	962	3c Francis Scott Key, 8/9/48, Frederick, MD (505,930) 2.00	2.25	3.00
	963	3c Salute to Youth, 8/11/48, DC (347,070)................2.00	2.25	3.00
	964	3c Oregon Territory, 8/14/48, Oregon City, OR		
		(365,898)..2.00	2.25	3.00

☐☐ 965	3c **Harlan Fiske Stone**, 8/25/48, Chesterfield, NH (362,170)................2.00		2.25	3.00
☐☐ 966	3c **Palomar Mountain Observatory**, 8/30/48, Palomar Mountain,CA (401,365)...........2.00		2.25	3.00
☐☐ 967	3c **Clara Barton**, 9/7/48, Oxford, MA (362,000) 2.00	.2.25	3.00	
☐☐ 968	3c **Poultry Industry**, 9/9/48, New Haven, CT (475,000)................2.00		2.25	3.00
☐☐ 969	3c **Gold Star Mothers**, 9/21/48, DC (386,064)...........2.00		2.25	3.00
☐☐ 970	3c **Fort Kearny**, 9/22/48, Minden, NE (429,633) 2.00		2.25	3.00
☐☐ 971	3c **Volunteer Firemen**, 10/4/48, Dover, DE (399,630)................4.00		4.25	5.00
☐☐	1st Mack (Mack Trucks) cachet 25.00			
☐☐ 972	3c **Indian Centennial**, 10/15/48, Muskogee, OK (459,528)................2.00		2.25	3.00
☐☐ 973	3c **Rough Riders**, 10/27/48, Prescott, AZ (399,198)...2.00		2.25	3.00
☐☐ 974	3c **Juliette Low**, 10/29/48, Savannah, GA (476,573) ..2.00		2.25	3.00
☐☐ 975	3c **Will Rogers**, 11/4/48, Claremore, OK (450,350) 2.00		2.25	3.00
☐☐	1st Kolor Kover cachet........................100.00			
☐☐ 976	3c **Fort Bliss**, 11/5/48, El Paso, TX (421,000)............2.00		2.25	3.00
☐☐	1st El Paso Stamp Club cachet...............20.00			
☐☐ 977	3c **Moina Michel**, 11/9/48, Athens, GA (374,090).......2.00		2.25	3.00
☐☐ 978	3c **Gettysburg Address**, 11/19/48, Gettysburg PA (511,990)................2.00		2.25	3.00
☐☐ 979	3c **American Turners**, 11/20/48, Cincinnati, OH (434,090)................2.00		2.25	3.00
☐☐	1st American Turners cachet, 11/21/48, Wash. DC.15.00			
☐☐ 980	3c **Joel Chandler Harris**, 12/9/48, Eatonton, GA (426,199) 2.00		2.25	3.00

1949

☐☐ 981	3c **Minnesota Territory**, 3/3/49, St. Paul, MN (458,750)................2.00		2.25	3.00
☐☐ 982	3c **Washington and Lee University**, 4/12/49, Lexington, VA (447,910)................2.00		2.25	3.00
☐☐ 983	3c **Puerto Rico Election**, 4/27/49, San Juan, PR (390,416)................2.00		2.25	3.00
☐☐ 984	3c **Annapolis Tercentenary**, 5/23/49, Annapolis, MD (441,802) 2.00		2.25	3.00
☐☐ 985	3c **G.A.R.**, 8/29/49, Indianapolis, IN (471,696)...........2.00		2.25	3.00
☐☐ 986	3c **Edgar Allan Poe**, 10/7/49, Richmond, VA (371,020)................2.00		2.25	3.00

1950

☐☐ 987	3c **Bankers**, 1/3/50, Saratoga Springs, NY (388,622).2.00		2.25	3.00
☐☐ 988	3c **Samuel Gompers**, 1/27/50, DC (332,023) 2.00		2.25	3.00
☐☐ 989	3c **National Capital Sesquicentennial (Freedom)**, 4/20/50, DC (371,743) 2.00		2.25	2.75
☐☐ 990	3c **National Capital Sesquicentennial (Executive)**, 6/12/50, DC (376,789) 2.00		2.25	2.75
☐☐ 991	3c **National Capital Sesquicentennial (Judicial)**, 8/2/50, DC (324,007)................2.00		2.25	2.75
☐☐ 992	3c **National Capital Sesquicentennial (Legislative)**, 11/22/50, DC (352,215) 2.00		2.25	2.75

967

968

969

970

971

972

973

974

975

976

977

978

979

980

981

982

983

984

986

985

987

988

989

SCOTT NUMBER	DESCRIPTION	SGL	CACHETED BLK	PL BLK
☐☐ 993	3c Railroad Engineers, 4/29/50, Jackson, TN (420,830)..3.00	3.00	3.50	4.00
☐☐ 994	3c Kansas City, Missouri, 6/3/50, Kansas City, MO (405,390)..2.00	2.00	2.25	2.75
☐☐ 995 ☐☐	3c Boy Scouts, 6/30/50, Valley Forge, PA (622,972)...3.00 1st Boy Scouts of America cachet..........................25.00	3.00	3.50	4.50
☐☐ 996	3c Indiana Territory, 7/4/50, Vincennes, IN (359,643)..2.00	2.00	2.25	2.75
☐☐ 997	3c California Statehood, 9/9/50, Sacramento, CA (391,919)..2.00	2.00	2.25	2.75

1951

SCOTT NUMBER	DESCRIPTION	SGL	CACHETED BLK	PL BLK
☐☐ 998 ☐☐	3c United Confederate Veterans, 5/30/51, Norfolk, VA (374,235) ....1.00 1st Dietz Printing Co. cachet...................................20.00	1.00	1.50	2.00
☐☐ 999	3c Nevada Centennial, 7/14/51, Genoa, NV (336,890)..2.00	2.00	2.25	2.75
☐☐ 1000	3c Landing of Cadillac, 7/24/51, Detroit, MI (323,094)..2.00	2.00	2.25	2.75
☐☐ 1001	3c Colorado Statehood, 8/1/51, Minturn, CO (311,568) 2.00	2.00	2.25	2.75
☐☐ 1002	3c American Chemical Society, 9/4/51, New York, NY (436,419)...2.00	2.00	2.25	2.75
☐☐ 1003 ☐☐	3c Battle of Brooklyn, 12/10/51, Brooklyn, NY (420,000)..2.00 1st Velvatone cachet 50.00	2.00	2.25	2.75

1952

SCOTT NUMBER	DESCRIPTION	SGL	CACHETED BLK	PL BLK
☐☐ 1004 ☐☐ ☐☐	3c Betsy Ross, 1/2/52, Philadelphia, PA (314,312).....2.00 1st Knoble/Bogert cachet ....75.00 1st Steelcraft cachet...30.00	2.00	2.25	2.75
☐☐ 1005	3c 4-H Clubs, 1/15/52, Springfield, OH (383,290) 2.00	2.00	2.25	2.75
☐☐ 1006 ☐☐ ☐☐	3c B. & O. Railroad, 2/28/52, Baltimore, MD (441,600)..2.00 1st M.W. Beck cachet ....20.00 1st T. Raquere cachet 20.00	2.00	2.25	2.75
☐☐ 1007 ☐☐	3c American Automobile Association, 3/4/52, Chicago, IL (520, 123)............................2.00 1st American Automobile Association cachet........15.00	2.00	2.25	2.75
☐☐ 1008	3c NATO, 4/4/52, DC (313,518)................................2.00	2.00	2.25	2.75
☐☐ 1009	3c Grand Coulee Dam, 5/15/52, Grand Coulee, WA (341,680) 2.00	2.00	2.25	2.75
☐☐ 1010	3c Lafayette, 6/13/52, Georgetown, SC (349,102)......2.00	2.00	2.25	2.75
☐☐ 1011	3c Mt. Rushmore Memorial, 8/11/52, Keystone, SD (337,027)..2.00	2.00	2.25	2.75
☐☐ 1012	3c Engineering Centennial, 9/6/52, Chicago, IL (318,483) 2.00	2.00	2.25	2.75
☐☐ 1013	3c Service Women, 9/11/52, DC (308,062)................2.00	2.00	2.25	2.75
☐☐ 1014	3c Gutenberg Bible, 9/30/52, DC (387,078) 2.00	2.00	2.25	2.75
☐☐ 1015	3c Newspaper Boys, 10/4/52, Philadelphia, PA (626,000)..2.00	2.00	2.25	2.75
☐☐ 1016	3c Red Cross, 11/21/52, New York, NY (439,252) 2.00	2.00	2.25	2.75

990

991

992

993

994

995

996

997

998

999

1000

1001

1002

1003

1004

**Values for various cachet makers can be determined
by using the Cachet Calculator which begins on page 40A.**

1st Velvatone cachet

1005

1006

1007

1008

1009

1010

1012

1011

1013

1014

1015

1016

1017

HOW TO USE THIS BOOK
The number in the first column is its Scott number or
identifying number. Following that is the denomination
of the stamp, description, date of issue, and the value.

1953

☐☐ 1017	3c National Guard, 2/23/53, DC (387,618) 2.00		2.25	2.75
☐☐ 1018	3c Ohio Sesquicentennial, 3/2/53, Chillicothe, OH			
	(407,983) 2.00		2.25	2.75
☐☐	1st Boerger cachet 25.00			
☐☐ 1019	3c Washington Territory, 3/2/53, Olympia, WA			
	(344,047) 1.00		1.00	1.50
☐☐	1st Tacoma Stamp Club cachet.............................20.00			
	1st Washington Territorial Centennial			
☐☐	Commission cachet.......................................15.00			
☐☐ 1020	3c Louisiana Purchase, 4/30/53, St. Louis, MO			
	(425,600) 2.00		2.25	2.75
☐☐ 1021	5c Opening of Japan Centennial, 7/14/53, DC			
	(320,541) 2.00		2.25	2.75
☐☐	1st Overseas Mailers cachet....................................60.00			
☐☐ 1022	3c American Bar Association, 8/24/53, Boston,			
	MA (410,036).................................2.00		2.25	2.75
☐☐ 1023	3c Sagamore Hill, 9/14/53, Oyster Bay, NY			
	(379,750) 2.00		2.25	2.75
☐☐ 1024	3c Future Farmers, 10/13/53, Kansas City, MO			
	(424,193) 2.00		2.25	2.75
☐☐ 1025	3c Trucking Industry, 10/27/53, Los Angeles, CA			
	(875,021).................................2.00		2.25	2.75
☐☐ 1026	3c General Patton, 11/11/53, Fort Knox, KY			
	(342,600) 1.75		2.50	3.50
☐☐	1st World Wars Tank Corps Association cachet . ..15.00			
☐☐ 1027	3c New York City, 11/20/53, New York, NY			
	(387,914) 2.00		2.25	2.75
☐☐ 1028	3c Gadsden Purchase, 12/30/53, Tucson, AZ			
	(363,250)................................2.00		2.25	2.75

1954

☐☐ 1029	3c Columbia University, 1/4/54, New York, NY			
	(550,745) 2.00		2.25	2.75

1954-68 Liberty Issue

☐☐ 1030	1/2c Benjamin Franklin, block of 6, 10/20/55, DC			
	(223,122)....................................		1.00	1.25
☐☐ 1031	1c George Washington, strip of 3, 8/26/54,			
	Chicago, IL (272,581) 1.00		1.00	1.50
☐☐ 1031A	1 1/4c Palace of the Governors, strip of 3,			
	6/17/60, Santa Fe, NM................................1.00		1.00	1.50
☐☐	1031A and 1054A on one cover..............................1.50			
	Total for Scott 1031A and 1054A is 501,848.			
☐☐ 1032	1 1/2c Mount Vernon, pair, 2/22/56, Mount			
	Vernon, VA (270,109)................................1.00		1.25	1.50
☐☐ 1033	2c Thomas Jefferson, pair, 9/15/54, San			
	Francisco, CA (307,300)................................1.00		1.25	1.50
☐☐ 1034	2 1/2c Bunker Hill Monument, pair, 6/17/59,			
	Boston, MA (315,060)................................1.00		1.25	1.50
☐☐ 1035	3c Statue of Liberty, 6/24/54, Albany, NY (340,001)..1.00		1.25	1.50
☐☐ 1035a	Statue of Liberty, booklet pane of 6, 6/30/54, DC			
	(131,839).................................5.00			

1st Boerger cachet    1st Overseas Mailers cachet

1018    1019    1020

1021    1022    1023

1024    1025    1026

1027    1028    1029

1031, 1054   1033, 1055   1036, 1058    1060

SCOTT NUMBER	DESCRIPTION	CACHETED SGL	BLK	PL BLK
☐☐ 1035b	**Statue of Liberty,** tagged, 7/6/66, DC 30.00			
☐☐ 1036	**4c Abraham Lincoln,** 11/19/54, New York, NY (374,064) 1.00	1.25	1.50
☐☐ 1036a	**Abraham Lincoln,** booklet pane of 6, 7/31/58, Wheeling, WV (135,825) 4.00		
☐☐ 1036b	**Abraham Lincoln,** tagged, DC (500) 75.00		
☐☐ 1037	**4 1/2c The Hermitage,** 3/16/59, Hermitage, TN (320,000) 1.00	1.25	1.50
☐☐ 1038	**5c James Monroe,** 12/2/54, Fredericksburg VA (255,650) 1.00	1.25	1.50
☐☐ 1039	**6c Theodore Roosevelt** 11/18/55, New York, NY (257,551) 1.00	1.25	1.50
☐☐ 1040	**7c Woodrow Wilson,** 1/10/56, Staunton, VA (200,111) 1.00	1.25	1.50
☐☐ 1041	**8c Statue of Liberty,** 4/9/54, DC (340,077) 1.00	1.25	1.50
☐☐ 1042	**8c Statue of Liberty,** (Giori press), 3/22/58, Cleveland, OH, (223,869) 1.00	1.25	2.00
	1st Cascade cachet 30.00		
☐☐ 1042A	**8c John J. Pershing,** 11/17/61, New York, NY (321,031) 1.00	1.25	2.00
☐☐ 1043	**9c The Alamo,** 6/14/56, San Antonio, TX (207,086) 1.50	2.00	3.00
☐☐ 1044	**10c Independence Hall,** 7/4/56, Philadelphia, PA (220,930) 1.00	1.25	2.00
☐☐ 1044b	**Independence Hall,** tagged, 7/6/66, DC 30.00		
☐☐ 1044A	**11c Statue of Liberty,** 6/15/61, DC (238,905) 1.00	1.25	2.00
☐☐ 1044c	**Statue of Liberty,** tagged, 1/11/67, DC 30.00		
☐☐ 1045	**12c Benjamin Harrison,** 6/6/59, Oxford, OH (225,869) 1.00	1.25	2.00
☐☐ 1045a	**Benjamin Harrison,** tagged, 5/6/68 ...... 25.00		
☐☐ 1046	**15c John Jay,** 12/12/58, DC (205,680) 1.00	1.50	2.00
☐☐ 1046a	**John Jay,** tagged, 7/6/66, DC 30.00		
☐☐ 1047	**20c Monticello,** 4/13/56, Charlottesville, VA (147,860) 1.20	1.75	2.50
☐☐ 1048	**25c Paul Revere,** 4/18/58, Boston, MA (196,530) 1.30	2.00	2.50
☐☐ 1049	**30c Robert E. Lee,** 9/21/55, Norfolk, VA (120, 166) 1.50	2.25	2.75
☐☐ 1050	**40c John Marshall,** 9/24/55, Richmond, VA (113,972) 1.75	2.50	3.00
☐☐ 1051	**50c Susan B. Anthony,** 8/25/55, Louisville, KY (110,220) 6.00	10.00	12.50
☐☐ 1052	**$1 Patrick Henry,** 10/7/55, Joplin, MO (80,191) 10.00	15.00	25.00
☐☐ 1053	**$5 Alexander Hamilton,** 3/19/56, Paterson, NJ (34,272) 55.00	90.00	125.00

SCOTT NUMBER	DESCRIPTION	CACHETED SGL	PR	L PR

1954-73 Liberty Coils

☐☐ 1054	**1c George Washington,** strip of 3, 10/8/54, Baltimore, MD (196,318)	1.00	1.50
☐☐ 1054A	**1 1/4c Palace of the Governors,** strip of 3, 6/17/60, Santa Fe, NM	1.00	1.75
☐☐ 1055	**2c Thomas Jefferson,** 10/22/54, St. Louis, MO (162,050)	1.00	1.50

1st Cascade cachet

1061

1062

1063

1065

1066

1064

1067

1068

1069

1070

1071

1072

1073

1074

1076

1077

1078

1080

1082

66

SCOTT NUMBER	DESCRIPTION	SGL	CACHETED PR	L PR
☐☐ 1055a	Thomas Jefferson, tagged, pair, 5/6/68, DC......		11.00	14.00
☐☐ 1056	2 1/2c Bunker Hill, 9/9/59, Los Angeles, CA			
	(198,680)		2.00	3.00
☐☐ 1057	3c Statue of Liberty, 7/20/54, DC (137,139)......	1.00	1.00	1.75
☐☐ 1058	4c Abraham Lincoln, 7/31/58, Mandan, ND			
	(184,079)	1.00	1.00	1.75
☐☐ 1059	4 1/2c The Hermitage, 5/1/59, Denver, CO			
	(202,454)	1.75	2.00	3.00
☐☐ 1059A	25c Paul Revere, 2/25/65, Wheaton, MD			
	(184,954)	1.20	2.00	3.00
☐☐ 1059b	Paul Revere, tagged, 4/3/73, New York, NY......	25.00		

SCOTT NUMBER	DESCRIPTION	SGL	CACHETED BLK	PL BLK

1954

☐☐ 1060	3c Nebraska Territory, 5/7/54, Nebraska City,			
	(401,015)	1.00	1.10	1.50
☐☐ 1061	3c Kansas Territory, 5/31/54, Fort Leavenworth,			
	KS (349,145)	1.00	1.10	1.50
☐☐ 1062	3c George Eastman, 7/12/54, Rochester, NY			
	(630,448)	1.00	1.10	1.50
☐☐ 1063	3c Lewis & Clark Expedition, 7/28/54, Sioux City,			
	IA (371,557)	1.00	1.10	1.50

1955

☐☐ 1064	3c Pennsylvania Academy of Fine Arts, 1/15/55			
	Philadelphia, PA (307,040)	1.00	1.10	1.50
☐☐ 1065	3c Land Grant Colleges, 2/12/55, East Lansing,			
	(419,241)	1.00	1.10	1.50
☐☐ 1066	8c Rotary International, 2/23/55, Chicago, IL			
	(350,625)	1.75	2.00	3.00
☐☐ 1067	3c Armed Forces Reserve, 5/21/55, DC (300,436)......	1.00	1.10	1.50
☐☐ 1068	3c New Hampshire, 6/21/55, Franconia, NH			
	(330,630)	1.00	1.10	1.50
☐☐	1st Texture Craft cachet......	35.00		
☐☐ 1069	3c Soo Locks, 6/28/55, Sault Sainte Marie, MI			
	(316,616)	1.00	1.10	1.50
☐☐ 1070	3c Atoms for Peace, 7/28/55, DC (351,940)	1.00	1.10	1.50
☐☐ 1071	3c Fort Ticonderoga, 9/18/55, Fort Ticonderoga,			
	NY (342,946)	1.00	1.10	1.50
☐☐ 1072	3c Andrew W. Mellon, 12/20/55, DC (278,897)	1.00	1.10	1.50

1956

☐☐ 1073	3c Benjamin Franklin, 1/17/56, Philadelphia, PA			
	(351,260)	1.00	1.10	1.50
☐☐	Poor Richard Station......	1.00	1.10	1.50
☐☐ 1074	3c Booker T. Washington, 4/5/56, Booker T.			
	Washington Birthplace, VA (272,659)	1.00	1.10	1.50
☐☐ 1075	3c & 8c FIPEX, Souvenir Sheet, 4/28/56,			
	New York, NY (429,327)	5.00		
☐☐ 1076	3c FIPEX, 4/30/56, New York, NY, (526,090)......	1.00	1.10	2.00

☐☐ 1077 3c Wildlife Conservation (Turkey), 5/5/56, Fond
du Lac, WI (292,121) 1.10   1.75   2.50

☐☐ 1078 3c Wildlife Conservation (Antelope), 6/22/56,
Gunnison, CO (294,731) 1.10   1.75   2.50

☐☐ 1079 3c Wildlife Conservation (Salmon), 11/9/56,
Seattle, WA (346,800) 1.10   1.75   2.50

☐☐ 1080 3c Pure Food and Drug Laws, 6/27/56, DC
(411,761) 1.00   1.00   1.50

☐☐ 1081 3c Wheatland, 8/5/56, Lancaster, PA (340,142) 1.00   1.10   1.50
☐☐ 1082 3c Labor Day, 9/3/56, Camden, NJ (338,450).............1.00   1.10   1.50
☐☐ 1083 3c Nassau Hall 9/22/56, Princeton, NJ (350,756) 1.00   1.10   1.50
☐☐ 1084 3c Devils Tower, 9/24/56, Devils Tower, WY
(285,090) 1.00   1.10   1.50

☐☐ 1085 3c Children, 12/15/56, DC (305,125) 1.00   1.10   1.50

1957

☐☐ 1086 3c Alexander Hamilton, 1/11/57, New York, NY
(305,117) 1.00   1.10   1.50

☐☐ 1087 3c Polio, 1/15/57, DC (307,630) 1.00   1.10   1.50
☐☐ 1088 3c Coast & Geodetic Survey, 2/11/57, Seattle, WA
(309,931) 1.00   1.10   1.50

☐☐ 1089 3c Architects, 2/23/57, New York, NY (368,840)........1.00   1.10   1.50
☐☐ 1090 3c Steel Industry, 5/22/57, New York, NY
(473,284) 1.00   1.10   1.50

☐☐ 1091 3c International Naval Review, 6/10/57, U.S.S.
Saratoga, Norfolk, VA (365,933) 1.00   1.10   1.50

☐☐ 1092 3c Oklahoma Statehood, 6/14/57, Oklahoma City,
OK (327,172) 1.00   1.10   1.50

☐☐ 1093 3c School Teachers, 7/1/57, Philadelphia, PA
(375,986) 1.00   1.10   1.50

☐☐   "Philadelpia" error cancel 8.00   10.00
☐☐ 1094 4c Flag, 7/4/57, DC (523,879) 1.00   1.10   1.50
☐☐ 1095 3c Shipbuilding, 8/15/57, Bath, ME (347,432) 1.00   1.10   1.50
☐☐ 1096 8c Ramon Magsaysay, 8/31/57, DC (334,558)............1.00   1.10   1.50
☐☐ 1097 3c Lafayette Bicentenary, 9/6/57, Easton, PA
(260,421) 1.00   1.10   1.50
        Fayetteville, NC (230,000)...........................1.00   1.10   1.50
        Louisville, KY (207,856) 1.00   1.10   1.50

☐☐ 1098 3c Wildlife Conservation (Whooping Cranes),
11/22/57, New York, NY (342,970)............................1.00   1.50   2.00
        New Orleans, LA (154,327)............................1.00   1.50   2.00
        Corpus Christi, TX (280,990) 1.00   1.50   2.00

☐☐ 1099 3c Religious Freedom, 12/27/57, Flushing NY
(357,770) 1.00   1.10   1.50

1958

☐☐ 1100 3c Gardening-Horticulture, 3/15/58, Ithaca, NY
(451,292) 1.00   1.10   1.50

☐☐ 1104 3c Brussels Fair, 4/17/58, Detroit, MI (428,073)........1.00   1.10   1.50
☐☐ 1105 3c James Monroe, 4/28/58, Montross, VA (326,988)..1.00   1.10   1.50
☐☐ 1106 3c Minnesota Statehood, 5/11/58, Saint Paul, MN
(475,522) 1.00   1.10   1.50

☐☐ 1107 3c Internati1nal Geophysical Year, 5/31/58,
Chicago, IL (397,000) 1.00   1.10   1.50

Subscribe To

SCOTT
Stamp Monthly

Each month it's a fascinating look at the people, places and events related to stamps. Time-saving hints, remarkable stamp discoveries and quirky amusing tales focusing on bizarre facets of the hobby, you'll find it all in Scott Stamp Monthly.

12 Issues $16.95

To subscribe call
1-800-488-5351

1079

1081

1083

1084

1085

1086

1087

1088

1089

1090

1091

1092

1096

1093

1094

1095

1097

1098

1099

1100

SCOTT NUMBER	DESCRIPTION	SGL	CACHETED BLK	PL BLK
☐☐ 1108	3c Gunston Hall, 6/12/58, Lorton, VA (349,801) 1.00		1.10	1.50
☐☐ 1109	3c Mackinac Bridge, 6/25/58, Mackinac,		1.10	1.50
	MI (445,605)..1.00		1.10	1.50
☐☐ 1110	4c Simon Bolivar, 7/24/58, DC.....................................1.00		1.10	1.50
☐☐ 1111	8c Simon Bolivar, 7/24/58, DC.....................................1.00		1.10	1.50
☐☐	Scott 1110-1111 on one cover 2.00			
	Total for Scott 1110-1111 is 708,777.			
☐☐ 1112	4c Atlantic Cable, 8/15/58, New York, NY (365,072).1.00		1.10	1.50

1958-59

☐☐ 1113	1c Lincoln Sesquicentennial, 2/12/59, Hodgenville,			
	KY (379,862)...		1.00	1.50
☐☐ 1114	3c Lincoln Sesquicentennial, pair, 2/27/59, New			
	York, NY (437,737)..1.00		1.10	1.50
☐☐ 1115	4c Lincoln-Douglas Debates, 8/27/58, Freeport, IL			
	(373,063)..1.00		1.10	1.50
☐☐	1st Western Cachets cachet 25.00			
☐☐ 1116	4c Lincoln Sesquicentennial, 5/30/59, DC			
	(894,887)..1.00		1.10	1.50

1958

☐☐ 1117	4c Lajos Kossnth, 9/19/58, DC.....................................1.00		1.10	1.50
☐☐ 1118	8c Lajos Kossuth, 9/19/58, DC.....................................1.00		1.10	1.50
☐☐	Scott 1117-1118 on one cover 2.00			
	Total for Scott 1117 and 1118 is 722,188.			
☐☐ 1119	4c Freedom of Press, 9/22/58, Columbia, MO			
	(411,752)..1.00		1.10	1.50
☐☐ 1120	4c Overland Mail, 10/10/58, San Francisco, CA			
	(352,760)..1.00		1.10	1.50
☐☐ 1121	4c Noah Webster, 10/16/58, West Hartford, CT			
	(364,608)..1.00		1.10	1.50
☐☐ 1122	4c Forest Conservation, 10/27/58, Tucson, AZ			
	(405,959)..1.00		1.10	1.50
☐☐ 1123	4c Fort Duquesne, 11/25/58, Pittsburgh, PA			
	(421,764)..1.00		1.10	1.50

1959

☐☐ 1124	4c Oregon Statehood, 2/14/59, Astoria, OR			
	(452,764)..1.00		1.10	1.50
☐☐ 1125	4c Jose de San Martin, 2/25/ 59, DC...........................1.00		1.10	1.50
☐☐ 1126	8c Jose de San Martin, 2/25/59, DC...........................1.00		1.25	1.50
☐☐	Scott 1125-1126 on one cover 2.00			
	Total for Scott 1125 and 1126 is 910,208.			
☐☐ 1127	4c NATO, 4/1/59, DC (361,040)....................................1.00		1.10	1.50
☐☐	1st Gold Craft cachet...35.00			
☐☐ 1128	4c Arctic Explorations, 4/6/59, Cresson, PA			
	(397,770)..1.00		1.10	. 1.50
☐☐ 1129	8c World Peace through World Trade, 4/20/59,			
	DC (503,618) 1.00		1.25	1.50
☐☐ 1130	4c Silver Centennial, 6/8/59, Virginia City, NV			
	(337,233)..1.00		1.10	1.50
☐☐ 1131	4c St. Lawrence Seaway, 6/26/59, Massena, NY			
	(543,211)..1.00		1.10	1.50
☐☐ 1132	4c Flag (49 stars), 7/4/59, Auburn, NY (523,773)......1.00		1.00	1.50

1104

1105

1106

1107

1108

1110-11

1109

1112

1115

1113

1114

1st Western Cachets cachet

1116

1117-18

**Values for various cachet makers can be determined
by using the Cachet Calculator which begins on page 40A.**

SCOTT NUMBER	DESCRIPTION	CACHETED SGL	BLK	PL BLK
☐☐ 1133	4c Soil Conservation, 8/26/59, Rapid City, SD		1.10	1.50
	(400,613) 1.00			
☐☐ 1134	4c Petroleum Industry, 8/27/59, Titusville, PA		1.10	1.50
	(801,859) 1.00			
☐☐	1st Col. Drake Philatelic Society cachet.............15.00			
☐☐ 1135	4c Dental Health, 9/14/59, New York, NY			
	(649,813) 4.00		4.25	4.75
☐☐ 1136	4c Ernst Reuter, 9/29/59 DC..............................1.00		1.10	1.50
☐☐ 1137	8c Ernst Reuter, 9/29/59 DC..............................1.00		1.25	1.50
☐☐	Scott 1136-1137 on one cover 2.00			
	Total for Scott 1136 and 1137 is 1,207,933.			
☐☐ 1138	4c Dr. Ephraim McDowell, 12/3/59, Danville, KY		1.10	1.50
	(344,603) 1.00			

1960-61

☐☐ 1139	4c American Credo, George Washington, 1/20/60,			
	Mount Vernon, VA (438,335)............................1.00		1.15	2.00
☐☐ 1140	4c American Credo, Benjamin Franklin, 3/31/60,			
	Philadelphia, PA (497,913).............................1.00		1.15	2.00
☐☐ 1141	4c American Credo, Thomas Jefferson, 5/18/60,			
	Charlottesville, VA (454,903)...........................1.00		1.15	2.00
☐☐ 1142	4c American Credo, Francis Scott Key, 9/14/60,			
	Baltimore, MD (501,129).................................1.00		1.15	2.00
☐☐ 1143	4c American Credo, Abraham Lincoln, 11/19/60,			
	New York, NY (467,780) 1.00		1.15	2.00
☐☐	1st Ritz cachet..20.00			
☐☐	1st National Urban League cachet.....................20.00			
☐☐	1st Springfield, (IL) Philatelic Society cachet.........15.00			
☐☐ 1144	4c American Credo, Patrick Henry, 1/11/61,			
	Richmond, VA (415,252)..................................1.00		1.15	2.00

1960

☐☐ 1145	4c Boy Scouts, 2/8/60, DC (1,419,955) 1.75		2.50	3.50
☐☐ 1146	4c Olympic Winter Games, 2/18/60, Olympic			
	Valley, CA (516,456) 1.00		1.10	1.50
☐☐ 1147	4c Thomas G. Masaryk, 3/7/60, DC.....................1.00		1.10	1.50
☐☐ 1148	8c Thomas G. Masaryk, 3/7/60, DC.....................1.00		1.25	1.50
☐☐	Scott 1147-1148 on one cover 2.00			
	Total for Scott 1147 and 1148 is 1,710,726.			
☐☐ 1149	4c World Refugee Year, 4/7/60, DC (413,298)............1.00		1.10	1.50
☐☐ 1150	4c Water Conservation, 4/18/60, DC			
	(648,988)...1.00		1.10	1.50
☐☐ 1151	4c SEATO, 5/31/60, DC (514,926) 1.10		1.00	1.50
☐☐ 1152	4c American Woman, 6/2/60, DC (830,385)...............1.00		1.10	1.50
☐☐ 1153	4c 50-Star Flag, 7/4/60, Honolulu, HI (820,900).......1.00		1.10	1.50
☐☐ 1154	4c Pony Express Centennial, 7/19/60,			
	Sacramento, CA (520,223)...............................1.00		1.10	1.50
☐☐ 1155	4c Employ the Handicapped, 8/28/60, New York,			
	NY (439,638) 1.00		1.10	1.50
☐☐ 1156	4c World Forestry Congress, 8/29/60, Seattle, WA			
	(350,848) 1.00		1.10	1.50
☐☐ 1157	4c Mexican Independence, 9/16/60, Los Angeles,			
	CA (360,297) 1.00		1.10	1.50
☐☐ 1158	4c U.S.-Japan Treaty, 9/28/60, DC (545,150)............1.00		1.10	1.50

1119

1122

1120

1121

1125-26

1127

1123

1124

1128

1129

1130

1131

1132

1134

1133

1135

1136-37

1138

1139-44

1145

1146

1147-48

1st Ritz cachet

1151

SCOTT NUMBER	DESCRIPTION	CACHETED SGL	BLK	PL BLK
☐☐ 1159	4c Ignacy Jan Paderewski, 10/8/60, DC	1.00	1.00	1.50
☐☐ 1160	8c Ignacy Jan Paderewski, 10/8/60, DC	1.00	1.25	1.50
☐☐	Scott 1159-1160 on one cover	2.00		
	Total for Scott 1159 and 1160 is 1,057,438.			
☐☐ 1161	4c Robert A. Taft 10/10/60, Cincinnati, OH (312,116)	1.00	1.10	1.50
☐☐ 1162	4c Wheels of Freedom, 10/15/60, Detroit, MI		1.10	1.50
	(380,551)	1.00		
☐☐ 1163	4c Boys' Clubs of America, 10/18/60, New York, NY (435,009)	1.00	1.10	1.50
☐☐ 1164	4c Automated Post Office, 10/20/60, Providence, RI (458,237)	1.00	1.10	1.50
☐☐ 1165	4c Gustaf Emil Mannerheim, 10/26/60, DC	1.00	1.10	1.50
☐☐ 1166	8c Gustaf Emil Mannerheim, 10/26/60, DC	1.00	1.25	1.50
☐☐	Scott 1165-1166 on one cover	2.00		
	Total for Scott 1165 and 1166 is 1,168, 770.			
☐☐ 1167	4c Camp Fire Girls, 11/1/60, New York, NY (324,944)	1.00	1.10	1.50
☐☐ 1168	4c Giuseppe Garibaldi, 11/2/60, DC	1.10	1.10	1.50
☐☐ 1169	8c Giuseppe Garibaldi, 11/2/60, DC	1.00	1.25	1.50
☐☐	Scott 1168-1169 on one cover	2.00		
	Total for Scott 1168 and 1169 is 1,001,490.			
☐☐ 1170	4c Walter F. George, 11/5/60, Vienna, GA (278,890)	1.00	1.10	1.50
☐☐ 1171	4c Andrew Carnegie, 11/25/60, New York, NY (318,180)	1.00	1.10	1.50
☐☐ 1172	4c John Foster Dulles, 12/6/60, DC (400,055)	1.00	1.10	1.50
☐☐ 1173	4c Echo I, 12/15/60, DC (583,747)	2.00	2.50	3.00

1961

☐☐ 1174	4c Mahatma Gandhi, 1/26/61, DC	1.00	1.10	1.50
☐☐ 1175	8c Mahatma Gandhi, 1/26/61, DC	1.00	1.25	1.50
☐☐	Scott 1174-1175 on one cover	2.00		
	Total for Scott 1174 and 1175 is 1,013,315.			
☐☐ 1176	4c Range Conservation, 2/2/61, Salt Lake City, UT (357,101)	1.00	1.10	1.50
☐☐ 1177	4c Horace Greeley, 2/3/61, Chappaqua, NY (359,205)	1.00	1.10	1.50

1961-65 Civil War Centennial

☐☐ 1178	4c Fort Sumter, 4/12/61, Charleston, SC (602,599)	1.25	1.35	2.00
☐☐ 1179	4c Battle of Shiloh, 4/7/62, Shiloh, TN (526,062)	1.25	1.35	2.00
☐☐ 1180	5c Battle of Gettysburg, 7/1/63, Gettysburg PA (600,205)	1.25	1.35	2.00
☐☐ 1181	5c Battle of Wilderness, 5/5/64, Fredericksburg, VA (450,904)	1.25	1.35	2.50
☐☐ 1182	5c Appomattox, 4/9/65, Appomattox, VA (653,121)	1.25	1.35	2.00

1961

☐☐ 1183	4c Kansas Statehood, 5/10/61, Council Grove, KS (480,561)	1.00	1.10	1.50
☐☐ 1184	4c George W. Norris, 7/11/61, DC (482,875)	1.00	1.10	1.50
☐☐ 1185	4c Naval Aviation, 8/20/61, San Diego, CA (416,391)	1.00	1.50	2.50

WORLD REFUGEE YEAR
UNITED STATES POSTAGE
1149

WATER CONSERVATION
UNITED STATES POSTAGE
1150

JULY 4 1960
4¢
U.S. POSTAGE
1153

THE AMERICAN WOMAN
U.S.POSTAGE 4¢
1152

1860·1960 PONY EXPRESS 4¢
1154

EMPLOY THE HANDICAPPED
4¢ UNITED STATES POSTAGE
1155

CHAMPION OF LIBERTY
4¢
UNITED STATES POSTAGE
1159-60

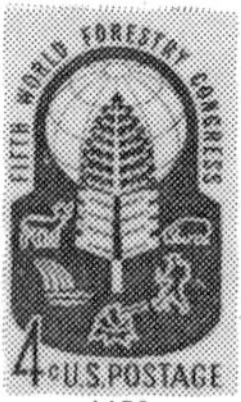

FIFTH WORLD FORESTRY CONGRESS
4¢ U.S. POSTAGE
1156

MEXICAN INDEPENDENCE 1810 1960
4¢ U.S. POSTAGE
1157

UNITED STATES JAPAN
U.S. POSTAGE 4
1158

UNITED STATES POSTAGE
4¢
1161

BOYS CLUBS OF AMERICA MOVEMENT
1860·1960 4¢ U.S. POSTAGE
1163

WHEELS OF FREEDOM
UNITED STATES POSTAGE 4
1162

U.S. POSTAGE FIRST AUTOMATED POST OFFICE IN THE UNITED STATES 4¢
1164

1910 1960 CAMP FIRE GIRLS
UNITED STATES POSTAGE 4¢
1167

CHAMPION OF LIBERTY
UNITED STATES POSTAGE 4¢
1165-66

CHAMPION OF LIBERTY
UNITED STATES POSTAGE 4¢
1168-69

UNITED STATES POSTAGE
4¢
1170

UNITED STATES POSTAGE 4¢
1171

UNITED STATES POSTAGE 4¢
1172

COMMUNICATIONS FOR PEACE
ECHO I U.S. POSTAGE 4¢
1173

CHAMPION OF LIBERTY
UNITED STATES POSTAGE 4¢
1174-75

RANGE CONSERVATION
THE TRAIL BOSS
UNITED STATES POSTAGE 4¢
1176

UNITED STATES POSTAGE
HORACE GREELEY 4¢
1177

CIVIL WAR CENTENNIAL FORT SUMTER
1861 1961
UNITED STATES POSTAGE 4¢
1178-82

			CACHETED	
☐☐ 1186	**4c Workmen's Compensation**, 9/4/61, Milwaukee, WI (410,236) 1.00		1.10	1.50
☐☐ 1187	**4c Frederic Remington**, 10/4/61, DC (723,443) 1.00		1.10	1.50
☐☐ 1188	**4c Republic of China**, 10/10/61, DC (463,900)...........1.00		1.10	1.50
☐☐ 1189	**4c Naismith-Basketball**, 11/6/61, Springfield, MA (479,917)................6.00		7.00	8.00
☐☐ 1190	**4c Nursing**, 12/28/61, DC (964,005) 8.00		8.50	10.00
☐☐	1st American Hospital Supply Corp. cachet...........20.00			

1962

☐☐ 1191	**4c New Mexico Statehood**, 1/6/62, Santa Fe, NM (365,330)....................1.00		1.10	1.50
☐☐	1st Glory cachet 25.00			
☐☐ 1192	**4c Arizona Statehood**, 2/14/62, Phoenix, AZ (508,216).......................1.00		1.10	1.50
☐☐	1st Vivid cachet 25.00			
☐☐	1st Tucson Chamber of Commerce cachet.............15.00			
☐☐ 1193	**4c Project Mercury**, 2/20/62, Cape Canaveral, FL (3,000,000).....................3.00		4.00	6.00
☐☐	Any city 5.00		6.00	7.00
☐☐	1st Marg cachet 25.00			
☐☐ 1194	**4c Malaria Eradication**, 3/30/62, DC (554, 175)........1.00		1.10	1.50
☐☐ 1195	**4c Charles Evans Hughes**, 4/11/62, DC (554,424) 1.00		1.10	1.50
☐☐ 1196	**4c Seattle World's Fair**, 4/25/62, Seattle, WA (771,856)....................1.00		1.10	1.50
☐☐	1st Top of the Needle, Inc. cachet.........................10.00			
☐☐	1st Boeing Employee's Stamp Club cachet 12.00			
☐☐ 1197	**4c Louisiana Statehood**, 4/30/62, New Orleans, LA (436,681)....................1.00		1.10	1.50
☐☐ 1198	**4c Homestead Act**, 5/20/62, Beatrice, NE (487,450)..1.00		1.10	1.50
☐☐ 1199	**4c Girl Scout Jubilee**, 7/24/62, Burlington, VT (634,347)....................3.00		3.50	4.00
☐☐ 1200	**4c Brien McMahon**, 7/28/62, Norwalk, CT (384,419).1.00		1.10	1.50
☐☐ 1201	**4c Apprenticeship**, 8/31/62, DC 1,003,548) 1.00		1.10	1.50
☐☐ 1202	**4c Sam Rayburn**, 9/16/62, Bonham, TX (401,042). ...1.00		1.10	1.50
☐☐ 1203	**4c Dag Hammarskjold**, 10/23/62, New York, NY (500,683)....................1.00		1.10	1.50
☐☐	1st Dag Hammarskjold Foundation cachet.............15.00			
☐☐	Inverted yellow, 10/26/62, Vanderveer Sta.,			
☐☐	Brooklyn, NY earliest known use..........................2000.			
☐☐ 1204	**4c Hanmarskjold Special Printing**, yellow inverted, 11/16/62, DC (c. 75,000) 6.00		7.50	10.00
☐☐ 1205	**4c Christmas**, 11/1/62, Pittsburgh, PA (491,312) 1.10		1.50	
☐☐ 1206	**4c Higher Education**, 11/14/62, DC (627,347) 1.00		1.10	1.50
☐☐ 1207	**4c Winslow Homer**, 12/15/62, Gloucester, MA (498,866)....................1.00		1.10	1.50

1963-66

☐☐ 1208	**5c Flag**, 1/9/63, DC (696,185) 1.00		1.10	1.50
☐☐ 1208a	**Flag**, tagged, 8/25/66, DC...........................25.00			

1962-66

☐☐ 1209	**1c Andrew Jackson**, 3/22/63, block of 5 or 6, New York, NY (392,363)................		1.00	1.50

1183 1184 1185

1186 1187 1188 1189 1190

1191 1192 1193 1195

1194

1198 1196 1197

1st Glory cachet

1st Marg cachet

HOW TO USE THIS BOOK
The number in the first column is its Scott number or identifying number. Following that is the denomination of the stamp, description, date of issue, and the value.

	1209a	Andrew Jackson, block of 5 or 6, tagged, 7/6/66, DC.25.00			
☐☐	1213	5c George Washington, 11/23/62, New York, NY			
		(360,531) 1.00			
☐☐	1213a	George Washington, booklet pane of 5, 11/23/62,			
		New York, NY (111,452) 4.00			
☐☐	1213b	George Washington, tagged, 10/28/63, Dayton, OH			
		& DC...25.00			
☐☐	1213c	George Washington, booklet pane of 5, tagged,			
		10/28/63, Dayton, OH 100.00			
☐☐		DC (750) 115.00			

☐☐	1225	1c Andrew Jackson, coil, pair & strip of 3,			
		5/31/63, Chicago, IL (238,952)...................		1.00	1.00
☐☐	1225a	Andrew Jackson, coil, pair & strip of 3, tagged,			
		7/6/66, DC		5.00	
☐☐	1229	5c George Washington, coil, 11/23/62, New York,			
		NY (184,627).....................................		1.00	1.00
☐☐	1229a	George Washington, coil, tagged, 10/28/63,			
		Dayton, OH & DC		30.00	
☐☐		Scott 1213b, 1213c, 1229a on one cover,			
		Dayton, OH.................................70.00			

1963

☐☐	1230	5c Carolina Charter, 4/6/63, Edenton, NC (426,200) .1.00	1.00	1.50
☐☐	1231	5c Food for Peace, 6/4/63, DC....................1.00	1.00	1.50
☐☐	1232	5c West Virginia Statehood, 6/20/63, Wheeling,		
		WV (413,389) 1.00	1.00	1.50
☐☐	1233	5c Emancipation Proclamation, 8/16/63, Chicago,		
		IL (494,886).....................................1.00	1.00	1.50
☐☐	1234	5c Alliance for Progress, 8/17/63, DC (528,095) 1.00	1.00	1.50
☐☐	1235	5c Cordell Hull, 10/5/63, Carthage, TN (391,631) 1.00	1.00	1.50
☐☐	1236	5c Eleanor Roosevelt, 10/11/63, DC (860,155) 1.00	1.00	1.50
☐☐	1237	5c Science, 10/14/63, DC (504,503)...............1.00	1.00	1.50
☐☐	1238	5c City Mail Delivery, 10/26/63, DC (544,806) 1.00	1.00	1.50
☐☐	1239	5c Red Cross Centenary, 10/29/63, DC (557,678)......1.00	1.00	1.50
☐☐	1240	5c Christmas, 11/1/63, Santa Claus, IN (458,619) 1.00	1.00	1.50
		1st Lily Spandorf cachet..........................20.00		
☐☐	1240a	Christmas, tagged, 1 1/2/63, DC (500) 60.00		
☐☐	1241	5c John James Audubon, 12/7/63, Henderson, KY		
		(518,855)...1.00	1.00	1.50

1964

☐☐	1242	5c Sam Houston, 1/10/64, Houston, TX (487,986).....1.00	1.00	1.50
☐☐		Mr. Zip Imprint......................................10.00	15.00	
		Scott 1242 was the first stamp to have Mr. Zip imprints.		
☐☐	1243	5c Charles M. Russell, 3/19/64, Great Falls, MT		
		(658,745)...1.00	1.00	1.50

1199

1200

1201

1202

1203

1204

1205

1206

1207

1209, 1225

1231

1208

1213, 1229

1230

1232

1233

1234

1235

1236

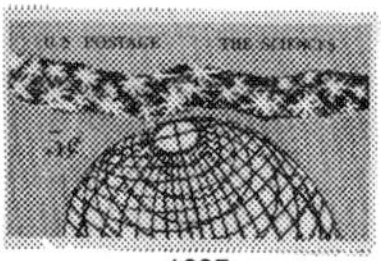

1237

1238

1239

1240

☐☐	1244	5c N.Y. World's Fair, 4/22/64, World's Fair, NY			
		(1,656,346) 1.00	1.00	1.50
☐☐		1st Sarzin Metallic cachet......................................30.00		
☐☐	1245	5c John Muir, 4/29/64, Martinez, CA (446,925) ...1.00	1.00	1.50
☐☐	1246	5c Kennedy Memorial, 5/29/64, Boston, MA			
		(2,003,096) 2.50	3.50	5.00
☐☐		Any city 2.50	3.50	5.00
☐☐		1st Cover Craft cachet...25.00		
☐☐	1247	5c New Jersey Tercentenary, 6/15/64, Elizabeth,			
		NJ (526,879)..1.00	1.00	1.50
☐☐	1248	5c Nevada Statehood, 7/22/64, Carson City, NV			
		(584,973) 1.00	1.00	1.50
☐☐	1249	5c Register & Vote, 8/1/64, DC (533,439) 1.00	1.00	1.50
☐☐	1250	5c Shakespeare, 8/14/64, Stratford, CT (524,053) 1.00	1.00	1.50
☐☐	1251	5c Drs. Mayo, 9/11/64, Rochester, MN (674,846) 2.00	2.25	2.75
☐☐	1252	5c American Music, 10/15/64, New York, NY			
		(466,107)...1.00	1.10	1.50
☐☐	1253	5c Homemakers, 10/26/64, Honolulu, HI			
		(435,392) 1.00	1.10	1.50
☐☐	1254	5c Holly, 11/9/64, Bethlehem, PA.............................1.00		
☐☐	1254a	Holly, tagged, 11/10/64, Dayton, OH......................20.00		
☐☐	1255	5c Mistletoe, 11/9/64, Bethlehem, PA........................1.00		
☐☐	1255a	Mistletoe, tagged, 11/10/64, Dayton, OH.................20.00		
☐☐	1256	5c Poinsettia, 11/9/64, Bethlehem, PA 1.00		
☐☐	1256a	Poinsettia, tagged, 11/10/64, Dayton, OH 20.00		
☐☐	1257	5c Sprig of Conifer, 11/9/64, Bethlehem, PA.............1.00		
☐☐	1257a	Sprig of Conifer, 11/10/64, Dayton, OH 20.00		
☐☐	1257b	Christmas, se-tenant (794,900)........................	3.00	4.00
☐☐	1257b	Christmas, tagged, se-tenant..........................	60.00	
☐☐	1258	5c Verrazano-Narrows Bridge, 11/21/64, Staten			
		Island, NY (619,780) 1.00	1.10	1.50
☐☐	1259	5c Fine Arts, 12/2/64, DC (558,046) 1.00	1.10	1.50
☐☐	1260	5c Amateur Radio, 12/15/64, Anchorage, AK............1.00	1.10	1.50

1965

☐☐	1261	5c Battle of New Orleans, 1/8/65, New Orleans, LA			
		(466,029)..1.00	1.10	1.50
☐☐	1262	5c Physical Fitness-Sokol, 2/15/65, DC (864,848) 1.00	1.10	1.50
☐☐	1263	5c Crusade Against Cancer, 4/1/65, DC (744,485).....1.00	1.10	1.50
☐☐	1264	5c Churchill Memorial, 5/13/65, Fulton, MO			
		(733,580)...1.00	1.10	1.50
☐☐	1265	5c Magna Carta, 6/15/65, Jamestown, VA			
		(479,065)...1.00	1.10	1.50
☐☐	1266	5c International Cooperation Year, 6/26/65, San			
		Francisco, CA (402,925).................................1.00	1.10	1.50
☐☐	1267	5c Salvation Army, 7/2/65, New York, NY (634,228) .1.00	1.10	1.50
☐☐	1268	5c Dante Alighieri, 7/17/65, San Francisco, CA			
		(424,893) 1.00	1.10	1.50
☐☐	1269	5c Herbert Hoover, 8/10/65, West Branch, IA			
		(698,182)...1.00	1.10	1.50
☐☐	1270	5c Robert Fulton, 8/19/65, Clermont, NY			
		(550,330)...1.00	1.10	1.50
☐☐	1271	5c Settlement of Florida, 8/28/65, St. Augustine,			
		FL (465,000)...1.00	1.10	1.50

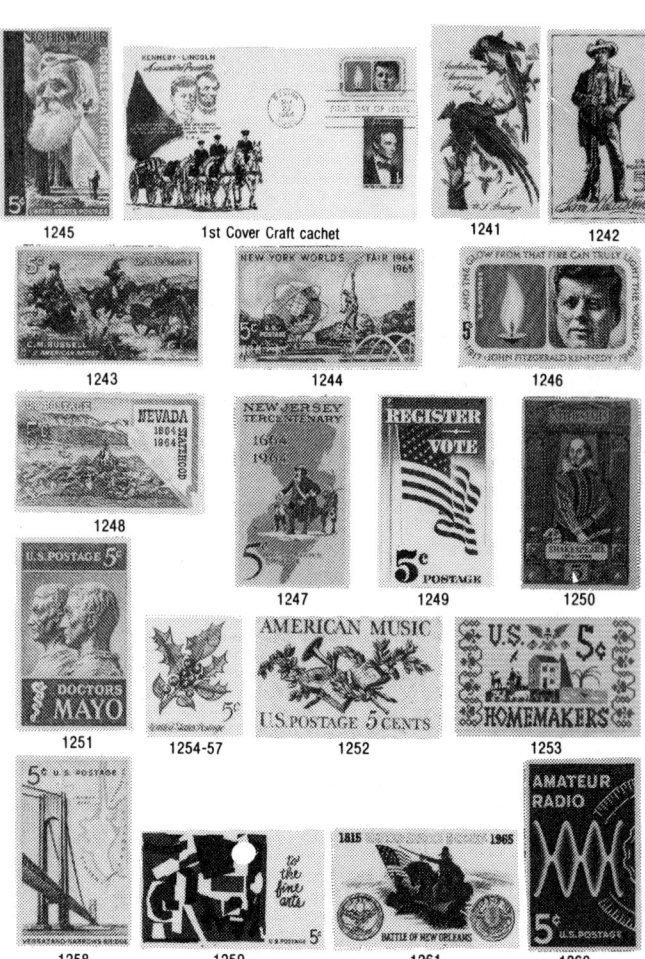

1245

1st Cover Craft cachet

1241

1242

1243

1244

1246

1248

1247

1249

1250

1251

1254-57

1252

1253

1258

1259

1261

1260

HOW TO USE THIS BOOK

The number in the first column is its Scott number or identifying number. Following that is the denomination of the stamp, description, date of issue, and the value.

☐☐	1272	5c Traffic Safety, 9/3/65, Baltimore, MD			
		(527,075) 1.00	1.00	1.10	1.50
☐☐	1273	5c John Singleton Copley, 9/17/65, DC (613,484) 1.00		1.10	1.50
☐☐	1274	11c International Telecommunication Union,			
		10/6/65, DC (332,818) 1.00		1.10	1.50
☐☐	1275	5c Adlai E. Stevenson, 10/23/65, Bloomington, IL			
		(755,656) 1.00		1.10	1.50
☐☐	1276	5c Christmas, 11/2/65, Silver Bell, AZ (705,039) 1.00		1.10	1.50
☐☐	1276a	Christmas, tagged, 11/15/65, DC (300c) 55.00			

1965-68 Prominent Americans

☐☐	1278	1c Thomas Jefferson block of 5 or 6, 1/12/68,			
		Jeffersonville, IN		1.00	1.00
☐☐	1278a	Thomas Jefferson, booklet pane of 8, 1/12/68,			
		Jeffersonville, IN 2.50			
☐☐		Dull gum, 3/1/71, DC...100.00			
		Total for Scott 1278, 1278a and 1299 is 655,680.			
☐☐	1278b	Thomas Jefferson. booklet pane of 4 plus 2 labels,			
		5/10/71, DC...15.00			
☐☐	1279	1 1/4c Albert Gallatin, 1/30/67, Gallatin, MO			
		(439,010)		1.00	1.00
☐☐	1280	2c Frank Lloyd Wright, strip of 3, 6/8/66, Spring			
		Green, WI (460,427)..1.00			
☐☐	1280a	Frank Lloyd Wright, booklet pane of 5 plus label,			
		1/8/68, Buffalo, NY (147,244)...................................4.00			
☐☐	1280c	Frank Lloyd Wright, booklet pane of 6, 5/7/71,			
		Spokane, WA 15.00			
☐☐		Dull gum, 10/31/75, Cleveland, OH 100.00			
☐☐	1281	3c Francis Parkman, 9/16/67, Boston, MA			
		(518,355)...		1.10	1.50
☐☐	1282	4c Abraham Lincoln, 11/19/65, New York, NY			
		(445,629)...		1.10	1.50
☐☐	1282a	Abraham Lincoln, tagged, 12/1/65, Dayton, OH 32.50			
☐☐		DC... 20.00			
☐☐	1283	5c George Washington, 2/22/66, DC (525,372)..........1.00		1.10	1.50
		1st B'nai B'rith Philatelic Service cachet 20.00			
☐☐	1283a	George Washington, tagged, 2/23/66, Dayton,			
		OH (c. 200) 75.00			
☐☐		DC...25.00			
☐☐	1283B	5c George Washington, Redrawn, 11/17/67,			
		New York, NY (328,983) 1.00		1.10	1.50
☐☐	1284	6c Franklin D. Roosevelt, 1/29/66, Hyde Park, NY			
		(448,631)..1.00		1.10	1.50
☐☐	1284a	Franklin D. Roosevelt,tagged, 12/29/66, DC............20.00			
☐☐	1284b	Franklin D. Roosevelt, booklet pane of S,			
		12/28/67, DC..3.00			
		Total for Scott 1284b and 1298 is 312,330.			
☐☐	1284c	Franklin D. Roosevelt, booklet pane of 5, 1/9/68,			
		DC...100.00			
☐☐	1285	8c Albert Einstein, 3/14/66, Princeton, NJ			
		(366,803)...1.50	2.00	2.75	
☐☐	1285a	Albert Einstein, tagged, 7/6/66, DC........................20.00			
☐☐	1286	10c Andrew Jackson, 3/15/67, Hermitage, TN			
		(255,945)..1.00	1.25	1.50	

1267 1262 1263 1264 1268

1265 1266

1269 1270 1272 1271

1274 1276

1273 1278, 1299 1287 1275

HOW TO USE THIS BOOK

The number in the first column is its Scott number or
identifying number. Following that is the denomination
of the stamp, description, date of issue, and the value.

84

SCOTT NUMBER	DESCRIPTION	SGL	BLK	PL BLK
☐☐ 1286A	12c Henry Ford, 7/30/68, Greenfield Village, MI (342,850)..........1.00		1.25	1.50
☐☐ 1287	13c John F. Kennedy, 5/29/67, Brookline, MA (391,195)..........1.50		2.00	2.75
☐☐ 1288	15c Oliver Wendell Holmes, 3/8/68, DC (322,970). ...1.00		1.25	1.50
☐☐ 1288B	15c Oliver Wendell Holmes, Redrawn, booklet single, 6/14/78, Boston, MA (387, 119)..........1.00		1.25	1.50
☐☐ 1288c	Oliver Wendell Holmes, booklet pane of 8..........3.00			
☐☐ 1289	20c George C. Marshall, 10/24/67, Lexington, VA (221,206)..........1.00		1.25	1.50
☐☐ 1289a	George C. Marshall, tagged, 4/3/73, New York, NY..25.00			
☐☐ 1290	25c Frederick Douglass, 2/14/67, DC (213,730) 1.25		1.25	1.75
☐☐ 1290a	Frederick Douglass, tagged, 4/3/73, New York, NY..25.00			
☐☐ 1291	30c John Dewey, 10/21/68, Burlington, VT (162,790)..........1.25		2.00	3.00
☐☐ 1291a	John Dewey, tagged, 4/3/73, New York, NY 25.00			
☐☐ 1292	40c Thomas Paine, 1/29/68, Philadelphia, PA (157,947)..........1.60		2.50	4.00
☐☐ 1292a	Thomas Paine, tagged, 4/3/73, New York, NY 15.00			
☐☐ 1293	50c Lucy Stone, 8/13/68, Dorchester, MA (140,410)..........3.25		4.00	7.50
☐☐ 1293a	Lucy Stone, tagged, 4/3/73, New York, NY..............30.00			
☐☐ 1294	$1 Eugene O'Neill, 10/16/67, New London, CT (103,102)..........7.50		10.00	15.00
☐☐ 1294a	Eugene O'Neill, tagged, 4/3/73, New York, NY 30.00			
☐☐ 1295	$5 John Bassett Moore, 12/3/66, Smyrna, DE (41,130)..........40.00		55.00	95.00
☐☐ 1295a	John Bassett Moore, tagged, 4/3/73, New York, NY..80.00			
	Total for 1059b, 1289a, 1290a, 1291a, 1292a, 1293a, 1294a, 1295a is 17,533.			

SCOTT NUMBER	DESCRIPTION	CACHETED SGL	PR	L PR

1966-68 Prominent Americans Coils
Perf. 10 Horizontally

☐☐ 1297	3c Francis Parkman, 11/4/75, Pendleton, OR (166,798)		1.00	1.50
☐☐ 1298	6c Franklin D. Roosevelt, 12/28/67, DC..........1.00		1.00	1.50

Perf. 10 Vertically

☐☐ 1299	1c Thomas Jefferson, pair & strip of 3, 1/12/68, Jeffersonville, IN		1.00	1.50
☐☐ 1303	4c Abraham Lincoln, pair, 5/28/66, Springfield, IL (322,563)		1.00	1.50
	1st A Hartford Cover cachet 20.00			
☐☐ 1304	5c George Washington, 9/8/66, Cincinnati, OH (245,400)..........1.00		1.00	1.50
☐☐ 1304C	5c George Washington, Redrawn, strip of 4, 3/31/81, earliest known use, DC 25.00			
☐☐ 1305	6c Franklin D. Roosevelt, 2/28/68, DC (317,199)..........1.00		1.00	1.50
☐☐ 1305E	15c Oliver Wendell Holmes 6/14/78, Boston, MA (387,119)..........1.00		1.25	1.50
☐☐	Scott 1288c, 1305E on one cover..........................6.50			

1306

1307

1308

1309

1310-11

1312

1313

1314

1315

1316

1318

1317

SCOTT NUMBER	DESCRIPTION	CACHETED SGL	PR	L PR
☐☐ 1305C	$1 Eugene O'Neill 1/12/73, Hempstead, NY (121,217)	5.00	7.00	9.00

SCOTT NUMBER	DESCRIPTION	CACHETED SGL	BLK	PL BLK

1966

SCOTT NUMBER	DESCRIPTION	CACHETED SGL	BLK	PL BLK
☐☐ 1306	5c Migratory Bird Treaty, 3/16/66, Pittsburgh, PA (555,485) 1.00		1.10	1.50
☐☐ 1307	5c Humane Treatment of Animals, 4/9/66, New York, NY (524,420)..1.00		1.10	1.50
☐☐ 1308	5c Indiana Statehood, 4/16/66, Corydon, IN (575,557) 1.00		1.10	1.50
☐☐ 1309	5c American Circus, 5/2/66, Delavan, WI (754,076) 2.50		3.00	4.50
	1st Cliff's Covers cachet 20.00			
☐☐ 1310	5c SIPEX, 5/21/66, DC (637,802) 1.00		1.10	1.50
☐☐ 1311	5c SIPEX, Souvenir Sheet, 5/23/66, DC (700,882).			1.00
☐☐ 1312	5c Bill of Rights, 7/1/66, Miami Beach, FL (562,920)..1.00		1.10	1.50
☐☐	1313 5c Polish Millennium, 7/30/66, DC (712,603)..1.00		1.10	1.50
☐☐ 1314	5c National Park Service, 8/25/66, Yellowstone National Park, WY (528,170) 1.00		1.10	1.50
☐☐ 1314a	National Park Service, tagged, 8/26/66, DC.............25.00			
☐☐ 1315	5c Marine Corps Reserve, 8/29/66, DC (585,923)......1.00		1.10	1.50
☐☐ 1315a	Marine Corps Reserve, tagged, 8/29/66, DC 25.00			
☐☐ 1316	5c General Federation of Women's Clubs, 9/12/66, New York, NY (383,334) 1.00		1.10	1.50
☐☐ 1316a	General Federation of Women's Clubs, tagged, 9/13/66, DC..25.00			
☐☐ 1317	5c Johnny Appleseed, 9/24/66, Leominster, MA (794,610)...1.00		1.10	1.50
☐☐ 1317a	Johnny Appleseed, tagged, 9/26/66, DC...................22.50			
☐☐ 1318	5c Beautification of America, 10/5/66, DC (564,440)..1.00		1.10	1.50
☐☐ 1318a	Beautification of America, tagged, 10/5/66, DC......25.00			
☐☐ 1319	5c Great River Road, 10/21/66, Baton Rouge, LA (330,933)...1.00		1.10	1.50
☐☐ 1319a	Great River Road, tagged, 10/22/66, DC...................25.00			
☐☐ 1320	5c Savings Bonds-Servicemen, 10/26/66, Sioux City, IA, (444,421) 1.00		1.10	1.50
	1st Border Croft cachet..25.00			
☐☐ 1320a	Savings Bonds-Servicemen, tagged, 10/27/66, DC ..25.00			
☐☐ 1321	5c Christmas, 11/1/66, Christmas, MI (537,650)........1.00		1.10	1.50
☐☐ 1321a	Christmas, tagged, 11/2/66, DC...................9.50			
☐☐ 1322	5c Mary Cassatt, 11/17/66, DC (593,389)...................1.00		1.10	1.50
☐☐ 1322a	Mary Cassatt, tagged, 11/17/66, DC 25.00			

1967

SCOTT NUMBER	DESCRIPTION	CACHETED SGL	BLK	PL BLK
☐☐ 1323	5c National Grange, 4/17/67, DC (603,460) 1.00		1.10	1.50
☐☐ 1324	5c Canada Centenary, 5/25/67, Montreal, Quebec (711,795)..1.00		1.10	1.50
☐☐ 1325	5c Erie Canal, 7/4/67, Rome, NY (784,611)................1.00		1.10	1.50

1319

1320

1321

1322

1323

1324

1325

1326

1327

1328

1330

1329

1331-32

☐☐ 1326	5c "Peace"-Lions, 7/5/67, Chicago, IL (393, 197) 1.00		1.10	1.50
☐☐ 1327	5c Henry David Thoreau, 7/12/67, Concord, MA (696,789) 1.00		1.10	1.50
☐☐ 1328	5c Nebraska Statehood, 7/29/67, Lincoln, NE (1,146,957)..1.00		1.10	1.50
☐☐ 1329	5c Voice of America, 8/1/67, DC (445,190) 1.00		1.10	1.50
☐☐ 1330	5c Davy Crockett, 8/17/67, San Antonio, TX (462,291) 1.00		1.10	1.50
☐☐ 1331	5c Space-walking astronaut, 9/29/67, Kennedy Space Center, FL 3.00			
☐☐ 1331a	Space Accomplishments, se-tenant pair, FL (667,267) 10.00		12.50	15.00
☐☐ 1332	5c Gemini 4 capsule, 9/29/67, Kennedy Space Center, FL 3.00			
☐☐ 1333	5c Urban Planning, 10/2/67, DC (389,009) 1.00		1.10	1.50
☐☐ 1334	5c Finland Independence, 10/6/67, Finland, MN (408,532) 1.00		1.10	1.50
☐☐ 1335	5c Thomas Eakins, 11/2/67, DC (648,054) 1.00		1.10	1.50
☐☐ 1336	5c Christmas, 11/6/67, Bethlehem, GA (462,118) 1.00		1.10	1.50
☐☐ 1337	5c Mississippi Statehood, 12/11/67, Natchez, MS (379,612) 1.00		1.10	1.50

1968-69

☐☐ 1338	6c Flag, Giori Press, 1/24/68, DC (412,120)................1.00		1.10	1.50
☐☐ 1338A	6c Flag, coil, 5/30/69, Chicago, IL (248,434) 1.00	pr 1.10	lpl 1.50
☐☐ 1338D	6c Flag, 8/7/70, Huck Press, DC (356,280). "Plate Block" value is for block of 4 with plate numbers 1.00		1.10	1.50
☐☐ 1338F	8c Flag, 5/10/71, DC. "Plate Block" value is for block of 4 with plate numbers 1.00		1.10	1.50
☐☐ 1338G	8c Flag, coil, 5/10/71, DC...1.00	pr 1.00	lpl 1.50
	Total for Scott 1338F-1338G is 235,543.			

1968

☐☐ 1339	6c Illinois Statehood, 2/12/68, Shawneetown, IL (761,640) 1.00		1.10	1.50
☐☐ 1340	6c Hemis Fair '68, 3/30/68, San Antonio, TX (469,909) 1.00		1.10	1.50
☐☐ 1341	$1 Airlift, 4/4/68, Seattle, WA (105,088) 7.50		9.50	15.00
☐☐ 1342	6c Youth-Elks, 5/1/68, Chicago, IL (354,711)..............1.00		1.10	1.50
☐☐ 1343	6c Law and Order, 5/17/68, DC (407,081)..................1.00		1.10	1.50
☐☐ 1344	6c Register and Vote, 6/27/68, DC (355,685)..............1.00		1.10	1.50
☐☐ 1345	6c Ft. Moultrie, 7/4/68, Pittsburgh, PA......................3.00			
☐☐ 1346	6c Ft. McHenry, 7/4/68, Pittsburgh, PA 3.00			
☐☐ 1347	6c Washington's Cruisers, 7/4/68, Pittsburgh, PA 3.00			
☐☐ 1348	6c Bennington, 7/4/68, Pittsburgh, PA......................3.00			
☐☐ 1349	6c Rhode Island, 7/4/68, Pittsburgh, PA....................3.00			
☐☐ 1350	6c First Stars & Stripes, 7/4/68, Pittsburgh, PA 3.00			
☐☐ 1351	6c Bunker Hill, 7/4/68, Pittsburgh, PA 3.00			
☐☐ 1352	6c Grand Union, 7/4/68, Pittsburgh, PA 3.00			
☐☐ 1353	6c Philadelphia Light Horse, 7/4/68, Pittsburgh, PA.3.00			
☐☐ 1354	6c First Navy Jack, 7/4/68, Pittsburgh, PA.................3.00			
☐☐ 1354a	Se-tenant strip 12.00			
	Total for Scott 1345-1354 is 2,924,962.			

1333

1334

1335

1336

1338

1337

1339

1341

1342

1340

1343

1344

1345-54

1356

1355

Values for various cachet makers can be determined by using the Cachet Calculator which begins on page 40A.

☐☐ 1355	6c Walt Disney, 9/11/68, Marceline, MO (499,505) 9.00		10.00	12.00
☐☐ 1356	6c Father Marquette, 9/20/68, Sault Sainte Marie MI (379,710)............1.00		1.10	1.50
☐☐ 1357	6c Daniel Boone, 9/26/68, Frankfort, KY (333,440)............1.00		1.10	1.50
☐☐ 1358	6c Arkansas River Navigation, 10/1/68, Little Rock, AR (358,025)............1.00		1.10	1.50
☐☐ 1359	6c Leif Erikson, 10/9/68, Seattle, WA (376,565) 1.00		1.10	1.50
☐☐ 1360	6c Cherokee Strip, 10/15/68, Ponca, OK (339,330)....1.00		1.10	1.50
☐☐ 1361	6c John Trumball, 10/18/68, New Haven, CT (378,285) 1.00		1.10	1.50
☐☐ 1362	6c Waterfowl Conservation, 10/24/68, Cleveland, OH (349,719)............1.00		1.10	1.50
☐☐	1st Ducks Unlimited, Inc. cachet 30.00			
☐☐ 1363	6c Christmas, tagged, 11/1/68, DC (739,055). "Plate Block" value is for block of 4 with plate numbers............1.00		1.10	1.50
☐☐ 1363a	6c Christmas, untagged, 11/2/68, DC............10.00			
☐☐ 1364	6c American Indian, 11/4/68, DC (415,964)............1.00		1.10	1.50

1969

☐☐ 1365	6c Capitol, Azaleas & Tulips, 1/16/69, DC 1.00			
☐☐ 1366	6c Washington Monument & Daffodils, 1/16/69, DC............1.00			
☐☐ 1367	6c Poppies & Lupines along Highway, 1/16/69, DC .1.00			
☐☐ 1368	6c Blooming Crabapples, 1/16/69, DC 1.00			
☐☐ 1368a	Se-tenant blocks, (1,094,184)		4.00	5.00
☐☐ 1369	6c American Legion, 3/15/59, DC (632,035) 1.00		1.25	2.00
☐☐ 1370	6c Grandma Moses, 5/1/69, DC (367,880)............1.00		1.25	2.00
☐☐ 1371	6c Apollo 8, 5/5/69, Houston, TX (908,634) 3.00		6.00	9.00
☐☐ 1372	6c W.C. Handy, 5/17/69, Memphis, TN (398,216). 1.00		1.25	2.00
☐☐ 1373	6c California Settlement, 7/16/69, San Diego, CA (530,210)............1.00		1.25	1.25
☐☐ 1374	6c John Wesley Powell, 8/1/69, Page, AZ (434,433)..1.00		1.25	2.00
☐☐ 1375	6c Alabama Statehood, 8/2/69, Huntsville, AL (485,801)............1.00		1.25	2.00
☐☐ 1376	6c Douglas Fir, 8/23/69, Seattle, WA............1.50			
☐☐ 1377	6c Lady's-slipper, 8/23/69, Seattle, WA............1.50			
☐☐ 1378	6c Ocotillo, 8/23/69, Seattle, WA 1.50			
☐☐ 1379	6c Franklinia, 8/23/69, Seattle, WA............1.50			
☐☐ 1379a	Se-tenant, (737,935)............		5.00	6.00
☐☐ 1380	6c Dartmouth College Case, 9/22/69, Hanover, NH (416,327)............1.00		1.00	1.50
☐☐ 1381	6c Professional Baseball, 9/24/69, Cincinnati, OH (414,942)............12.00		13.00	15.00
☐☐ 1382	6c Intercollegiate Football, 9/26/69, New Brunswick, NJ (414,860)............7.00		8.00	10.00
☐☐ 1383	6c Dwight D. Eisenhower, 10/14/69, Abilene, KS (1,009,560) 1.00		1.00	1.50
☐☐ 1384	6c Christmas, 11/3/69, Christmas, FL (555,550). "Plate Block" value is for block of 4 with plate number.............1.00		1.00	1.50

1357

1358

1360

1359

1361

1362

1363

1364

1365-68

1369

1370

1371

1372

1373

1374

1375

1380

1376-79

1381

1382

☐☐ 1384a	**Christmas,** Precancel, New Haven, Memphis, Baltimore, 11/4/69 (250) 35.00			
☐☐ 1385	**6c Hope for Crippled,** 11/20/69, Columbus, OH (342,676)...1.00	1.00	1.50
☐☐ 1386	**6c William M. Harnett,** 12/3/69, Boston, MA (408,860)...1.00	1.00	1.50

1970

☐☐ 1387	**6c American Bald Eagle,** 5/6/70, New York, NY........1.50		
☐☐ 1388	**6c African Elephant Herd,** 5/6/70, New York, NY 1.50		
☐☐ 1389	**6c Tlingit Chief,** Ceremonial Canoe, 5/6/70, New York, NY..1.50		
☐☐ 1390	**6c Brontosaurus,** Stegosaurus & Allosaurus 5/6/70, New York, NY..1.50		
☐☐ 1390a	**Se-tenant,** (834,260)..	4.00	5.00
☐☐ 1391	**6c Maine Statehood,** 7/9/90, Portland, ME (472,165)...1.00	1.00	1.50
☐☐ 1392	**6c Wildlife Conservation,** 7/20/70, Custer, SD (309,418)...1.00	1.25	2.00

1970-74

☐☐ 1393	**6c Dwight D. Eisenhower,** 8/6/70, DC 1.00	1.00	1.50
☐☐ 1393a	**Dwight D. Eisenhower,** booklet pane of 8, 8/6/70, DC...3.00		
☐☐ 1393a	**Dwight D. Eisenhower,** booklet pane of 8, dull gum, 3/1/71, DC..50.00		
☐☐ 1393b	**Dwight D. Eisenhower,** booklet pane of 5 plus labels, 8/6/70, DC...1.50		
☐☐	Scott 1393a, 1393b (two different slogans in label) 3 panes on one FDC, 8/6/70, DC ....11.50 *Total for Scott 1393-1393b, 1401 is 823,540.*		
☐☐ 1393D	**7c Beajamin Franklin,** 10/20/72, Philadelphia, PA (309,276)...1.00	1.00	1.50
☐☐ 1394	**8c Dwight D. Eisenhower,** 5/10/71, DC 1.00	1.00	1.50
☐☐ 1395	**8c Dwight D. Eisenhower,** 5/10/71, DC 1.00	1.00	1.50
☐☐ 1395a	**Dwight D. Eisenhower,** booklet pane of 8, 5/10/71, DC...3.00		
☐☐ 1395b	**Dwight D. Eisenhower,** booklet pane of 6, 5/10/71, DC...3.00		
☐☐	Scott 1395a, 1395b on one cover, 5/10/72, DC ....5.00 *Total for Scott 1394-1395b, 1402 is 813,947.*		
☐☐ 1395c	**Dwight D. Eisenhower,** booklet pane of 4 plus labels, 1/28/72, Casa Grande, AZ............................2.25		
☐☐ 1395d	**Dwight D. Eisenhower,** booklet pane of 7 plus label, 1/28/72, Casa Grande, AZ 2.00		
☐☐	Scott 1395c, 1395d on one cover.............................3.00		
☐☐ 1396	**8c USPS Emblem,** 7/1/71, DC 1.00	1.00	1.50
☐☐	Unofficial city...— *Washington, D. C post office had "First Day of Issue" postmark, but Scott 1396 was available at every post office on 7/1/71. More than 18,000 different cities are known with first day postmarks out of 39,521 possible. Values of the individual covers range from $1.*		
☐☐ 1397	**14c Fiorello H. LaGuardia,** 4/24/72, New York, NY (180,114)...1.00	1.25	1.75

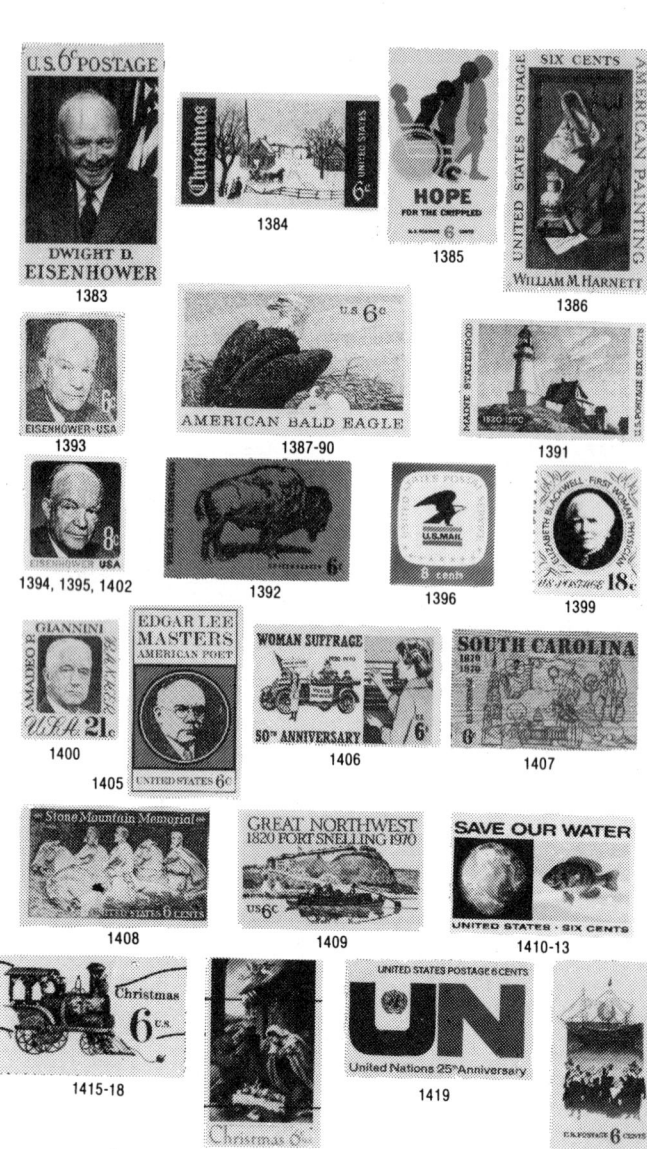

U.S. 6¢ POSTAGE

DWIGHT D. EISENHOWER

1383

Christmas
UNITED STATES
6¢
1384

HOPE
FOR THE CRIPPLED
6¢
1385

SIX CENTS
UNITED STATES POSTAGE
AMERICAN PAINTING
WILLIAM M. HARNETT
1386

EISENHOWER·USA 6¢
1393

U.S. 6¢
AMERICAN BALD EAGLE
1387-90

MAINE STATEHOOD
1820-1970
1391

EISENHOWER USA 8¢
1394, 1395, 1402

6¢
1392

U.S. POSTAL
U.S. MAIL
8 cents
1396

ELIZABETH BLACKWELL FIRST WOMAN PHYSICIAN
U.S. POSTAGE 18¢
1399

AMADEO P. GIANNINI
U.S.A. 21¢
1400

EDGAR LEE MASTERS
AMERICAN POET
UNITED STATES 6¢
1405

WOMAN SUFFRAGE
50TH ANNIVERSARY 6¢
1406

SOUTH CAROLINA
1670 1970
6¢
1407

Stone Mountain Memorial
UNITED STATES 6 CENTS
1408

GREAT NORTHWEST
1820 FORT SNELLING 1970
US 6¢
1409

SAVE OUR WATER
UNITED STATES · SIX CENTS
1410-13

Christmas
6¢ U.S.
1415-18

Christmas 6¢
1414

UNITED STATES POSTAGE 6 CENTS
UN
United Nations 25th Anniversary
1419

1620 THE LANDING OF THE PILGRIMS 1970
U.S.POSTAGE 6 CENTS
1420

94

☐☐ 1398	16c Ernie Pyle, 5/7/71, DC (444,410) 1.00		1.25	1.50
☐☐ 1399	18c Elizabeth Blackwell, 1/23/74, Geneva, NY			
	(217,938)...1.00		1.50	2.50
☐☐ 1400	21c Amadeo Giannini, 6/27/73, San Mateo, CA			
	(282,520)..1.00		1.50	2.50

1970-71 Coils

☐☐ 1401	6c Dwight D. Eisenhower, 8/6/70, DC......................1.00		prl.25	lp2.00
☐☐ 1402	8c Dwight D. Eisenhower, 5/10/71, DC 1.00		prl.25	lp2.00

1970

☐☐ 1405	6c Edgar Lee Masters, 8/22/70, Petersburg, IL			
	(372,804)..1.00		1.00	1.50
☐☐ 1406	6c Woman Suffrage, 8/26/70, Adams, MA			
	(508,142)..1.00		1.00	1.50
☐☐ 1407	6c South Carolina, 9/12/70, Charleston, SC			
	(533,000)..1.00		1.00	1.50
☐☐ 1408	6c Stone Mountain Memorial, 9/19/70, Stone			
	Mountain, GA (558,546)..1.00		1.00	1.50
☐☐ 1409	6c Fort Snelling, 10/17/70, Fort Snelling, MN			
	(497,611)..1.00		1.00	1.50
☐☐ 1410	6c Globe & Wheat, 10/28/70, San Clemente, CA........1.25			
☐☐ 1411	6c Globe & City, 10/28/70, San Clemente, CA 1.25			
☐☐ 1412	6c Globe & Bluegill, 10/28/70, SanClemente, CA 1.25			
☐☐ 1413	6c Globe & Seagull, 10/28/70, San Clemente, CA 1.25			
☐☐ 1413a	Se-tenant, (1,033,147). "Plate Block" value is for			
	block of 4 with plate numbers		3.00	4.00
☐☐ 1414	6c Christmas, 11/5/70, DC. "Plate Block" value			
	is for block of 4 with plate numbers.......................1.40		1.75	3.00
☐☐ 1414a	Christmas, precanceled, 11/5/70, DC 10.00			
☐☐ 1415	6c Tin & Cast-iron Locomotive, 11/5/70, DC.............1.40			
☐☐ 1415a	Tin & Cast-iron Locomotive, precanceled 2.50			
☐☐ 1416	6c Toy Horse on Wheels, 11/5/70, DC......................1.40			
☐☐ 1416a	Toy Horse on Wheels, precanceled............................2.50			
☐☐ 1417	6c Mechanical Tricycle, 11/5/70, DC........................1.40			
☐☐ 1417a	Mechanical Tricycle, precanceled.............................2.50			
☐☐ 1418	6c Doll Carriage, 11/5/70, DC.................................1.40			
☐☐ 1418a	Doll Carriage, precanceled......................................2.50			
☐☐ 1418b	Se-tenant, "Plate Block" value is for block of 4			
	with plate numbers		3.50	5.00
☐☐ 1418c	Se-tenant, precanceled..		6.00	
☐☐	Scott 1414a-1418a set of 5 on one cover 35.00			
	Total for Scott 1414-1418 or 1414a-1418a is 2,014,450.			
☐☐ 1419	6c United Nations, 11/20/70, New York, NY			
	(474,070)..1.00		1.00	1.50
☐☐ 1420	6c Landing of the Pilgrims, 11/21/70, Plymouth,			
	MA (629,850)...1.00		1.00	1.50
☐☐ 1421	6c Disabled Veterans, 11/24/70, Cincinnati, OH,			
	or Montgomery, AL 1.00		1.00	1.50
☐☐ 1422	6c U.S. Servicemen, 11/24/70, Cincinnati, OH, or			
	Montgomery, AL..1.00		1.00	1.50
☐☐	Scott 1421-1422 on one cover 1.20		1.75	2.50
	476,610 covers were postmarked in Cincinnati; 336,417 in Montgomery.			

1421

1422

1423

1424

1425

1st Bazaar cachet

1st Colorano Silk cachet

1426

1427-30

1433

1431

1434-35

1432

1436

1437

1438

1439

1440-43

1444

1445

1446

1447

1971

☐☐ 1423	6c **American Wool Industry**, 1/19/71, Las Vegas, NV (379,911)..1.00	1.00	1.50
☐☐	1st Bazaar cachet...25.00		
☐☐	1st Colomno Silk cachet.............................175.00		
☐☐ 1424	6c **Gen. Douglas MacArthur**, 1/26/71, Norfolk, VA (720,035)...1.00	1.00	1.50
☐☐ 1425	6c **Blood Donor**, 3/12/71, New York, NY (644,497)...1.00	1.00	1.50
☐☐ 1426	8c **Missouri Sesquicentennial**, 5/8/71, Independence, MO (551,000). "Plate Block" value is for block of 4 with plate numbers.............1.00	1.25	1.50
☐☐ 1427	8c **Trout**, 6/12/71, Avery Island, LA............1.25		
☐☐ 1428	8c **Alligator**, 6/12/71, Avery Island, LA........1.25		
☐☐ 1429	8c **Polar Bear & Cubs**, 6/12/71, Avery Island, LA......1.25		
☐☐ 1430	8c **California Condor**, 6/12/71, Avery Island, LA........1.25		
☐☐ 1430a	Se-tenant (679,483)..	3.00	5.00
☐☐ 1431	8c **Antarctic Treaty**, 6/23/71, DC (419,200) 1.00	1.25	1.50
☐☐ 1432	8c **American Revolution Bicentennial**, 7/4/71, DC (434,930) 1.00	1.25	1.50
☐☐	1st Medallion cachet 25.00		
☐☐ 1433	8c **John Sloan**, 8/2/71, Lock Haven, PA (482,265). 1.00	1.25	1.50
☐☐ 1434a	8c **Space Achievement Decade**, se-tenant pair, 8/2/71, Kennedy Space Center, FL (1,403,644)........2.50	3.25	4.00
☐☐	Houston, TX (811,560), pair 2.50	3.25	4.00
☐☐	Huntsville, AL (524,000), pair...................3.00	4.00	5.00
☐☐	1st Manned Space Flight Covers cachet 15.00		
☐☐	1st Swanson cachet.......................................15.00		
☐☐ 1436	8c **Emily Dickinson**, 8/28/71, Amherst, MA (498, 180)...1.00	1.25	1.50
☐☐ 1437	8c **San Juan**, 9/12/71, San Juan, PR (501,688) 1.00	1.25	1.50
☐☐ 1438	8c **Prevent Drug Abuse**, 10/4/71, Dallas, TX (425,330). "Plate Block" value is for block of 4 with plate numbers 1.00	1.25	1.50
☐☐ 1439	8c **CARE**, 10/27/71, New York, NY (402,121). "Plate Block" value is for block of 4 with plate numbers...1.00	1.25	1.50
☐☐ 1440	8c **Decatur House**, 10/29/71, DC.................1.25		
☐☐ 1441	8c **Whaling Ship Charles W. Morgan**, 10/29/71, DC..1.25		
☐☐ 1442	8c **Cable Car**, 10/29/71, DC........................1.25		
☐☐ 1443	8c **San Xavier del Bac Mission**, 10/29/71, DC....1.25		
☐☐ 1443a	Se-tenant, (783,242).......................................	3.00	4.00
☐☐ 1444	8c **Christmas**, 11/10/71, DC (348,038)........1.00	1.25	1.50
☐☐ 1445	8c **Christmas**, 11/10/71, DC (580,062)........1.00	1.25	1.50
☐☐	Scott 1444-1445 on one cover 1.20		

1972

☐☐ 1446	8c **Sidney Lanier**, 2/3/72, Macon, GA (394,800).........1.00	1.25	1.50
☐☐ 1447	8c **Peace Corps**, 2/11/72, DC (453,660), "Plate Block" value is for block of 4 with plate numbers...1.00	1.25	1.50

1453

1448-51

1452

1455

1454

1456-59

1460-62

1463

1464-67

1468

1469

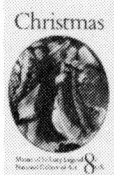

1470

1471

1472

1474

1st Coulson cachet

1473

1484-87

1475

1476-79

1480-83

National Parks Centennial

☐☐	1451a	2c Cape Hatteras National Seashore, se-tenant, 4/5/72, Hatteras, NC (505,697)		1.25	2.00
☐☐	1452	6c Wolf Trap Farm, 6/26/72, Vienna, VA (403,396)...1.00		1.25	1.50
☐☐	1453	8c Old Faithful, 3/1/72, Yellowstone National Park, WY...1.00		1.25	1.50
☐☐		DC (847,500)...1.00		1.25	1.50
☐☐	1454	15c Mt. McKinley, 7/28/72, Mt. McKinley National Park, AK (491,456)...1.00		1.25	2.00
☐☐	1455	8c Family Planning, 3/18/72, New York, NY (691,385)...1.00		1.25	1.50
☐☐	1456	8c Glass Blower, 7/4/72, Williamsburg, VA...1.00			
☐☐	1457	8c Silversmith, 7/4/72, Williamsburg, VA...1.00			
☐☐	1458	8c Wigmaker, 7/4/72, Williamsburg, VA...1.00			
☐☐	1459	8c Hatter, 7/4/72, Williamsburg, VA...1.00			
☐☐	1459a	Se-tenant, (1,914,976)...		2.50	3.50
☐☐	1460	6c Olympics, 8/17/72, DC. "Plate Block" value is for block of 4 with plate numbers...1.00		1.25	1.50
☐☐	1461	8c Winter Olympics, 8/17/72, DC. "Plate Block" value is for block of 4 with plate numbers...1.00		1.25	1.50
☐☐	1462	15c Olympics, 8/17/72, DC. "Plate Block" value is for block of 4 with plate numbers...1.00		1.50	2.00
		Scott 1460-1462 and C85 on one cover...2.00			
		Total for Scott 1460-1462 and C85 is 971,536.			
☐☐	1463	8c Parent Teacher Association, 9/15/72, San Francisco, CA (523,454)...1.00		1.25	1.50
☐☐	1464	8c Far Seals, 9/20/72 Warm Springs, OR...1.50			
☐☐	1465	8c Cardinal, 9/20/72 Warm Springs, OR...1.50			
☐☐	1466	8c Brown Pelican, 9/20/72 Warm Springs, OR...1.50			
☐☐	1467	8c Bighorn Sheep, 9/20/72 Warm Springs, OR...1.50			
☐☐	1467a	Se-tenant, (733,778)...		3.00	5.00
☐☐	1468	8c Mail Order, 9/27/72, Chicago, IL (759,666). "Plate Block" value is for block of 4 with plate numbers...1.00		1.25	2.00
☐☐	1469	8c Osteopathic Medicine, 10/9/72, Miami, FL (607, 160). "Plate Block" value is for block of 4 with plate numbers...1.00		1.25	2.00
☐☐	1470	8c Tom Sawyer, 10/13/72, Hannibal, MO (459,013)...1.00		1.25	2.00
		1st Coulson cachet...15.00			
☐☐	1471-1472	8c Christmas, 11/9/72, DC, either stamp...1.00		1.25	2.00
		Scott 1471-1472 on one cover (718,821 total for both)...2.00			
☐☐	1473	8c Pharmacy, 11/10/72, Cincinnati, OH (804,320). ...4.00		4.50	6.00
☐☐	1474	8c Stamp Collecting, 11/17/72, New York, NY (434,680)...1.00		1.25	1.50

1973

☐☐	1475	8c Love, 1/26/73, Philadelphia, PA (422,294). "Plate Block" value is for block of 4 with plate numbers...1.00		1.25	1.50

Progress in Electronics
1500-02

Copernicus
1473 - 1973
8¢ US
1488

U.S. POSTAL SERVICE 8¢
1489-98

Harry S. Truman
U.S Postage 8 cents
1499

Lyndon B. Johnson
United States
8 cents
1503

RURAL AMERICA
10¢
1504-06

Christmas
Raphael
National Gallery
of Art
8¢
1507

US. 8¢
CHRISTMAS
1508

UNITED 10 STATES
1509, 1519

We hold these Truths
UNITED STATES 10¢
1510, 1520

V·F·W·
75th Anniversary
VETERANS of SPANISH
AMERICAN and OTHER
FOREIGN WARS · U.S.
10¢
1525

10¢
Robert Frost
AMERICAN POET
1526

IT ALL DEPENDS ON
ZIP CODE
1511

6+3¢
U.S. Postage
1518

HORSE RACING
U.S. postage 10 cents
1528

US 10¢
Skylab
1529

EXPO'74 · US 10¢
PRESERVE THE ENVIRONMENT
1527

Letters
mingle souls
Raphael
10¢ US
1530-37

10¢
1538-41

FIRST KENTUCKY
SETTLEMENT
FORT HARROD
1774   1974
1542

CONSERVATION
UNITED STATES
1547

100

Communications in Colonial Times

			SGL	BLK	PL BLK
□□	1476	8c Pamphleteer, 2/16/73, Portland, OR (431,784)	1.00	1.25	1.50
□□	1477	8c Broadside, 4/13/73, Atlantic City, NJ (423,437)	1.00	1.25	1.50
□□	1478	8c Postrider, 6/22/73, Rochester, NY (586,850)	1.00	1.25	1.50
□□	1479	8c Drummer, 9/28/73, New Orleans, LA (522,427)	1.00	1.25	1.50
□□	1480	8c British merchantman, 7/4/73, Boston, MA	1.00		
□□	1481	8c British three-master, 7/4/73, Boston, MA	1.00		
□□	1482	8c Boats & ship's hulk 7/4/73, Boston, MA	1.00		
□□	1483	8c Boat & dock, 7/4/73, Boston, MA	1.00		
□□	1483a	Se-tenant, (897,870)		3.00	4.00

American Arts

			SGL	BLK	PL BLK
□□	1484	8c George Gershwin, 2/28/73, Beverly Hills, CA (448,814). "Plate Block" value is for block of 4 with plate numbers	1.00	1.25	1.50
□□	1485	8c Robinson Jeffers, 8/13/73, Carmel, CA (394,261). "Plate Block" value is for block of 4 with plate numbers	1.00	1.25	1.50
□□	1486	8c Henry O. Tanner, 9/10/73, Pittsburgh, PA (424,065). "Plate Block" value is for block of 4 with plate numbers	1.00	1.25	1.50
□□	1487	8c Willa Cather, 9/20/73, Red Cloud, NE (435,784). "Plate Block" value is for block of 4 with plate numbers	1.00	1.25	2.00
□□	1488	8c Nicolaus Copernicus, 4/23/73, DC (734,190)	1.00	1.25	1.50
□□	1489	8c Stamp Counter, 4/30/73, any city	1.00		
□□	1490	8c Mail Collection, 4/30/73, any city	1.00		
□□	1491	8c Letter Facing on Conveyor Belt, 4/30/73, any city	1.00		
□□	1492	8c Parcel Post Sorting, 4/30/73, any city	1.00		
□□	1493	8c Mail Canceling, 4/30/73, any city	1.00		
□□	1494	8c Manual Letter Routing, 4/30/73, any city	1.00		
□□	1495	8c Electronic Letter Routing, 4/30/73, any city	1.00		
□□	1496	8c Loading Mail on Truck, 4/30/73, any city	1.00		
□□	1497	8c Mailman, 4/30/73, any city	1.00		
□□	1498	8c Rural Mail Delivery, 4/30/73, any city	1.00		
		Any block of 4/block of 4 with plate number		1.25	2.00
		Strip of 10 on one cover	5.00		
□□	1499	8c Harry S. Truman, 5/8/73, Independence, MO (938,636)	1.00	1.25	1.50
□□	1500	6c Electronics, 7/10/73, New York, NY	1.00	1.25	1.50
□□	1501	8c Electronics, 7/10/73, New York, NY	1.00	1.25	1.50
□□	1502	15c Electronics, 7/10/73, New York, NY	1.00	1.25	1.75
		Scott 1500-1502 and C86 on one cover	3.00		
		Total for Scott 1500-1502 and C86 is 1,197, 700.			
□□	1503	8c Lyndon B. Johnson, 8/27/73, Austin, TX (701,490)	1.00	1.25	1.50

1973-74 Rural America

			SGL	BLK	PL BLK
□□	1504	8c Angus Cattle, 10/5/73, St. Joseph, MO (521,427)	1.00	1.25	1.50
□□	1505	10c Chautauqua, 8/6/74, Chautauqua, NY (411,105)	1.00	1.25	1.50
□□	1506	10c Wheat, 8/16/74, Hillsboro, KS (468,280)	1.00	1.25	1.50

10c

Retarded Children
Can Be Helped

1549

10c
'Bicentennial' Era

1543-46

1548

Christmas 10c U.S.

1551

Peace on Earth
Christmas 10

1552

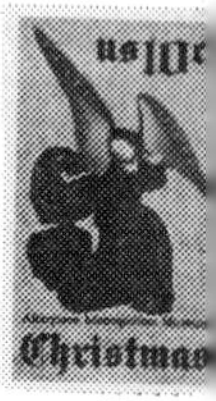

us 10c
Christmas

1550

Benjamin West
American artist
10 cents U.S. postage

1553

D.W. GRIFFITH

1555

PIONEER ★ JUPITER
US 10c

1556

Paul Laurence
Dunbar
American poet
10 cents U.S. postage

1554

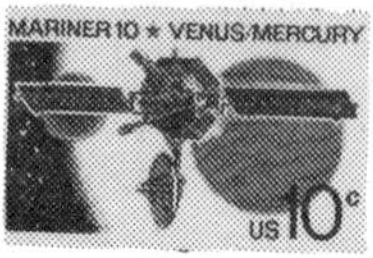

MARINER 10 ★ VENUS/MERCURY
US 10c

1557

UNITED STATES
collective bargaining
out of conflict 10c

1558

Bunker Hill 1775 by Trumbull
US Bicentennial 10c

1564

Continental Congress
8

Sybil Ludington Youthful Heroine

1559-62

Lexington & Concord 1775 by Sandham
US Bicentennial 10cents

1563

CONTINENTAL MARINES
US 10c

1565-68

us 10c
APOLLO SOYUZ 1975

APOLLO SOYUZ SPACE TEST PROJECT
10c

1569-70

1st Gothic Covers cachet

USA 10c
INTERNATIONAL WOMEN'S YEAR

1571

102

1973

		SGL	BLK	PL BLK
☐☐ 1507	8c Christmas, 11/7/73, DC 1.00		1.25	1.50
☐☐ 1508	8c Christmas, 11/7/73, DC 1.00		1.25	1.50
	Scott 1507-1508 on one cover			
	(807,468 total for both) 1.00			

1973-74

☐☐ 1509	10c Crossed Flags, 12/8/73, San Francisco, CA.			
	"Plate Block" value is for block of 4 with plate			
	numbers 1.00		1.25	1.50
	Total for Scott 1509 and 1519 is 341,528.			
☐☐ 1510	10c Jefferson Memorial, 12/14/73, DC 1.00		1.25	1.50
☐☐ 1510b	Jefferson Memorial, booklet pane of 5 plus labels,			
	12/14/73, DC...2.25			
☐☐ 1510c	Jefferson Memorial, booklet pane of 8, 12/14/73, DC .2.50			
☐☐ 1510d	Jefferson Memorial, booklet pane of 6, 8/5/74,			
	Oakland, CA 3.00			
	Total for Scott 1510, 1510b, 1510c, and 1520 is 686,300.			
☐☐ 1511	10c Zip Code, 1/4/74, DC (335,220). "Plate Block"			
	value is for block of 4 with plate numbers 1.00		1.00	1.50
☐☐ 1518	6.3c Liberty Bell, coil, 10/1/74, DC (221,141).............		prl.00	lpl.50
☐☐ 1519	10c Crossed Flags, coil, 12/8/73, DC 1.00		prl.00	lpl.50
☐☐ 1520	10c Jefferson Memorial, coil, 12/14/73, DC...............1.00		prl.25	lpl.50

1974

☐☐ 1525	10c Veterans of Foreign Wars, 3/11/74, DC			
	(543,598)..1.00		1.25	1.50
☐☐ 1526	10c Robert Frost, 3/26/74, Derry, NH (500,425)....1.00		1.25	1.50
☐☐ 1527	10c EXPO '74, 4/18/74, Spokane, WA (565,548).			
	"Plate Block" value is for block of 4 with plate			
	numbers 1.00		1.25	1.50
☐☐ 1528	10c Horse Racing, 5/4/74, Louisville, KY			
	(623,983) 2.00		2.50	3.50
☐☐	1st Henry Koehler cachet 15.00			
☐☐ 1529	10c Skylab, 5/14/74, Houston, TX (972,326)..............1.50		2.50	3.50
☐☐ 1530	10c Michelangelo, 6/6/74, DC...................................1.00			
☐☐ 1531	10c Five Feminine Virtues, 6/6/74, DC 1.00			
☐☐ 1532	10c Old Scraps, 6/6/74, DC.......................................1.00			
☐☐ 1533	10c The Lovely Reader, 6/6/74, DC 1.00			
☐☐ 1534	10c Lady Writing Letter, 6/6/74, DC 1.00			
☐☐ 1535	10c Inkwell & Quill, 6/6/74, DC................................1.00			
☐☐ 1536	10c Mrs. John Douglas, 6/6/74, DC...........................1.00			
☐☐ 1537	10c Don Antonio Noriega, 6/6/74, DC.......................1.00			
	Any block of 4/block of 4 with plate numbers		1.25	2.00
	Strip of 8 on one cover...4.00			
	Total for Scott 1530-1537 is 1,374,765.			
☐☐ 1538	10c Petrified Wood, 6/13/74, Lincoln, NE 1.00			
☐☐ 1539	10c Tourmaline, 6/13/74, Lincoln, NE.......................1.00			
☐☐ 1540	10c Anethyst 6/13/74, Lincoln, NE 1.00			
☐☐ 1541	10c Rhedochrosite, 6/13/74, Lincoln, NE 1.00			
☐☐ 1541a	Se-tenant (865,368)..		2.50	4.00
☐☐ 1542	10c Kentucky Settlement, 6/15/74, Harrodsburg			
	KY (478,239) 1.00		1.25	1.50

1572-75

1576

1579-80

1577-78

1584

1592, 1617

1593

1596

1599, 1619

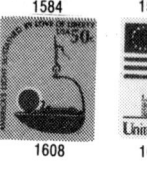

1608

1622, 1625

HOW TO USE THIS BOOK

The number in the first column is its Scott number or identifying number. Following that is the denomination of the stamp, description, date of issue, and the value.

☐☐ 1543	10c Carpenter's Hall, 7/4/74, Philadelphia, PA 1.00			
☐☐ 1544	10c "We ask but for peace," 7/4/74, Philadelphia, PA...1.00			
☐☐ 1545	10c "Deriving their just powers," 7/4/74, Philadelphia, PA...1.00			
☐☐ 1546	10c Independence Hall, 7/4/74, Philadelphia, PA......1.00			
☐☐ 1546a	Se-tenant (2,124,957)......................		2.75	3.50
☐☐ 1547	10c Energy Conservation, 9/23/74, Detroit, MI (587,210)...1.00		1.25	1.50
☐☐ 1548	10c Legend of Sleepy Hollow, 10/10/74, North Tarrytown, NY (514,836) 1.00		1.25	1.50
☐☐ 1549	10c Retarded Children, 10/12/74, Arlington, TX (412,882)..1.00		1.25	1.50
☐☐ 1550	10c Christmas, 10/23/74, New York, NY. "Plate Block" value is for block of 4 with plate numbers...1.00		1.25	1.50
☐☐ 1551	10c Chrismms, 10/23/74, New York, NY. "Plate Block" value is for block of 4 with plate numbers...1.00		1.25	1.50
☐☐	Scott 1550-1551 on one cover 1.00			
☐☐ 1552	10c Christnuts, self-adhesive, 11/15/74, New York, NY (477,410). "Plate Block" value is for block of 4 with plate numbers...1.00		1.25	1.50
☐☐	1st Glen cachet..20.00			

1975 American Arts

☐☐ 1553	10c Benjamin West, 2/10/75, Swarthmore, PA (465,017). "Plate Block" value is for block of 4 with plate numbers...1.00		1.25	1.50
☐☐ 1554	10c Paul Laurence Dunbar, 5/1/75, Dayton, OH (397,347). "Plate Block" value is for block of 4 with plate numbers...1.00		1.25	1.50
☐☐ 1555	10c D.W. Griffith, 5/27/75, Beverly Hills, CA (424,167)...1.00		1.25	1.50
☐☐ 1556	10c Pioneer-Jupiter, 2/28/75, Mountain View, CA (594,896)...2.00		2.50	4.00
☐☐ 1557	10c Mariner 10, 4/4/75, Pasadena, CA (563,636) 2.00		2.50	4.00
☐☐ 1558	10c Collective Bargaining, 3/13/75, DC (412,329). "Plate Block" value is for block of 4 with plate numbers...1.00		1.25	1.50
☐☐ 1559	8c Sybil Ludington, 3/25/75, Carmel, NY (394,550). "Plate Block" value is for block of 4 with plate numbers...1.00		1.25	1.50
☐☐ 1560	10c Salem Poor, 3/25/75, Cambridge, MA (415,565). "Plate Block" value is for block of 4 with plate numbers...1.00		1.25	1.50
☐☐ 1561	10c Haym Salomon, 3/25/75, Chicago, IL (447,630). "Plate Block" value is for block of 4 with plate numbers...1.00		1.25	1.50
☐☐ 1562	18c Peter Francisco, 3/25/75, Greensboro, NC (415,000). "Plate Block" value is for block of 4 with plate numbers...1.00		1.25	1.50
☐☐	Scott 1559-1562 set on one cover, any city 5.00			
☐☐ 1563	10c Lexington-Concord Battle, 4/19/75, Lexington, MA, or Concord, MA (975,020). "Plate Block" value is for block of 4 with plate numbers.............1.00		1.25	1.50
☐☐	Dual cancel..2.00			

☐☐ 1564 10c **Battle of Bunker Hill,** 6/17/75, Charlestown,
MA, (557,130). "Plate Block" value is for block of
4 with plate numbers...1.00   1.25   1.50

☐☐ 1565 10c **Soldier with Flintlock Musket,** 7/4/75, DC..........1.00
☐☐ 1566 10c **Sailor with Grappling Hook,** 7/4/75, DC 1.00
☐☐ 1567 10c **Marine with Musket,** 7/4/75, DC 1.00
☐☐ 1568 10c **Militiaman,** 7/4/75, DC.......................................1.00
☐☐ 1568a **Se-tenant,** (1,134, 831). "Plate Block" value is for
block of 4 with plate numbers 2.50   3.50

☐☐ 1569 10c **Apollo,** Soyuz before link-up, 7/15/75,
Kennedy Space Center, FL 2.00

☐☐ 1569a **Se-tenant,** (1,427,046)...4.00   5.00   6.00
☐☐ 1570 10c **Apollo,** Soyuz after link-up, 7/15/75 Kennedy
Space Center, FL 1.25

☐☐ 1571 10c **International Women's Year,** 8/26/75, Seneca
Falls, NY (476,769). "Plate Block" value is for
block of 4 plate numbers 1.00   1.25   1.50
☐☐   1st Gothic Covers cachet...................................20.00
☐☐ 1572 10c **Stagecoach & Trailer Truck,** 9/3/75,
Philadelphia, PA..1.00

☐☐ 1573 10c **Locomotives,** 9/3/75, Philadelphia, PA 1.00
☐☐ 1574 10c **Early Mail Plane,** Jet, 9/3/75, Philadelphia, PA...1.00
☐☐ 1575 10c **Satellite, Dishes,** 9/3/75, Philadelphia, PA 1.00
☐☐ 1575a **Se-tenant,** (969,999), "Plate Block" value is for block
of 4 with plate numbers 1.25   1.50

☐☐ 1576 10c **World Peace through Law,** 9/29/75, DC
(386,736) 1.00   1.25   1.50

☐☐ 1577 10c **"Banking,"** coins, 10/6/75, New York, NY 1.00
☐☐ 1577a **Se-tenant,** (555, 580) "Plate Block" value is for
block of 4 with plate numbers 1.10   1.00   1.50
☐☐ 1578 10c **"Commerce,"** coins, 10/6/75, New York, NY........1.00
☐☐ 1579 10c **Christmas,** 10/14/75, DC, "Plate Block" value
is for block of 4 with plate numbers.......................1.00   1.25   1.50
☐☐ 1580 10c **Christmas,** 10/14/75, DC, "Plate Block" value
is for block of 4 with plate numbers.......................1.00   1.25   1.50
☐☐   Scott 1579-1580 on one cover (730,079).................2.00

1975-81 Americana Issue

☐☐ 1581 1c **Inkwell & Quill,** multiple for First Class rate,
12/8/77, St. Louis, MO 1.00   1.00
☐☐ 1582 2c **Speaker's Stand,** multiple for First Class rate,
12/8/77, St. Louis, MO 1.00   1.00
☐☐ 1584 3c **Early Ballot Box,** multiple for First Class rate,
12/8/77, St. Louis, MO 1.00   1.00
☐☐ 1585 4c **Books,** Bookmark & Eyeglasses, multiple for
First Class rate, 12/8/77, St. Louis, MO............................   1.00   1.00
         Total for Scott 1581-1585 is 530,033.
☐☐ 1590 9c **Dome of the Capitol,** booklet single plus postage
for First Class rate, 3/11/77, New York, NY...................   8.00
☐☐ 1591 9c **Dome of the Capitol,** perf. 11 x 10 1/2, multiple
for First Class rate, 11/24/75, DC (190,117)`............1.00   1.25   1.50
☐☐ 1592 10c **Contemplation of Justice,** multiple for First
Class rate, 11/17/77, New York, NY (359,050).........1.00   1.25   1.75

SCOTT NUMBER	DESCRIPTION	CACHETED SGL	BLK	PL BLK
☐☐ 1593	11c **Early American Printing Press**, multiple for First Class rate, 11/13/75, Philadelphia, PA (217,755)...1.00	1.25	1.75
☐☐ 1594	12c **Torch**, multiple for First Class rate, 4/8/81, Dallas, TX...1.00	1.25	1.75
	Total for Scott 1594 and 1816 is 280,930.			
☐☐ 1595	13c **Liberty Bell**, booklet single, 10/31/75, Cleveland, OH...1.00		
☐☐ 1595a	**Liberty Bell**, booklet pane of 6, 10/31/75, Cleveland, OH...2.00		
☐☐ 1595b	**Liberty Bell**, booklet pane of 7 + label, 10/31/75, Cleveland, OH.............................2.75		
☐☐ 1595c	**Liberty Bell**, booklet pane of 8, 10/31/75, Cleveland, OH...2.50		
	Total for Scott 1595a-1595c is 256, 734.			
☐☐ 1595d	**Liberty Bell**, booklet pane of 5 + label, 4/2/76, Liberty, MO (92,223) 2.25	·	
☐☐ 1596	13c **Eagle & Shield**, 12/1/75, Juneau, AK (418,272). "Plate Block" value is for block of 4 with plate numbers.....................................1.00	1.25	1.75
☐☐ 1597	15c **Ft. McHenry Flag**, 6/30/78, Baltimore, MD. "Plate Block" value is for block of 4 with plate numbers...1.00	1.25	1.75
☐☐ 1598	15c **Ft. McHenry Flag**, booklet single, 6/30/78, Baltimore, MD 1.00		
☐☐ 1598a	**Ft. McHenry Flag booklet pane of 8**.....................2.50			
	Total for Scott 1597-1598 and 1618C is 315,359.			
☐☐ 1599	16c **Head, Statue of Liberty**, 3/31/78, New York, NY..1.00	1.25	1.75
	Total for Scott 1599 and 1619 is 376,338.			
☐☐ 1603	24c **Old North Church**, 11/14/75, Boston, MA (208,973)1.00	1.25	1.75
☐☐ 1604	28c **Ft. Nisqually**, 8/11/78, Tacoma, WA (159,639) 1.25	1.75	3.00
☐☐ 1605	29c **Sandy Hook Lighthouse**, 4/14/78, Atlantic City, NJ (193,476)......................................1.25	1.50	2.50
☐☐ 1606	30c **Morris Township School No. 2**, 8/27/79, Devils Lake, ND (186,882) 1.25	1.50	2.50
☐☐ 1608	50c **Iron "Betty" Lamp**, 9/11/79, San Juan, PR (159,540)..1.50	2.00	3.00
☐☐ 1610	$1 **Rush Lamp & Candle Holder**, 7/2/79, San Francisco, CA (255,575).............................3.00	4.50	7.50
☐☐ 1611	$2 **Kerosene Table Lamp**, 11/16/78, New York, NY (173,596) 7.00	8.50	10.00
☐☐ 1612	$5 **Railroad Lantern**, 8/23/79, Boston, MA (129,192)..15.00	20.00	25.00

1975-79 Americana Coils

SCOTT NUMBER	DESCRIPTION	CACHETED SGL	PR	L PR
☐☐ 1613	3.1c **Guitar**, 10/25/79, Shreveport, LA (230,403)..............	1.00	1.00
☐☐ 1614	7.7c **Saxhorns**, 11/20/76, New York, NY (285,298)..........	1.00	1.00
☐☐ 1615	7.9c **Drum**, 4/23/76, Miami, FL (193,270)	1.00	1.00
☐☐ 1615C	8.4c **Piano**, 7/13/78, Interlochen, MI (200,392).................	1.00	1.00
☐☐ 1616	9c **Dome of the Capitol**, 3/5/76, Milwaukee, WI (128,171)..	1.00	1.00

☐ 1617	10c **Contemplation of Justice**, 11/4/77, Tampa, FL (184,954)		1.00	1.00
☐	1st Bill Ressl cachet	15.00		
☐	1st Sandra's Cachets cachet	15.00		
☐ 1618	13c **Liberty Bell**, 11/25/75, Allentown, PA (320,387)	1.00	1.00	1.00
☐ 1618C	15c **Ft. McHenry Flag**, 6/30/78, Boston, MA	1.00 ...... 1.00	1.00	
☐ 1619	16c **Statue of Liberty Head**, 3/31/78, New York,NY	1.00	1.00	1.00

1975-77

☐ 1622	13c **Flag over Independence Hall**, 11/15/75, Philadelphia, PA, "Plate Block" value is for block of 4 with plate numbers	1.00	1.25	1.75
☐ 1623	13c **Flag over Capitol**, booklet single, perf. 11x10 1/2, 3/11/77, New York, NY	1.00		
☐ 1623a	**Flag over Capitol** booklet pane of 7 + 1 Scott 1590, 3/11/77, New York, NY	30.00		
☐ 1623b	**Flag over Capitol** booklet single, perf. 10, 3/11/77, New York, NY	1.50		
☐ 1623c	**Flag over Capitol** booklet pane of 7 + 1 Scott 1590a, 3/11/77, New York, NY	12.50		
	Total for all versions of Scott 1623 is 242.208.			

☐ 1625	13c **Flag over Independence Hall**, coil, 11/15/75, Philadelphia, PA		1.00	1.00
	Total for Scott 1622 and 1625 is 362,959.			

1976

☐ 1629	13c **Drummer boy**, 1/1/76, Pasadena, CA	1.75		
☐ 1630	13c **Old Drummer**, 1/1/76, Pasadena, CA	1.75		
☐ 1631	13c **Fifer**, 1/1/76, Pasadena, CA	1.75		
☐ 1631a	**Se-tenant**, (1,013,067). "Block"value is for block of 6. "Plate Block" value is for block of 6 with plate numbers		2.00	2.25
☐	1st Postmasters of America cachet	30.00		
☐ 1632	13c **Interphil '76**, 1/17/76, Philadelphia, PA (519,902)	1.00	1.25	1.75
☐ 1633	13c **Delaware**, 2/23/76, DC	1.25		
☐ 1634	13c **Pennsylvania**, 2/23/76, DC	1.25		
☐ 1635	13c **New Jersey**, 2/23/76, DC	1.25		
☐ 1636	13c **Georgia**, 2/23/76, DC	1.25		
☐ 1637	13c **Connecticut**, 2/23/76, DC	1.25		
☐ 1638	13c **Massachusetts**, 2/23/76, DC	1.25		
☐ 1639	13c **Maryland**, 2/23/76, DC	1.25		
☐ 1640	13c **South Carolina**, 2/23/76, DC	1.25		
☐ 1641	13c **New Hampshire**, 2/23/76, DC	1.25		
☐ 1642	13c **Virginia**, 2/23/76, DC	1.25		
☐ 1643	13c **New York**, 2/23/76, DC	1.25		
☐ 1644	13c **North Carolina**, 2/23/76, DC	1.25		
☐ 1645	13c **Rhode Island**, 2/23/76, DC	1.25		

1623

1629-31

1st Postmasters of America cachet

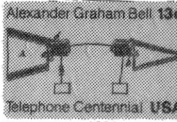

1632

1633-82

1683

Commercial Aviation

CHEMISTRY

1684

1685

1686

1687

1688

JULY 4,
1691-9

1689

1690

1st Metropolitan FDC Society cachet

**Values for various cachet makers can be determined
by using the Cachet Calculator which begins on page 40A.**

			CACHETED		
		DESCRIPTION	SGL	BLK	PL BLK
1646	13c Vermont, 2/23/76, DC	1.25		
1647	13c Kentucky, 2/23/76, DC	1.25		
1648	13c Tennessee, 2/23/76, DC	1.25		
1649	13c Ohio, 2/23/76, DC	1.25		
1650	13c Louisiana, 2/23/76, DC	1.25		
1651	13c Indiana, 2/23/76, DC	1.25		
1652	13c Mississippi, 2/23/76, DC	1.25		
1653	13c Illinois, 2/23/76, DC	1.25		
1654	13c Alabama, 2/23/76, DC	1.25		
1655	13c Maine, 2/23/76, DC	1.25		
1656	13c Missouri, 2/23/76, DC	1.25		
1657	13c Arkansas, 2/23/76, DC	1.25		
1658	13c Michigan, 2/23/76, DC	1.25		
1659	13c Florida, 2/23/76, DC	1.25		
1660	13c Texas, 2/23/76, DC	1.25		
1661	13c Iowa, 2/23/76, DC	1.25		
1662	13c Wisconsin, 2/23/76, DC	1.25		
1663	13c California, 2/23/76, DC	1.25		
1664	13c Minnesota, 2/23/76, DC	1.25		
1665	13c Oregon, 2/23/76, DC	1.25		
1666	13c Kansas, 2/23/76, DC	1.25		
1667	13c West Virginia, 2/23/76, DC	1.25		
1668	13c Nevada, 2/23/76, DC	1.25		
1669	13c Nebraska, 2/23/76, DC	1.25		
1670	13c Colorado, 2/23/76, DC	1.25		
1671	13c North Dakota, 2/23/76, DC	1.25		
1672	13c South Dakota, 2/23/76, DC	1.25		
1673	13c Montana, 2/23/76, DC	1.25		
1674	13c Washington, 2/23/76, DC	1.25		
1675	13c Idaho, 2/23/76, DC	1.25		
1676	13c Wyoming, 2/23/76, DC	1.25		
1677	13c Utah, 2/23/76, DC	1.25		
1678	13c Oklahoma, 2/23/76, DC	1.25		
1679	13c New Mexico, 2/23/76, DC	1.25		
1680	13c Arizona, 2/23/76, DC	1.25		
1681	13c Alaska, 2/23/76, DC	1.25		
1682	13c Hawaii, 2/23/76, DC	1.25		
	Complete set of 50	75.00		
1682a	Se-tenant, complete pane on one cover	50.00		
	Canceled at state capitals	2.00		
	Canceled at state capitals, complete set of 50	100.00		
	2/23/76, dual cachets (State & DC)	125.00		

Total for Scott 1633-1682 is 3,514,070.

1683	13c Telephone Centenary, 3/10/76, Boston, MA (662,515)	1.00	1.25	1.50
1684	13c Commercial Aviation, 3/19/76, Chicago, IL (631,555). "Plate Block" value is for block of 4 with plate numbers	1.00	1.25	1.50
	1st hfb cachet	15.00		

**Values for various cachet makers can be determined
by using the Cachet Calculator which begins on page 40A.**

111

1695-98

1699

1700

1701

1702

1st Carrollton cachet

1705

1704

1st Doris Gold cachet

1710

1706-09

1st GAMM cachet

1st Spectrum cachet

HOW TO USE THIS BOOK

The number in the first column is its Scott number or identifying number. Following that is the denomination of the stamp, description, date of issue, and the value.

112

☐☐ 1685 **13c Chemistry,** 4/6/76, New York, NY (557,600).
"Plate Block" value is for block of 4 with
plate numbers 1.00 1.25 1.50

☐☐ 1686 **13c Surrender of Cornwallis,** souvenir sheet,
5/29/76, Philadelphia, PA.......................................6.00

☐☐ 1687 **18c Declaration of Independence,** souvenir sheet,
5/29/76, Philadelphia, PA.......................................7.50

☐☐ 1688 **24c Washington Crossing the Delaware,** souvenir
sheet, 5/29/76, Philadelphia, PA 8.50

☐☐ 1689 **31c Washington at Valley Forge,** souvenir sheet,
5/29/76, Philadelphia, PA.......................................9.50
Scott 1686a-1689e, any single from sheets 1.00
Total for Scott 1686-1689 is 879,890.

☐☐ 1690 **13c Benjamin Franklin,** 6/1/76, Philadelphia, PA 1.00 1.25 1.50
In Combo with Canadian issue, dual cancels...........1.25
1st Metropolitan FDC Society cachet 10.00

☐☐ 1691 **13c Declaration of Independence,** 7/4/76,
Philadelphia, PA...1.00

☐☐ 1692 **13c Declaration of Independence,** 7/4/76,
Philadelphia, PA...1.00

☐☐ 1693 **13c Declaration of Independence,** 7/4/76,
Philadelphia, PA...1.00

☐☐ 1694 **13c Declaration of Independence,** 7/4/76,
Philadelphia, PA...1.00

☐☐ 1694a **Se-tenant,** "Plate Block" value is for block of 8
with plate numbers 2.00 2.50
Total for Scott 1691-1694 is 2,093,880.

☐☐ 1695 **13c Diving,** 7/16/76, Lake Placid, NY 1.00
☐☐ 1696 **13c Skiing,** 7/16/76, Lake Placid, NY.........................1.00
☐☐ 1697 **13c Running,** 7/16/76, Lake Placid, NY......................1.00
☐☐ 1698 **13c Skating,** 7/16/76, Lake Placid, NY 1.00
☐☐ 1698a **Se-tenant,** (1,140,189). "Plate Block" value is for
block of 4 with plate numbers 2.00 2.50

☐☐ 1699 **13c Clara Maass,** 8/18/76, Belleville, NJ
(646,506). "Plate Block" value is for block of 4 with
plate numbers 1.00 1.25 1.50

☐☐ 1700 **13c Adolph S. Ochs,** 9/18/76, New York, NY
(582,580)..1.00 1.25 1.50

☐☐ 1701 **13c Christmas (Nativity),** 10/27/76, Boston, MA.
"Plate Block" value is for block of 4 with plate
numbers 1.00 1.25 1.50

☐☐ 1702 **13c Christmas ("Winter Pastime"),** 10/27/76,
Boston, MA. "Plate Block" value is for block of 4
with plate numbers...1.00 1.25 1.50
Scott 1701-1702 set on one cover............................1.20

☐☐ 1703 **13c Christmas ("Winter Pastime"),** 10/27/76,
Boston, MA. "Plate Block" value is for block of 4
with plate numbers...1.00 1.25
Total for Scott 1701-1703 is 330,450.

1977

☐☐ 1704 **13c Washington at Princeton,** 1/3/77, Princeton,
NJ (695,335). "Plate Block" value is for block of 4
with plate numbers...1.00 1.25 1.50
1st Carrollton cachet...20.00

1st Tudor House cachet

1711

US Bicentennial 13c

1716

1st Comic Cachets

1st Ham cachet

1712-15

1717-20

1721

1722

1723-24

1725

HOW TO USE THIS BOOK

The number in the first column is its Scott number or identifying number. Following that is the denomination of the stamp, description, date of issue, and the value.

114

☐☐ 1705	13c **Sound Recording**, 3/23/77, DC (632,216)............1.00		1.25	1.50
	1st Weddle cachet...250.00			
☐☐ 1706	13c **Zia Pot**, 4/13/77, Santa Fe, NM.........................1.00			
☐☐ 1707	13c **San Ildefonso Pot**, 4/13/77, Santa Fe, NM...........1.00			
☐☐ 1708	13c **Hopi Pot**, 4/13/77, Santa Fe, NM 1.00			
☐☐ 1709	13c **Acoma Pot**, 4/13/77, Santa Fe, NM...................1.00			
☐☐ 1709a	**Se-tenant**, (1,194, 554). "Plate Block" value is for			
	block of 4 with plate numbers		2.00	3.00
☐☐	1st Jack Davis Covers cachet...................................45.00			
☐☐	"Sante Fe" error in cancel.....................................10.00	12.00		
☐☐ 1710	13c **Lindbergh Flight**, 5/20/77, Roosevelt Field			
	Sta., NY (3,985,989). "Plate Block" value is for			
	block of 4 with plate numbers.................................1.00		1.25	2.00
☐☐	1st Doris Gold cachet 50.00			
☐☐	1st GAMM cachet..60.00			
☐☐	1st Spectrum cachet..25.00			
☐☐	1st Tudor House cachet 20.00			
☐☐	1st Global Cachets..20.00			
☐☐	1st Z-Silk cachet...20.00			
☐☐ 1711	13c **Colorado Statehood**, 5/21/77, Denver, CO			
	(510, 880). "Plate Block" value is for block of 4			
	with plate numbers 1.00		1.25	1.50
☐☐ 1712	13c **Swallowtail**, 6/6/77, Indianapolis, IN..................1.00			
☐☐ 1713	13c **Checkerspot**, 6/6/77, Indianapolis, IN 1.00			
☐☐ 1714	13c **Dogface**, 6/6/77, Indianapolis, IN 1.00			
☐☐ 1715	13c **Orange-tip**, 6/6/77, Indianapolis, IN....................1.00			
☐☐ 1715a	**Se-tenant**, (1,218,278). "Plate Block" value is for			
	block of 4 with plate numbers		2.00	3.00
☐☐	1st Comic cachet...20.00			
☐☐	1st Ham cachet 450.00			
☐☐ 1716	13c **Lafayette**, 6/13/77, Charleston, SC (514,506)......1.00		1.25	1.50
☐☐ 1717	13c **Seamstress**, 7/4/77, Cincinnati, OH 1.00			
☐☐ 1718	13c **Blacksmith**, 7/4/77, Cincinnati, OH.....................1.00			
☐☐ 1719	13c **Wheelwright**, 7/4/77, Cincinnati, OH...................1.00			
☐☐ 1720	13c **Leatherworker**, 7/4/77, Cincinnati, OH...............1.00			
☐☐ 1720a	**Se-tenant**, (1,263,568). "Plate Block" value is for			
	block of 4 with plate numbers 1.75		2.50	
☐☐ 1721	13c **Peace Bridge**, 8/4/77, Buffalo, NY (512,995)........1.00		1.25	1.50
☐☐	U.S. and Canadian stamps on one cover,			
	U.S. cancel...2.00			
☐☐	Dual U.S. and Canadian cancels 3.00			
☐☐ 1722	13c **Battle of Oriskany**, 8/6/77, Herkimer, NY			
	(605,906). "Plate Block" value is for block of 4			
	with plate numbers...1.00		1.25	1.50
☐☐ 1723	13c **Energy Conservation**, 10/20/77, DC 1.00			
☐☐ 1723a	**Se-tenant**, "Plate Block" value is for block of 4			
	with plate numbers...1.25		1.25	1.50
☐☐ 1724	13c **Energy Development**, 10/20/77, DC 1.00			
	Total for Scott 1723-1724 is 410,299.			
☐☐ 1725	13c **Alta California**, 9/9/77, San Jose, CA			
	(709,457)...1.00		1.25	1.50
☐☐ 1726	13c **Articles of Confederation**, 9/30/77, York, PA			
	(605,455)..1.00		1.25	1.50
☐☐ 1727	13c **Talking Pictures**, 10/6/77, Hollywood, CA			
	(570,195)...1.00		1.25	1.65

1726   1727

US Bicentennial 13 cents
1728

1729   1730   1734

1731   1732

1st Calhoun Collector's Society Gold Foil Cachet

1733   1735

1st Rob Cuscaden cachet

1st Western Silk Cachets

HOW TO USE THIS BOOK
The number in the first column is its Scott number or identifying number. Following that is the denomination of the stamp, description, date of issue, and the value.

☐☐ 1728	13c **Surrender at Saratoga**, 10/7/77, Schuylerville, NY (557,529). "Plate Block" value is for block of 4 with plate numbers 1.00		1.25	1.50
☐☐ 1729	13c **Christmas (Valley Forge)**, 10/21/77, Valley Forge, PA (583,139). "Plate Block" value is for block of 4 with plate numbers 1.00		1.25	1.50
☐☐	1st HJS cachet...15.00			
☐☐ 1730	13c **Christmas (mailbox)**, 10/21/77, Omaha, NE (675,786). "Plate Block" value is for block of 4 with plate numbers 1.00		1.25	1.50
☐☐	Scott 1729-1730 on one cover 3.00			
☐☐	Scott 1729-1730 on one cover with dual cancels ...4.00			

1978

☐☐ 1731	13c **Carl Sandburg**, 1/6/78, Galesburg, IL (493,826)..1.00		1.25	1.50
☐☐	1st Calhoun Collector's Society Gold Foil Cachet...15.00			
☐☐	1st Rob Cuscaden cachet 15.00			
☐☐	1st Western Silk cachet..35.00			
☐☐	1st Nova cachet..15.00			
☐☐	1st Susan Richardson cachet 15.00			
☐☐ 1732	13c **Captain Cook**, 1/20/78, Honolulu, HI, or Anchorage, AK 1.00		1.25	1.50
☐☐ 1732a	**Se-tenant**...1.50		1.75	2.00
☐☐ 1733	13c **Resolution & Discovery**, 1/20/78, Honolulu, HI, or Anchorage, AK...1.00		1.25	1.50
☐☐	Scott 1732-1733 on one cover with dual cancel......2.00			
☐☐	1st K.M.C. Venture cachet....................................50.00			
	Total for Scott 1732-33 is 1,496,659.			
☐☐ 1734	13c **Indian Head Penny**, 1/11/78, Kansas City, MO (512,426)..1.00		1.25	2.00

1978-80 Regular Issues

☐☐ 1735	(15c) **"A" & Eagle**, non-denominated, 5/22/78, Memphis, TN...1.00		1.25	1.50
☐☐	1st G. Peltin cachet 30.00			
☐☐ 1736	(15c) **"A" & Eagle**, non-denominated, booklet single, 5/22/78, Memphis, TN 1.00		1.25	1.50
☐☐ 1736a	**"A" & Eagle**, booklet pane of 8......................2.50			
☐☐ 1737	15c **Roses**, booklet single, 7/11/78, Shreveport, LA, (445,003) 1.00			
☐☐ 1737a	**Roses**, booklet pane of 8................................2.50			
☐☐ 1738	15c **Windmills**, 2/7/80, Lubbock, TX, booklet single...1.00			
☐☐ 1739	15c **Windmills**, 2/7/80, Lubbock, TX, booklet single...1.00			
☐☐ 1740	15c **Windmills**, 2/7/80, Lubbock, TX, booklet single...1.00			
☐☐ 1741	15c **Windmills**, 2/7/80, Lubbock, TX, booklet single...1.00			
☐☐ 1742	15c **Windmills**, 2/7/80, Lubbock, TX, booklet single...1.00			
☐☐ 1742a	**Booklet pane of 10** 3.50			
	Total for Scott 1738-1742 is 708,411.			

☐☐ 1743	(15c) "A" & Eagle, coil, 5/22/78, Memphis, TX 1.00	pr 1.00		lp 1.50
☐☐	1st Kribbs Kover cachet................................40.00			
	Total for Scott 1735, 1736 and 1743 is 689,049.			
☐☐ 1744	13c Harriet Tubman, 2/1/78, DC (493,495) "Plate Block" value is for block of 4 with plate numbers...1.00		1.25	2.00
☐☐ 1745	13c Quilt design, 3/8/78, Charleston, WV 1.00			
☐☐ 1746	13c Quilt design, 3/8/78, Charleston, WV 1.00			
☐☐ 1747	13c Quilt design, 3/8/78, Charleston, WV 1.00			
☐☐ 1748	13c Quilt design, 3/8/78, Charleston, WV 1.00			
☐☐ 1748a	Se-tenant, (1,081,827), "Plate Block" value is for block of 4 with numbers		2.00	3.00
☐☐	1st F. Collins cachet................................500.00			
☐☐ 1749	13c Ballet, 4/26/78, New York, NY 1.00			
☐☐ 1750	13c Theatre Dance, 4/26/78, New York, NY 1.00			
☐☐ 1751	13c Folk Dance, 4/26/78, New York, NY...................1.00			
☐☐ 1752	13c Modern Dance, 4/26/78, New York, NY..............1.00			
☐☐ 1752a	Se-tenant, (1,626,493) "Plate Block" value is for block of 4 with plate numbers		1.75	2.50
☐☐	1st Andrews cachet..............................25.00			
☐☐	1st Annable cachet................................15.00			
☐☐	1st Great Picture Covers cachet...........................20.00			
☐☐ 1753	13c French Alliance, 5/4/78, York, PA (705,240) 1.00		1.25	1.50
☐☐ 1754	13c Early Cancer Detection, 5/18/78, DC (535,584)..1.00		1.25	1.50
☐☐ 1755	13c Jimmie Rodgers, 5/24/78, Meridian, MS (599,287). "Plate Block" value is for block of 4 with plate numbers..1.00		1.25	1.50
☐☐ 1756	15c George M. Cohen, 7/3/78, Providence, RI (740,750). "Plate Block" value is for block of 4 with plate numbers..1.00		1.25	1.50
☐☐	1st Richard S. Byron cachet...........................15.00			
☐☐ 1757	13c CAPEX Souvenir Sheet, 6/10/78, Toronto, Ontario (1,994,067)..2.75			
☐☐ 1757a	13c Cardinal 1.00			
☐☐ 1757b	13c Mallard 1.00			
☐☐ 1757c	13c Canada Goose 1.00			
☐☐ 1757d	13c Blue jay..1.00			
☐☐ 1757e	13c Moose...1.00			
☐☐ 1757f	13c Chipmunk 1.00			
☐☐ 1757g	13c Red Fox..1.00			
☐☐ 1757h	13c Raccoon 1.00			
☐☐ 1758	15c Photography, 6/26/78, Las Vegas, NV (684,987). "Plate Block" value is for block of 4 with plate numbers..1.00		1.25	1.50
☐☐ 1759	15c Viking Missions to Mars, 7/20/78, Hampton, VA (805,051)..2.00		2.50	3.00
☐☐	1st Softones cachet 20.00			
☐☐ 1760	15c Great gray Owl, 8/26/78, Fairbanks, AK.............1.00			
☐☐ 1761	15c Saw-whet Owl, 8/26/78, Fairbanks, AK 1.00			
☐☐ 1762	15c Barrod Owl, 8/26/78, Fairbanks, AK 1.00			
☐☐ 1763	15c Great Horned Owl, 8/26/78, Fairbanks, AK 1.00			
☐☐ 1763a	Se-tenant, (1,690,474)..		2.00	2.50
☐☐ 1764	15c Giant Sequoia, 10/9/78, Hot Springs National Park, AR..1.00			

1st F. Collins Cachet

1744

1749-52

1st Andrews Cachet cachet

US Bicentennial 13c
1753

1754

JIMMIE RODGERS
Performing Arts 13c
1755

GEORGE M. COHAN
Performing Arts USA 13c
1756

Photography USA 15c
1758

Viking missions to Mars
USA 15c
1759

1st Softones cachet

GRAY BIRCH
USA 15c
1764-67

1760-63

**Values for various cachet makers can be determined
by using the Cachet Calculator which begins on page 40A.**

SCOTT NUMBER	DESCRIPTION	CACHETED SGL	BLK	PL BLK
☐☐ 1765	15c White Pine, 10/9/78, Hot Springs National Park, AR...1.00			
☐☐ 1766	15c White Oak, 10/9/78, Hot Springs National Park, AR...1.00			
☐☐ 1767	15c Gray Birch, 10/9/78, Hot Springs National Park, AR...1.00			
☐☐ 1767a	Se-tenant, (1,139,100)................................		2.00	2.50
☐☐ 1768	15c Christmas (Madonna), 10/18/78, DC (553,064)...1.00		1.25	1.50
☐☐ 1769	15c Christmas (Hobby Horse), 10/18/78, Holly, MI (603,008). "Plate Block" value is for block of 4with plate numbers...........................1.00		1.25	1.50
☐☐	Scott 1768-1769 on one cover 3.00			
☐☐	Scott 1768-1769 dual cancels....................4.00			

1979

☐☐ 1770	15c Robert F. Kennedy, 1/12/79, DC (624,582) 2.00		2.50	3.50
☐☐	1st Bittings cachet.....................................20.00			
☐☐	1st DRC cachet 50.00			
☐☐ 1771	15c Martin Luther King, Jr. 1/13/79, Atlanta, GA (726, 149). "Plate Block" value is for block of 4 with plate numbers.....................................1.00		1.25	1.50
☐☐ 1772	15c International Year of the Child, 2/15/79, Philadelphia, PA (716,782)........................1.00		1.25	1.50
☐☐ 1773	15c John Steinbeck, 2/27/79, Salinas, CA (709,073)...1.00		1.25	1.50
☐☐ 1774	15c Albert Einstein, 3/4/79, Princeton, NJ (641,423)...1.50		2.00	3.00
☐☐ 1775	15c Coffeepot, 4/19/79, Lancaster, PA......................1.00			
☐☐ 1776	15c Tea Caddy, 4/19/79, Lancaster, PA......................1.00			
☐☐ 1777	15c Sugar Bowl, 4/19/79, Lancaster, PA 1.00			
☐☐ 1778	15c Coffeepot, 4/19/79, Lancaster, PA......................1.00			
☐☐ 1778a	Se-tenant, (1,581,963). "Plate Block" value is for block of 4 with plate numbers		2.00	2.50
☐☐ 1779	15c Virginia Rotunda, 6/4/79, Kansas City, MO 1.00			
☐☐ 1780	15c Baltimore Cathedral, 6/4/79, Kansas City,MO.....1.00			
☐☐ 1781	15c Boston State House, 6/4/79, Kansas City, MO. 1.00			
☐☐ 1782	15c Philadelphia Exchange, 6/4/79, Kansas City,MO 1.00			
☐☐ 1782a	Se-tenant, (1,219,258)................................		2.00	2.50
☐☐ 1783	15c Persistent Trillium, 6/7/79, Milwaukee, WI 1.00			
☐☐ 1784	15c Hawaiian Wild Broadbean 6/7/79, Milwaukee, WI 1.00			
☐☐ 1785	15c Contra Costa Wallflower, 6/7/79, Milwaukee, WI 1.00			
☐☐ 1786	15c Antioch Dunes Evening Primrose, 6/7/79, Milwaukee, WI 1.00			
☐☐ 1786a	Se-tenant, (1,436,268). "Plate Block" value is for block of 4 with plate numbers		2.00	2.50
☐☐ 1787	15c Seeing Eye Dogs, 6/15/79, Morristown, NJ (588,826). "Plate Block" value is for block of 4 with plate numbers.....................................1.00		1.25	1.50
☐☐ 1788	15c Special Olympics, 8/9/79, Brockport, NY (651,344). "Plate Block" value is for block of 4 with plate numbers.....................................1.00		1.25	1.50

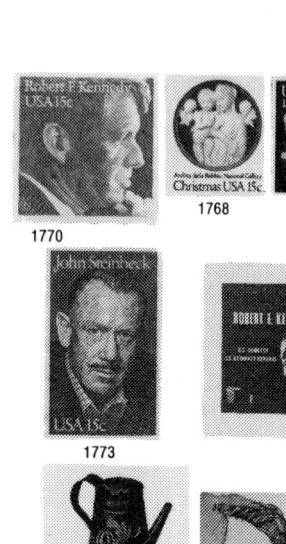

1770

Christmas USA 15c
1768

1769

USA 15c
International Year of the Child
1772

Martin Luther King Jr.
Black Heritage USA 15c
1771

John Steinbeck
USA 15c
1773

1st Bittings cachet

Einstein
USA 15c
1774

Pennsylvania Toleware
Folk Art USA 15c
1775-8

1st DRC cachet

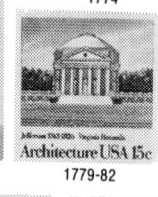

Jefferson 1743-1826 Virginia Rotunda
Architecture USA 15c
1779-82

Endangered Flora
15c
USA
1783-6

USA 15c
Seeing For Me
1787

Special Olympics
Skill · Sharing · Joy
USA 15c
1788

I have not yet begun to fight
John Paul Jones
US Bicentennial 15c
1789

USA
10c
1790

USA
15c
1795-8

Christmas USA 15c
1799

Christmas
15c USA
1800

USA 15c
HONORING VIETNAM VETERANS
NOV 11 1979
1802

122

☐☐	1789	15c John Paul Jones, 9/23/79, Annapolis, MD, perf. 11x12. "Plate Block" value is for block of 4 with plate numbers 1.00	1.25	1.50
☐☐	1789a	John Paul Jones, perf. 11. "Plate Block" value is for block of 4 with plate numbers 1.00	1.25	1.50
☐☐		1st D. Cunningham cachet......................................5.00		
		Total for Scott 1789 and 1789a is 587,018.		
☐☐	1790	10c Olympic Games, 9/5/79, Olympia, WA (305, 122). "Plate Block" value is for block of 4 with plate numbers 1.00	1.50	2.00
☐☐	1791	15c Running, 9/28/79, Los Angeles, CA....................1.00		
☐☐	1792	15c Swimming, 9/28/79, Los Angeles, CA 1.00		
☐☐	1793	15c Rowing, 9/28/79, Los Angeles, CA 1.00		
☐☐	1794	15c Equestrian, 9/28/79, Los Angeles, CA 1.00		
☐☐	1794a	Se-tenant, (1,561,366). "Plate Block" value is for block of 4 with plate numbers	2.00	2.50
☐☐	1795	15c Speed Skating, 2/1/80, Lake Placid, NY 1.00		
☐☐	1796	15c Downhill Skiing, 2/1/80, Lake Placid, NY...........1.00		
☐☐	1797	15c Ski Jump, 2/1/80, Lake Placid, NY 1.00		
☐☐	1798	15c Hockey, 2/1/80, Lake Placid, NY 1.00		
☐☐	1798a	Se-tenant, (1,166,302). "Plate Block" value is for block of 4 with plate numbers	2.00	2.50
☐☐	1799	15c Christmas (Madonna & Child), 10/18/79, DC (686,990). "Plate Block" value is for block of 4 with plate numbers 1.00	1.25	1.50
☐☐	1800	15c Christmas (Santa Claus), 10/18/79, North Pole, AK (511,829). "Plate Block" value is for block of 4 with plate numbers 1.00	1.25	2.00
☐☐		Scott 1799-1800 on one cover 2.00		
☐☐		Scott 1799-1800 on one cover, dual cancels............3.00		
☐☐	1801	15c Will Rogers, 11/4/79, Claremore, OK (1,643,151). "Plate Block" value is for block of 4 with plate numbers 1.00	1.25	1.50
☐☐		1st Jemm Covers cachet 25.00		
☐☐	1802	15c Vietnam Veterans, 11/11/79, DC (445,934). "Plate Block" value is for block of 4 with plate numbers 2.50	3.00	4.00
☐☐		1st Brennan cachet 15.00		
☐☐	1803	15c W.C. Fields, 1/29/80, Beverly Hills, CA (633,303). "Plate Block" value is for block of 4 with plate numbers 1.25	1.50	2.50
☐☐		1st Gill Craft cachet 35.00		
☐☐		1st Kover Kids cachet 12.00		
☐☐	1804	15c Benjamin Banneker, 2/15/80, Annapolis, MD (647,126). "Plate Block" value is for block of 4 with plate numbers 1.00	1.25	1.50
☐☐		1st Queensbury cachet..20.00		
☐☐	1805	15c "Letters Preserve Memories," 2/25/80, DC.........1.00		
☐☐	1806	15c "P.S. Write Soon," 2/25/80, DC 1.00		
☐☐	1807	15c "Letters Lift Spirits," 2/25/80, DC......................1.00		
☐☐	1808	15c "P.S. Write Soon," 2/25/80, DC 1.00		
☐☐	1809	15c "Letters Shape Opinions," 2/25/80, DC...............1.00		
☐☐	1810	15c "P.S. Write Soon," 2/25/80, DC 1.00		
☐☐	1810a	Se-tenant, (1,083,360) on single cover 2.50		

Note: Marginal markings require 12 stamps, plate blocks 36.

WILL ROGERS
Performing Arts USA 15c
1801

W.C. FIELDS
Performing Arts USA 15c
1803

Benjamin Banneker
Black Heritage USA 15c
1804

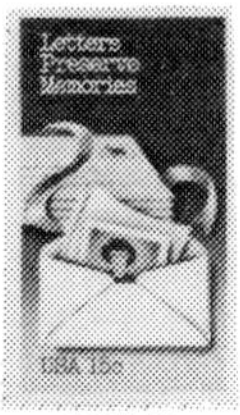

Letters Preserve Memories
USA 15c
1805-10

THE ABILITY TO WRITE, A ROOT OF DEMOCRACY
USA 1c
1811

JOHN J. BRENNAN JR.
P.O. BOX 433
ELMWOOD PARK, N.J. 07407
The Buddies

1st Brennan cachet

W.C. FIELDS

1st Gill Craft cachet

B US Postage
1818-20

Frances Perkins USA 15c
1821

Dolley Madison USA 15c
1822

Emily Bissell
Crusader Against Tuberculosis
USA 15c
1823

USA 15c
HELEN KELLER
ANNE SULLIVAN
1824

Veterans Administration
VA
Fifty Years of Service
USA 15c
1825

1st American Postal Arts Society Cachet (Post/Art)

1st D.J. Graf Cachet

HOW TO USE THIS BOOK

The number in the first column is its Scott number or identifying number. Following that is the denomination of the stamp, description, date of issue, and the value.

SCOTT NUMBER	DESCRIPTION	CACHETED PR	L PR

1980-81 Americana Coils

	Scott	Description	PR	L PR
☐☐	1811	1c Inkwell & Quill, 3/6/80, New York, NY (262,921)	1.00	1.00
☐☐	1813	3.5c Weaver Violins, 6/23/80, Williamsburg PA	1.00	1.00
		Total for Scott 1813 and U590 is 716,988.		
☐☐	1816	12c Torch, 4/8/81, Dallas, TX	1.00	1.00
		Total for Scott 1594 and 1816 is 280,930.		

SCOTT NUMBER	DESCRIPTION	SGL	CACHETED BLK	PL BLK
☐☐ 1818	(18c) "B" & Eagle, 3/15/81, San Francisco, CA 1.00		1.25	1.65
☐☐ 1819	(18c) "B" & Eagle, booklet single, 3/15/81, San Francisco, CA 1.00			
☐☐ 1819a	"B" & Eagle, booklet pane of 8 .... 3.00			
☐☐ 1820	(18c) "B" & Eagle coil, 3/15/81, San Francisco,CA 1.00		1.25	1.65
	Total for Scott 1818-1820, U592 and UX88 is 511,688.			

1980

☐☐ 1821	15c Frances Perkins, 4/10/80, DC (678,966) 1.00	1.25	1.50
	1st Samuel Gompers Stamp Club cachet 12.00		
☐☐ 1822	15c Dolley Madison, 5/20/80, DC (331,048) 1.00	1.25	1.50
	1st American Postal Arts Society cachet (Post/Art) 20.00		
☐☐	1st D.J. Graf cachet... 20.00		
☐☐ 1823	15c Emily Bissell, 5/31/80, Wilmington, DE (649,509) 1.00	1.25	2.00
☐☐ 1824	15c Helen Keller, 6/27/80, Tuscumbia, AL (713,061) 1.00	1.25	1.65
☐☐ 1825	15c Veterans Administration, 7/21/80, DC (634,101) 1.00	1.25	1.50
☐☐ 1826	15c Bernardo de Galvez, 7/23/80, New Orleans, LA (658,061) 1.00	1.25	1.50
☐☐ 1827	15c Brain Coral, Beaugregory Fish, 8/26/80, Charlotte Amalie, VI 1.00		
☐☐ 1828	15c Elkhorn Coral, Porkfish, 8/26/80, Charlotte Amalie, VI 1.00		
☐☐ 1829	15c Chalice Coral, Moorish Idol 8/26/80, Charlotte Amalie, VI.................................... 1.00		
☐☐ 1830	15c Finger Coral, Sabertooth Blenny, 8/26/80, Charlotte Amalie, VI.................................... 1.00		
☐☐ 1830a	Se-tenant, (1,195,126) "Plate Block" value is for block of 4 with plate numbers	2.00	2.50
☐☐ 1831	15c Organized Labor, 9/1/80, DC (759,973). "Plate Block" value is for block of 4 with plate numbers. 1.00	1.25	1.50

Addressed covers sell for about 75% of catalogue value.

1826   1827-30   1831   1832   1833

1834-7   1838-41   1842   1843

1845   1860   1866   1874   1875

**Values for various cachet makers can be determined
by using the Cachet Calculator which begins on page 40A.**

☐☐ 1832 15c **Edith Wharton**, 9/5/80, New Haven, CT
(633,917)..1.00 1.25 1.50

☐☐ 1833 15c **American Education**, 9/12/80, DC (672,592).
"Plate Block" value is for block of 4 with plate
numbers...1.00 1.25 1.50

☐☐ 1834 15c **Bella Bella Tribe**, 9/25/80, Spokane, WA 1.00

☐☐ 1835 15c **Chilkat Tlingit Tribe**, 9/25/80, Spokane, WA 1.00

☐☐ 1836 15c **Tlingit Tribe**, 9/25/80, Spokane, WA 1.00

☐☐ 1837 15c **Bella Coola Tribe**, 9/25/80, Spokane, WA...........1.00

☐☐ 1837a **Se-tenant**, (2, 195, 136). "Plate Block" value is for
block of 4 with plate numbers 2.00 2.50

☐☐ 1838 15c **Smithsonian**, 10/9/80, New York, NY 1.00

☐☐ 1839 15c **Trinity Church**, 10/9/80, New York, NY..............1.00

☐☐ 1840 15c **Penn Academy**, 10/9/80, New York, NY..............1.00

☐☐ 1841 15c **Lyndhurst**, 10/9/80, New York, NY 1.00

☐☐ 1841a **Se-tenant**, (2,164,721)... 2.00 2.50

☐☐ 1842 15c **Christmas (Madonna & Child)**, 10/31/80, DC
(718,614). "Plate Block" value is for block of 4
with plate numbers....................................1.00 1.25 1.50

☐☐ 1843 15c **Christmas (Wreath & Toys)**, 10/31/80,
Christmas, MI (755,108). "Plate Block" value is
for block of 4 with plate numbers 1.00 1.25 1.50

☐☐ Scott 1842-1843 on one cover 3.00

☐☐ Scott 1842-1843 on one cover, dual cancels............4.00

1980-85 Great Americans

☐☐ 1844 1c **Dorothea Dix**, 9/23/83, Hampden, ME
(164,140).. 1.00 1.00

☐☐ 1845 2c **Igor Stravinsky**, 11/18/82, New York, NY
(501,719).. 1.00 1.00

☐☐ 1st Phil-Mart cachet......................................15.00

☐☐ 1846 3c **Henry Clay**, 7/13/83, DC (204,320) 1.00 1.00

☐☐ 1847 4c **Carl Schurz**, 6/3/83, Watertown, WI (165,010) 1.00 1.00

☐☐ 1848 5c **Pearl Buck**, 6/23/83, Hillsboro, WV (231,852) 1.00 1.00

☐☐ 1849 6c **Walter Lippmann**, 9/19/85, Minneapolis, MN
(371,990)..1.00 1.00 1.50

☐☐ 1850 7c **Abraham Baldwin**, 1/25/85, Athens, GA
(402,285)..1.00 1.25 1.50

☐☐ 1st RTI cachet..20.00

☐☐ 1851 8c **Henry Knox**, 7/25/85, Thomaston, ME
(315,937)..1.00 1.25 1.50

☐☐ 1852 9c **Sylvanus Thayer**, 6/7/85, Braintree, MA
(345,649)..1.00 1.25 1.50

☐☐ 1853 10c **Richard Russell**, 5/31/84, Winder, GA
(183,581)..1.00 1.25 1.65

☐☐ 1854 11c **Alden Partridge**, 2/12/85, Northfield, VT
(442,311)..1.00 1.25 1.65

☐☐ 1855 13c **Crazy Horse**, 1/15/82, Crazy Horse, SD................1.00 1.25 1.65

☐☐ 1856 14c **Sinclair Lewis**, 3/21/85, Sauk Centre, MN
(308,612)..1.00 1.25 1.65

☐☐ 1857 17c **Rachel Carson**, 5/28/81, Springdale, PA
(273,686)..1.00 1.25 1.75

☐☐ 1858 18c **George Mason**, 5/7/81, Gunston Hall, VA
(461,937)..1.00 1.25 1.75

Rose USA 18c

1876-9

1880-9
1949

1894

Mail Wagon 1880s
USA 9.3c

1903

Fire Pumper
1860s
USA 20c

1908

Exploring
the Moon

USA 18c

1912-9

The Gift of Self

USA
18c

American Red Cross

1910

SAVINGS AND LOANS

USA 18c

1911

Professional
Management

USA 18c

1920

1st Double A Cachet

Save Wetland Habitats

USA
8c

1921-4

USA 18c

Disabled doesn't mean Unable

1925

Alcoholism
You can beat it!
USA 18c

1927

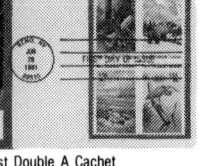

1926

Babe Zaharias

USA
18c

1932

Bobby Jones

USA
18c

1933

Architecture USA 18c

1928-31

FREDERIC REMINGTON
American
Sculptor

8c
USA

1934

USA 18c

1935-36

18c USA

1937-38

SCOTT NUMBER	DESCRIPTION	SGL	CACHETED BLK	PL BLK
☐☐ 1859	19c Sequoyah, 12/27/80, Tahlequah, OK (241,325) ...1.00		1.25	1.75
☐☐ 1860	20c Ralph Bunche, 1/12/82, New York, NY................1.00		1.25	1.75
☐☐ 1861	20c Thomas Gallaudet, 6/10/83, West Hartford,			
	CT (261,336)..1.00		1.25	1.75
☐☐ 1862	20c Harry S Truman, 1/26/84, DC (267,631) 1.00		1.25	1.75
☐☐	1st Caricature cachet..25.00			
☐☐ 1863	22c John J. Audubon, 4/23/85, New York, NY			
	(516,249)..1.00		1.35	2.00
☐☐ 1864	30c Frank Laubach, 9/2/84, Benton, PA (118,974). ...1.25		1.35	2.00
☐☐ 1865	35c Charles Drew, 6/3/81, DC (383,882) 1.25		2.00	3.00
☐☐ 1866	37c Robert Millikan, 1/26/82, Pasadena, CA 1.25		2.00	3.00
☐☐ 1867	39c Grenville Clark, 3/20/85, Hanover, NH			
	(297,797)..1.25		2.00	3.00
☐☐ 1868	40c Lillian Gilbreth, 2/24/84, Montclair, NJ			
	(110,588)..1.25		2.00	3.00
☐☐ 1869	50c Chester W. Nimitz, 2/22/85, Fredericksburg,			
	TX (376,166) 2.00		3.00	3.50
☐☐	1st Gulf Coast FDC Group cachet...........................15.00			

1981

☐☐ 1874	15c Everett Dirksen, 1/4/81, Pekin, IL (665,755).......1.00		1.25	1.50
☐☐ 1875	15c Whitney Moore Young, Jr., 1/30/81, New			
	York, NY (963,870)...1.00		1.25	1.50
☐☐ 1876	18c Rose, 4/23/81, Ft. Valley, GA..............................1.00			
☐☐ 1877	18c Camellia, 4/23/81, Ft. Valley, GA 1.00			
☐☐ 1878	18c Dahlia, 4/23/81, Ft. Valley, GA..........................1.00			
☐☐ 1879	18c Lily, 4/23/81, Ft. Valley, GA...............................1.00			
☐☐ 1879a	Se-tenant (1,966,599).....................................		2.50	3.00
☐☐ 1880	18c Bighorn, 5/14/81, Boise, ID.................................1.00			
☐☐ 1881	18c Puma, 5/14/81, Boise, ID 1.00			
☐☐ 1882	18c Harbor seal, 5/14/81, Boise, ID 1.00			
☐☐ 1883	18c Bison, 5/14/81, Boise, ID....................................1.00			
☐☐ 1884	18c Brown bear, 5/14/81, Boise, ID..........................1.00			
☐☐ 1885	18c Polar bear, 5/14/81, Boise, ID............................1.00			
☐☐ 1886	18c Elk, 5/14/81, Boise, ID..1.00			
☐☐ 1887	18c Moose, 5/14/81, Boise, ID...................................1.00			
☐☐ 1888	18c White-tailed deer, 5/14/81, Boise, ID 1.00			
☐☐ 1889	18c Pronghorn, 5/14/81, Boise, ID 1.00			
☐☐ 1889a	Booklet pane of 10 (1,641,749)...................................5.00			
☐☐ 1890	18c Flag and Anthem, 4/24/81, Portland,ME.			
	"Plate Block" value is for block of 4 with			
	plate numbers 1.00		1.25	1.50
☐☐ 1891	18c Flag and Anthem, coil, 4/24/81, Portland, ME....1.00 pr1.25			
☐☐ 1892	6c Field of Stars, booklet single, 4/24/81,			
	Portland, ME..1.00			
☐☐ 1893	18c Flag and Anthem, booklet single, 4/24/81,			
	Portland, ME..1.00			
☐☐ 1893a	Flag and Anthem, booklet pane of 8			
	(6 Scott 1893 + 2 Scott 1892).................................2.50			
	Total for all versions Scott 1890-1893 is 691,526.			
☐☐ 1894	20c Flag over Supreme Court, 12/17/81, DC.			
	"Plate Block" value is for block of 4 with plate			
	numbers 1.00		1.25	1.50
☐☐ 1895	20c Flag over Supreme Court, coil, 12/17/81, DC 1.00 pr1.25			

SCOTT NUMBER	DESCRIPTION	CACHETED SGL	BLK	PL BLK
☐☐ 1896	20c **Flag over Supreme Court,** booklet single, 12/17/81, DC..1.00		1.25	1.50
☐☐ 1896a	**Flag over Surpeme Court,** booklet pane of 6............6.00			
☐☐	Scott 1894, 1895, 1896a on one cover 7.00			
☐☐ 1896b	**Flag over Supreme Court,** booklet pane of 10, 6/1/82 ....10.00			

SCOTT NUMBER	DESCRIPTION	CACHETED SGL	PL	L PR

1981-84 Transportation Coils

☐☐ 1897	1c **Omnibus,** 8/19/83, Arlington, VA (109,436)................		1.00	12.50
☐☐ 1897A	2c **Locomotive,** 5/20/82, Chicago, IL (290,020)		1.00	12.50
☐☐ 1898	3c **Handcar,** 3/25/83, Rochester, NY (77,900).................		1.00	12.50
☐☐ 1898A	4c **Stagecoach,** 8/19/82, Milwaukee, WI (152,940)		1.00	10.00
☐☐ 1899	5c **Motorcycle,** 10/10/83, San Francisco, CA (188,240)		1.00	12.50
☐☐ 1900	5.2c **Sleigh,** 3/21/83, Memphis, TN (141,979)		1.00	25.00
☐☐	Combination with Scott U604		1.00	25.00
☐☐ 1900a	**Sleigh,** untagged (Bureau precanceled), 3/21/83	200.00		800.00
☐☐ 1901	5.9c **Bicycle,** 2/17/82, Wheeling, WV (814,419)		1.00	20.00
☐☐ 1901a	**Bicycle,** untagged (Bureau precanceled), 2/17/82	300.00		*1,000*
☐☐ 1902	7.4c **Baby Buggy,** 4/7/84, San Diego, CA (187,797).......		1.00	
☐☐ 1902a	**Baby Buggy,** untagged (Bureau precanceled), 4/7/84	*500.00*		
☐☐ 1903	9.3c **Mail Wagon,** 12/15/81, Shreveport, LA (199,645)		1.00	20.00
☐☐ 1903a	**Mail Wagon,** untagged (Bureau precanceled), 12/15/81	500.00		*1,500*
☐☐ 1904	10.9c **Hansom Cab,** 3/26/82, Chattanooga, TN		1.00	25.00
☐☐ 1904a	**Hansom Cab,** untagged (Bureau precanceled), 3/26/82	500.00		*2,500*
☐☐ 1905	11c **Railroad Caboose,** 2/3/84, Chicago, IL (172,753) 1.00		1.00	
☐☐ 1906	17c **Electric Auto,** 6/25/81, Greenfield Village, MI (239,458) 1.00		1.25	17.50
☐☐	1st Four Flags Cover Group cachet 12.00			
☐☐ 1907	18c **Surrey,** 5/18/81, Notch, MO (207,801) 1.00		1.25	30.00
☐☐ 1908	20c **Fire Pumper,** 12/10/81, Alexandria, VA (304,668) 1.00		1.25	30.00

SCOTT NUMBER	DESCRIPTION	CACHETED SGL	BLK	PL BLK

1983

☐☐ 1909	$9.35 **Eagle and Moon,** 8/12/83, booklet single, Kennedy Space Center, FL (77,858)....................60.00			
☐☐	Flown on Space Shuttle, (not FDC) 30.00			
☐☐ 1909a	**Eagle and Moon,** booklet pane of 3.....................175.00			

1981

☐☐ 1910	18c **American Red Cross,** 5/1/81, DC (874,972).........1.00		1.25	1.50

130

3 x 5 FDC INVENTORY INDEX CARDS

These 3 x 5 FDC Inventory Index Cards let you keep a detailed history of your first day cover collection. They also contain a special section for keeping a 10-year history of price trends.

To order these handy FDC Inventory Index Cards just drop us a note stating the quantity wanted, your name and address for UPS shipment, along with appropriate payment for the quantity ordered. With Visa or MasterCard you can phone or fax us your order.

Michael A. Mellone
Box 206 - Dept. S, Stewartsville, NJ 08886
Phone: 908-479-4614 - Fax: 908-479-6158

- - - - - - - - - - - - - - - - - - - -

ORDER FORM

□ 100 cards   □ 500 cards   □ 1000 cards
for $6.00   for $16.95   for $24.95

NAME:_____

ADDRESS:_____

CITY:_____

STATE & ZIP:_____

CARD #:_____

EXPIRATION DATE:_____

SIGNATURE:_____

Mail to: ## Michael A. Mellone
Box 206 - Dept. S, Stewartsville, NJ 08886
Phone: 908-479-4614 - Fax: 908-479-6158

131

1st Court of Honor cachet

1st Pugh Cachet

1st M.J. Philatelics cachet

1939

1941

1950

1946-48

1952

1953-2002

1940

1951

2003

**Values for various cachet makers can be determined
by using the Cachet Calculator which begins on page 40A.**

SCOTT NUMBER	DESCRIPTION	SGL	CACHETED BLK	PL BLK
☐☐ 1911	18c Savings Loans Sesquicentennial, 5/8/81, Chicago, Il. (740,910)	1.00	1.25	1.50
☐☐ 1912	18c Moon Walk, 5/21/81, Kennedy Space Center,FL	1.00		
☐☐ 1913	18c Columbia Launch, 5/21/81, Kennedy Space Center, FL	1.00		
☐☐ 1914	18c Columbia Releasing Satellite, 5/21/81, Kennedy Space Center, FL	1.00		
☐☐ 1915	18c Skylab, 5/21/81, Kennedy Space Center, FL	1.00		
☐☐ 1916	18c Pioneer II, 5/21/81, Kennedy Space Center, FL	1.00		
☐☐ 1917	18c Columbia & Booster, 5/21/81, Kennedy Space Center, FL	1.00		
☐☐ 1918	18c Columbia in Orbit, 5/21/81, Kennedy Space Center, FL	1.00		
☐☐ 1919	18c Space Telescope, 5/21/81, Kennedy Space Center, FL	1.00		
☐☐ 1919a	Se-tenant, (7,027,549)		1.25	4.00
☐☐ 1920	18c Professional Management, 6/18/81, Philadelphia, PA (713,096)	1.00	1.00	1.50
☐☐	1st Garik Covers cachet	30.00		
☐☐ 1921	18c Great Blue Heron, 6/26/81, Reno, NV	1.00		
☐☐ 1922	18c Badger, 6/26/81, Reno, NV	1.00		
☐☐ 1923	18c Grizzly Bear, 6/26/81, Reno, NV	1.00		
☐☐ 1924	18c Ruffed Grouse, 6/26/81, Reno, NV	1.00		
☐☐ 1924a	Se-tenant, (2,327,609)		2.50	3.00
☐☐	1st Double A cachet	20.00		
☐☐ 1925	18c International Year of the Disabled, 6/29/81, Milford, MI (714,244)	1.00	1.25	1.50
☐☐ 1926	18c Edna St. Vincent Millay, 7/10/81, Austefiitz, NY (725,978)	1.00	1.25	1.50
☐☐ 1927	18c Alcoholism, 8/19/81, DC. "Plate Block" value is for block of 4 with plate numbers	1.00	1.25	1.50
☐☐	1st Uncovers cachet	25.00		
☐☐ 1928	18c New York University Library, 8/28/81, New York, NY	1.00		
☐☐ 1929	18c Biltmore House, 8/28/81, New York, NY	1.00		
☐☐ 1930	18c Palace of the Arts, 8/28/81, New York, NY	1.00		
☐☐ 1931	18c National Farmer's Bank, 8/28/81, New York, NY	1.00		
☐☐ 1931a	Se-tenant, (1,998,208)		2.50	3.00
☐☐ 1932	18c Mildred Didrikson Zaharias, 9/22/81, Pinehurst, NC	5.00	5.50	6.00
☐☐ 1933	18c Robert Tyre Jones, 9/22/81, Pinehurst, NC	8.00	8.50	9.00
☐☐	Scott 1932-1933 on one cover	9.00		
	Total for Scott 1932-1933 is 1,231,543.			
☐☐ 1934	18c Frederic Remington, 10/9/81, Oklahoma City, OK (1,367,009)	1.00	1.25	1.50
☐☐ 1935	18c James Hoban, 10/13/81, DC	1.00	1.25	1.50
☐☐ 1936	20c James Hoban, 10/13/81, DC	1.00	1.25	1.50
☐☐	Scott 1935-1936 on one cover	3.00		
☐☐	Scott 1935-1936 on one cover with Irish Hoban stamp	9.00		
	Total for Scott 1935-1936 is 635,012.			
☐☐ 1937	18c Battle of Yorktown, 10/16/81, Yorktown, VA	1.00		
☐☐ 1938	18c Battle of Virginia Capes, 10/16/81, Yorktown,VA.	1.00		

SCOTT NUMBER	DESCRIPTION	CACHETED		
		SGL	BLK	PL BLK
1938a	Se-tenant..1.00		1.50	2.00
	Total for Scott 1937-1938 is 1,098,278.			
1939	(20c) Christmas (Botticelli), 10/28/81, Chicago, IL			
	(481,395)...1.00		1.25	1.50
	1st Court of Honor cachet.................................15.00			
1940	(20c) Christmas (Bear & Sleigh), 10/28/81,			
	Christmas Valley, OR (517,989).........................1.00		1.25	1.50
	Scott 1939-1940 on one cover, one cancel 2.00		3.00	4.00
	Scott 1939-1940 on one cover, dual cancels...........3.00		4.00	
1941	20c John Hanson, 11/5/81, Frederick, MD			
	(605,616) 1.00		1.25	1.50
1942	20c Barrel Cactus, 12/11/81, Tucson, AZ................1.00			
1943	20c Agave, 12/11/81, Tucson, AZ...........................1.00			
1944	20c Beavertail Cactas, 12/11/81, Tucson, AZ...........1.00			
1945	20c Saguaro, 12/11/81, Tucson, AZ........................1.00			
1945a	Se-tenant, (1,770,187)..		2.50	3.00
	1st Pugh cachet..65.00			
1946	(20c) "C" and Eagle, 10/11/81, Memphis, TN..........1.00		1.25	1.50
1947	(20c) "C" and Eagle, coil, 10/11/81, Memphis, TN 1.00	prl.25		lpl.50
1948	(20c) "C" and Eagle, booklet single, 10/11/81,			
	Memphis, TN...1.00			
1948a	"C" and Eagle, booklet pane of 10............................3.50			
	Total for Scott 1946-1948, U594 and UX92 is 304,404.			

1982

1949	20c Bighorn Sheep, booklet single, 1/8/82,			
	Bighorn, MT 1.00			
	1st New Direxions cachet....................................20.00			
1949a	Bighorn Sheep, booklet pane of 10............................6.00			
1950	20c Franklin D. Roosevelt, 1/30/82, Hyde Park, NY..1.00		1.25	1.50
	1st Aurora Covers cachet....................................15.00			
1951	20c Love, 2/1/82, Boston, MA (325,727)...................1.00		1.25	1.50
	1st Chaczyk Cachets & Covers cachet...................30.00			
1952	20c George Washington, 2/22/82, Mount Vernon,			
	VA...1.00		1.25	1.50
	1st M.J. Philatelic cachet 10.00			
	1st Ricale cachet..20.00			
1953	20c Alabama, 4/14/82, DC.....................................1.25			
1954	20c Alaska, 4/14/82, DC..1.25			
1955	20c Arizona, 4/14/82, DC.......................................1.25			
1956	20c Arkansas, 4/14/82, DC.....................................1.25			
1957	20c California, 4/14/82, DC....................................1.25			
1958	20c Colorado, 4/14/82, DC.....................................1.25			
1959	20c Connecticut, 4/14/82, DC.................................1.25			
1960	20c Delaware, 4/14/82, DC.....................................1.25			
1961	20c Florida, 4/14/82, DC..1.25			
1962	20c Georgia, 4/14/82, DC.......................................1.25			
1963	20c Hawaii, 4/14/82, DC..1.25			
1964	20c Idaho, 4/14/82, DC 1.25			
1965	20c Illinois, 4/14/82, DC 1.25			
1966	20c Indiana, 4/14/82, DC.......................................1.25			
1967	20c Iowa, 4/14/82, DC...1.25			
1968	20c Kansas, 4/14/82, DC..1.25			
1969	20c Kentucky, 4/14/82, DC.....................................1.25			

	Scott Number	Description	SGL	BLK	PL BLK
☐☐	1970	20c Louisiana, 4/14/82, DC 1.25			
☐☐	1971	20c Maine, 4/14/82, DC 1.25			
☐☐	1972	20c Maryland, 4/14/82, DC 1.25			
☐☐	1973	20c Massachusetts, 4/14/82, DC............1.25			
☐☐	1974	20c Michigan, 4/14/82, DC 1.25			
☐☐	1975	20c Minnesota, 4/14/82, DC 1.25			
☐☐	1976	20c Mississippi, 4/14/82, DC 1.25			
☐☐	1977	20c Missouri, 4/14/82, DC 1.25			
☐☐	1978	20c Montana, 4/14/82, DC 1.25			
☐☐	1979	20c Nebraska, 4/14/82, DC 1.25			
☐☐	1980	20c Nevada, 4/14/82, DC 1.25			
☐☐	1981	20c New Hampshire, 4/14/82, DC 1.25			
☐☐	1982	20c New Jersey, 4/14/82, DC............1.25			
☐☐	1983	20c New Mexico, 4/14/82, DC............1.25			
☐☐	1984	20c New York, 4/14/82, DC............1.25			
☐☐	1985	20c North Carolina, 4/14/82, DC 1.25			
☐☐	1986	20c North Dakota, 4/14/82, DC 1.25			
☐☐	1987	20c Ohio, 4/14/82, DC............1.25			
☐☐	1988	20c Oklahoma, 4/14/82, DC............1.25			
☐☐	1989	20c Oregon, 4/14/82, DC 1.25			
☐☐	1990	20c Pennsylvania, 4/14/82, DC............1.25			
☐☐	1991	20c Rhode Island, 4/14/82, DC............1.25			
☐☐	1992	20c South Carolina, 4/14/82, DC............1.25			
☐☐	1993	20c South Dakota, 4/14/82, DC 1.25			
☐☐	1994	20c Tennessee, 4/14/82, DC............1.25			
☐☐	1995	20c Texas, 4/14/82, DC............1.25			
☐☐	1996	20c Utah, 4/14/82, DC............1.25			
☐☐	1997	20c Vermont, 4/14/82, DC 1.25			
☐☐	1998	20c Virginia, 4/14/82, DC............1.25			
☐☐	1999	20c Washington, 4/14/82, DC............1.25			
☐☐	2000	20c West Virginia, 4/14/82, DC 1.25			
☐☐	2001	20c Wisconsin, 4/14/82, DC............1.25			
☐☐	2002	20c Wyoming, 4/14/82, DC 1.25			
☐☐		Complete set of 50 ....65.00			
☐☐		Cancels of state capitals, any single 1.50		2.00	
☐☐		Complete set of 50 state capitals 80.00			
☐☐	2002a	Complete pane............30.00			
☐☐	2003	20c U.S.-Netherlands, 4/20/82, DC. "Plate Block" value is for block of 4 with plate numbers 1.00		1.25	1.50
☐☐		Combination with Netherlands stamp 7.50			
☐☐	2004	20c Library of Congress, 4/21/82, DC............1.00		1.25	1.50
☐☐	2005	20c Consumer Education, coil, 4/27/82, DC............1.00	pr1.25		lp25.00
☐☐	2006	20c Solar Energy, 4/29/82, Knoxville, TN 1.00			
☐☐	2007	20c Synthetic Fuels, 4/29/82, Knoxville, TN 1.00			
☐☐	2008	20c Breeder Reactor, 4/29/82, Knoxville, TN............1.00			
☐☐	2009	20c Fossil Fuels, 4/29/82, Knoxville, TN 1.00			
☐☐	2009a	Se-tenant............		2.50	3.00
☐☐	2010	20c Horatio Alger, 4/30/82, Willow Grove, PA 1.00		1.25	1.50
☐☐	2011	20c Aging Together, 5/21/82, Sun City, AZ (510,677)............1.00		1.25	1.50
☐☐	2012	20c The Barrymores, 6/8/82, New York, NY............1.00		1.25	1.50
☐☐	2013	20c Dr. Mary E. Walker, 6/10/82, Oswego, NY............1.00		1.25	1.50
☐☐	2014	20c International Peace Gardens, 6/30/82, Dunseith, ND............1.00		1.25	1.50

Library of Congress USA 20c
2004

Wise shoppers stretch dollars
Consumer Education USA 20c
2005

USA 20c
Solar energy Knoxville World's Fair
2006-9

Horatio Alger
USA 20c
2010

THE BARRYMORES
Performing Arts USA 20c
2012

Aging together
USA 20c
2011

International Peace Garden
1932 1982 USA 20c
2014

Dr. Mary Walker
Army Surgeon
Medal of Honor USA 20c
2013

Touro Synagogue
Newport RI 1763
To bigotry, no sanction. To persecution, no assistance.
George Washington
USA 20c
2017

USA 20c
Wolf Trap Farm Park for the performing arts
2018

America's
A B C
Libraries
X Y Z
USA 20c
Legacies To Mankind
2015

Frank Lloyd Wright 1867-1959 Fallingwater Mill Run PA
Architecture USA 20c
2019-22

FRANCIS of ASSISI 1182-1982 USA 20c
2023

Jackie Robinson
Black Heritage USA 20c
2016

HOW TO USE THIS BOOK

The number in the first column is its Scott number or identifying number. Following that is the denomination of the stamp, description, date of issue, and the value.

	Scott	Description	SGL	BLK	PL BLK
☐☐	2015	20c America's Libraries, 7/13/82, Philadelphia, PA...1.00		1.25	1.50
☐☐		1st WSC cachet....................15.00			
☐☐	2016	20c Jackie Robinson, 8/2/82, Cooperstown, NY.........8.00		9.00	10.00
☐☐		1st Armadillo Covers cachet 30.00			
☐☐	2017	20c Touro Synagogue, 8/22/82, Newport, RI			
		(517,264). "Plate Block" value is for block of 4			
		with plate numbers....................1.00		1.25	1.65
☐☐	2018	20c Wolf Trap Farm Park, 9/1/82, Vienna, VA			
		(764,361) 1.00		1.25	1.50
☐☐	2019	20c Fallingwater, 9/30/82, DC..............1.00			
☐☐	2020	20c Illinois Institute of Technology, 9/30/82, DC.......1.00			
☐☐	2021	20c Gropius House, 9/30/82, DC..............1.00			
☐☐	2022	20c Dulles Airport, 9/30/82, DC 1.00			
☐☐	2022a	Se-tenant, (1,552,567)...............		2.50	3.00
☐☐	2023	20c St. Francis of Assisi, 10/7/82, San Francisco,			
		CA (530,275)...................1.00		1.25	1.50
☐☐	2024	20c Ponce de Leon, 10/12/82, San Juan, PR			
		(530,275). "Plate Block" value is for block of 4			
		with plate numbers...................1.00		1.25	1.50
☐☐	2025	13c Christmas (Kitten & Puppy), 11/3/82,			
		Danvers, MA (239,219) 1.00		1.25	1.50
☐☐	2026	20c Christmas (Madonna & Child), 10/28/82, DC			
		(462,982). "Plate Block" value is for block of 4			
		with plate numbers....................1.00		1.25	1.50
☐☐	2027	20c Children & Sleds, 10/28/82, Snow, OK 1.00			
☐☐	2028	20c Children & Snowman, 10/28/82, Snow, OK.........1.00			
☐☐	2029	20c Children Playing, 10/28/82, Snow, OK 1.00			
☐☐	2030	20c Children Decorating Tree, 10/28/82, Snow, OK...1.00			
☐☐	2030a	Se-tenant, (676,950)........................		2.50	3.00
☐☐		Scott 2026-2030, either city..................1.50			
☐☐		Scott 2026-3030 dual cancels 2.50			

1983

	Scott	Description	SGL	BLK	PL BLK
☐☐	2031	20c Science & Industry, 1/19/83, Chicago, IL			
		(526,693) 1.00		1.25	1.50
☐☐	2032	20c Intrepid, Albuquerque, NM & DC........................1.00			
☐☐	2033	20c Balloons Ascending, Albuquerque, NM, & DC. ...1.00			
☐☐	2034	20c Balloons Ascending, Albuquerque, NM, & DC. ...1.00			
☐☐	2035	20c Explorer II, Albuquerque, NM, & DC...................1.00			
☐☐	2035a	Se-tenant, (989,305)................................		2.50	3.00
☐☐	2036	20c U.S.-Sweden, 3/24/83, Philadelphia, PA			
		(526,373) 1.00		1.25	1.50
☐☐		1st Panda cachet......................30.00			
☐☐		Combination cover with Swedish issue....................5.00			
☐☐	2037	20c Civilian Conservation Corps, 4/5/83, Luray,			
		VA (483,824)...................1.00		1.25	1.50
☐☐	2038	20c Joseph Priestley, 4/13/83, Northumberland, PA			
		(673,266) 1.00		1.25	1.50
☐☐	2039	20c Voluntarism, 4/20/83, DC (574,708). "Plate			
		Block" value is for block of 4 with plate numbers...1.00		1.25	1.50

2024

2025

2026

2027-30

2031

2036

2032-5

2037

2039

2038

2040

2041

2042

2043

2044

2046

2047

HOW TO USE THIS BOOK
The number in the first column is its Scott number or
identifying number. Following that is the denomination
of the stamp, description, date of issue, and the value.

☐☐ 2040	20c U.S.-Germany, 4/29/83, Germantown, PA			
	(611,109) 1.00		1.25	1.50
☐☐	Combination cover with German issue 6.00			
☐☐ 2041	20c Brooklyn Bridge, 5/17/83, Brooklyn, NY			
	(815,085)...1.00		1.25	1.50
☐☐ 2042	20c T.V.A., 5/18/83, Knoxville, TN (837,588).			
	"Plate Block" value is for block of 4 with plate			
	numbers 1.00		1.25	1.50
☐☐ 2043	20c Physical Fitness, 5/14/83, Houston, TX			
	(501,336). "Plate Block" value is for block of 4			
	with plate numbers 1.0		1.25	1.50
☐☐ 2044	20c Scott Joplin, 6/9/83, Sedalia, MO (472,667) 1.00		1.25	1.50
☐☐ 2045	20c Medal of Honor, 6/7/83, DC (1,623,995)............1.00		1.25	1.50
☐☐ 2046	20c Babe Ruth, 7/6/83, Chicago, IL (1,277,907)......6.00		6.50	8.00
☐☐	1st Eastern Covers, Inc., cachet............................15.00			
☐☐	1st Dome cachet...25.00			
☐☐ 2047	20c Nathaniel Hawthorne, 7/8/83, Salem, MA			
	(442,793)..1.00		1.25	1.50
☐☐ 2048	13c Discus, 7/28/83, South Bend, IN 1.00			
☐☐ 2049	13c High Jump, 7/28/83, South Bend, IN..................1.00			
☐☐ 2050	13c Archery, 7/28/83, South Bend, IN 1.00			
☐☐ 2051	13c Boxing, 7/28/83, South Bend, IN 1.00			
☐☐ 2051a	Se-tenant, (909,332)...		2.50	3.00
☐☐ 2052	20c Signing of Treaty of Paris, 9/2/83, DC			
	(651,208)..1.00		1.25	1.50
☐☐	1st TF cachet..25.00			
☐☐ 2053	20c Civil Service, 9/9/83, DC (422,206) 1.00		1.25	1.50
☐☐ 2054	20c Metropolitan Opera, 9/14/83, New York, NY			
	(807,609)..1.00		1.25	1.50
☐☐	1st Desert Sun cachet.......................................15.00			
☐☐ 2055	20c Charles Steinmetz, 9/21/83, DC.......................1.00			
☐☐ 2056	20c Edwin Armstrong, 9/21/83, DC 1.00			
☐☐ 2057	20c Nikola Tesla, 9/21/83, DC 1.00			
☐☐ 2058	20c Philo T. Farnsworth, 9/21/83, DC....................1.00			
☐☐ 2058a	Se-tenant, (1,006,516)....................................		2.50	3.00
☐☐ 2059	20c First American streetcar, 10/8/83,			
	Kennebunkport, ME...1.00			
☐☐ 2060	20c Electric Streetcar, 10/8/83, Kennebunkport, ME.1.00			
☐☐ 2061	20c "Bobtail" Horsecar, 10/8/83, Kennebunkport,			
	ME...1.00			
☐☐ 2062	20c St. Charles Streetcar, 10/8/83, Kennebunkport,			
	ME...1.00			
☐☐ 2062a	Se-tenant, (1,116,909).....................................		2.50	3.00
☐☐ 2063	20c Christmas (Madonna & Child), 10/28/83, DC			
	(361,874)..1.00		1.25	1.50
☐☐ 2064	20c Christmas (Santa Claus), 10/28/83, Santa			
	Claus, IN (388,749). "Plate Block" value is for			
	block of 4 with plate numbers 1.00		1.25	1.50
☐☐ 2065	20c Martin Luther, 11/11/83, DC (463,777) 1.50		2.00	2.50

1984

☐☐ 2066	20c Alaska Statehood, 1/3/84, Fairbanks, AK			
	(816,591)..1.00		1.25	1.50
☐☐ 2067	20c Ice Dancing, 1/6/84, Lake Placid, NY 1.00			

USA 20c
Medal of Honor

2045

"Olympics"
USA
13c

2048-2051

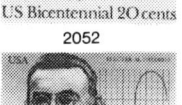
Treaty of Paris 1783
US Bicentennial 20 cents

2052

CIVIL
SERVICE
1883
1983
USA 20c

2053

METROPOLITAN OPERA
1883   1983   USA   20c

2054

Charles Steinmetz
20c

2055-2058

USA 20c
First American streetcar, New York City 1832

2059-2062

Season's Greetings   USA 20c

2064

Christmas USA 20c

Raphael, detail, National Gallery

2063

Martin Luther

1483-1983   USA 20c

2065

USA 20c
1959 1984
Alaska Statehood

2066

Olympics
USA
20c

2067-2070

FEDERAL DEPOSIT
INSURANCE
CORPORATION

2071

LO♥E
LO♥E
LO♥E
LO♥E
LO♥E
USA 20c

2072

Carter G. Woodson
Black Heritage USA 20c

2073

SOIL AND WATER
CONSERVATION

USA 20c

2074

ACT OF 1934
USA 20c

2075

NATIONAL ARCHIVES
USA

2081

140

	Scott Number	Description	SGL	BLK	PL BLK
☐☐	2068	20c Alpine Skiing, 1/6/84, Lake Placid, NY 1.00			
☐☐	2069	20c Nordic Skiing, 1/6/84, Lake Placid, NY 1.00			
☐☐	2070	20c Hockey, 1/6/84, Lake Placid, NY 1.00			
☐☐	2070a	Se-tenant, (1,245,807)...		2.50	3.00
☐☐	2071	20c Federal Deposit Insurance Corporation,			
		1/12/84, DC (536,329)..1.00		1.25	1.50
☐☐	2072	20c Love, 1/31/84, DC (327,727). "Plate Block"			
		value is for block of 4 with plate numbers 1.00		1.25	1.50
☐☐	2073	20c Carter Woodson, 2/1/84, DC (387,583)...............1.00		1.25	1.50
☐☐	2074	20c Soil & Water Conservation, 2/6/84, Denver,			
		CO (426,101) 1.00		1.25	1.50
☐☐	2075	20c Credit Union Act, 2/10/84, Salem, MA			
		(523,583)...1.00		1.25	1.50
☐☐	2076	20c Wild Pink Orchid, 3/5/84, Miami, FL..................1.00			
☐☐	2077	20c Yellow Lady's Slipper Orchid, 3/5/84, Miami, FL..1.00			
☐☐	2078	20c Spreading Pogonia Orchid, 3/5/84, Miami, FL....1.00			
☐☐	2079	20c Pacific Calpyso Orchid, 3/5/84, Miami, FL.........1.00			
☐☐	2079a	Se-tenant, (1,063,237)...		2.50	3.00
☐☐	2080	20c Hawaii Statehood, 3/12/84, Honolulu, HI			
		(546,930)..1.00		1.25	1.50
☐☐	2081	20c National Archives, 4/16/84, DC (414,415)...........1.00		1.25	1.50
☐☐	2082	20c Diving, 5/4/84, Los Angeles, CA...........................1.00			
☐☐	2083	20c Long Jump, 5/4/84, Los Angeles, CA....................1.00			
☐☐	2084	20c Wrestling, 5/4/84, Los Angeles, CA......................1.00			
☐☐	2085	20c Kayak, 5/4/84, Los Angeles, CA 1.00			
☐☐	2085a	Se-tenant, (1,172,313)...2.50		3.00	
☐☐	2086	20c New Orleans World Exposition, 5/11/84, New			
		Orleans, LA (467,408)..1.00		1.25	1.50
☐☐	2087	20c Health Research, 5/17/84, New York, NY			
		(845,007)...1.00		1.25	1.50
☐☐	2088	20c Douglas Fairbanks, 5/23/84, Denver, CO			
		(547, 134). "Plate Block" value is for block of 4			
		with plate numbers 1.00		1.25	1.50
☐☐	2089	20c Jim Thorpe, 5/24/84, Shawnee, OK (568,544) 6.00		7.00	9.00
☐☐	2090	20c John McCormack, 6/6/84, Boston, MA			
		(464,117)...1.00		1.25	1.50
☐☐	2091	20c St. Lawrence Seaway, 6/26/84, Massena, NY			
		(550,173)...1.00		1.25	1.50
☐☐	2092	20c Waterfowl Preservation Act, 7/2/84, Des			
		Moines, IA (549,388)..1.00		1.25	1.50
		1st George Van Natta cachet..................................35.00			
☐☐	2093	20c Roanoke Voyages, 7/13/84, Manteo, NC			
		(443,725)...1.00		1.25	1.50
☐☐	2094	20c Herman Melville, 8/1/84, New Bedford, MA			
		(379,293)...1.00		1.25	1.50
☐☐	2095	20c Horace A. Moses, 8/6/84, Bloomington, IN			
		(459,386). "Plate Block" value is for block of 4			
		with plate numbers 1.00		1.25	1.50
☐☐	2096	20c Smokey the Bear, 8/13/84, Capitan, NM			
		(506,833)...2.00		3.00	4.00
		1st Long Island Cover Society cachet....................15.00			
☐☐	2097	20c Roberto Clemente, 8/17/84, Carolina, PR			
		(547,387)...8.00		8.50	10.00
☐☐	2098	20c Beagle & Boston Terrier, 9/7/84, New York, NY..1.00			

Hawaii Statehood 1959-1984

USA 20c

2080

USA 20c

Wildpink *Arethusa bulbosa*

2076-2079

2082-2085

USA 20c

Louisiana World Exposition

USA 20c

Fresh water as a source of Life

2086

Health Research USA 20c

2087

USA 20c

2091

Preserving Wetlands 1934 1984

USA 20c

2092

DOUGLAS FAIRBANKS

Performing Arts USA 20c

2088

Jim Thorpe

USA 20c

2089

JOHN McCORMACK

Performing Arts USA 20c

2090

Roanoke Voyages North Carolina 1584

USA 20c

2093

Herman Melville

USA 20c

2094

Horace Moses
Founder, Junior Achievement
USA 20c

2095

SMOKEY

USA 20c

2096

Roberto Clemente

P

USA 20c

2097

Values for various cachet makers can be determined by using the Cachet Calculator which begins on page 40A.

☐☐ 2099	20c Chesapeake Bay Retriever & Cocker Spaniel, 9/7/84, New York, NY 1.00			
☐☐ 2100	20c Alaskan Malamute & Collie, 9/7/84, New York, NY 1.00			
☐☐ 2101	20c Black & Tan Coonhound & American Foxhound, 9/7/84, New York, NY......................................1.00			
☐☐ 2101a	Se-tenant, (1,157,373)..		2.50	3.00
	1st Heartland FDC cachet 20.00			
☐☐ 2102	20c Crime Prevention, 9/26/84, DC (427,564) 1.00		1.25	1.50
☐☐ 2103	20c Hispanic Americans, 10/31/84, DC (416,796) 1.00		1.25	1.50
☐☐ 2104	20c Family Unity, 10/1/84, Shaker Heights, OH (400,659). "Plate Block" value is for block of 4 with plate numbers 1.00		1.25	1.50
☐☐ 2105	20c Eleanor Roosevelt, 10/11/84, Hyde Park, NY (479,919)...1.00		1.25	1.50
☐☐ 2106	20c Nation of Readers, 10/16/84, DC (437,559) 1.00		1.25	1.50
☐☐ 2107	20c Christmas (Madonna), 10/30/84, DC (386,385)...1.00		1.25	1.50
☐☐ 2108	20c Christmas (Santa Claus), 10/30/84, Jamaica, NY (430,843)..1.00		1.25	1.50
☐☐ 2109	20c Vietnam Veterans' Memorial, 11/10/84, DC (434,489)...1.00		1.25	1.50

1985

☐☐ 2110	22c Jerome Kern, 1/23/85, New York, NY (503,855)...1.00		1.25	1.50
☐☐ 2111	(22c) "D" & Eagle, 2/1/85, Los Angeles, CA...............1.00		1.25	1.50
☐☐ 2112	(22c) "D" & Eagle, coil, 2/1/85, Los Angeles, CA.......1.00	pr1.25		
☐☐ 2113	(22c) "D" & Eagle, booklet single, 2/1/85, Los Angeles, CA 1.00			
☐☐ 2113a	"D" & Eagle, booklet pane of 10................................7.50			
	Total for Scott 2111-2113a is 513,027.			
☐☐ 2114	22c Flag over Capitol Dome, 3/29/85, DC..................1.00		1.25	1.50
☐☐ 2115	22c Flag over Capitol Dome, coil, 3/29/85 DC 1.00	pr1.25		
☐☐ 2115b	22c Flag over Capitol Dome, pre-phosphored, coil, 3/29/85, DC...—	pr5.00		
	Total for Scott 2114-2115 is 268,161.			
☐☐ 2116	22c Flag over Capitol Dome, booklet single, 3/29/85, Waubeka, WI (234,318) 1.00			
☐☐ 2116a	Flag over Capitol Dome, booklet pane of 5 ....3.50			
☐☐ 2117	22c Frilled Dogwinkle, 4/4/85, Boston, MA 1.00			
☐☐ 2118	22c Reticulated Helmet, 4/4/85, Boston, MA............1.00			
☐☐ 2119	22c New England Neptune, 4/4/85, Boston, MA........1.00			
☐☐ 2120	22c Calico Scallop, 4/4/85, Boston, MA....................1.00			
☐☐ 2121	22c Lightning Whelk, 4/4/85, Boston, MA 1.00			
☐☐ 2121a	Booklet pane of 10...7.50			
	Total for Nos. 2117-2121 is 426,290.			
☐☐ 2122	$10.75 Eagle & Half Moon, 4/29/85, San Francisco, CA (93,154)...50.00			
☐☐ 2122a	Eagle & Half Moon, booklet pane of 3..................125.00			

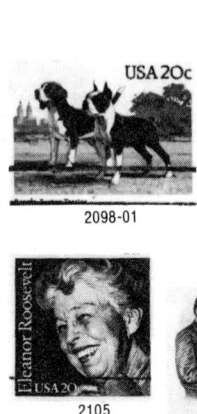

USA 20c

2098-01

TAKE A BITE OUT OF CRIME

2102

Hispanic Americans

A Proud Heritage USA 20

2103

2104

Eleanor Roosevelt

USA 20c

2105

A Nation of Readers

USA 20c

2106

Christmas USA 20c

Fra Filippo Lippi, National Gallery

2107

USA 20c

Season's Greetings

2108

Domestic Mail

D US Postage

2111

JEROME KERN

Performing Arts USA

2110

Vietnam Veterans Memorial USA 20c

2109

USA 22

New England Neptune

2117-21

USA 22

2114

Tricycle 1880s
6 USA

2126

USA $10.75

2122

Mary McLeod Bethune

Black Heritage USA 22

2137

Iceboat 1880s
USA 14

2134

Mallard Decoy

Folk Art USA 22

2138-41

22 USA

Winter Special Olympics

2142

22 USA

Rural Electrification Administration

2144

144

1985-88 Transportation Coils

☐☐ 2123	3.4c School Bus, 6/8/85, Arlington, VA (131,480) ....—		1.00	12.50
☐☐ 2123a	School Bus, untagged (Bureau precanceled), 6/8/85, Arlington, VA, earliest known use ....—		—	—
☐☐ 2124	4.9c Buckboard, 6/21/85, Reno, NV.............................—		1.00	13.50
☐☐ 2124a	Buckboard, untagged (Bureau precanceled), 6/21/85, DC, earliest known use ....—		—	—
☐☐ 2125	5.5c Star Route Truck, 11/1/86, Ft. Worth, TX (136,021)...—		1.00	
☐☐ 2125a	Star Route Truck, untagged (Bureau precanceled), 11/1/86, DC ....—		5.00	
☐☐ 2126	6c Tricycle, untagged (Bureau precanceled), 5/6/85, Childs, MD (151,494)...		1.00	
☐☐ 2127	7.1c Tractor, 2/6/87, Sarasota, FL (167,555) ....—		1.00	
☐☐ 2127a	Tractor, untagged (Bureau precancel "Nonprofit Org." in black), 2/6/87, Sarasota, FL 5.00			
☐☐ 2127a	Tractor, untagged (Bureau precancel "Nonprofit 5-Digit Zip+4" in black), 5/26/89, Rosemont, FL......1.00			
☐☐ 2128	8.3c Ambulance, 6/21/85, Reno, NV ....—		1.00	10.00
☐☐ 2128a	Ambulance, untagged (Bureau precanceled), 6/21/85, DC, earliest known use ....—		—	—
☐☐ 2129	8.5c Tow Truck, 1/24/87, Tucson, AZ (224,285)...........—		1.00	
☐☐ 2129a	Tow Truck, untagged (Bureau precanceled), 1/24/87, DC ....—		5.00	
☐☐ 2130	10.1c Oil Wagon, 4/18/85, Oil Center, NM....................—		1.00	
☐☐ 2130a	Oil Wagon, untagged (black Bureau precancel), 4/18/85, DC, earliest known use ....—		—	
☐☐ 2130a	Oil Wagon, untagged (red Bureau precancel), 6/27/88, DC ....—		1.00	
☐☐ 2131	11c Stutz Super Bearcat, 6/11/85, Baton Rouge, LA (135,037)..—		1.00	15.00
☐☐ 2132	12c Stanley Steamer, 4/2/85, Kingfield, ME, (173,998)...—		1.00	12.50
☐☐ 2132a	Stanley Steamer, untagged (Bureau precanceled), 4/2/85, DC ....—		—	—
☐☐ 2133	12.5c Pushcart, 4/18/85, Oil Center, NM......................—		1.25	
	Total for Scott 2130 and 2133 is 319,953.			
☐☐ 2133a	Pushcart, untagged (Bureau precanceled), 4/18/85, DC ....—		—	
☐☐ 2134	14c Ice Boat, 3/23/85, Rochester, NY (324,710) ....—		1.25	15.00
	1st C.L. cachets 15.00			
☐☐ 2135	17c Dog Sled, 8/20/86, Anchorage, AK (112,009).........—		1.25	
☐☐ 2136	25c Bread Wagon, 11/22/86, Virginia Beach, VA (151,950)..1.25		1.25	

Uncached covers sell for about 10% of catalogue value.

2143

2146

2147

2152

2153

2145

2149

2150

2154

2155-58

2159

2160-63

2164

2165

2166

Values for various cachet makers can be determined by using the Cachet Calculator which begins on page 40A.

SCOTT NUMBER	DESCRIPTION	CACHETED SGL	BLK	PL BLK

1985-86

☐☐ 2137	22c Mary McLeod Bethune, 3/5/85, DC (413,244).......1.00		1.25	1.50
☐☐ 2138	22c Broadbill Decoy, 3/22/85, Shelburne, VT...............1.00			
☐☐ 2139	22c Mallard Decoy, 3/22/85, Shelburne, VT 1.00			
☐☐ 2140	22c Canvasback Decoy, 3/22/85, Shelburne, VT 1.00			
☐☐ 2141	22c Redhead Decoy, 3/22/85, Shelburne, VT...............1.00			
☐☐ 2141a	Se-tenant, (923,249)		2.75	3.50
☐☐ 2142	22c Winter Special Olympics, 3/25/85, Park City, UT (253,074)...1.00		1.25	1.50
☐☐ 2143	22c Love, 4/17/85, Hollywood, CA (283,072) 1.00		1.25	1.50
☐☐ 2144	22c Rural Electrificafion Administration, 5/11/85, Madison, SD (472,895). "Plate Block" value is for block of 4 with plate numbers 1.00		1.25	1.50
☐☐ 2145	22c Ameripex '86, 5/25/85, Rosemont, IL (457,038) ...1.00		1.25	1.50
☐☐ 2146	22c Abigail Adams, 6/14/85, Quincy, MA (491,026) 1.00		1.25	1.50
☐☐ 2147	22c Frederic Auguste Bartholdi, 7/18/85, New York, NY (594,896) 1.00		1.25	1.50

SCOTT NUMBER	DESCRIPTION	CACHETED SGL	PR
☐☐ 2149	18c George Washington & Monument, 11/6/85, ... (376,238)..1.25		
☐☐ 2149a	George Washington & Monument, untagged (Bureau precanceled), 11/6/85...............................		5.00
☐☐ 2150	21.1c Envelopes, 10/22/85, DC (119,941)..................................1.25		
☐☐ 2150a	Envelopes, untagged (Bureau precanceled), 10/22/85, DC..		5.00

SCOTT NUMBER	DESCRIPTION	CACHETED SGL	BLK	PL BLK
☐☐ 2152	22c Korean War Veterans, 7/26/85, DC (391,754) 1.00		1.25	1.50
☐☐ 2153	22c Social Security Act, 8/14/85, Baltimore, MD (265,143)...1.00		1.25	1.50
☐☐ 2154	22c World War I Veterans, 8/26/85, Milwaukee,WI ...1.00		1.25	1.50
☐☐ 2155	22c Quarter Horse, 9/26/85, Lexington, KY 1.25			
☐☐ 2156	22c Morgan, 9/26/85, Lexington, KY 1.25			
☐☐ 2157	22c Saddlebred, 9/26/85, Lexington, KY......................1.25			
☐☐ 2158	22c Appaloosa, 9/26/85, Lexington, KY 1.25			
☐☐ 2158a	Se-tenant, (1,135,368)		5.00	6.00
☐☐ 2159	22c Public Education in America, 10/1/85, Boston, MA (356,030) 1.00		1.25	1.50
☐☐ 2160	22c YMCA Youth Camping, 10/7/85, Chicago, IL.........1.00			
☐☐ 2161	22c Boy Scouts, 10/7/85, Chicago, IL...........................1.00			
☐☐ 2162	22c Big Brothers/Big Sisters, 10/7/85, Chicago, IL.....1.00			
☐☐ 2163	22c Camp Fire, Inc., 10/7/85, Chicago, IL....................1.00			
☐☐ 2163a	Se-tenant, (1,202,541)		2.50	3.00
☐☐ 2164	22c Help End Hunger, 10/15/85, DC (299,485)............1.00		1.25	1.50
☐☐ 2165	22c Christmas (Madonna & Child), 10/30/85, Detroit, MI 1.00		1.25	1.50
☐☐ 2166	22c Christmas (Poinsettia), 10/30/85, Nazareth, MI (524,929) 1.00		1.25	1.50

2167

2168

2170

2171

2172

2177

2179

2183

2191

2194

2195

2198-2201

2202

2203

2204

2205-09

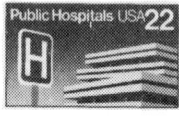

2210

2220-23

2216a

2217a

2211

2224

2218a

2219a

148

☐☐ 2167	22c Arkansas Statehood, 1/3/86, Little Rock, AR			
	(364,729)..1.00		1.25	1.50
☐☐	1st LMG cachets.......................................30.00			

1986-93 Great Americans

☐☐ 2168	1c Margaret Mitchell, 9/17/86, Atlanta, GA			
	(316,764)..1.00		1.00	1.50
☐☐ 2169	2c Mary Lyon, 2/28/87, S. Hadley, MA (349,831) 1.00		1.00	1.50
☐☐ 2170	3c Dr. Paul Dudley White, 9/15/86, Washington,DC....1.00		1.00	1.50
☐☐ 2171	5c Father Flanagan, 7/14/86, Boys Town, NE			
	(367,883)..1.00		1.00	1.50
☐☐ 2172	5c Hugo Black, 2/27/86, DC (303,012)...........................1.00		1.00	1.50
	1st Key Kachets cachet.....................................20.00			
☐☐ 2173	5c Luiz Munoz Marin, 2/18/90, San Juan, PR 1.00		1.00	1.00
☐☐ 2176	10c Red Cloud, 8/15/87, Red Cloud, NE (300,472) 1.00		1.25	1.50
☐☐ 2177	14c Julia Ward Howe, 2/12/87, Boston, MA			
	(454,829)..1.00		1.25	1.50
☐☐ 2178	15c Buffalo Bill Cody, 6/6/88, Cody, WY			
	(356,395)..1.00		1.25	1.50
☐☐ 2179	17c Belva Ann Lockwood, 6/18/86, Middleport, NY			
	(249,215)..1.00		1.25	1.65
☐☐ 2180	21c Chester Carlson, 10/21/88, Rochester, NY			
	(288,073)..1.00		1.25	1.65
☐☐ 2182	23c Mary Cassatt, 11/4/88, Philadelphia, PA			
	(322,537)..1.00		1.25	1.65
☐☐ 2183	25c Jack London, 1/11/86, Glen Ellen, CA			
	(358,686)..1.25		1.25	1.65
☐☐ 2183a	Jack London, booklet pane of 10, 5/3/88,			
	San Francisco, CA..6.00			
☐☐ 2184	28c Sitting Bull, 9/14/89, Rapid City, SD			
	(126,777)..1.25		1.50	1.75
☐☐ 2184A	29c Earl Warren, Mar. 9, 1992 (175,517)...................1.25			
☐☐ 2184B	29c Thomas Jefferson, Apr. 13, 1993			
	Charlottesville,... 1.25			
☐☐ 2185	35c Dennis Chavez, Apr. 3, 1991, Albuquerque, NM			
	(285,570).. 1.25			
☐☐ 2186	40c Claire Chennault, Sept. 6, 1990, Monroe, LA			
	(186,761)..1.50			
☐☐ 2188	45c Harvey Cushing, June 17, 1988, Cleveland, OH			
	(135,140)..1.25			
☐☐ 2190	52c Hubert Humphrey, June 3, 1991,			
	Minneapolis, MN (93,391) 1.35			
☐☐ 2186	40c Claire Lee Channault, 9/6/90, Monroe, LA 1.25		1.75	2.25
☐☐ 2188	45c Harvey Cushing, 6/17/88, Cleveland, OH			
	(135,140)..1.25		2.00	2.50
☐☐ 2191	56c John Harvard, 9/3/86, Boston, MA......................1.25		2.50	3.00
☐☐ 2192	65c Hap Arnold, 11/5/88, Gladwyne, PA (129,829) 1.50		3.00	3.50
☐☐ 2194	$1 Dr. Bernard Revel, 9/23/86, New York, NY 2.00		4.50	5.00
☐☐ 2194A	$1 Johns Hopkins, 6/7/89, Baltimore, MD			
	(159,049)..3.00		4.50	6.00
☐☐ 2195	$2 William Jennings Bryan, 3/19/86, Salem, IL			
	(123,430)..5.00		10.00	15.00
☐☐ 2196	$5 Bret Harte, 8/25/87, Twain Harte, CA			
	(111,431)..15.00		24.00	30.00

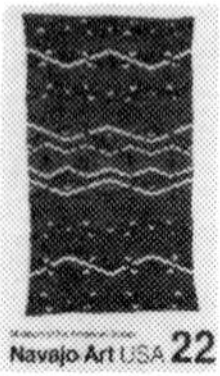

Navajo Art USA 22

2235-38

T.S.Eliot
22 USA

2239

Wood Carving: Highlander Figure
Folk Art USA 22

2240-43

1837-1987 Michigan Statehood

2246

CHRISTMAS
22 USA
Perugino, National Gallery

2244

GREETINGS

2245

22 USA
Pan American Games Indianapolis 1987

2247

LOVE
22

2248

Jean Baptiste
Pointe Du Sable
22
Black Heritage USA

2249

Enrico
Caruso
22 USA

2250

22

2251

Conestoga Wagon
1800s
USA 3

2253

Milk Wagon 1900s
5 USA

2255

Canal Boat 1880s
10 USA

2259

Racing Car 1911
USA
17.5

2264

Congratulations! USA 22

2267-74

1887-1987
Uniting Communities USA 22

2275

22 USA

2276

22 USA
Barn Swallow

2286-2335

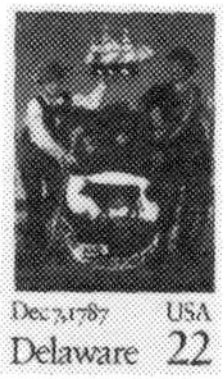

Dec 7, 1787   USA
Delaware 22

2336

Dec 12, 1787
Pennsylvania

2337

Dec 18, 1787   USA
New Jersey 22

2338

150

☐☐ 2197 25c **Jack London,** booklet single, 5/3/88,
San Francisco, CA..1.25

☐☐ 2197a **Jack London,** booklet pane of 6...................................4.00
Total for Scott 2183a, 2197, and 2197a is 94,655.

1986

☐☐ 2198 22c **Handstamped Cover,** Memorabilia, 1/23/86
State College, PA..1.00

☐☐ 2199 22c **Boy & Stamp Collection,** 1/23/86
State College, PA..1.00

☐☐ 2200 22c **Scott U.S. 836,** Sweden 268 & 271, 1/23/86
State College, PA..1.00

☐☐ 2201 22c **Scott U.S. 2216,** 1/23/86 State College, PA............1.00

☐☐ 2201a **Booklet pane of 4**..5.00

☐☐ 2201b **Booklet pane of 4, black omitted on 2198, 2201** ...500.00
Total for Scott 2198-2201 is 675,924.

☐☐ 2202 22c **Love,** 1/30/86, New York, NY...............................1.00 | 1.25 | 1.50
1st Cat-Chet cachet..30.00

☐☐ 2203 22c **Sojourner Truth,** 2/4/86, New Paltz, NY
(342,985)..1.00 | 1.25 | 1.50

☐☐ 2204 22c **Republic of Texas,** 3/2/86, San Antonio, TX
(380,450)..1.00 | 1.25 | 1.50

☐☐ 2205 22c **Muskellunge,** 3/21/86, Seattle, WA 1.00
☐☐ 2206 22c **Atlantic Cod,** 3/21/86, Seattle, WA........................1.00
☐☐ 2207 22c **Largemouth Bass,** 3/21/86, Seattle, WA 1.00
☐☐ 2208 22c **Bluefin Tuna,** 3/21/86, Seattle, WA.......................1.00
☐☐ 2209 22c **Catfish,** 3/21/86, Seattle, WA..................................1.00
☐☐ 2209a **Booklet pane of 5**..2.50
☐☐   1st Ohio Cachetmakers Association cachet 15.00
Total for Scott 2205-2209 is 988, 184.

☐☐ 2210 22c **Public Hospitals,** 4/11/86, New York, NY
(403,665)..1.00 | 1.25 | 1.50

☐☐ 2211 22c **Duke Ellington,** 4/29/86, New York, NY
(397,894)..1.00 | 1.25 | 1.50

☐☐ 2216 **Sheet of 9,** 5/22/86, Chicago, IL 4.00
☐☐ 2216a 22c **George Washington**..1.00
☐☐ 2216b 22c **John Adams**..1.00
☐☐ 2216c 22c **Thomas Jefferson** 1.00
☐☐ 2216d 22c **James Madison** 1.00
☐☐ 2216e 22c **James Monroe**..1.00
☐☐ 2216f 22c **John Quincy Adams** 1.00
☐☐ 2216g 22c **Andrew Jackson**..1.00
☐☐ 2216h 22c **Martin Van Buren** 1.00
☐☐ 2216I 22c **William H. Harrison** 1.00
☐☐ 2217 **Sheet of 9,** 5/22/86, Chicago, IL 4.00
☐☐ 2217a 22c **John Tyler** 1.00
☐☐ 2217b 22c **James Knox Polk** 1.00
☐☐ 2217c 22c **Zachary Taylor** 1.00
☐☐ 2217d 22c **Millard Fillmore** 1.00
☐☐ 2217e 22c **Franklin Pierce** 1.00
☐☐ 2217f 22c **James Buchanan**..1.00
☐☐ 2217g 22c **Abraham Lincoln** 1.00
☐☐ 2217h 22c **Andrew Johnson** 1.00
☐☐ 2217i 22c **Ulysses S. Grant**..1.00

22
USA
January 2, 1788
Georgia
2339

22
USA
January 9, 1788
Connecticut
2340

22
USA
Feb 6, 1788
Massachusetts
2341

April 28, 1788 USA
Maryland 22
2342

Friendship
with Morocco
1787-1987
USA 22
2349

William Faulkner
USA 22
2350

Lacemaking USA 22
2351-54

U.S. Constitution
1787-1987 22 USA
2360

CPA
22
USA
2361

The Bicentennial
of the Constitution of
the United States
of America
1787-1987   USA 22
2355-59

Stourbridge Lion
1829   USA 22
2362-66

CHRISTMAS
22
USA
Moroni, National Gallery
2367

USA 22 GREETINGS
2368

22 USA
2369

Happy Bicentennial
Australia!
1788
1988   USA 22
2370

James Weldon
Johnson
22
2371

USA 22
Siamese Cat, Exotic Shorthair Cat
2372-75

22
USA
KNUTE ROCKNE
2376

152

SCOTT NUMBER	DESCRIPTION	CACHETED SGL	BLK	PL BLK
2218	Sheet of 9, 5/22/86, Chicago, IL	4.00		
2218a	22c Rutherford B. Hayes	1.00		
2218b	22c James A. Garfield	1.00		
2218c	22c Chester A. Arthur	1.00		
2218d	22c Grover Cleveland	1.00		
2218e	22c Benjamin Harrison	1.00		
2218f	22c William McKinley	1.00		
2218g	22c Theodore Roosevelt	1.00		
2218h	22c William H. Taft	1.00		
2218i	22c Woodrow Wilson	1.00		
2219	Sheet of 9, 5/22/86, Chicago, IL	4.00		
2219a	22c Warren G. Harding	1.00		
2219b	22c Calvin Coolidge	1.00		
2219c	22c Herbert Hoover	1.00		
2219d	22c Franklin Delano Roosevelt	1.00		
2219e	22c White House	1.00		
2219f	22c Harry S. Truman	1.00		
2219g	22c Dwight D. Eisenhower	1.00		
2219h	22c John F. Kennedy	1.00		
2219i	22c Lyndon B. Johnson	1.00		
	Total for Scott 2216-2219 and 2216a-2219i is 9,009,599.			
2220	22c Elisha Kent Kane, 5/28/86, North Pole, AK	1.00		
2221	22c Adolphus W. Greely, 5/28/86, North Pole, AK	1.00		
2222	22c Vilhjalmur Stefansson, 5/28/86, North Pole, AK	1.00		
2223	22c Robert E. Peary & Matthew Henson, 5/28/86, North Pole, AK	1.00		
2223a	Se-tenant, (760,999)		2.50	3.00
2224	22c Statue of Liberty, 7/4/86, New York, NY (1,540,308)	2.00	2.50	3.50

SCOTT NUMBER	DESCRIPTION	CACHETED SGL	PR
	1986-87 Transportation Coils		
2225	1c Omnibus, re-engraved, 11/26,86, DC (57,845)	—	1.00
2226	2c Locomotive, re-engraved, 3/6/87, Milwaukee, WI (169,484)	—	1.00
2228	4c Stagecoach, re-engraved, 8/15/86, DC, earliest known use		150.00
2231	8.3c Ambulance, re-engraved, 8/24/86, DC, earliest known use		150.00

SCOTT NUMBER	DESCRIPTION	CACHETED SGL	BLK	PL BLK
	1986			
2235	22c Navajo Art, 9/4/86, Window Rock, AZ	1.00		
2236	22c Navajo Art, 9/4/86, Window Rock, AZ	1.00		
2237	22c Navajo Art, 9/4/86, Window Rock, AZ	1.00		
2238	22c Navajo Art, 9/4/86, Window Rock, AZ	1.00		
2238a	Se-tenant, (1,102,520)		2.50	3.00
2239	22c T.S. Eliot, 9/26/86, St. Louis, MO (304,764)	1.00	1.25	1.50
2240	22c Highlander Figure, 10/1/86, DC	1.00		
2241	22c Ship Figurehead, 10/1/86, DC	1.00		

2377

2390-93

2379

2378

2380

2386-89

2394

2395-98

2399

2400

SCOTT NUMBER	DESCRIPTION	CACHETED SGL	BLK	PL BLK
☐☐ 2242	22c Nautical Figure, 10/1/86, DC	1.00		
☐☐ 2243	22c Cigar-store Figure, 10/1/86, DC	1.00		
☐☐ 2243a	Se-tenant, (629,399)		2.50	3.00
☐☐ 2244	22c Christmas (Madonna & Child), 10/24/86, DC (467,999)	1.00	1.25	1.50
☐☐ 2245	22c Christmas (Winter Village), 10/24/86 Snow Hill, MD (504,851)	1.00	1.25	1.50

1987

SCOTT NUMBER	DESCRIPTION	CACHETED SGL	BLK	PL BLK
☐☐ 2246	22c Michigan Statehood, 1/26/87, Lansing, MI (379,117)	1.00	1.25	1.50
☐☐ 2247	22c Pan American Games, 1/29/87, Indianapolis, IN (344,731)	1.00	1.25	1.50
☐☐ 2248	22c Love, 1/30/87, San Francisco, CA (333,329)	1.00	1.25	1.50
☐☐ 2249	22c Jean Baptiste Pointe du Sable, 2/20/87, Chicago, IL (313,054)	1.00	1.25	1.50
☐☐ 2250	22c Enrico Caruso, 2/27/87, New York, NY (389,834)	1.00	1.25	1.50
☐☐ 2251	22c Girl Scouts, 3/12/87, DC (556,391)	1.00	1.25	1.50

SCOTT NUMBER	DESCRIPTION	CACHETED SGL	PR

1987-88 Transportation Coils

SCOTT NUMBER	DESCRIPTION	CACHETED SGL	PR
☐☐ 2252	3c Conestoga Wagon, 2/29/88, Conestoga, PA (155,203)	—	1.00
☐☐	1st Gil Lewis cachet	18.00	
☐☐ 2253	5c Milk Wagon, 9/25/87, Indianapolis, IN	—	1.00
☐☐ 2254	5.3c Elevator, 9/16/88, New York, NY (142,705)	—	1.00
☐☐ 2255	7.6c Carreta, 8/30/88, San Jose, CA (140,024)	—	1.00
☐☐ 2256	8.4c Wheel Chair, 8/12/88, Tucson, AZ (136,337)	—	1.00
☐☐ 2257	10c Canal Boat, 4/11/87, Buffalo, NY (171,952)	—	1.00
☐☐ 2258	13c Patrol Wagon, 10/29/88, Anaheim, CA (132,928)	—	1.25
☐☐ 2259	13.2c Coal Car, 7/19/88, Pittsburgh, PA (123,965)	—	1.25
☐☐ 2260	15c Tugboat, 7/12/88, Long Beach, CA (134,926)	—	1.25
☐☐	1st One Fifty-Five Co. cachet	25.00	
☐☐ 2261	16.7c Popcorn Wagon, 7/7/88, Chicago, IL (117,908)	—	1.25
☐☐ 2262	17.5c Racing Car, 9/25/88, Indianapolis, IN	—	1.25
☐☐ 2262a	Racing Car, untagged (Bureau precanceled)	—	5.00
☐☐ 2263	20c Cable Car, 10/28/88, San Francisco, CA (150,068)	—	1.25
☐☐ 2264	20.5c Fire Engine, 9/28/88, San Angelo, TX (123,043)	—	1.25
☐☐ 2265	21c Railroad Mail Car, 8/16/88, Santa Fe, NM (124,430)	—	1.25
☐☐ 2266	24.1c Tandem Bicycle, 10/26/88, Redmond, WA (136,593)	—	1.25

SCOTT NUMBER	DESCRIPTION	CACHETED SGL	BLK	PL BLK

1987

SCOTT NUMBER	DESCRIPTION	CACHETED SGL	BLK	PL BLK
☐☐ 2267	22c "Congratulations," 4/20/87, Atlanta, GA	1.00		
☐☐ 2268	22c "Get Well," 4/20/87, Atlanta, GA	1.00		
☐☐ 2269	22c "Thank You," 4/20/87, Atlanta, GA	1.00		
☐☐ 2270	22c "Love You, Dad," 4/20/87, Atlanta, GA	1.00		
☐☐ 2271	22c "Best Wishes," 4/20/87, Atlanta, GA	1.00		

2401

2402, 2442, 2567, 2617, 2746

2403

2404

2410

2405-2409

2411

2412-2415

2416

2417

2418

2419

2420

2421

2422-2425

2426, 2512

2427, 2514
2578, 2710

2428-2429,
2515-2516,
2579-2585,
2711-2719

2433

2431

☐☐ 2272	22c "Happy Birthday," 4/20/87, Atlanta, GA..............1.00		
☐☐ 2273	22c "Love You, Mother," 4/20/87, Atlanta, GA 1.00		
☐☐ 2274	22c "Keep In Touch," 4/20/87, Atlanta, GA................1.00		
☐☐ 2274a	Booklet pane of 10...4.00		
	Total for Scott 2267-2274 is 1,588, 129.		
☐☐ 2275	22c United Way Centenary, 4/28/87, DC (556,391)...1.00	1.25	2.00
☐☐ 2276	22c Flag & Fireworks, booklet single, 5/9/87, Denver, CO (398,855)...1.00	1.25	2.00
☐☐ 2276a	Flag & Fireworks, booklet pane of 20......................12.00		
☐☐ 2277	(25c) "E" & Earth, 3/22/88, DC.................................1.25	1.25	2.00
☐☐ 2278	25c Flag and Clouds, 5/6/88, Boxborough, MA (131,265)..1.25	1.25	2.00
☐☐ 2279	(25c) "E" and Earth, coil, 3/22/88, DC 1.25		
☐☐ 2280	25c Flag Over Yosemite, coil, 5/20/88, Yosemite, CA (144,339)..1.25		
☐☐ 2281	25c Honeybee, coil, 9/2/88, Omaha, NE (122,853)...1.25		
☐☐	1st Ralph J. Pohl cachet 15.00		
☐☐ 2282	(25c) "E" & Earth, booklet single, 3/22/88, DC 1.25		
☐☐ 2282a	"E" & Earth, booklet pane of 10................................6.00		
	Total for Scott 2277, 2279 and 2282 is 363,639.		
☐☐ 2283	25c Pheasant, booklet single, 4/29/88, Rapid City, SD (167,053) 1.25		
☐☐ 2283a	Pheasant, booklet pane of 10....................................6.00		
☐☐ 2284	25c Owl, booklet single, 5/28/88, Arlington, VA..........1.25		
☐☐ 2285	25c Grosbeak, booklet single, 5/28/88, Arlington, VA 1.25		
☐☐ 2285b	Booklet pane of 10...6.00		
	Total for Scott 2284-2285 is 272,359.		
☐☐ 2285A	25c Flag and Clouds, booklet single, 7/5/88, DC (117,303)...1.25		
☐☐ 2285c	Flag and Clouds, booklet pane of 6 ....4.00		
☐☐ 2286	22c Barn Swallow, 6/13/87, Toronto, ONT 1.00		
☐☐ 2287	22c Monarch Butterfly, 6/13/87, Toronto, ONT 1.00		
☐☐ 2288	22c Bighorn Sheep, 6/13/87, Toronto, ONT.................1.00		
☐☐ 2289	22c Broad-tailed Hummingbird, 6/13/87, Toronto, ONT 1.00		
☐☐ 2290	22c Cottontail, 6/13/87, Toronto, ONT.......................1.00		
☐☐ 2291	22c Osprey, 6/13/87, Toronto, ONT............................1.00		
☐☐ 2292	22c Mountain Lion, 6/13/87, Toronto, ONT 1.00		
☐☐ 2293	22c Luna Moth, 6/13/87, Toronto, ONT 1.00		
☐☐ 2294	22c Mule Deer, 6/13/87, Toronto, ONT 1.00		
☐☐ 2295	22c Gray Squirrel, 6/13/87, Toronto, ONT...................1.00		
☐☐ 2296	22c Armadillo, 6/13/87, Toronto, ONT........................1.00		
☐☐ 2297	22c Eastern Chipmunk, 6/13/87, Toronto, ONT 1.00		
☐☐ 2298	22c Moose, 6/13/87, Toronto, ONT.............................1.00		
☐☐ 2299	22c Black Bear, 6/13/87, Toronto, ONT 1.00		
☐☐ 2300	22c Tiger Swallowtail, 6/13/87, Toronto, ONT 1.00		
☐☐ 2301	22c Bobwhite, 6/13/87, Toronto, ONT 1.00		
☐☐ 2302	22c Ringtail, 6/13/87, Toronto, ONT 1.00		
☐☐ 2303	22c Red-winged Blackbird, 6/13/87, Toronto,ONT 1.00		
☐☐ 2304	22c American Lobster, 6/13/87, Toronto, ONT............1.00		
☐☐ 2305	22c Black-tailed Jack Rabbit, 6/13/87, Toronto, ONT 1.00		

2434-2438

IDAHO

USA 25 1890

2439

L O V E

2440-2441,
2535-2536, 2618

Wyoming

2444

2443

The WIZARD of Oz

2445-2448

Marianne Moore

American Poet 1887-1972

2449

2475, 2522

$2 USA

2476

2481-2494

2501-2505

OLYMPIAN

2496-2500

Federated States of Micronesia

2506-2507

1990

Killer Whale

2508-2511

Dwight David Eisenhower

USA 25

2513

F Flower

2517-2520
2524-2527

This U.S. stamp, along with 25¢ of additional U.S. postage, is equivalent to the 'F' stamp rate

2521

2523, 2523A

2529

2530

2528

USA 29

2531

50 USA

Switzerland Founded 1291

2532

Vermont

2533

158

☐☐ 2306	22c Scarlet Tanager, 6/13/87, Toronto, ONT	1.00	
☐☐ 2307	22c Woodchuck, 6/13/87, Toronto, ONT	1.00	
☐☐ 2308	22c Roseate Spoonbill, 6/13/87, Toronto, ONT	1.00	
☐☐ 2309	22c Bald Eagle, 6/13/87, Toronto, ONT	1.00	
☐☐ 2310	22c Alaskan Brown Bear, 6/13/87, Toronto, ONT	1.00	
☐☐ 2311	22c Iiwi, 6/13/87, Toronto, ONT	1.00	
☐☐ 2312	22c Badger, 6/13/87, Toronto, ONT	1.00	
☐☐ 2313	22c Pronghorn, 6/13/87, Toronto, ONT	1.00	
☐☐ 2314	22c River Otter, 6/13/87, Toronto, ONT	1.00	
☐☐ 2315	22c Ladybug, 6/13/87, Toronto, ONT	1.00	
☐☐ 2316	22c Beaver, 6/13/87, Toronto, ONT	1.00	
☐☐ 2317	22c White-tailed Deer, 6/13/87, Toronto, ONT	1.00	
☐☐ 2318	22c Blue Jay, 6/13/87, Toronto, ONT	1.00	
☐☐ 2319	22c Pika, 6/13/87, Toronto, ONT	1.00	
☐☐ 2320	22c Bison, 6/13/87, Toronto, ONT	1.00	
☐☐ 2321	22c Snowy Egret, 6/13/87, Toronto, ONT	1.00	
☐☐ 2322	22c Gray Wolf, 6/13/87, Toronto, ONT	1.00	
☐☐ 2323	22c Mountain Goat, 6/13/87, Toronto, ONT	1.00	
☐☐ 2324	22c Deer Mouse, 6/13/87, Toronto, ONT	1.00	
☐☐ 2325	22c Black-tailed Prairie Dog, 6/13/87, Toronto, ONT	1.00	
☐☐ 2326	22c Box Turtle, 6/13/87, Toronto, ONT	1.00	
☐☐ 2327	22c Wolverine, 6/13/87, Toronto, ONT	1.00	
☐☐ 2328	22c American Elk, 6/13/87, Toronto, ONT	1.00	
☐☐ 2329	22c California Sea Lion, 6/13/87, Toronto, ONT	1.00	
☐☐ 2330	22c Mockingbird, 6/13/87, Toronto, ONT	1.00	
☐☐ 2331	22c Raccoon, 6/13/87, Toronto, ONT	1.00	
☐☐ 2332	22c Bobcat, 6/13/87, Toronto, ONT	1.00	
☐☐ 2333	22c Black-footed Ferret, 6/13/87, Toronto, ONT	1.00	
☐☐ 2334	22c Canada Goose, 6/13/87, Toronto, ONT	1.00	
☐☐ 2335	22c Red Fox, 6/13/87, Toronto, ONT	1.00	
☐☐	1st Bennett Cachetoon cachet	30.00	
☐☐	Complete Set	50.00	
☐☐ 2335a	Pane of 50	30.00	

1987-90 Ratification of the Constitution

☐☐ 2336	22c Delaware, 7/4/87, Dover, DE (505,770)	1.75	2.00	2.50
☐☐ 2337	22c Pennsylvania, 8/26/87, Harrisburg, PA (367,184)	1.75	2.00	2.50
☐☐ 2338	22c New Jersey, 9/11/87, Trenton, NJ (432,899)	1.75	2.00	2.50
☐☐ 2339	22c Georgia, 1/6/88, Atlanta, GA (467,804)	1.75	2.00	2.50
	1st 7-1-71 Chapter 50 cachet	15.00		
☐☐ 2340	22c Connecticut, 1/9/88, Hartford, CT (379,706)	1.75	2.00	2.50
☐☐ 2341	22c Massachusetts, 2/6/88, Boston, MA (412,616)	1.75	2.00	2.50
☐☐ 2342	22c Maryland, 2/15/88, Annapolis, MD (376,403)	1.75	2.00	2.50
☐☐ 2343	25c South Carolina, 5/23/88, Columbia, SC (322,938)	1.75	2.00	2.50
☐☐ 2344	25c New Hampshire, 6/21/88, Concord, NH (374,402)	1.75	2.00	2.50
☐☐ 2345	25c Virginia, 6/25/88, Williamsburg, VA(474,079)	1.75	2.00	2.50
☐☐ 2346	25c New York, 7/26/88, Albany, NY (385,793)	1.75	2.00	2.50
☐☐ 2347	25c North Carolina, 8/22/89, Fayetteville, NC (392,953)	1.75	2.00	2.50
☐☐ 2348	25c Rhode Island, 5/29/90, Pawtucket, RI (305,566)	1.75	2.00	2.50

2534

2537

2559, 2697, 2765

2545-2549

2540-2542

2539

2543

2550

2551-2552

2558

2560

2561

2562-2566

2568-2577

2594, 2594B

2595-2597

2604-2606

2607

2608-2608B

2609

2616

2619

2620-2629

160

1987

	Scott	Description	SGL	BLK	PL BLK
☐☐	2349	22c U.S.-Morocco Diplomatic Relations,			
		7/17/87, DC (372,814)................................1.00		1.25	1.50
☐☐		1st Anagram cachet.............................25.00			
☐☐	2350	22c William Faulkner, 8/3/87, Oxford, MS			
		(480,024)..1.00		1.25	1.50
☐☐	2351	22c Lacemaking, 8/14/87 Ypsilanti, MI........1.00			
☐☐	2352	22c Lacemaking, 8/14/87 Ypsilanti, MI........1.00			
☐☐	2353	22c Lacemaking, 8/14/87 Ypsilanti, MI........1.00			
☐☐	2354	22c Lacemaking, 8/14/87 Ypsilanti, MI........1.00			
☐☐	2354a	Se-tenant.....................................		2.75	3.50
☐☐	2355	22c "The Bicentennial," 8/28/87, DC..........1.50			
☐☐	2356	22c "We the People," 8/28/87, DC.............1.50			
☐☐	2357	22c "Establish Justice," 8/28/87, DC.........1.50			
☐☐	2358	22c "And Secure," 8/28/87, DC................1.50			
☐☐	2359	22c "Do Ordain," 8/28/87, DC.................1.50			
☐☐	2359a	Booklet pane of 5............................9.00			
		Total for Scott 2355-2359 is (1,008,799).			
☐☐	2360	22c Signing of the Constitution, 9/17/87,			
		Philadelphia, PA (719,975) 1.00		1.25	1.50
☐☐		1st Alexia cachet............................30.00			
☐☐		1st Olde Well cachet.........................35.00			
☐☐	2361	22c Certified Public Accounting, 9/21/87,			
		New York, NY 5.00		6.00	8.00
☐☐	2362	22c Stourbridge Lion, 10/1/87, Baltimore, MD ...1.00			
☐☐	2363	22c Best Friend of Charleston, 10/1/87,			
		Baltimore, MD................................1.00			
☐☐	2364	22c John Bull, 10/1/87, Baltimore, MD........1.00			
☐☐	2365	22c Brother Jonathan, 10/1/87, Baltimore, MD ...1.00			
☐☐	2366	22c Gowan & Marx, 10/1/87, Baltimore, MD 1.00			
☐☐	2366a	Booklet pane of 5............................3.00			
		Total for Scott 2362-2366 is 976,694.			
☐☐	2367	22c Christmas (Madonna & Child), 10/23/87,			
		DC (320,406)................................1.00		1.25	1.50
☐☐	2368	22c Christmas (Ornaments), 10/23/87,			
		Anaheim, CA (375,858).......................1.00		1.25	1.50

1988

	Scott	Description	SGL	BLK	PL BLK
☐☐	2369	22c 1988 Winter Olympics, 1/10/88, Anchorage, AK			
		(395, 198)..................................1.00		1.25	1.50
☐☐	2370	22c Australia Bicentennial, 1/26/88, DC			
		(523,465)...................................1.00		1.25	1.50
☐☐	2371	22c James Weldon Johnson, 2/2/88, Nashville, TN			
		(465,282)...................................1.00		1.25	1.50
☐☐	2372	22c Siamese & Exotic Shorthair, 2/5/88,			
		New York, NY 2.50			
☐☐	2373	22c Abyssinian & Himalayan, 2/5/88, New York, NY..2.50			
☐☐	2374	22c Maine Coon & Burmese, 2/5/88, New York,NY 2.50			
☐☐	2375	22c American Shorthair & Persian, 2/5/88,			
		New York, NY 2.50			
☐☐	2375a	Se-tenant(872,734)		6.00	8.00
☐☐	2376	22c Knute Rockne, 3/9/88, Notre Dame, IN			
		(404,311)...................................4.00		4.50	5.00

	SCOTT NUMBER	DESCRIPTION	SGL	BLK	PL BLK
☐☐	2377	25c Francis Ouimet, 6/13/88, Brookline, MA (383,168)....................4.00		4.50	5.00
☐☐	2378	25c Love, 7/4/88, Pasadena, CA (399,038)........1.25		1.50	1.75
☐☐	2379	45c Love, 8/8/88, Shreveport, LA (121,808)........1.25		2.00	2.50
☐☐	2380	25c Summer Olympics, 8/9/88, ColoradoSprings, CO (402,616)....................1.25		1.50	1.75
☐☐	2381	25c 1928 Locomobile, 8/25/88, Detroit, MI 1.25			
☐☐	2382	25c 1929 Pierce-Arrow, 8/25/88, Detroit, MI 1.25			
☐☐	2383	25c 1931 Cord, 8/25/88, Detroit, MI....................1.25			
☐☐	2384	25c 1932 Packard, 8/25/88, Detroit, MI................1.25			
☐☐	2385	25c 1935 Duesenberg, 8/25/88, Detroit, MI........1.25			
☐☐	2385a	Booklet pane of 5....................3.00			
		Total for Scott 2381-2385 is 875,801.			
☐☐	2386	25c Nathaniel Palmer, 9/14/88, DC....................1.25			
☐☐	2387	25c Lt. Charles Wilkes, 9/14/88, DC 1.25			
☐☐	2388	25c Richard E. Byrd, 9/14/88, DC 1.25			
☐☐	2389	25c Lincoln Ellsworth, 9/14/88, DC 1.25			
☐☐	2389a	Se-tenant, (720,537)........		3.00	3.50
☐☐	2390	25c Deer, 10/1/88, Sandusky, OH 1.50			
☐☐	2391	25c Horse, 10/1/88, Sandusky, OH 1.50			
☐☐	2392	25c Camel, 10/1/88, Sandusky, OH 1.50			
☐☐	2393	25c Goat, 10/1/88, Sandusky, OH 1.50			
☐☐	2393a	Se-tenant, (856,380)		3.50	4.00
☐☐	2394	$8.75 Eagle in Flight, 10/6/88, Terre Haute, IN (66,558)....................25.00		37.50	50.00
☐☐		Sheet of 20....................350.00			
☐☐	2395	25c "Happy Birthday," 10/22/88, King of Prussia, PA.1.25			
☐☐	2396	25c "Best Wishes," 10/22/88, King of Prussia, PA.......1.25			
☐☐	2396a	Booklet pane of 6 (3 No. 2395 +3 No. 2396)..............4.00			
☐☐	2397	25c "Thinking of You," 10/22/88, King of Prussia, PA....................1.25			
☐☐	2398	25c "Love You," 10/22/88, King of Prussia, PA........1.25			
☐☐	2398a	Booklet pane of 6 (3 No. 2397 + 3 No. 2398)..............4.00			
		Total for Scott 2395-2398 is 126, 767.			
☐☐	2399	25c Christmas (Madonna), 10/20/88, Washington, DC (247,291)....................1.25		1.50	1.75
☐☐	2400	25c Christmas (Sleigh & Village), 10/20/88, Berlin, NH (412,213)....................1.25		1.50	1.75

1989

☐☐	2401	25c Montana Statehood, 1/15/89, Helena, MT (353,319)....................1.25		1.50	1.75
☐☐		1st Steve Wilson cachet 30.00			
☐☐	2402	25c A. Philip Randolph, 2/3/89, New York, NY (363,174)....................1.25		1.50	1.75
☐☐	2403	25c North Dakota Statehood, 2/21/89, Bismarck,ND (306,003)....................1.25		1.50	1.75
☐☐	2404	25c Washington Statehood, 2/22/89, Olympia,WA (445,174)....................1.25		1.50	1.75
☐☐	2405	25c Experiment 3/3/89, New Orleans, LA....................1.25			
☐☐	2406	25c Phoenix, 3/3/89, New Orleans, LA 1.25			
☐☐	2407	25c New Orleans, 3/3/89, New Orleans, LA................1.25			
☐☐	2408	25c Washington, 3/3/89, New Orleans, LA................1.25			
☐☐	2409	25c Walk in the Water, 3/3/89, New Orleans,LA 1.25			

☐☐ 2409a Booklet pane of 5...4.00
Total for Scott 2405-2409 is 981,674.

☐☐ 2410 **25c World Stamp Expo '89. 3/16/89,** New York,NY
(296,310)..1.25 1.50 1.75

☐☐ 2411 **25c Arturo Toscanini,** 3/25/89, New York, NY
(309,441)..1.25 1.50 1.75

1989-90

☐☐ 2412 **25c House of Representatives,** 4/4/89, DC(327,755)...1.25 1.50 1.75
☐☐ 2413 **25c Senate,** 4/6/89, DC (341,288)...............................1.25 1.50 1.75
☐☐ 2414 **25c Executive Branch,** 4/30/89, Mount Vernon,VA
(387,644)..1.25 1.50 1.75
☐☐ 2415 **25c Supreme Court,** 2/2/90, DC 1.25 1.50 1.75

1989

☐☐ 2416 **25c South Dakota Statehood,** 5/3/89, Pierre, SD
(348,370)..1.25 1.50 1.75

☐☐ 2417 **25c Lou Gehrig,** 6/10/89, Cooperstown, NY
(694,227)...2.50 3.00 3.50
☐☐ 1st Edken cachet 20.00

☐☐ 2418 **25c Ernest Hemingway,** 7/17/89, Key West, FL
(345,436)..1.25 1.50 1.75

☐☐ 2419 **$2.40 Moon Landing,** 7/20/89, DC (208,982)...............7.00 12.00 17.50

☐☐ 2420 **25c Letter Carriers,** 8/30/89, Milwaukee, WI
(372,241)..1.25 1.50 1.75

☐☐ 2421 **25c Bill of Rights,** 9/25/89, Philadelpha, PA
(900,384)..1.25 1.50 1.75

☐☐ 2422 **25c Tyrannosaurus Rex,** 10/1/89, Orlando, FL 1.25
☐☐ 2423 **25c Pteranodon,** 10/1/89, Orlando, FL.........................1.25
☐☐ 2424 **25c Stegosaurus,** 10/1/89, Orlando, FL 1.25
☐☐ 2425 **25c Brontosaurus,** 10/1/89, Orlando, FL 1.25
☐☐ 2425a **Se-tenant,** (871,634) 3.00 3.50
☐☐ 2426 **25c America,** 10/12/89, San Juan, PR (215,285) 1.25 1.50 1.75
☐☐ 2427 **25c Christmas (Madonna & Child),** 10/19/89,DC
(395,321)...1.25 1.50 1.75

☐☐ 2427a **Booklet pane of 6**..6.00
☐☐ 2428 **25c Christmas (Sleigh),** 10/19/89, Westport, CT.........1.25 1.50 1.75
☐☐ 2429 **25c Christmas (Sleigh),** booklet single, 10/19/89,
Westport, CT..1.25

☐☐ 2429a **Booklet pane of 10**...6.00
Total for Scott 2428-2429a was 345, 931.

☐☐ 2431 **25c Eagle & Shield,** self-adhesive, booklet single,
11/10/89, Virginia Beach, VA.....................................1.25

☐☐ 2433 **90c World Stamp Expo,** souvenir sheet of 4,
11/17/89, DC 10.00

☐☐ 2434 **25c Stagecoach,** 11/19/89, DC 1.25
☐☐ 2435 **25c Paddlewheel Steamer,** 11/19/89, DC....................1.25
☐☐ 2436 **25c Biplane,** 11/19/89, DC...1.25
☐☐ 2437 **25c Depot-hack type Automobile,** 11/19/89, DC 1.25
☐☐ 2437a **Se-tenant,** (916,389) 3.00 3.50
☐☐ 2438 **25c Traditional Mail Delivery,** souvenir sheet of 4,
11/27/89, DC (241,634)..2.00

1990

☐☐	2439	25c Idaho Statehood, 1/6/90, Boise, ID (252,493)...1.25		1.50	1.75
☐☐	2440	25c Love, 1/18/90, Romance, AR.................................1.25		1.50	1.75
☐☐	2441	25c Love, booklet single, 1/18/90, Romance, ID 1.25			
☐☐	2441a	Love, booklet pane of 10 ....7.00			
		Total for Scott 2440-2441a was 257, 788.			
☐☐	2442	25c Ida B. Wells, 2/1/90, Chicago, IL (229,226)...........1.25		1.50	1.75
☐☐	2443	25c Beach Umbrella, booklet single, 2/3/90, Sarasota, FL..1.50			
☐☐	2443a	Beach Umbrella, booklet pane of 10 (72,286)............8.00			
☐☐	2444	25c Wyoming Statehood, 2/23/90, Cheyenne, WY (317,654)...1.25		1.50	1.75
☐☐	2445	25c The Wizard of Oz, 3/23/90, Hollywood, CA..........3.00			
☐☐	2446	25c Gone with the Wind, 3/23/90, Hollywood,CA.........3.00			
☐☐	2447	25c Beau Geste, 3/23/90, Hollywood, CA....................1.25			
☐☐	2448	25c Stagecoach, 3/23/90, Hollywood, CA....................1.25			
☐☐	2448a	Se-tenant (863,079)		7.00	9.00
☐☐	2449	25c Marianne Moore, 4/18/90, Brooklyn, NY (390,535)...1.25		1.50	1.75

1990-91 Transportation Coil

☐☐	2451	4c Steam Carriage, 1/25/91, Tucson, AZ.......................— pr 1.00			
☐☐	2452	5c Circus Wagon, 8/31/90, Syracuse, NY (71,806)..— pr 1.00			
☐☐	2452B	5c Circus Wagon, photogravure, Dec. 8, 1992 Cincinnati, OH...1.25			
☐☐	2453	5c Canoe, engraved, May 25, 1991, Secaucus, NJ (108,634)...1.25			
☐☐	2454	5c Canoe, photogravure, Oct. 22, 1991, Secaucus, NJ..1.25			
☐☐	2457	10c Tractor Trailer, May 25, 1991, Secaucus, NJ (84,717)...1.25			
☐☐	2464	23c Lunch Wagon, Apr. 12, 1991, Columbus, OH (115,830)..1.25			
☐☐	2468	$1 Seaplane, 4/20/90, Phoenix, AZ ....3.00 pr 4.00			

1990

☐☐	2470	25c Admiralty Head, WA, 4/26/90, DC 1.50			
☐☐	2471	25c Cape Hatteras, NC, 4/26/90, DC............................1.50			
☐☐	2472	25c West Quoddy Head, ME, 4/26/90, DC....................1.50			
☐☐	2473	25c American Shoals, FL, 4/26/90, DC 1.50			
☐☐	2474	25c Sandy Hook, NJ, 4/26/90, DC 1.50			
☐☐	2474a	Booklet pane of 5 (805, 133).......................................4.00			
☐☐	2475	25c Flag, plastic self-adhesive, 5/18/90, Seattle, WA (97,567)...1.25			
☐☐	2476	$2 Bobcat, 6/1/90, Arlington, VA (49,660) 7.00		11.00	15.00
☐☐	2478	29c Red Squirrel, June 25, Milwaukee, WI................1.25			
☐☐	2481	1c Kestrel, 6/22/91, Aurora, CO (77,781) 1.25			
☐☐	2482	3c Eastern Bluebird, 6/22/91, Aurora, CO (76,149)..1.25			
☐☐	2487	19c Fawn, 3/11/91, (100,212).....................................1.25			
☐☐	2489	30c Cardinal, 6/22/91, Aurora, CO (101,290) 1.25			
☐☐	2491	45c Pumpkinseed Sunfish, 12/2/92, ...1.75			

			CACHETED	
		SGL	BLK	PL BLK
☐☐ 2493	29c Wood Duck, 4/12/91, Columbus, OH 1.25			
☐☐ 2493a	Booklet pane of 10...5.00			
☐☐ 2494	29c Wood Duck, 4/12/91, Columbus, OH 1.25			
☐☐ 2494a	Booklet pane of 10...5.00			
	First day cancel was applied to 205,305 covers bearing one or more of Nos. 2493-2494, 2493a-2494a.			
☐☐ 2496	25c Jesse Owens, 7/6/90, Minneapolis, MN 1.25			
☐☐ 2497	25c Ray Ewry, 7/6/90, Minneapolis, MN 1.25			
☐☐ 2498	25c Hazel Wightman, 7/6/90, Minneapolis, MN 1.25			
☐☐ 2499	25c Eddie Eagan, 7/6/90, Minneapolis, MN 1.25			
☐☐ 2500	25c Helene Madison, 7/6/90, Minneapolis, MN 1.25			
	Strip of 5, (1,143,404)..3.00		5.00	6.00
☐☐ 2501	25c Assiniboin, 8/17/90, Cody, WY......................1.25			
☐☐ 2502	25c Cheyenne, 8/17/90, Cody, WY.......................1.25			
☐☐ 2503	25c Comanche, 8/17/90, Cody, WY......................1.25			
☐☐ 2504	25c Flathead, 8/17/90, Cody, WY 1.25			
☐☐ 2505	25c Shoshone, 8/17/90, Cody, WY 1.25			
☐☐ 2505a	Booklet pane of 10 (979,580) 6.00			
☐☐ 2506	25c Federated States of Micronesia, 9/28/90,DC....1.25			
☐☐ 2507	25c Republic of the Marshall Islands, 9/28/90,DC...1.25			
☐☐ 2507a	Se-tenant...2.00		2.50	3.00
	Total for Scott 2506-2507a was 343,816.			
☐☐ 2508	25c Killer Whales, 10/3/90, Baltimore, MD 1.25			
☐☐ 2509	25c Northern Sea Lions, 10/3/90, Baltimore, MD 1.25			
☐☐ 2510	25c Sea Otter, 10/3/90, Baltimore, MD 1.25			
☐☐ 2511	25c Common Dolphin, 10/3/90, Baltimore, MD 1.25			
☐☐ 2511a	Se-tenant (706,047)		4.00	4.50
☐☐ 2512	25c Grand Canyon, 10/12/90, Grand Canyon, AZ (164, 190) 1.25		1.50	1.75
☐☐ 2513	25c Dwight D. Eisenhower, 10/13/90, Abilene, KS (487,988)...1.25		1.50	1.75
☐☐ 2514	25c Christmas (Madonna & Child), 10/18/90, DC (378,383)..1.25		1.50	1.75
☐☐ 2515	25c Christmas (Tree), sheet stamp, 10/18/90, Evergreen, CO...1.25		1.50	1.75
☐☐ 2516	25c Christmas (Tree), booklet single, 10/18/90, Evergreen, CO...1.25			
☐☐ 2516a	Booklet pane of 10..6.00			
	Total for Scott 2515-2516a was 230,586.			

1991-92

☐☐ 2517	(29c) Flower, non-denominated sheet stamp, 1/22/91, DC 1.25		1.50	1.75
☐☐ 2518	(29c) Flower, non-denominated coil stamp, 1/22/91, DC 1.25			
☐☐ 2519	(29c) Flower, non-denominated booklet single (printed by BEP), 1/22/91, DC..................................1.25			
☐☐ 2519a	Booklet pane of 10...6.00			
☐☐ 2520	(29c) Flower, non-denominated booklet single (printed by KCS), 1/22/91, DC..................................1.25			
☐☐ 2520	Booklet pane of 10...6.00			
☐☐ 2521	(4c) Make-up rate, non-denominated, text only, 1/22/91, DC 1.25		1.50	1.75

ONLY THIS ONE HAS IT ALL...

Handpainted First Day Covers (FDCs) have enjoyed dramatic appreciation over the last few years! Nothing need stand in YOUR way of reaping the many benefits and rewards of having a COMPLETE collection of intrinsically valuable, handpainted FDCs of the United States Postal Service (USPS). PUGH CACHETS will shoulder the responsibility of making certain the deadlines are met and GUARANTEE you receive an FDC of YOUR satisfaction for as many or as few new issues as you choose.

PUGH CACHETS is NOW accepting a limited number of applications for Automatic Shipment Accounts (ASA). As an ASA subscriber you will receive:

★ A TRULY limited edition FDC for EVERY new issue of the USPS that you choose; commemorative or definitive, postal card, embossed envelope, etc. You may choose to take one each of ALL items, or just the ones of interest - such as a special topic.

★ The strongest GUARANTEE of absolute satisfaction available in the hobby (you may return ANY cover, at ANY time, for ANY reason - with a copy of the original invoice - for an IMMEDIATE, NO QUESTIONS ASKED, refund or exchange)!

★ A series of rare works of art, that are meticulously and individually handcrafted, handpainted (with watercolors and by air brush), and hand cancelled.

★ The assurance that your covers are tastefully, sequentially numbered and autographed - on the face - like the works of art they are, proving their authenticity and "limited" edition.

★ In addition to each FDC, a detailed narrative - of enormous educational value - on the background and history of the stamp subject matter as well as technical production data.

★ Covers are shipped UNaddressed - under separate cover - to assure each arrives in YOUR hands in pristine condition. PLUS we provide prompt service with detailed computer record keeping on EVERY shipment.

★ The right to discontinue at ANY time without ANY adverse consequences.

We maintain a strong nationwide dealer network that assures a strong secondary market that in some cases has resulted in resales of as much as 3,500% of the original single item, but you are NEVER under any obligation to purchase an unwanted FDC - regardless the reason. Many buyers buy duplicates and report that the sale of one can OFTEN be sold to cover the cost of several.

FOR COMPLETE DETAILS, FREE COVER & FREE 4-COLOR BROCHURE, SEND 52¢ SASE TODAY!

PUGH CACHETS, INC.

P.O. Box 8789, The Woodlands, TX 77387-8789
or CALL (713) 363-9135
Member: ASDA, AFDCS, APS, TxPA, COPO, IFSDA, et. al.

☐☐ 2522 **(29c) Flag**, non-denominated ATM single, self-adhesive, 1/22/91, DC 1.25

☐☐ 2523 **29c Flag over Mt. Rushmore**, engraved, 1/29/91 Mt. Rushmore, SD (233,793) 1.25   1.50

☐☐ 2523A **29c Flag over Mt. Rushmore**, photogravure, 7/4/91 Mt. Rushmore, SD (80,662) 1.25   1.50

☐☐ 2524 **29c Flower**, 4/5/91 Rochester, NY (132,233) 1.25   1.50   1.75

☐☐ 2525 **29c Flower**, roulette 10 coil, 4/5/91 Rochester, NY (144,750)...1.25   1.50

☐☐ 2526 **29c Flower**, perf. 10 coil, 3/3/92 Rochester, NY (35,877)...1.25   1.50

☐☐ 2527 **29c Flower**, bklt. single, 5/5/91 Rochester, NY................1.25   1.50

☐☐ 2527a **Booklet pane of 10**..6.00

First day cancel was applied to 16,975 covers bearing one or more of Nos. 2527-2527a.

☐☐ 2528 **29c Flag and Olympic Rings**, bklt. single, 4/21/91 Atlanta, GA 1.25

☐☐ 2528a **Booklet pane of 10**..5.00

☐☐ 2529 **19c Fishing Boat**, 8/8/91 (82,698).............................1.25

☐☐ 2530 **19c Balloon**, 5/17/91 Denver, CO................................1.25

☐☐ 2530a **Booklet pane of 10**..6.00

First day cancel was applied to 96,351 covers bearing one or more of Nos. 2530-2530a.

☐☐ 2531 **29c Flags on Parade**, 5/30/91 Waterloo, NY (104,046) .1.25   1.50   1.75

☐☐ 2531A **29c Liberty Torch**, 6/25/91 New York, NY (68,456) 1.25

1991-93

☐☐ 2532 **50c Switzerland**, 2/22/91 (316,047)...............................1.35   1.75   2.50

☐☐ 2533 **29c Vermont**, 3/1/91, Bennington, VT (308,105) 1.25   1.50   1.75

☐☐ 2534 **29c Savings Bonds**, 4/30/91 (341,955)........................1.25   1.50   1.75

☐☐ 2535 **29c Love**, 5/9/91, Honolulu, HI (336,132) 1.25   1.50   1.75

☐☐ 2536 **29c Love**, bklt. single, 5/9/91, Honolulu, HI 1.25

☐☐ 2536a **Booklet pane of 10**..5.00

First day cancel was applied to 43,336 covers bearing one or more of Nos. 2536-2536a.

☐☐ 2537 **52c Love**, 5/9/91, Honolulu, HI (90,438) 1.35   1.75   2.00

☐☐ 2538 **29c William Saroyan**, 5/22/91, Fresno, CA (334,373) ...1.25   1.50   1.75

☐☐ 2539 **$1 USPS & Olympic Rings**, 9/29/91, Orlando, FL (69,241)..2.25   6.00   7.50

☐☐ 2540 **$2.90 Eagle & Olympic Rings**, 7/7/91, San Diego, CA (79,555)...4.50   40.00   50.00

☐☐ 2541 **$9.95 Eagle & Olympic Rings**, 6/16/91, Sacramento, CA (68,657)...................................12.50   85.00   100.00

☐☐ 2542 **$14 Eagle**, 8/31/91, Hunt Valley, MD (54,727) 18.50   125.00   150.00

☐☐ 2543 **$2.90 Futuristic Space Shuttle**, 6/3/93 Kennedy Space Center, FL.................................4.50   40.00   50.00

☐☐ 2549a **29c Fishing Flies booklet pane of 5**, 5/31/91, Cuddebackville, NY (1,045,726) 3.00

☐☐ 2545-2549, any single 1.25

☐☐ 2550 **29c Cole Porter**, 6/8/91, Peru, IN (304,363)....................1.25   1.50   1.75

☐☐ 2551 **29c Desert Storm/ Desert Shield**, 7/2/91, ...1.50   1.75   2.50

☐☐ 2552 **29c Desert Storm/ Desert Shield**, bklt. single, 7/2/91,..1.50

☐☐ 2552a **Booklet pane of 5**..4.00

First day cancel was applied to 860,455 covers
bearing one or more of Nos. 2551-2552, 2552a.

☐☐ 2557a 29c **Summer Olympics**, 7/12/91, Los Angeles, CA
(886,984)..3.00

☐☐ 2553-2557, **any single** 1.25

☐☐ 2558 29c **Numismatics**, 8/13/91, Chicago, IL (288,519) 1.25   1.50   1.75

☐☐ 2559 29c **World War II Souvenir Sheet of 10**, 9/3/91,
Phoenix, AZ (1,832,967) 6.00

☐☐ 2559a-2559j, **any single** 1.25

☐☐ 2560 29c **Basketball**, 8/28/91, Springfield, MA (295,471) 2.00   2.50   3.50

☐☐ 2561 29c **District of Columbia**, 9/7 (299,989) 1.25   1.50   1.75

☐☐ 2566a 29c **Comedians booklet pane of 10**, 8/29/91,
Hollywood, CA...5.00

☐☐ 2562-2566, **any single** 1.25

First day cancel was applied to 954,293 covers
bearing one or more of Nos. 2562-2566a.

☐☐ 2567 29c **Jan Matzeliger**, 9/15/91, Lynn, MA (289,034)..........1.25   1.50   1.75

☐☐ 2577a 29c **Space Exploration booklet pane of 10**, 10/1/91,
Pasadena, CA...5.00

☐☐ 2568-2577, **any single** 1.25

First day cancel was applied to 1,465,111 covers
bearing one or more of Nos. 2568-2577a.

☐☐ 2578 (29c) **Christmas (religious)**, 10/17/91, Houston, TX.......1.25   1.50   1.75

☐☐ 2579 (29c) **Christmas (secular)**, 10/17/91, Santa, ID
(169,750)...1.25   1.50   1.75

☐☐ 2581b (29c) **Christmas booklet pane of 4**, 10/17/91,
Santa, ID...2.50

☐☐ 2580-2581, **any single** 1.25

☐☐ 2582 (29c) **Christmas, bklt. single**, 10/17/91, Santa, ID 1.25

☐☐ 2582a **Booklet pane of 4**...2.50

☐☐ 2583 (29c) **Christmas, bklt. single**, 10/17/91, Santa, ID 1.25

☐☐ 2583a **Booklet pane of 4**...2.50

☐☐ 2584 (29c) **Christmas, bklt. single**, 10/17/91, Santa, ID 1.25

☐☐ 2584a **Booklet pane of 4**...2.50

☐☐ 2585 (29c) **Christmas, bklt. single**, 10/17/91, Santa, ID 1.25

☐☐ 2585a **Booklet pane of 4**...2.50

☐☐ 2594 29c **Pledge of Allegiance**, black denomination,
9/8/92, Rome, NY...1.25

☐☐ 2594a **Booklet pane of 10**...5.00

First day cancel was applied to 61,464 covers
bearing one or more of Nos. 2594-2594a.

☐☐ 2595 29c **Eagle & Shield**, brown denomination, 9/25/92,
Dayton, OH...1.25

☐☐ 2596 29c **Eagle & Shield**, green denomination, 9/25/92,
Dayton, OH...1.25

☐☐ 2597 29c **Eagle & Shield**, red denomination, 9/25/92,
Dayton, OH...1.25

First day cancel was applied to 65,822 covers
bearing one or more of Nos. 2595-2597.

☐☐ 2604 (10c) **Eagle & Shield**, Bulk Rate USA, 11/13/91,
Kansas City, MO..1.25   1.50

☐☐ 2605 (10c) **Eagle & Shield**, USA Bulk Rate, 5/29/93,
Secaucus, NJ..1.25   1.50

☐☐ 2606 (10c) **Eagle & Shield**, gold eagle, 5/29/93,
Secaucus, NJ..1.25   1.50

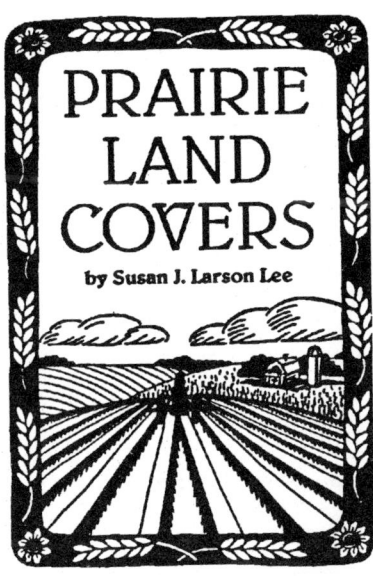

Scott Number	Description	SGL	BLK	PL BLK
☐☐ 2607	23c Flag, 9/27/91	1.25	1.50	
☐☐ 2608	23c Reflected Flag, 7/21/92, Kansas City, MO (35,673)	1.25	1.50	
☐☐ 2608A	23c Reflected Flag, 7mm "23" 10/9/92, Kansas City, MO	1.25	1.50	
☐☐ 2608B	23c Reflected Flag, 8 1/2mm "First Class" 5/14/93, Denver, CO	1.25	1.50	
☐☐ 2609	29c Flag and White House, 4/23/92 (56,505)	1.25	1.50	

1992

Scott Number	Description	SGL	BLK	PL BLK
☐☐ 2615a	29c Winter Olympics, 1/11/92, Orlando, FL (1,062,048)	3.00		
☐☐ 2611-2615,	any single	1.25		
☐☐ 2616	29c World Columbian Stamp Expo, 1/24/92, Rosemont, IL (309,729)	1.25	1.50	1.75
☐☐	1st Info cachet	20.00		
☐☐ 2617	29c W.E.B. Du Bois, 1/31/92, Atlanta, GA (196,219)	1.25	1.50	1.75
☐☐ 2618	29c Love, 2/6/92, Loveland, CO (218,043)	1.25	1.50	1.75
☐☐ 2619	29c Olympic Baseball, 4/3/92, Atlanta, GA (105,996)	1.50	1.75	2.00
☐☐ 2623a	29c Voyages of Columbus, 4/24/92, Christiansted, VI (509,170)	2.75		
☐☐ 2620-2623,	any single	1.25		
☐☐ 2624	First Sighting of Land Souvenir Sheet of 3, 5/22/92, Chicago, IL	3.00		
☐☐ 2624a	1c	1.25		
☐☐ 2624b	4c	1.25		
☐☐ 2624c	$1	2.00		
☐☐ 2625	Claiming a New World Souvenir Sheet of 3, 5/22/92, Chicago, IL	9.00		
☐☐ 2625a	2c	1.25		
☐☐ 2625b	3c	1.25		
☐☐ 2625c	$4	8.00		
☐☐ 2626	Seeking Royal Support Souvenir Sheet of 3, 5/22/92, Chicago, IL	2.00		
☐☐ 2626a	5c	1.25		
☐☐ 2626b	30c	1.25		
☐☐ 2626c	50c	1.50		
☐☐ 2627	Royal Favor Restored Souvenir Sheet of 3, 5/22/92, Chicago, IL	6.25		
☐☐ 2627a	6c	1.25		
☐☐ 2627b	8c	1.25		
☐☐ 2627c	$3	6.00		
☐☐ 2628	Reporting Discoveries Souvenir Sheet of 3, 5/22/92, Chicago, IL	4.50		
☐☐ 2628a	10c	1.25		
☐☐ 2628b	15c	1.25		
☐☐ 2628c	$2	4.00		
☐☐ 2629	$5 Christopher Columbus Souvenir Sheet, 5/22/92, Chicago, IL	10.00		
	First day cancel was applied to 211,142 covers bearing one or more of Nos. 2624-2629.			
☐☐ 2630	29c New York Stock Exchange, 5/17/92, New York, NY (261,897)	1.25	1.50	1.75
☐☐ 2634a	29c Space Accomplishments, 5/29/92, Chicago, IL	2.75		
☐☐ 2631-2634,	any single	1.25		

First day cancel was applied to 277,853 covers
bearing one or more of Nos. 2631-2634a.

☐☐ 2635 29c Alaska Highway, 5/30/92, Fairbanks, AK

(186,791)..1.25　　1.50　　1.75

☐☐ 2636 29c Kentucky, 6/1/92, Danville, KY (251,153) ....1.25　　1.50　　1.75

☐☐ 2641a 29c Summer Olympics, 6/11/92, Baltimore, MD...............

(713,942)...3.00

☐☐ 2637-2641, any single...1.25

☐☐ 2646a 29c Hummingbirds booklet pane of 5, 6/15/92, ...4.00

☐☐ 2642-2646, any single..1.25

First day cancel was applied to 995,278 covers
bearing one or more of Nos. 2642-2646a.

☐☐ 2696a 29c Wildflowers, 7/24/92, Columbus, OH

(3,693,972)...30.00

☐☐ 2647-2696, any single...1.25

☐☐ 2697 29c World War II Souvenir Sheet of 10, 8/17/92,

Indianapolis, IN (1,734,880) 8.00

☐☐ 2697a-2697j, any single...1.25

☐☐ 2698 29c Dorothy Parker, 8/22/92, West End, NJ (266,323)..1.25　　1.50　　1.75

☐☐ 2699 29c Theodore von Karman, 8/31 (256,986) ....1.25　　1.50　　1.75

☐☐ 2703a 29c Minerals, 9/17/92 (681,416) 2.75

☐☐ 2700-2703, any single...1.25

☐☐ 2704 29c Juan Rodriguez Cabrillo, 9/28/92, San Diego, CA

(290,720)...1.25　　1.50　　1.75

☐☐ 2709a 29c Wild Animals booklet pane of 5, 10/1/92,

New Orleans, LA..3.25　　8.00

☐☐ 2705-2709, any single...1.50

First day cancel was applied to 604,205 covers
bearing one or more of Nos. 2705-2709a.

☐☐ 2710 29c Christmas (religious), 10/22 ....1.25　　1.50　　1.75

☐☐ 2710a Booklet pane of 10...7.25

First day cancel was applied to 201,576 covers
bearing one or more of Nos. 2710-2710a.

☐☐ 2714a 29c Christmas (secular), 10/22/92, Kansas City, MO....2.75

☐☐ 2711-2714, any single...1.25

☐☐ 2718a 29c Christmas (secular) booklet pane of 4, 10/22/92,

Kansas City, MO 2.75

☐☐ 2715-2718, any single...1.25

First day cancel was applied to 461,937 covers
bearing one or more of Nos. 2711-2714, 2715-2718
and 2718a.

☐☐ 2719 29c Christmas (secular), self-adhesive, 10/28/92,

New York, NY (48,873)..1.25

☐☐ 2720 29c Chinese New Year, 11/30/92, San Francisco, CA .....1.25　　1.50　　1.75

1993

☐☐ 2721 29c Elvis (Presley), 1/8/93, Memphis, TN, AM

cancellation ....1.50　　1.75　　1.85

☐☐ Any city, PM cancellation ....1.25　　1.50　　1.75

☐☐ 2722 29c Oklahoma!, 3/30/93, Oklahoma City, OK................1.25　　1.50　　1.75

☐☐ 2723 29c Hank Williams, 6/9/93, Nashville, TN ....1.25　　1.50　　1.75

☐☐ 2730a 29c Rock & Roll/Rhythm & Blues Musicians, ...

6/16/93, Cleveland, OH or Santa Monica CA 5.00

☐☐ Any other city 5.00

☐☐ 2724-2730, any single...1.25

☐☐ **Any single, any other city**..1.25
      Value for No. 2730a is also for any se-tenant
      configuration of seven different stamps.

☐☐ **2737a 29c Rock & Roll/Rhythm & Blues Musicians** booklet
      pane of 8, 6/16/93, Cleveland, OH or
      Santa Monica CA 5.25

☐☐ **Any other city** 5.25

☐☐ **2731-2737, any single**...1.25

☐☐ **Any single, any other city**..5.25

☐☐ **2737b 29c Rock & Roll/Rhythm & Blues Musicians** booklet
      pane of 4, 6/16/93, Cleveland, OH or
      Santa Monica CA 2.75

☐☐ **Any other city** 2.75

☐☐ **2745a 29c Space Fantasy** booklet pane of 5, 1/25/93,
      Huntsville, AL 3.25

☐☐ **2741-2745, any single**...1.25

☐☐ **2746 29c Percy Lavon Julian**, 1/29/93, Chicago, IL 1.25   1.50   1.75

☐☐ **2747 29c Oregon Trail**, 2/12/93, Salem, OR 1.25   1.50   1.75
      No. 2747 was also available on the first day of issue
      in 36 cities along the route of the Oregon Trail.

☐☐ **2748 29c World University Games**, 2/25/93, Buffalo, NY.......1.25   1.50   1.75

☐☐ **2749 29c Grace Kelly**, 3/24/93, Beverly Hills, CA 1.25   1.50   1.75

☐☐ **2753a 29c Circus**, 4/6/93...3.50

☐☐ **2750-2753, any single**...1.25

☐☐ **2754 29c Cherokee Strip Land Run**, 4/17/93, Enid, OK.........1.25   1.50   1.75

☐☐ **2755 29c Dean Acheson**, 4/21/93, ...1.25   1.50   1.75

☐☐ **2759a 29c Sporting Horses**, 5/1/93, Louisville, KY 2.75

☐☐ **2756-2759, any single**...1.25

☐☐ **2764a 29c Garden Flowers** booklet pane of 5, 5/15/93,
      Spokane, WA...3.25

☐☐ **2760-2764, any single**...1.25

☐☐ **2765 29c World War II Souvenir Sheet of 10**, 5/31/93, ...7.00

☐☐ **2765a-2765j, any single**...1.25

☐☐ **2766 29c Joe Louis**, 6/22/93, Detroit, MI....................1.25   1.50   1.75

☐☐ **2770a 29c Broadway Musicals** booklet pane of 4,
      7/14/93, New York, NY 3.25

☐☐ **2767-2770, any single**...1.25

☐☐ **2782a 29c National Postal Museum**, 7/30/93.....................2.75

☐☐ **2779-2782, any single**...1.25

☐☐ **2784a 29c Deafness/Sign Language**, 9/20/93, Burbank CA ...2.00

☐☐ **2783-2784, any single**...1.25

☐☐ **2788a 29c Classic Books**, 10/23/93, Louisville, KY 2.75

☐☐ **2785-2788, any single**...1.25

☐☐ **2789 29c Christmas (religious)**, 10/21/93, Raleigh, NC.............1.25   1.50   1.75

☐☐ **2790 29c Christmas (religious)**, booklet single, 10/21/93,
      Raleigh, NC...1.25

☐☐ **2790a Booklet pane of 4** 2.00

☐☐ **2794a 29c Christmas (secular)**, sheet stamps, 10/23/93,
      New York, NY 2.75

☐☐ **2791-2794, any single** 1.25

☐☐ **2798a 29c Christmas (secular)** booklet pane of 10,
      10/21/93, New York, NY 6.50

☐☐ **2798b 29c Christmas (secular)** booklet pane of 10,
      10/21/93, New York, NY 6.50

☐☐ **2795-2798, any single** 1.25

☐☐ 2799 29c Christmas (snowman), large self-adhesive,
10/28/93, New York, NY..............................1.25

☐☐ 2800 29c Christmas (soldier), self-adhesive, 10/28/93,
New York, NY..............................1.25

☐☐ 2801 29c Christmas (jack-in-the-box), self-adhesive,
10/28/93, New York, NY..............................1.25

☐☐ 2802 29c Christmas (reindeer), self-adhesive, 10/28/93,
New York, NY..............................1.25

☐☐ 2799-2802 on one cover 2.50

☐☐ 2803 29c Christmas (snowman), small self-adhesive,
10/28/93, New York, NY..............................1.25

☐☐ 2804 29c Mariana Islands, 11/4/93, Saipan, MP ....1.25 | 1.50 | 1.75

☐☐ 2805 29c Columbus' Landing in Puerto Rico, 11/19/93,
San Juan, PR..............................1.25 | 1.50 | 1.75

☐☐ 2806 29c AIDS Awareness, 12/1/93, New York, NY ....1.25 | 1.50 | 1.75

☐☐ 2806a 29c AIDS Awareness, booklet single,
perf. 11 vert., 12/1/93, New York, NY 1.25

☐☐ 2806b Booklet pane of 5..3.25

1994

☐☐ 2811a 29c Winter Olympics, 1/6/94, Salt Lake City, UT 3.00

☐☐ 2807-2811, any single..1.25

☐☐ 2812 29c Edward R. Murrow, 1/21/94, Pullman, WA..............1.25 | 1.50 | 1.75

☐☐ 2813 29c Love, self-adhesive, 1/27/94, Loveland, OH.............1.25

☐☐ 2814 29c Love, booklet single, 2/14/94, Niagara Falls, NY......1.25

☐☐ 2814a Booklet pane of 10..6.50

☐☐ 2814C 29c Love, 6/11/94, Niagara Falls, NY...........................1.25 | 1.50 | 1.75

☐☐ 2815 52c Love, 2/14/94, Niagara Falls, NY.............................1.35 | 2.75 | 3.00

☐☐ 2816 29c Dr. Allison Davis, 2/1/94, Williamstown, MA ....1.25 | 1.50 | 1.75

☐☐ 2817 29c Chinese New Year, 2/5/94, Pomona, CA...................1.25 | 1.50 | 1.75

☐☐ 2818 29c Buffalo Soldiers, 4/22/94, Dallas, TX......................1.25 | 1.50 | 1.75

No. 2818 was also available on the first day of issue in forts
in Kansas, Texas and Arizona.

☐☐ 2828a 29c Silent Screen Stars, 4/27/94, San Francisco, CA ...6.50

☐☐ 2819-2828, any single..1.25

☐☐ 2833a 29c Garden Flowers booklet pane of 5, 4/28/93,
Cincinnati, OH..............................3.25

☐☐ 2829-2833, any single..1.25

☐☐ 2834 29c World Cup Soccer, 5/26/94, New York, NY ....1.25 | 1.50 | 1.75

☐☐ 2835 40c World Cup Soccer, 5/26/94, New York, NY ....1.25 | 2.25 | 2.50

☐☐ 2836 50c World Cup Soccer, 5/26/94, New York, NY ....1.35 | 2.50 | 2.75

☐☐ 2838 29c World War II Souvenir Sheet of 10, 6/6/94,
USS Normandy..............................6.50

☐☐ 2838a-2838j, any single..1.25

No. 2838 was also available on the first day of issue in 13 other locations.

☐☐ 2839 29c Norman Rockwell, 7/1/94, Stockbridge, MA............1.25 | 1.50 | 1.75

☐☐ 2840 50c Norman Rockwell Souvenir Sheet of 4, 7/1/94,
Stockbridge, MA 3.00

☐☐ 2840a-2840d, any single..1.35

☐☐ 2841 29c Moon Landing Sheet of 12, 7/20/94 ....6.50

☐☐ 2841a single stamp..1.35

☐☐ 2842 $9.95 Moon Landing, 7/20/94 ....12.50 | 85.00 | 100.00

☐☐ 2847a 29c Locomotives booklet pane of 5, 7/28/93,
Chama, NM..............................3.25

☐☐ 2843-2847, any single..1.25

☐☐ 2848 29c George Meany, 8/16/94 ....1.25 | 1.50 | 1.75

C1-C3   C7-C9   C10

AIR POST
1918

☐☐	C1	**6c Jenny**, 12/10/18, DC ....17,500.	—	—	—	
☐☐		Washington, DC 12/16/18............2000.	—	—	—	
☐☐		Philadelphia, PA 12/16/18............2000.	—	—	—	
☐☐		New York, NY 12/16/18.............2000.	—	—	—	
☐☐	C2	**16c Jenny**, 7/ll/18, DC..............22,500.	—	—	—	
☐☐		Washington, DC 7/15/18............800.00	—	—	—	
☐☐		Philadelphia, PA 7/15/18 ....800.00	—	—	—	
☐☐		New York, NY 7/15/18..............800.00	—	—	—	
☐☐	C3	**24c Jenny**, 5/13/18, DC..............27,500.	—	—	—	
☐☐		Washington, DC 5/15/18............750.00	—	—	—	
☐☐		Philadelphia, PA 5/15/18...........750.00	—	—	—	
☐☐		New York, NY 5/15/18..............750.00	—	—	—	

The earliest date listed under C1-C3 is the first day of issue. The other date is the first flight for the three different air mail rates of 1918.

1923

☐☐	C4	**8c Propeller**, 8/15/23, DC 400.00	700.00	—	—	
☐☐	C5	**16c Insignia**, 8/17/23, DC 600.00	1150.	—	—	
☐☐	C6	**24c Biplane**, 8/21/23, DC...........750.00	2000.	—	—	

1926-27

☐☐	C7	**10cMap**, 2/13/26, DC 75.00	150.00	—	—	
☐☐		Chicago, IL 85.00	160.00	—	—	
☐☐		Cleveland, OH 125.00	200.00	—	—	
☐☐		Dearborn, MI 125.00	200.00	—	—	
☐☐		Detroit, MI......................75.00	160.00	—	—	
☐☐		Unofficial city 150.00	—	—	—	

FDC/first flight covers on 2/15/26 sell for 25% more than values listed.

☐☐	C8	**15c Map**, 9/18/26, DC 90.00	150.00	500.00	—	
☐☐	C9	**20c Map**, 1/25/27, DC 100.00	175.00	—	—	
☐☐		New York, NY......................125.00	200.00	—	—	
☐☐		1st Albert E. Gorham cachet ....—	—	250.00	—	
☐☐	C10	**10c Lindbergh's Plane**, 6/18/27, DC......25.00	30.00	150.00	—	
☐☐		Detroit, MI......................35.00	40.00	150.00	—	
☐☐		Little Falls, MN 35.00	40.00	150.00	—	
☐☐		St. Louis, MO 25.00	30.00	150.00	—	
☐☐		Air Mail Field, Chicago, unofficial 150.00	—	—	—	
☐☐		Any other unofficial city...............150.00	—	150.00	—	
☐☐		1 st Milton Mauck cachet ....—	—	200.00	—	
☐☐	C10a	**Lindbergh's Plane**, booklet pane of 3,				
☐☐		5/26/28, DC 825.00		—		
☐☐		Cleveland Mid. Phil. Sta 800.00		—		
☐☐		Plus Scott 645, Cleveland Mid. Phil. Sta .....1000.		—		

179

C11

C12, C16, C17, C19

C13, C15

C18

C20-C22

C23

C24

C25, C35

C32

C33, C37, C39, C41

C34

C38

C40

C42

C45

C46

C47

C48, C50

C49

C51, C52, C60, C61

SCOTT NUMBER	DESCRIPTION	UNCACHETED SGL	BLK	CACHETED SGL	BLK
C10a	**Lindbergh's Plane**, booklet single, DC 110.00		—		
	Cleveland Mid. Phil. Sta 100.00		—		
	Plus Scott 645 ....150.00		—		

Lindbergh booklet pane FDC's and Scott C10a plus 645 FDC's are both known on Garfield Perry Shield Eagle and Biplane general purpose cacheted envelopes. These sell for a 10% to 20% premium over uncacheted FDCS.

1928

C11	**5c Beacon**, 7/25/28, DC(pair) 50.00	60.00	175.00	—	
	With single stamp and postage due stamp 100.00	—	250.00	—	
	Unofficial city (pair) 175.00	—	250.00	—	
	Single stamp with no postage due 150.00	—	350.00	—	

1930

C12	**5c WingedGlobe**, 2/10/30, DC 12.00	14.00	100.00	—	
C13	**65c Zeppelin**, 4/19/30, DC ....1200.	2400.	1600.	4000.	
C14	**$1.30 Zeppelin**, 4/19/30, DC ....1000.	1800.	1200.	2500.	
C15	**$2.60 Zeppelin**, 4/19/30, DC ....1100.	2400.	1500.	3000.	
C13-C15	complete set on one cover ....15,000.	—	—	—	
C13-C15	complete set of pl# sgl on one cover ....20,000.	—	—	—	

FDC's flown on Zeppelin flights sell for a premium.

1931-32

C16	**5c Winged Globe**, 8/19/31, DC 175.00	300.00	350.00	—	
C17	**8c Winged Globe**, 9/26/32, DC 15.00	18.00	40.00	50.00	

1933

C18	**50c Zeppelin**, 10/2/33, New York, NY				
	(3,500) 125.00	225.00	300.00	450.00	
	Akron, OH 10/4/33 ....275.00	400.00	425.00	650.00	
	Washington, DC, 10/5/33 ....225.00	350.00	450.00	575.00	
	Miami, FL, 10/6/33 ....150.00	250.00	325.00	450.00	
	Chicago, IL, 10/7/33 ....275.00	375.00	400.00	550.00	

FDC's flown on a Zeppelin flight sell for a premium.

1934

C19	**6c Winged Globe**, Baltimore, MD, 6/30/34 ..175.00	—	600.00	—	
	New York, NY 800.00	—	1500.	—	
	Brooklyn, NY ....1200.	—	1700.	—	
	7/1/34, DC 8.00	10.00	35.00	45.00	
	Unofficial city 20.00	—	—	—	

1935

C20	**25c China Clipper**, 11/22/35, San				
	Francisco, CA (15,000) 17.50	20.00	45.00	55.00	
	DC (10,910) 20.00	22.50	50.00	60.00	

1937

C21	**20c China Clipper**, 2/15/37, DC 20.00	22.50	50.00	55.00	
C22	**50c China Clipper**, 2/15/37, DC 20.00	22.50	.55.00	60.00	
	Both on one cover 37.50	40.00	110.00	165.00	

Total for Scott C21 and C22 is 40,000.

C54

C53

C55

C56

C57, C59, C62, C63

C64-C65

C67

C68

C66

C69

C70

C71

C72-C73

C74

C77

C78, C82

C84

1st Readers Digest cachet

C79, C83

SCOTT NUMBER	DESCRIPTION	UNCACHETED		CACHETED	
		SGL	BLK	SGL	BLK

1938

☐☐ C23	6c **Eagle Holding Shield**, 5/14/38, Dayton,				
	OH (116,443)...10.00		12.00	20.00	30.00
☐☐	St. Petersburg, FL (95,121).........................10.00		12.00	20.00	30.00
☐☐	DC, 5/15/38 ....3.50				

1939

☐☐ C24	30c **Winged Globe**, 5/16/39, New York,				
	NY (63,634)..20.00		30.00	50.00	70.00

SCOTT NUMBER	DESCRIPTION	CACHETED		
		SGL	BLK	PL BLK

1941-44

☐☐ C25	6c **Plane**, 6/25/41, DC (99,986)........................2.25		4.00	8.00
☐☐ C25a	**Plane**, booklet pane of 3, 3/18/43, DC (50,216)........25.00			
☐☐ C25a	**Plane**, booklet single 10.00			
☐☐ C26	8c **Plane**, 3/21/44, DC (147,484).......................3.75		5.00	8.00
☐☐ C27	10c **Plane**, 8/15/41, Atlantic City, NJ (87,712)...........&.00		10.00	15.00
☐☐ C28	15c **Plane**, 8/19/41, Baltimore, MD (74,000)............10.00		15.00	25.00
☐☐ C29	20c **Plane**, 8/27/41, Philadelphia, PA (66,225)........12.50		17.50	25.00
☐☐ C30	30c **Plane**, 9/25/41, Kansas City, MO (57,175) 20.00		25.00	35.00
☐☐ C31	50c **Plane**, 10/29/41, St. Louis, MO (54,580)............40.00		50.00	60.00

1946

☐☐ C32	5c **DC-4**, 9/25/46, DC 2.00		4.00	6.00
☐☐	1st William W. Bayless cachet 15.00		—	—
	Total for Scott C32 and UC14 is 396,639.			

1947

☐☐ C33	5c **DC4**, 3/26/47, DC (342,634) 2.00		3.00	5.00
☐☐ C34	10c **Pan Am. Bldg.**, 8/30/47, DC (265,773) 2.00		3.00	5.00
☐☐	1st Glenn L. Martin Co. cachet 20.00			
☐☐ C35	15c **N.Y. Skyline**, 8/20/47, New York, NY			
	(230,338)..2.00		4.00	6.00
☐☐ C36	25c **Bay Bridge**, 7/30/47, San Francisco, CA			
	(201,762)..2.75		5.75	8.50

1948

☐☐ C37	5c **DC4**, coil, 1/15/48, DC (192,084)....................2.00		pr3.50	1p4.50
☐☐ C38	5c **Map**, 7/31/48, New York, NY (371,265)................1.75		2.75	3.75

1949

☐☐ C39	6c **DC-4**, 1/18/49, DC (266,790)........................1.50		2.50	3.50
☐☐ C39a	**DC-4**, booklet pane of 3, 11/18/49, New York,			
	NY 9.00			
☐☐ C40	6c **Alexandria Bicentennial**, 5/11/49, Alexandria,			
	VA (386,717)..1.25		2.00	3.00
☐☐ C41	6c **DC-4**, coil, 8/25/49, DC (240,386) 1.25		pr2.50	1p4.00
☐☐ C42	10c **P.O. Bldg.**, 11/18/49, New Orleans, LA			
	(270,000)..1.75		2.75	3.75

SCOTT NUMBER	DESCRIPTION	SGL	CACHETED BLK	PL BLK
☐☐ C43	15c Globes & Doves, 10/7/49, Chicago, IL (246,833)................2.25		4.00	7.00
☐☐	1st Jack Knight Air Mail Society cachet...............30.00			
☐☐ C44	25c Boeing Stratocruiser, 11/30/49, Seattle, WA (220,215).................3.00		4.00	7.00
☐☐ C45	6c Wright Bros., 12/17/49, Kitty Hawk, NC (378,585)................3.50		5.00	8.00

1952

☐☐ C46	80c Diamond Head, 3/26/52, Honolulu, HI (89,864)................17.50		25.00	45.00

1953

☐☐ C47	6c Powered Flight, 5/29/53, Dayton, OH (359,050)....1.50		2.50	3.50

1954

☐☐ C48	4c Eagle, 9/3/54, Philadelphia, PA (295,720)..............1.00		1.50	2.50

1957

☐☐ C49	6c Air Force, 8/1/57, DC (356,683) 1.75		2.75	3.75

1958

☐☐ C50	5c Eagle, 7/31/58, Colorado Springs, CO, (207,954)....1.00		2.50	3.50
☐☐	1st United States Air Force Academy cachet........18.00			
☐☐ C51	7c Blue Jet, 7/31/58, Phila. PA, (204,401) 1.00		2.50	3.50
☐☐ C51a	Blue Jet, booklet pane of 6, 7/31/58, San Antonio, TX (119,769)................9.50			
☐☐ C52	7c Blue Jet, coil, 7/31/58, Miami, FL(181,603)..........1.00	pr2.00	lp3.00

1959

☐☐ C53	7c Alaska, 1/3/59, Juneau, AK (489,752)...................1.00		1.75	2.75
☐☐	1st Gastineau Stamp Club cachet.........................12.00			
☐☐ C54	7c Balloon, 8/17/59, Lafayette, IN (383,556) 1.10		2.75	3.75
☐☐ C55	7c Hawaii, 8/21/59, Honolulu, HI (533,464)...............1.00		2.50	3.50
☐☐ C56	10c Pan Am. Games, 8/27/59, Chicago, IL (302,206)................1.00		2.00	3.00

1959- 66

☐☐ C57	10c Liberty Bell, 6/10/60, Miami, FL (246,509)..........1.25		2.00	4.00
☐☐ C58	15c Statue of Liberty, 11/20/59, New York, NY (259,412)................1.25		2.00	4.00
☐☐ C59	25c Lincoln, 4/22/60, San Francisco, CA (211,235) ..1.75		2.75	4.75
☐☐ C59a	Lincoln, tagged, 12/29/66, DC (3,000).....................25.00		—	—

1960

☐☐ C60	7c Red Jet, 8/12/60, Arlington, VA (247,190) 1.00		1.00	2.50
☐☐ C60a	Red Jet, booklet pane of 6, 8/19/60, St. Louis, MO (143,363)................9.50			
☐☐ C61	7c Red Jet, coil, 10/22/60, Atlantic City, NJ (197,995)................1.00	pr1.25	lp3.00

1961- 67

☐☐ C62	13c Liberty Bell, 6/28/61, New York, NY (316,166)...1.00		1.00	2.75

SCOTT NUMBER	DESCRIPTION	SGL	BLK	PL BLK
☐☐ C62a	Liberty Bell, tagged, 2/15/67, DC	25.00	—	—
☐☐ C63	15c Statue of Liberty, 1/13/61, Buffalo, NY (192,976)	1.00	2.50	3.50
☐☐ C63a	Statue of Liberty, tagged, 1/11/67, DC	25.00	—	—

1962-65

☐☐ C64	8c Capitol, 12/5/62, DC (288,355)	1.00	1.00	2.50
☐☐ C64a	8c Capitol, tagged, 8/1/63, Dayton, OH (262,720)	2.00	2.50	4.00
☐☐	1st National Cash Register Co. cachet	15.00		
☐☐ C64b	Capitol, booklet pane of 5 + label, 12/5/62, DC (146,835)	2.00		
☐☐ C65	8c Capitol, coil, 12/5/62, DC(220,173)	1.00	pr1.00	lp2.75
☐☐ C65a	Capitol, coil, tagged, 1/14/65, New Orleans, LA	25.00		

1963

☐☐ C66	15c Montgomery Blair, 5/3/63, Silver Spring MD (260,031)	1.10	2.50	3.50
☐☐ C67	6c Bald Eagle, 7/12/63, Boston, MA (268,265)	1.00	1.00	2.50
☐☐ C67a	Bald Eagle, tagged, 2/15/67, DC	25.00	—	—
☐☐ C68	8c Amelia Earhart, 7/24/63, Atchison, KS (437,996)	1.75	2.25	2.75
☐☐	1st The Ninety-Nines, Inc., cachet	15.00		

1964

☐☐ C69	8c Robert H. Goddard, 10/5/64, Roswell, NM (421,020)	1.75	2.25	2.75

1967

☐☐ C70	8c Alaska, 3/30/67, Sitka, AK (554,784)	1.00	1.00	2.50
☐☐	1st Sheldon Jackson College cachet	15.00		
☐☐ C71	20c Audubon, 4/26/67, New York, NY (227,930)	2.00	3.50	4.50

1968

☐☐ C72	10c 50-Star Runway, 1/5/68, San Francisco, CA	1.00	1.00	2.50
☐☐ C72b	50-Star Runway, booklet pane of 8, 1/5/68, DC	3.50		
☐☐ C72c	50-Star Runway, booklet pane of 5 plus Mail Early Tab, 1/6/68, DC	125.00		
☐☐ C72c	50-Star Runway, booklet pane of 5 plus Zip Tab, 1/6/68, DC	125.00		
☐☐ C73	10c 50-Star Runway, coil 1/5/68 San Francisco, CA	1.00	pr1.50	1p2.50
	Total for Scott C72- C73 is 814, 140.			
☐☐ C74	10c Jenny, 5/15/68, DC (521,084)	1.50	2.75	3.75
☐☐	1st Readers Digest cachet	15.00	—	—
☐☐ C75	20c "USA," 11/22/68, NewYork, NY (276,244)	1.10	2.75	3.75

1969

☐☐ C76	10c First Man on Moon, 9/9/69, DC (8,743,070)	4.50	6.00	9.00
☐☐	1st Dow-Unicover cachet	12.00		

1971-73

☐☐ C77	9c Delta Plane, 5/15/71, Kitty Hawk, NC	1.00	1.25	2.50
	Total for Scott C77 and UXC10 is 379,442.			
☐☐ C78	11c Jet, 5/7/71, Spokane, WA	1.00	1.25	2.50

C75, C81   C76   C85

C86   C87   C88

C89   C90   C99

C98   C100   C105-8   C101-4

C113   C114

C115   C116

C118   C119

SCOTT NUMBER	DESCRIPTION	SGL	CACHETED BLK	PL BLK
☐☐ C78a	Jet, booklet pane of 4 + 2 labels, 5/7/71, Spokane, WA 1.75			
☐☐ C79	13c Winged Envelope, 11/16/73, New York, NY (282,550)...........1.00		1.25	2.50
☐☐ C79a	Winged Envelopes, booklet pane of 5 + label, 12/27/73, Chicago, IL 1.75			
☐☐ C80	17c Statue of Liberty, 7/13/71 Lakehurst, NJ (172,269)...........1.00		1.25	2.50
☐☐ C81	21c "USA," 5/21/71, DC (293,140)...........1.00		1.25	2.50
☐☐ C82	11c Jet, coil, 5/7/71, Spokane, WA 1.00		pr1.25	lp2.50
	Total for Scott C78, C78a and C82 is 464, 750.			
☐☐ C83	13c Winged Envelope, coil 12/27/73, Chicago, IL.......1.00		1.25	2.00
	Total for Scott C79a and C83 is 204,756.			

1972

☐☐ C84	11c City of Refuge, 5/3/72, Honaunau, (364,816)...........1.00		1.25	2.50
☐☐ C85	11c Olympics, 8/17/72, DC 1.00		1.25	2.50
	Total for Scott 1460-1462 and C85 is 971,536.			

1973

☐☐ C86	11c Electronics, 7/10/73, New York, NY 1.00		1.25	2.50
	Total for set Scott 1500-1502 and C86 is 1,197,700.			

1974

☐☐ C87	18c Statue of Liberty, 1/11/74, Hempstead, NY (216,902)...........1.00		1.25	2.50
☐☐	1st James Hogg cachet 15.00			
☐☐ C88	26c Mt. Rushmore, 1/2/74, Rapid City, SD (210,470)...........1.25		1.50	2.75

1976

☐☐ C89	25c Plane and Globes, 1/2/76, Honolulu, HI.............1.25		1.50	2.75
☐☐ C90	31c Plane, Globe and Flag, 1/2/76, Honolulu, HI.......1.25		1.50	3.00
☐☐	Scott C89 & C90 on one cover 3.00			

1978

☐☐ C91	31c Wright Bros., 9/23/78, Dayton, OH 3.00			
☐☐ C92	31c Wright Bros., 9/23/78, Dayton, OH 3.00			
☐☐ C92a	Se-tenant...........4.00		5.00	6.00

1979

☐☐ C93	21c Octave Chanute, 3/29/79, Chanute, KS 3.00			
☐☐ C94	21c Octave Chanute, 3/29/79, Chanute, KS 3.00			
☐☐ C94a	Se-tenant...........4.00		5.00	6.00
	Total for Scott C93 and C94 is 459,235.			
☐☐ C95	25c Wiley Post, 11/20/79, Oklahoma City, OK...........3.00			
☐☐ C96	5c Wiley Post, 11/20/79, Oklahoma City, OK...........3.00			
☐☐ C96a	Se-tenant...........4.00		5.00	6.00
☐☐ C97	31c Olympics, 11/1/79, Colorado Springs, CO...........1.25		1.65	2.35

1980

☐☐ C98	40c Philip Mazzei, 10/13/80, DC...........1.35		2.75	4.00

SCOTT NUMBER	DESCRIPTION	SGL	CACHETED BLK	PL BLK
☐☐ C99	28c Blanche Smart Scott, 12/30/80, Hammondsport, NY (238,502)...............1.25		1.50	2.75
☐☐ C100	35c Glenn Curtiss, 12/30/80, Hammondsport, NY (208,502)...............1.25		1.75	3.00
☐☐	Scott C99 & C100 on one cover 2.50		—	—

1983

☐☐ C101	28c Gymnastics, 6/17/83, San Antonio, TX...............1.25		—	—
☐☐ C102	28c Hurdles, 6/17/83, San Antonio, TX...............1.25		—	—
☐☐ C103	28c Basketball, 6/17/83, San Antonio, TX 1.25		—	—
☐☐ C104	28c Soccer, 6/17/83, San Antonio, TX...............1.25		—	—
☐☐ C104a	Se-tenant, (901,028) ....—		3.75	4.50
☐☐ C105	40c Shot Put, 4/8/83, Los Angeles, CA 1.35		—	—
☐☐ C106	40c Gymnastics, 4/8/83, Los Angeles, CA...............1.35		—	—
☐☐ C107	40c Swimming, 4/8/83, Los Angeles, CA...............1.35		—	—
☐☐ C108	40c Weight lifting, 4/8/83, Los Angeles, CA...............1.35		—	—
☐☐ C108a	Se-tenant, (1,001,657) ....—		5.00	6.00
☐☐ C109	35c Fencing, 11/4/83, Colorado Springs, CO...............1.25		—	—
☐☐ C110	35c Cycling, 11/4/83, Colorado Springs, CO...............1.25		—	—
☐☐ C111	35c Volleyball, 11/4/83, Colorado Springs, CO...........1.25		—	—
☐☐ C112	35c Pole Vaulting, 11/4/83, Colorado Springs, CO.....1.25		—	—
☐☐ C112a	Se-tenant, (897,729) ....—		4.50	5.50

1985

☐☐ C113	33c Alfred Verville, 2/13/85, Garden City, NY 1.25		1.75	2.50
☐☐ C114	39c Lawrence & Elmer Sperry, 2/13/85, Garden City, NY 1.35		1.75	2.50
☐☐ C115	44c Transpacific Air Mail, 2/15/85, San Francisco, CA (269,229)...............1.35		2.25	2.50
☐☐ C116	44c Junipero Serra, 8/22/85, San Diego, CA (254,977)...............1.35		2.25	2.50

1988

☐☐ C117	44c Settling of New Sweden, 3/29/88, Wilmington, DE (213,445)...............1.35		2.25	2.50
☐☐ C118	45c Samuel P. Langley, 5/14/88, San Diego, CA.......1.40		2.25	2.50
☐☐ C119	36c Igor Sikorsky, 6/23/88, Stratford, CT (162,986)...............1.25		2.00	2.50

1989

☐☐ C120	45c French Revolution Bicentennial, 7/14/89, DC (309,975)...............1.40		2.25	2.50
☐☐ C121	45c America, 10/12/89, San Juan, PR (93,569) 1.40		2.25	2.50
☐☐ C122	45c Spacecraft, 11/28/89, DC...............1.50		—	—
☐☐ C123	45c Hover Car, 11/28/89, DC...............1.50		—	—
☐☐ C124	45c Moon Rover, 11/28/89, DC 1.50		—	—
☐☐ C125	45c Space Shuttle, 11/28/89, DC...............1.50		—	—
☐☐ C125a	Se-tenant, (765,479) ....—		6.00	7.00
☐☐ C126	45c Futuristic Mail Delivery, souvenir sheet, 11/24/89, DC (237,826)...............6.00		—	—

1990

☐☐ C127	45c America, 10/12/90, Grand Canyon, AZ (137,068) 1.75		2.25	2.50

1991

☐☐	C128 50c Harriet Quimby, 4/27/91, Plymouth, MI 1.75		2.25	2.50
☐☐	C129 40c William T. Piper, 5/17/91, Denver, CO 1.75		2.25	2.50
☐☐	C130 50c Antarctic Treaty, 6/21/91 ....1.75		2.25	2.50
☐☐	C131 50c Bering Land Bridge, 10/12/91, Anchorage, AK.....1.75		2.25	2.50

Cachet values in this catalogue are for an average cacheted First Day Cover. Some FDC's, depending on the cachet, can sell for many times the catalogue value, while others sell for less. The Cachet Calculator lists cachetmakers, the dates they produced FDC's and a market value multiplier. The Calculator begins on page 40A.

AIRPOST SPECIAL DELIVERY

CE1-CE2   E1   E12-E13, E15-E18

E14, E19   E22-E23

E20-E21

FA1

1934

☐☐	CE1	16c Great Seal, 8/30/34, Chicago, IL (AAMS Convention Sta.) (40,171) 30.00	35.00	40.00
☐☐		DC, 8/31/34 .... 15.00	17.50	22.50

For Scott CE1 design imperforate, see Scott 771.

1936

☐☐	CE2	16c Great Seal, 2/10/36, DC (72,981) 25.00	27.50	32.50

SPECIAL DELIVERY
1885

☐☐ E1   **10c Messenger,** at special delivery offices, 10/1/1885......8000.

1888

☐☐ E2   **10c Messenger,** at any post office, 12/18/1888, earliest known use .... —

1893

☐☐ E3   **10c Messenger,** 2/11/1893, earliest known use .... —

1894

☐☐ E4   **10c Messenger,** unwmkd, 11/21/1894, earliest known use ... —

1895-99

☐☐ E5   **10c Messenger,** wmk USPS, 10/3/1895, earliest known use .. —

1903

☐☐ E6   **10c Bicycle,** perf. 12, dbl-line wmk, 1/22/03, earliest known use .... —

1908

☐☐ E7 10c Mercury, 12/14/08, earliest known use ....—

1911

☐☐ E8 10c Bicycle, perf. 12, sgl-line wmk, 1/14/11,
earliest known use ....—

1914

☐☐ E9 10c Bicycle, perf. 10, sgl-line wmk, 10/26/14,
earliest known use ....—

1916

☐☐ E10 10c Bicycle, perf. 10, unwrnk, 11/4/16, earliest known use ..—

1917

☐☐ E11 10c Bicycle, perf. 11, unwmk, 6/12/17, earliest known use ...—

1922

☐☐ E12 10c Motorcycle, perf. 11, 7/12/22 ....400.00   —

1925

☐☐ E13 15c Motorcycle, perf. 11, 4/11/25 ....225.00   375.00
☐☐ E14 20c P.O. Truck, perf. 11, 4/25/25 ....100.00   200.00

1927-41

☐☐ E15 10c Motorcycle, perf. 11 x 10 1/2, 11/29/27, DC 90.00   200.00
☐☐ E15 Motorcycle, electric eye, perf 11 x 10 1/2, 9/8/41, DC......25.00   35.00
*Values given for Scott E15 Electric Eye are for covers
with sheet salvage with Electric Eye markings.*

1931

☐☐ E16 15c Motorcycle, perf. 11 x 10 1/2, 8/13/31, DC 125.00   200.00
☐☐ Easton, PA, 8/6/31 ....1000.   —
*8/6/31 is the earliest known use of Scott E16,
8/13/31 is the first day of sale at the Philatelic Agency.*

1944

☐☐ E17 13c Motorcycle, 10/30/44, DC...12.50   15.00
☐☐ E18 17c Motorcycle, 10/30/44, DC...12.50   15.00
☐☐ Scott E17 & E18 on one cover ....15.00   —
Total for Scott E17 and E18 is 158,863

1951

☐☐ E19 20c P.O. Truck, 11/30/51, DC (33,139)................................5.00   8.00

1954-57

☐☐ E20 20c Letter, 10/13/54, Boston, MA (194,043)........................3.00   5.00
☐☐ E21 30c Letter, 9/3/57, Indianapolis, IN (111,451)....................2.25   4.25

1969-71

☐☐ E22 45c Arrows, 11/21/69, New York, NY(192,391).................3.50   6.00
☐☐ E23 60c Arrows, 5/10/71, Phoenix, AZ (129,562)......................3.50   6.00

CERTIFIED MAIL/REGISTRATION

☐☐ FA1 15c Certified Mail, 6/6/55, DC (176,308) 3.25   5.00
☐☐ F1   10c Registry, 12/1/11, any city ....9000.   —

SPECIAL HANDLING

QE1-QE4

Q2

J68

J88

SCOTT NUMBER	DESCRIPTION	CACHETED SGL	UNCACHETED BLK	UNCACHETED SGL
☐☐ QE1	10c Special Handling, 6/25/28 ....45.00		65.00	200.00
☐☐ QE2	15c Special Handling, 6/25/28 ....45.00		65.00	200.00
☐☐ QE3	20c Special Handling, 6/25/28 ....45.00		65.00	200.00
☐☐ QE4	25c Special Handling, 4/11/25 ....225.00		275.00	300.00
☐☐	Scott QE4 & E13 on one cover, 4/11/25..............1300.00			1500.00

PARCEL POST

Parcel Post Service (fourth class) began January 1, 1913, and these stamps were issued for that service only. The 1c, 2c, 4c and 5c are known with January 1, 1913, postmarks — the 2c undoubtedly for fourth class usage, the others possible but unproven. Beginning July 1, these stamps could be used for any purpose, thus a few first class FDCs were prepared for some of the lower denominations. There was not an official first day city for either date.

		4th Class (1/1/13)	1st Class (7/1/13)
☐☐ Q1	1c Post Office Clerk, any city.................................—		1500.
	Scott Q1 known on picture postcard.		
☐☐ Q2	2c City Carrier, any city ....—		1500.
☐☐ Q3	3c Railway Postal Clerk, any city ....—		3000.
☐☐ Q4	4c Rural Carrier, any city ....—		3000.
☐☐ Q5	5c Mail Train, any city ....—		3000.
	Scott Q4 & Q5 on wrapper ....—		—

SCOTT NUMBER	DESCRIPTION	CACHETED SGL	BLK

OFFICIALS
1983-85

☐☐ O127	1c Great Seal, 1/12/83, DC.....................................1.00		1.25
☐☐ O128	4c Great Seal, 1/12/83, DC.....................................1.00		1.25
☐☐ O129	13c Great Seal, 1/12/83, DC...................................1.00		1.25
☐☐ O129A	14c Great Seal, 5/15/85 DC....................................1.00		1.25
☐☐ O130	17c Great Seal, 1/12/83, DC...................................1.00		1.25
☐☐ O132	$1 Great Seal, 1/12/83, DC 2.25		6.00
☐☐ O133	$5 Great Seat, 1/12/83, DC 12.50		20.00

SCOTT NUMBER	DESCRIPTION	CACHETED SGL	BLK
0135	20c Great Seal Coil,1/12/83, DC 1.00		pr1.25
	Scott O127-0129, 0130-0135 on one cover.................15.00		
	Scott O127-0129, 0130-0135 on Official Postal Card (Scott UZ2) or envelope (Scott UO73) 18.00		
0136	22c Great Seal Coil, 5/15/85, DC 1.00		pr1.25
0138	(14c) Great Seal, 2/4/85, DC 1.00		1.25

SCOTT NUMBER	DESCRIPTION	CACHETED SGL	PR

1988

0138A	15c Great Seal Coil, 6/11/88, Corpus Christi, TX 1.00		1.25
0138B	20c Great Seal Coil, 5/19/88, DC.......................................1.00		1.25
0139	(22c) Great Seal, 2/4/85, DC...1.00		1.25
0140	(25c) Great Seal Coil, 3/22/88, DC.....................................1.25		1.50
0141	25c Great Seal Coil, 6/11/88, Corpus Christi, TX 1.25		1.50

SCOTT NUMBER	DESCRIPTION	CACHETED SGL	BLK

1989

0143	1c Great Seal, typographed, 7/5/89, DC..............................1.00		1.10

1991

0144	(29c) Great Seal, non-denominated, 1/22/91, DC..............1.25		1.50
0145	29c Great Seal, 5/24/91, Seattle, WA..................................1.25		1.50
0146	4c Great Seal, 4/6/91, Oklahoma City, OK 1.25		1.50
0147	19c Great Seal, 5/24/91, Seattle, WA..................................1.25		1.50
0148	23c Great Seal, 5/24/91, Seattle, WA..................................1.25		1.50

POSTAGE DUE
1925

		SINGLE
J68	1/2c Dull Red, 4/15/25, earliest known use	—

1959

J88	1/2c Red and Black, 6/19/59	70.00
J89	1c Red and Black, 6/19/59	70.00
J90	2c Red and Black, 6/19/59	70.00
J91	3c Red and Black, 6/19/59	70.00
J92	4c Red and Black, 6/19/59	70.00
J93	5c Red and Black, 6/19/59	100.00
J94	6c Red and Black, 6/19/59	100.00
J95	7c Red and Black, 6/19/59	100.00
J96	8c Red and Black, 6/19/59	100.00
J97	10c Red and Black, 6/19/59	100.00
J98	30c Red and Black, 6/19/59	100.00
J99	50c Red and Black, 6/19/59	100.00
J100	$1 Red and Black, 6/19/59	100.00
J101	$5 Red and Black, 6/19/59	150.00

1978-85

J102	11c Red and Black, 1/2/78...	5.00

☐☐ J103	13c Red and Black, 1/2/78...	5.00
☐☐ J104	17c Red and Black, 6/10/85...	5.00

POSTAL NOTES

☐☐ PN1	1c Black, 2/1/45, on complete 3 part money order form..........	40.00
☐☐ PN1-PN18	1c to 90c Black, 2/1/45 on 18 money order forms	450.00
	Last day covers of this service also exist, dated 3/31/51.	
	These sell for $15-$20.	

POSTAL SAVINGS
1941

☐☐ PS11	10c Red, 5/1/41, any city...	175.00

REVENUES

These examples of Revenue FD's are postmarked with fiscal
rather than postal cancellations.

1898

☐☐ R154	1c Green, Franklin, 7/1/98...	—
☐☐ R155	2c Washington, 7/1/98	—
☐☐ R166	4c Rose Battleship, 7/1/98...	—

HUNTING PERMIT STAMPS

The following are not postage stamp items. They are listed here
only for collectors' interest.

☐☐ RW3	$1 Canada Geese, 7/1/36, Warren, NJ.......................................	700.00
☐☐ RW43	$5 Canada Geese, 7/1/76, any city.......................................	100.00
☐☐ RW46	$7.50 Green-winged Teal, 7/1/79, any city	100.00
☐☐ RW47	$7.50 Mallards, 7/1/80, any city	100.00
☐☐ RW48	$7.50 Ruddy Ducks, 7/1/81, any city	75.00
☐☐ RW49	$7.50 Canvas Backs, 7/1/82, any city	55.00
☐☐ RW50	$7.50 Pintail, 7/1/83, any city..	50.00
☐☐ RW51	$7.50 Wigeons, 7/1/84, any city...	50.00
☐☐ RW52	$7.50 Cinnamon Teal, 7/1/85, any city	45.00
☐☐ RW53	$7.50 Fulvous Whistling Duck, 7/1/86, any city.......................	35.00
☐☐ RW54	$10 Redheads, 7/1/87, any city..	35.00
☐☐ RW55	$10 Snow Goose, 7/1/88, any city...	30.00
☐☐ RW56	$12.50 Lesser Scaup, 6/30/89, any city...................................	30.00
☐☐ RW57	$12.50 Black Bellied Whistling Duck, 6/30/90, any city..........	—

**Cachet values in this catalogue are for an average cacheted
First Day Cover. Some FDC's, depending on the cachet, can sell
for many times the catalogue value, while others sell for less.
The Cachet Calculator lists cachetmakers, the dates
they produced FDC's and a market value multiplier.
The Calculator begins on page 40A.**

ENVELOPES

Sizes of U.S. Envelope FD's are as follows: Size 5 — 89x160mm,
Size 6 3/4 - 92x165mm, Size 7 - 98x225mm, Size 7 1/2 —
99x190mm, Sizes 8 and 10 — 105x240mm, Size 13 — 95x171mm.
Where a paper difference is shown, the watermark of "Standard
Quality" is similar to Watermark 28 and "Extra Quality" is similar
to Watermark 29.

    Note that all cachets on postal stationery are add-ons until a
grace period for cancels was allowed beginning in 1982.

U481, U436-9,   U522   U523-28   U532-4,
U529-31   U536, U544

U541-2   U543   U546

1861

☐☐ U35   **3c George Washington**, pink, 8/10/1861,
             earliest known use ....—

1876

☐☐ U221 **3c Centennial**, green, 5/10/1876, earliest known use,
             Centennial cancel, size 3, wmk 3 ....3500.

1883

☐☐ U227 **2c George Washington**, 10/2/1883, size 5, wmk 6,
             earliest known use 350.00

1886

☐☐ U293 **2c U.S. Grant**, letter sheet, 8/18/1886,
             earliest known use ....—

1916-32

☐☐ U436a **3c George Washington**, white paper, extra quality,
             6/16/32, DC, size 5, die 1, wmk 29 ....75.00   —
☐☐   size 8, die 1, wmk 29 ....18.00   —
☐☐ U436e **3c George Washington**, white paper, extra quality,
             6/16/32, DC, size 5, die 7, wmk 29 ....12.00   15.00
☐☐   size 13, die 7, wmk 29 ....75.00   —

□□ U436f	3c George Washington, white paper, extra quality, 6/16/32, DC, size 5, die 9, wmk 29 ....12.00	50.00
□□	size 13, die9, wmk 29 ....18.00	—
□□ U437a	3c George Washington, amber paper, 7/13/32, DC, size 5, wmk 28, standard quality 50.00	—
□□	7/19/32, DC, size 5, wmk 29, extra quality 35.00	—
□□ U439	3c George Washington, blue paper, 7/13/32, DC, size 5, wmk 28, standard quality 40.00	—
□□	size 13, wmk 28, standard quality 65.00	—
□□	9/9/32, DC, size 8, wmk 28, standard quality 85.00	—
□□ U439a	3c George Washington, blue paper, 7/19/32, DC, extra quality, size 5, wmk 29 ....40.00	

1921

□□ U446	2c on 3c George Washington, 5/21/21, earliest known use ....—	

1925

□□ U481	1 1/2c George Washington, 3/19/25, DC, size 5, wmk 27 ....35.00	
□□	size 8, wmk 27 ....70.00	—
□□	size 13, wmk 26 ....50.00	—
□□	size 5, wmk 27 with Scott 553, 582 & 598 ....150.00	
□□	size 8, wmk 27 with Scott 553, 582 & 598 ....125.00	
□□	size 13, wmk 26 with Scott 553 ....60.00	—
□□ U495	1 1/2c on 1c Benjamin Franklin, 6/1/25, DC size 5 ....50.00	—
□□	6/3/25, DC, size 8 ....65.00	—
□□	6/2/25, DC, size 13 ....60.00	—
□□ U515	1 1/2c on lc Benjamin Franklin, 8/1/25, Des Moines, IA, size 5, die 1 ....50.00	
□□ U521	1 1/2c on 1c Benjamin Franklin, 10/22/25, DC, size 5, die 1, wmk 25 ....100.00	—

1926

□□ U522a	2c Liberty Bell, 7/27/26, Philadelphia, PA, size 5, wmk 27 ....20.00	30.00
□□	7/27/26, DC, size 5, wmk 27 ....22.50	32.50
□□	7/27/26, unofficial city, size 5, wmk 27 ....35.00	45.00

1932

□□ U523	1c Mount Vernon, 1/1/32, DC, size 5, wmk 29 ....10.00	16.00
□□	size 8, wmk 29 ....12.50	18.50
□□	size 13, wmk 29 ....10.00	16.00
□□ U524	1 1/2c Mount Vernon, 1/1/32, DC, size 5,wmk 29 ....10.00	16.00
□□	size 8, wmk 29 ....12.50	18.50
□□	size 13, wmk 29 ....10.00	16.00
□□ U525	2c Mount Vernon, 1/1/32, DC, size 5, wmk 29 ....8.00	15.00
□□	size 8, wmk 29 ....10.00	15.00
□□	size 13, wmk 29 ....8.00	15.00
□□ U526	3c Mount Vernon, 6/16/32, DC, size 5, wmk 29 ....18.00	20.00
□□	size 8, wmk 29 ....25.00	40.00
□□	size 13, wmk 29 ....20.00	30.00
□□ U527	4c Mount Vernon, 1/1/32, DC, size 8, wmk 29 ....30.00	40.00

			UNCACHETED	CACHETED
☐☐	U528	5c Mount Vernon, 1/1/32, DC, size 5, wmk 29 ....18.00		20.00
☐☐		size 8, wmk 29...20.00		22.00
☐☐	U529	6c George Washington, white paper, 8/18/32, Los		
		Angeles, CA, size 8, wmk 29 ....15.00		—
☐☐		8/19/32, DC, size 7, wmk 29 ....20.00		—
☐☐		8/19/32, DC, size 9, wmk 29 ....20.00		—
☐☐	U530	6c George Washington, amber paper, 8/18/32, Los		
		Angeles, CA, size 8, wmk 29 ....15.00		—
☐☐		8/19/32, DC, size 7, wmk 29 ....20.00		—
☐☐		8/19/32, DC, size 9, wmk 29 ....20.00		—
☐☐		size 8, wmk 29, with Scott 723 pair.............................25.00		—
☐☐	U531	6c George Washington, blue paper, 8/18/32, DC, size 8,		
		wmk 29...15.00		—
☐☐		8/19/32, DC. size 7, wmk 29 ....20.00		—
☐☐		8/19/32. DC. size 9, wmk 29 ....20.00		—

1950

			UNCACHETED	CACHETED
☐☐	U532	1c Benjamin Franklin, 11/16/50, New York, NY, size 13, wmk 42..1.50		2.50
☐☐	U533a	2c George Washington, 11/17/50, New York, NY, size 13, wmk 42..1.65		2.50
☐☐	U534a	3c George Washington, die 1, 11/18/50, New York, NY, size 13, wmk 42 ....1.50		2.50
☐☐	U534b	3c George Washington, die 2, 11/19/50, New York, NY, size 8, wmk 42 ....5.00		8.00

1952

☐☐	U535	1 1/2c George Washington, 10/21/52, Dover or Kenvil, NJ, size 13, wmk 42, earliest known use..............................—		—

1958

☐☐	U536	4c Benjamin Franklin, 7/31/58, Montpelier, VT (163,746), size 6 3/4, wmk 46...................................1.00		1.50
☐☐		size 8, wmk 46 (not a slogan cancel) 60.00		—
☐☐		size 13, wmk 46 (not a slogan cancel) 60.00		—
☐☐		7/31/58, Wheeling, WV, size 6 3/4, wmk 46 with Scott 1036a...35.00		—
☐☐		size 13, window (not a slogan cancel)...........................25.00		—
☐☐	U540	3c + 1c George Washington (U534c), 7/22/58, Kenvil, NJ, size 8, wmk 46, die 3, earliest known use..............50.00		—

1960

☐☐	U541	1 1/4c Benjamin Franklin, 6/25/60, Birmingham, AL (211,500), size 6 3/4, wmk 46...1.00		1.25
☐☐	U542	2 1/2c George Washington, 5/28/60, Chicago, IL (196,977), size 6 3/4, wmk 46...1.00		1.25
☐☐	U543	4c Pony Express Rider, 7/19/60, St. Joseph, MO (407,160), size 6 3/4, wmk 46...1.00		1.25
☐☐		7/19/60, Sacramento, CA, with Scott 1154, size 6 3/4, wmk 46..3.50		5.00

Values for various cachet makers can be determined by using the Cachet Calculator which begins on page 40A.

U547, U548,
U548A, U556

U549, U552

U550, U553

U551, U561

U554

U555, U562

U557

U563

U564

U565

U567

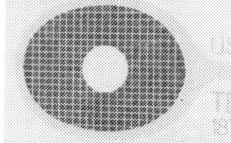

U569

U568

U571-75

U576

U581

U584

198

1962

☐☐ **U544** **5c Abraham Lincoln**, 11/19/62, Springfield, IL
(163,258), size 6 3/4, wmk 48 ....1.00   1.25

☐☐ **U546** **5c New York World's Fair**, 4/22/64, World's Fair, NY
(466,422), size 6 3/4, wmk 48 ....1.00   1.25

1965-69

☐☐ **U547** **1 1/4c Liberty Bell**, 1/6/65, DC, size 6 3/4, wmk 49 ....1.00   1.00
☐☐   1/8/65, DC, size 10, wmk 48 (not a slogan cancel)...........9.00   15.00
☐☐ **U548** **1 4/10c Liberty Bell**, 3/26/68, Springfield, MA
(134,832), size 6 3/4, wmk 49 ....1.00   1.00
☐☐   3/27/68, DC, size 10, wmk 48 (not a slogan cancel).........5.00   8.00
☐☐ **U548A** **1 6/10c Liberty Bell**, 6/16/69, DC, size 6 3/4, wmk 47 ......1.00   1.00
☐☐   size 10, wmk 49 (not a slogan cancel) 1.25   1.75
☐☐ **U549** **4c Old Ironsides**, 1/6/65, DC, size 6 3/4, wmk 49 ....1.00   1.00
☐☐   1/8/65, DC, size 6 3/4, window, wmk 49.........................9.00   15.00
☐☐   size 10, wmk 49 (not a slogan cancel) 9.00   15.00
☐☐   size 10, window, wmk 49 (not a slogan cancel) 9.00   15.00
      Total for Scott U547 and U549 is 451,960.

☐☐ **U550** **5c Eagle**, 1/5/65, Williamsburg, PA (246,496), size 6 3/4,
wmk 49...1.00   1.00
☐☐   1/8/65, DC, size 6 3/4, window, wmk 49.........................9.00   15.00
☐☐   size 10, wmk 49 (not a slogan cancel) 9.00   15.00
☐☐   size 10, window, wmk 49 (not a slogan cancel) 9.00   15.00
☐☐ **U550a** **Eagle**, tagged, 8/15/67, DC & Dayton, OH, size 6 3/4,
wmk 50...3.50   5.00
☐☐   size 6 3/4, window, wmk 48 ....3.50   5.00
☐☐   size 10, wmk 48 (not a slogan cancel) 3.50   5.00
☐☐   size 10, wmk 49, Dayton only (not a slogan cancel) 4.50   7.50
☐☐   size 10, window, wmk 49 (not a slogan cancel) 3.50   5.00
☐☐ **U551** **6c Statue of Liberty**, 1/4/68, New York, NY (184,784),
size 6 3/4, wmk 47 or 48 ....1.00   1.25
☐☐   1/5/68, DC, size 6 3/4, window, wmk 48 or 49 ....2.50   3.00
☐☐   size 10, wmk 47 (not a slogan cancel) 2.50   3.00
☐☐   size 10, window, wmk 49 ....2.50   3.00
☐☐   11/15/68, DC, new shiny plastic window, size 6 3/4,
window, wmk 48 (not a slogan cancel) 3.00   5.00

1968

☐☐ **U552** **4c + 2c Old Ironsides**, 2/5/68, DC, size 6 3/4, wmk 50.......5.00   7.50
☐☐   size 6 3/4, window, wmk 48 ....5.00   7.50
☐☐   size 10, wmk 47...5.00   7.50
☐☐   size 10, window, wmk 49 ....5.00   7.50
☐☐ **U553** **5c + 1c Eagle**, 2/5/68, DC, size 6 3/4, wmk 49....................5.00   7.50
☐☐   size 10, window, wmk 49 ....5.00   7.50
☐☐ **U553a** **Eagle**, tagged, 2/5/68, DC, size 6 3/4, wmk 48...................5.00   7.50
☐☐   size 10, wmk 47 or 49...5.00   7.50
☐☐   size 10, window, wmk 49 ....5.00   7.50

1970

☐☐ **U554** **6c Moby Dick**, 3/7/70, New Bedford, MA (433,777)
size 6 3/4, wmk 47 ....1.00   1.25

1971

☐☐ U555 **6c Youth Conference**, 2/24/71, DC, (264,559), size 6 3/4,
           wmk 49 ....1.00   1.00
☐☐ U556 **1 7/10c Liberty Bell**, 5/10/71, Baltimore, MD (150,767),
           size 6 3/4, wmk 48A 1.00   1.00
☐☐   5/10/71, DC, size, 6 3/4, wmk 49 with Scott 1394 ....9.00   15.00
☐☐   5/10/71, Phoenix, AZ, size 6 3/4, wmk 48A, with Scott
           E23 ....18.00   30.00
☐☐   5/10/71, DC, size 6 3/4, combo with Scott 1283 ....2.00   3.00
☐☐   5/11/71, DC, size10, wmk 47 or 49 ....7.50   12.00
☐☐   5/11/71, DC, size 10, wmk 48A 3.50   6.00
☐☐ U557 **8c Eagle**, 5/6/71, Williamsburg, PA (193,000), size 6 3/4,
           wink 48A 1.00   1.00
☐☐   size 6 3/4, wmk 49 ....—   2.50
☐☐   size 10, wmk 49 ....2.00   3.50
☐☐   size 10, window, wmk 47 ....2.00   3.50
           Some size 10, wmk 47 were canceled without any
           authority at Williamsburg, PA, on 5/6/71.
☐☐ U561 **6c + (2c) Statue of Liberty**, 5/16/71, DC, size 6 3/4,
           wmk 47 ....2.00   4.00
☐☐   size 6 3/4, wmk 48A, (25 known) 15.00   25.00
☐☐   size 6 3/4, wmk 49 ....2.50   4.00
☐☐   size 6 3/4, window, wmk 47 ....2.00   3.00
☐☐   size 10, wmk 48A 2.00   3.00
☐☐   size 10, wmk 49 ....3.50   6.00
☐☐   size 10, window, wmk 47 ....2.00   3.00
☐☐   size 10, window, wmk 49 ....3.00   5.00
☐☐ U562 **6c + (2c) Youth Conference**, 5/16/71, DC, size 6 3/4,
           wmk 47 ....20.00   30.00
☐☐   size 6 3/4, wmk 49 ....2.50   5.00
☐☐ U563 **8c Bowling**, 8/21/71, Milwaukee, WI (281,342),
           size 6 3/4, wmk 49 ....1.00   1.25
☐☐   size 10, wmk 49 ....1.00   2.00
☐☐ U564 **8c Aging Conference**, 11 / 15/71, DC (125,000),
           size 6 3/4, wmk 48A 1.00   1.00

1972

☐☐ U565 **8c International Transportation Exposition**, 5/2/72, DC,
           size 6 3/4, wmk 47 ....2.50   3.00
☐☐   size 6 3/4, wmk 49 ....1.00   1.00

1973

☐☐ U566 **8c + 2c Eagle**, 12/1/73, DC, size 6 3/4, wmk 47 or 49 ......1.50   2.50
☐☐   size 6 3/4, window, wmk 48A ....7.50   —
☐☐   size 6 3/4, window, wmk 49 ....3.00   4.50
☐☐   size 10, wmk 47 ....3.00   4.50
☐☐   size 10, window, wmk 47 ....3.00   4.50
☐☐ U567 **10c Liberty Bell**, 12/5/73, Philadelphia, PA (147,141),
☐☐   size 6 3/4, wmk 47, old knife depth 58mm 1.00   1.00
☐☐   size 6 3/4, wmk 47, new knife depth 51mm 1.00   1.50
☐☐   size 10, wmk 47 ....1.00   1.50
☐☐   size 10, window, wmk 47 ....1.00   1.50

1974

☐☐ U568 1 8/10c **Volunteer Yourself**, 8/23/74, Cincinnati, OH,

size 6 3/4, wmk 47 ....1.00	1.00
☐☐ | size 10, wmk 47 ....1.00 | 1.50 |

☐☐ U569 10c **Tennis Centenary**, 8/31/74, Forest Hills, NY

(245,000), size 6 3/4, wmk 49 ....1.00	1.25
☐☐ | size 10, wmk 49 ....1.00 | 3.00 |
☐☐ | 9/3/74, DC, size 6 3/4, window, wmk 49...........................2.50 | 4.00 |
☐☐ | size 10, window, wmk 49 ....2.50 | 4.00 |

Note: Window envelopes were sold and canceled on the first day, contrary to regulations.

1975-76 Bicentennial Era

☐☐ U571 10c **Seafaring Tradition**, 10/13/75, Minneapolis, MN

(255,304), size 6 3/4 ....1.00	1.00
☐☐ | size 10 ....1.00 | 1.25 |

☐☐ U572 13c **American Homemaker**, 2/2/76, Biloxi, MS

(196,647), size 6 3/4 ....1.00	1.00
☐☐ | size 10 ....1.00 | 1.25 |

☐☐ U573 13c **American Farmer**, 3/15/76, New Orleans, LA

(214,563), size 6 3/4 ....1.00	1.00
☐☐ | size 10 ....1.00 | 1.25 |

☐☐ U574 13c **American Doctor**, 6/30/76, Dallas, TX, size 6 3/4 ....1.00 | 1.00

☐☐ | size 10 ....1.00 | 1.25

☐☐ U575 13c **American Craftsman**, 8/6/76, Hancock, MA,

size 6 3/4 ....1.00	1.00
☐☐ | size 10 ....1.00 | 1.25 |

1975

☐☐ U576 13c **Liberty Tree**, 11/8/75, Memphis, TN (226,824)

size 6 3/4, wmk 48A..1.00	1.00
☐☐ | size 10, wmk 47...1.00 | 1.25 |

1976-78

☐☐ U577 2c **Star and Pinwheel**, 9/10/76, Hempstead, NY

(81,388), size 6 3/4, wmk 48A or 49 ....1.00	1.00
☐☐ | size 10, wmk 48A..1.00 | 1.25 |

☐☐ U578 2.1c **(Non-Profit)**, 6/3/77, Houston, TX (120,280)

size 6 3/4, wmk 47 ....1.00	1.00
☐☐ | size 10, wmk 47...1.00 | 1.25 |

☐☐ U579 2.7c **(Non-Profit)**, 7/5/78, Raleigh, NC (92,687),

size 6 3/4, wmk 47 ....1.00	1.00
☐☐ | size 10, wmk 47...1.00 | 1.25 |

☐☐ U580 (15c) **"A" & Eagle**, 5/22/78, Memphis, TN, size 6 3/4

wmk 47 ....1.00	1.50
☐☐ | size 6 3/4, wmk 48A..1.00 | 1.00 |
☐☐ | size 6 3/4, wmk 47 or 48A ....1.25 | 2.00 |
☐☐ | size 10, wmk 47 or 49 ....1.00 | 1.25 |
☐☐ | size 10, window, wmk 47 or 49.......................1.25 | 2.00 |
☐☐ | size 6 3/4, wmk 48A with sheet, coil & booklet pane ......5.00 | 10.00 |

U587

U590

U593

U595

U598

U602

U606

U607

U608

U609

202

☐☐ U581 **15c Uncle Sam**, 6/3/78, Williamsburg, PA (176,000),

size 6 3/4, wmk 47 or 49..1.00	1.00
size 6 3/4, window, wmk 47 ....1.25	2.00
size 10, wmk 47 or 48A..1.00	1.25
size 10, window, wmk 48A or 49 ....1.25	2.00
12/2/80, eku with luminescent bar, size 10, window,	
wmk 47 or 49...—	—

1976

☐☐ U582 **13c Bicentennial**, 10/15/76, Los Angeles, CA (277,222),

size 6 3/4, wmk 48A...2.00	3.00
size 6 3/4, wmk 49 ....1.00	1.00
size 6 3/4, wmk 49, dark green ....—	7.50
size 10, wmk 49..1.00	1.25

1977

☐☐ U583 **13c Golf**, 4/7/77, Augusta, GA (252,000), size 6 3/4,

wmk 49 ....1.00	7.00
size 10, wmk 49..1.00	7.00
4/8/77, DC, size 6 3/4, window, wmk 49...................2.00	7.50
size 10, window, wmk 49...2.00	7.50

☐☐ U584 **13c Energy Conservation**, 10/20/77, Ridley Park, PA, San Francisco,

size 6 3/4, wmk 49 ....1.00	1.00
size 6 3/4, window, wmk 49 ....1.50	2.50
size 10, wmk 49..1.00	1.25.
size 10, window, wmk 49...1.50	2.50
10/20/77, DC, with Scott 1723-1724, all sizes.................3.50	4.00

☐☐ U585 **13c Energy Development**, 10/20/77, Ridley Park, PA, San Francisco,

size 6 3/4, wmk 49 ....1.00	1.00
size 6 3/4, window, wmk 49 ....1.50	2.50
size 10, wmk 49..1.00	1.25
size 10, window, wmk 49...1.50	2.50
10/20/77, DC, with Scott 1723-1724, all sizes.................3.50	4.00
Total for Scott U584 and U585 is 353,515.	

1978

☐☐ U586 **15c on 16c USA**, 7/28/78, Williamsburg, PA, (193, 153),

size 6 3/4, wmk 47 ....1.00	1.00
size 10, wmk 47..1.00	1.25

☐☐ U587 **15c Auto Racing**, 9/2/78, Ontario, CA (209,147),

size 6 3/4, wmk 49 ....1.00	1.00
size 10, wmk 49..1.00	1.25

☐☐ U588 **15c on 13c Liberty Tree**, 11/22/78, Williamsburg, PA

(137,500), size 6 3/4, wmk 47 ....1.00	1.00
size 10, wmk 47..1.00	1.25
size 6 3/4, window, wmk 47 ....1.25	2.00
size 10, window, wmk 48A..1.25	2.00

1979-82

☐☐ U589 **3.1c (Non-Profit)**, 5/18/79, Denver, CO (117,575)

size 6 3/4, wmk 48A...1.00	1.00
size 6 3/4, window, wmk 48 ....1.25	2.00
size 10, wmk 49..1.00	1.25
size 10, window, wmk 49...1.25	2.00

		UNCACHETED	CACHETED
☐☐ U590	3.5c (Non-Profit), 6/23/80, Williamsburg, PA, size 6 3/4, wmk 49	1.00	1.00
☐☐	size 10, wmk 48A or 49	1.00	1.25
	Note: Window envelopes were sold and canceled on the First Day, contrary to regulations.		
☐☐ U591	5.9c (Non-Profit), 2/17/82, Wheeling, WV, size 6 3/4, wmk 47, 48A or 49	1.00	1.25
☐☐	size 6 3/4, window, wmk 47	1.25	2.00
☐☐	size 10, wmk 47, 48A or 49	1.00	1.50
☐☐ U592	(18c) "B" & Eagle, 3/15/81, Memphis, TN (179,171), size 6 3/4, wmk 47, 48A, or 49	1.00	1.00
☐☐	size 6 3/4, window, wmk 47, 48A, or 49	1.25	2.00
☐☐	size 10, wmk 47, 48A or 49	1.00	1.25
☐☐	size 10, window, wmk 47 or 49	1.25	2.00
☐☐	3/15/81, San Francisco, CA, With Scott 1818-1820 on any of the above	1.50	2.00
☐☐ U593	18c Star, 4/2/81, Star City, IN (160,439), size 6 3/4, wmk 47 or 49	1.00	1.00
☐☐	size 10, wmk 47, 48A or 49	1.00	1.25
☐☐ U594	(20c) "C" & Eagle, 10/11/81, Memphis, TN (304,404), size 6 3/4, wmk 47 or 49	1.00	1.25
☐☐	size 10, wmk 47, 48A or 49	1.00	1.50
	Note: Window envelopes were sold and canceled with the "FDOI" cancel contrary to announced policy.		

1979

		UNCACHETED	CACHETED
☐☐ U595	15c Veterinary Medicine, 7/24/79, Seattle, WA (209,658), size 6 3/4, wmk 49	1.00	1.00
☐☐	size 10, wmk 49	1.00	1.25
☐☐ U596	15c Olympic Games, 12/10/79, E. Rutherford, NJ (179,336), size 6 3/4, wmk 49	1.00	1.25
☐☐	size 10, wmk 49	1.00	1.50

1980

		UNCACHETED	CACHETED
☐☐ U597	15c Bicycling, 5/16/80, Baltimore, MD (173,978) size 6 3/4, wmk 49	1.00	1.25
☐☐	size 10, wmk 49	1.00	1.50
☐☐ U598	15c America's Cup Yacht Races, 9/15/80, Newport, RI, (192,220), size 6 3/4, wmk 49	1.00	1.25
☐☐	size 10, wmk 49	1.00	1.50
☐☐ U599	15c Honey Bee, 10/10/80, Paris, IL, (202,050) size 6 3/4, wmk 49	1.00	1.00
☐☐	size 10, wmk 49	1.00	1.25

1981-82

		UNCACHETED	CACHETED
☐☐ U600	18c Remember the Blinded Veteran, 8/13/81, Arlington, VA (175,966), size 6 3/4, wmk 49	1.00	1.00
☐☐	size 10, wmk 49	1.00	1.25
☐☐ U601	20c Capitol Dome, 11 / 13/81, Los Angeles, CA, size 6 3/4, wmk 48A or 49 and window	1.00	1.25
☐☐	size 10, wmk 47 or 49	1.00	1.50
☐☐	1/26/82, with luminescent bar, size 10, wmk 47, earliest known use	—	—

1982

☐☐ U602 **20c Great Seal,** 6/15/82, DC, (163,905), size 6 3/4,
   wmk 49..1.00   1.25
☐☐   size 10, wmk 49..1.00   1.50
☐☐ U603 **20c Purple Heart,** 8/6/82, DC, (110,679), size 6 3/4,
   wmk 49..1.00   1.25
☐☐   size 10, wmk 49..1.00   1.50

1983

☐☐ U604 **5.2c (Non-Profit),** 3/21/83, Memphis, TN, size 6 3/4,
   wmk 47, 48A or 49..1.00   1.25
☐☐   size 6 3/4, window, wmk 49 ....1.00   1.50
☐☐   size 10, wmk47..1.00   1.50
☐☐   size 10, window, wmk 47 ....1.00   1.50
☐☐ U605 **20c Paralyzed Veterans,** 8/3/83, Portland, OR,
   size 6 3/4 ....1.00   1.25
☐☐   size 10 ....1.00   1.50

1984

☐☐ U606 **20c Small Business,** 5/7/84, DC, size 6 3/4........................1.00   1.25
☐☐   size 10 ....1.00   1.50

1985

☐☐ U607 **(22c) "D" & Eagle,** 2/1/85, DC, size 6 3/4, wmk 47,
   48A or 49..1.00   1.25
☐☐   size 6 3/4, window, wmk 47, 48A or 49 ....1.00   1.50
☐☐   size 10, wmk 47, 48A or 49 ....1.00   1.50
☐☐   size 10, window, wmk 47 ....1.00   1.50
☐☐ U608 **22c Bison,** 2/25/85, DC, size 6 3/4, wmk 47, 48A or 49......1.00   1.25
☐☐   size 6 3/4, window, wmk 47, 48A or 49 ....1.00   1.50
☐☐   size 10, wmk 47, 48A or 49 ....1.00   1.50
☐☐   size 10, window, wmk 48A or 49 ....1.00   1.50
☐☐ U609 **6e U.S.S. Constitution,** 5/3/85, DC, size 6 3/4, wmk 47,
   48A or 49..1.00   1.25
☐☐   size 10, wmk 47, 48A or 49 ....1.00   1.50

1986

☐☐ U610 **8.5c The Mayflower,** 12/4/86, Plymouth, MA (105,164),
   size 6 3/4 and window, wmk 48A, 49 or 50 ....1.00   1.25
☐☐   size 10, wmk 48A, 49 or 50 ....1.00   1.50

1988

☐☐ U611 **25c Stars,** 3/26/88, Star, MS, (29,393) size 6 3/4 ....1.25   1.25
☐☐   size 10 ....1.25   1.50
☐☐ U612 **8.4c Sea Gulls & U.S. Frigate Constellation,** 4/12/88,
   Baltimore, MD, size 6 3/4 (41,420)....................................1.00   1.00
☐☐   size 10 ....1.00   1.50
☐☐ U613 **25c Snowflake,** 9/8/88, Snowflake, AZ, wmk 50 ....1.25   1.25

1989

☐☐ U614 **25c Stars in "perforated" square,** 3/10/89 Cleveland,
   OH, size 9, wmk 50 ....1.25   1.25
☐☐ U615 **25c Stars in 'circle,** 7/10/89, DC, size 9, unwmk.................1.25   1.25

☐☐ U616	25c **Love**, 9/22/89, McLean, VA (69,498), size 9, unwmk ...1.25	1.25
☐☐ U617	25c **Space Station**, hologram, 12/3/89, DC,	
	size 9, unwmk...1.25	1.25

1990

☐☐ U618	25c **Football**, hologram, 9/9/90, Green Bay, WI	
	(54,589), size 10, unwmk 1.25	1.25

1991

☐☐ U619	29c **Star**, 1/24/91, DC, size 6 3/4 and window,	
	wmk 48A, 49 or 50...1.25	1.25
☐☐ U620	11.1c **Birds**, 5/3/91, Boxborough, MA, size 6 3/4	
	and window, wmk 48A, 49 or 50 .... 1.25	1.25
☐☐	size 10 and window, wmk 47, 48A or 49 ....1.25	1.25
☐☐ U621	29c **Love**, 5/9/91, Honolulu, HI, size 6 3/4, unwmk 1.25	1.25
☐☐	size 10, unwmk...1.25	1.25
☐☐ U622	29c **Magazine Industry**, 10/7/91, Naples, FL,	
	size 10, unwmk...1.25	1.25
☐☐ U623	29c **Star**, 7/20/91, DC, size 9, and window	
	(left or right), unwmk....................................... 1.25	1.25
☐☐ U624	29c **Geese**, 11/8/91, Virginia Beach, VA, size 6 3/4,	
	wmk 49 or 50.. 1.25	1.25
☐☐	1/21/92, size 10, wmk 49 or 50 ....1.25	1.25

1992

☐☐ U625	29c **Space Shuttle**, 1/21/92, Virginia Beach, VA,	
	size 10, unwmk 1.25	1.25
☐☐ U626	29c **Western Americana**, 4/10/92, Dodge City, KS,	
	size 10, unwmk 1.25	1.25
☐☐ U627	29c **Environment**, 4/22/92, Chicago, IL, size 10,	
	unwmk.. 1.25	1.25
☐☐ U628	19.9c **Bulk Rate Star**, 5/19/92, Las Vegas, NV,	
	size 10, unwmk 1.25	1.25
☐☐ U629	29c **Wheelchair**, 7/22/92, DC, size 6 3/4, unwmk.............. 1.25	1.25
☐☐	size 10, unwmk...1.25	1.25

1993

☐☐ U630	29c **Kitten**, 10/2/93, King of Prussia, PA, size 10,	
	unwmk.. 1.25	1.25

UC1-7

UC14, UC18, UC26

UC16

UC25

UC17

UC32

UC33-34

UC36

UC35

UC37

UC38-39

UC42

UC40-45

UC43

UC44-44a

208

AIR POST ENVELOPES & AIR LETTER SHEETS

1929

☐☐ UC1	5c Blue, 1/12/29, DC, size 13, wmk 28 ....40.00		100.00
☐☐	2/1/29, DC, size 5, wmk 28 ....45.00		—
☐☐	Size 8, wmk 28 ....65.00		—

1934

☐☐ UC3	6c Orange, 7/1/34, DC, size 8, wmk 33...........................25.00		—
☐☐	Size 13, wmk 33 ....14.00		—

1932

☐☐ UC7	8c Olive green, 9/26/32, DC, size 8, wmk 30a.................30.00		—
☐☐	Size 13, wmk 30a 11.00		—

1946

☐☐ UC10	5c on 6c Orange, 10/1/46, Aiea Heights, HI, size 13, die 2a, wmk 41..100.00		—
☐☐ UC11	5c on 6c Orange, 10/1/46, Aiea Heights, HI, size 13, die 2b...150.00		—
☐☐ UC12	5c on 6c Orange, 10/1/46, Aiea Heights, HI, APO & New York, NY, size 13, die 2c, wmk 41......................75.00		—
☐☐ UC13	5c on 6c Orange, 10/1/46, Aiea Heights, HI, size 13, die 3, wmk 41...75.00		—
☐☐ UC14	5c Skymaster, 9/25/46, DC, size 13, wmk 41 ....1.50		2.50

1947

☐☐ UC16	10c Skymaster Letter Sheet, 4/29/47, DC (162,802)........3.00		5.00
☐☐ UC17	5c Stamp Cent. - Type I, 5/21/47, New York, NY size 13, wmk 41..1.25		2.50
☐☐ UC17a	5c Stamp Cent. - Type II, 5/21/47, New York, NY size 13, wmk 41..1.25		2.50
	Total for Scott UC17 and UC17a is 306,660.		

1950

☐☐ UCI8	6c Skymaster, 9/22/50, Phila. PA (74,006), size 13, wmk 43..1.00		1.50

1952

☐☐ UC22	6c on 5c Carmine (UC15), die 2, 8/29/52, Norfolk, VA, size 13, wmk 41...20.00		30.00

1956

☐☐ UC25	6c FIPEX, 5/2/56, New York, NY (363,239), size 13, wmk 45, with short clouds 1.00		1.50
☐☐	Size 13, wmk 45, with long clouds...................................1.00		1.50

1958

☐☐ UC26	7c Skymaster, 7/31/58, Dayton, OH (143,428), size 6 3/4, wink 46, straight left wing............................1.00		1.00
☐☐	Size 6 3/4, wmk 46, crooked left wing 1.00		3.00
☐☐	Size 8, wmk 46 ....35.00		—

SCOTT NUMBER	DESCRIPTION	UNCACHETED	CACHETED
☐☐ UC32a	10c Jet Airliner letter sheet, Type I, 9/12/58, St. Louis, MO (92,400) 1.25		2.50
☐☐ UC33	7c Blue, 11/21/58, New York, NY (208,980), size 6 3/4, wmk 46 ....1.00		1.00

1960

| ☐☐ UC34 | 7c Jet, carmine, 8/18/60, Portland, OR (196,851), size 6 3/4, wmk 46 ....1.00 | | 1.00 |

1961

| ☐☐ UC35 | 11c Jet Airliner letter sheet, 6/16/61, Johnstown, PA (163,460) ....1.00 | | 1.75 |

1962

| ☐☐ UC36 | 8c Jet, 11/17/62, Chantilly, VA (194,810), size 6 3/4, wmk 47 (not a slogan cancel).....1.00 | | 1.00 |

1965-67

☐☐ UC37	8c Jet Triangle, 1/7/65, Chicago, IL (226, 178) size 6 3/4, wmk 49 ....1.00		1.00
	1/8/65, DC, size 10, wmk 49 ....9.00		15.00
☐☐ UC37a	Jet Triangle, tagged, 8/15/67, Dayton, OH & DC, size 6 3/4, wmk 48 ....3.50		6.00
☐☐	Size 10, wmk 49 (not a slogan cancel) 4.50		7.50

1965

| ☐☐ UC38 | 11c Kennedy letter sheet, 5/29/65, Boston, MA (337,422) ....1.00 | | 1.75 |

1967

☐☐ UC39	13c Kennedy letter sheet, 5/29/67, Chicago, IL (211,387) 1.00		1.75
☐☐	5/29/67, Boston, MA 5.00		7.50
☐☐	5/29/67, Brookline, MA......................5.00		7.50

1968

☐☐ UC40	10c Jet Triangle, 1/8/68, Chicago, IL (157,553), size 6 3/4, wmk 48 (not a slogan cancel) 1.00		1.00
☐☐	1/9/68, DC, size 10, wmk 49 ....4.50		7.50
☐☐ UC41	8c + 2c Jet Triangle, 2/5/68, DC, size 6 3/4, wmk 49.....5.00		10.00
	size 10, wmk 49 ....5.00		10.00
☐☐ UC42	13c Human Rights letter sheet, 12/3/68, DC (145,898)...1.25		2.50

1971

☐☐ UC43	11c Jet, 5/6/71, Williamsburg, PA (187,000), size 6 3/4, wmk 49..............................1.00		1.00
☐☐	Size 10, wmk 49 (not a slogan cancel) 3.50		6.00
☐☐ UC44	15c Birds letter sheet, 5/28/71, Chicago, IL (130,669).....1.00		1.25
☐☐ UC44a	15c Birds letter sheet, "Aerogramme" added, Philadelphia, PA 1.00		1.25
☐☐ UC45	10c + 1c Jet Triangle, 6/28/71, DC, size 6 3/4 wmk 47, 48A, or 49................................5.00		10.00
☐☐	Size 10, wmk 49 ....5.00		10.00

postage 15c

UC46

13c USAirmail

UC47

18 CENTS

UC48

postage 18c

UC49

USA/22c

UC50

UC52

30c

UC53-54

USA 36

UC58

USA 36

UC59

SCOTT NUMBER	DESCRIPTION	UNCACHETED	CACHETED

1973

☐☐ UC46	15c **Ballooning letter sheet**, 2/10/73, Albuquerque, NM (210,000).................................1.00		1.25
☐☐ UC47	13c **Bird in Flight**, 12/1/73, Memphis, TN (132,658) size 6 3/4, wmk 47 ....1.00		1.00
☐☐	12/28/73, size 10, earliest known use 3.00		

1974

| ☐☐ UC48 | 18c **"USA" letter sheet**, 1/4/74, Atlanta, GA (119,615)....1.00 | | 1.25 |
| ☐☐ UC49 | 18c **NATO letter sheet**, 4/4/74, DC ....1.00 | | 1.25 |

1976

| ☐☐ UC50 | 22c **"USA" letter sheet**, 1/16/76, Tempe, AZ (118,303) ..1.00 | | 1.25 |

1978

| ☐☐ UC51 | 22c **"USA" letter sheet**, 11/3/78, St. Petersburg, FL (86,099) ....1.00 | | 1.25 |

1979

| ☐☐ UC52 | 22c **Olympics letter sheet**, 12/5/79, Bay Shore, NY (129,221) ....1.00 | | 1.50 |

1980

| ☐☐ UC53 | 30c **"USA" letter sheet**, 12/29/80, San Francisco, CA......1.25 | | 1.50 |

1981

| ☐☐ UC54 | 30c **"USA" letter sheet**, 9/21/81, Honolulu, HI.................1.25 | | 1.50 |

1982

| ☐☐ UC55 | 30c **"USA" & Globe letter sheet**, 9/16/82, Seattle, WA ....1.25 | | 1.50 |

1983

| ☐☐ UC56 | 30c **World Communications letter sheet**, 1/7/83, Anaheim, CA..1.25 | | 1.50 |

1985

☐☐ UC57	30c **Olympics letter sheet**, 10/14/85, Los Angeles, CA.....1.25		1.50
☐☐ UC58	36c **Landsat letter sheet**, 2/14/85, Goddard Flight Center, MD..1.25		1.50
☐☐ UC59	36c **Urban Skyline letter sheet**, 5/21/85, DC 1.25		1.50
☐☐ UC60	36c **Comet Tail letter sheet**, 12/4/85, Hannibal, MO........1.25		1.50

1988

| ☐☐ UC61 | 39c **Envelope letter sheet**, 5/9/88, Miami, FL (27,446)....1.25 | | 1.50 |

1989

| ☐☐ UC62 | 39c **Montgomery Blair letter sheet**, 11/20/89, DC...........1.25 | | 1.50 |

1991

| ☐☐ UC63 | 45c **Eagle letter sheet**, 5/17/91, Denver, CO, blue or white paper ....1.35 | | 2.00 |

OFFICIAL MAIL
1983

☐☐	U073 20c Eagle, 1/12/83, DC, size 10, wmk 47 ....1.25		2.00
☐☐	Size 10, window, wmk 47 ....1.75		3.00

1985

☐☐	U074 22c Eagle, 2/26/85, DC, size 10, wmk 47, 48A or 49 ....1.00		1.50
☐☐	Size 10, window, wmk 47, 48A or 49 ....1.25		2.00

1987

☐☐	U075 22c Eagle, 3/2/87, DC, savings bond size 2.00		3.00
☐☐	Window 2.50		4.00

1988

☐☐	U076 (25c)"E" Eagle, 3/22/88, DC, size 10 ....1.25		1.50
☐☐	Window 1.25		2.00
☐☐	U077 25c Eagle, 4/11/88, DC, size 10, wmk 48A, 49 or 50 ....1.25		1.50
☐☐	Window, wmk 48A, 49 or 50 ....1.25		2.00
☐☐	U078 25c Eagle, 4/11/88, DC (12,017), savings bond size 1.25		1.50
☐☐	Window 1.25		2.00
	Total for Scott U077 and U078 was 12,017.		

1990

☐☐	U079 45c Eagle, 3/17/90, Springfield, VA (5,956), passport size 1.50		2.00
☐☐	U080 65c Eagle, 3/17/90, Springfield, VA (6,922), passport size 1.75		2.25
☐☐	U081 45c Eagle, self-sealing, 8/10/90, DC (7,160), passport size 1.50		2.00
☐☐	U082 65c Eagle, self-sealing, 8/10/90, DC (6,759), passport size 1.75		2.25

1991

☐☐	U083 (29c) Eagle, non-denominated, 1/22/91, savings bond size 1.25		1.50
☐☐	U084 29c Eagle, 4/6/91, size 10, wmk 48A, 49 or 50 ....1.25		1.50
☐☐	Size 10, window, wmk 48A, 49, or 50 ....1.25		1.50
☐☐	U085 29c Eagle, 4/17/91, savings bond size, wmk 51 ....1.25		1.50

1992

☐☐	U086 52c Consular Service, 7/10/92, passport size, logo on back at left, unwmk 1.25		1.50
☐☐	3/2/94, passport size, logo on back at right, unwmk 1.25		1.50
☐☐	U087 75c Consular Service, 7/10/92, passport size, logo on back at left, unwmk 1.25		1.50
☐☐	3/2/94, passport size, logo on back at right, unwmk 1.25		1.50

Values for various cachet makers can be determined by using the Cachet Calculator which begins on page 40A.

UX1, UX3,
UX65

UX21

UX37

UX38

UX43

UX44

UX45, UY16

UX46, UY17

UX48

UX49, UX54,
UY19, UY20

UX50

UX51

UX52

UX53

UX56

UX58, UY22

UX62

UX63

UX67

HOW TO USE THIS BOOK
The number in the first column is its Scott number or
identifying number. Following that is the denomination
of the stamp, description, date of issue, and the value.

POSTAL CARDS
1873

☐☐ UX1   1c Liberty, 5/13/1873, Boston, New York or DC ....2250.   —

1875

☐☐ UX5   1c Liberty, unwmk, 9/30/1875 ....1200.   —
1910

☐☐ UX21   1c William McKinley, 2/13/10, any city ....125.00   —

1926

☐☐ UX37   3c William McKinley, 2/1/26, DC ....250.00   —

1951

☐☐ UX38   2c Benjamin Franklin, 11/16/51, New York, NY
     (170,000) 1.25   2.50

1952

☐☐ UX39   2c on 1c Thomas Jefferson (UX27), 1/1/52, DC 12.50   25.00
☐☐ UX40   2c on 1c Abraham Lincoln, (UX28), 3/22/52, DC ....100.00   —
     Scott UX40 went on sale at the Philatelic Agency
     3/22/52 and some were canceled that day. It is
     believed that the 1/1/52 cancels are not legitimate.
☐☐ UX43   2c Abraham Lincoln, 7/31/52, DC (125,400) 1.00   1.75

1956

☐☐ UX44   2c FIPEX, 5/4/56, New York, NY (537,474) 1.00   1.25
☐☐ UX45   4c Statue of Liberty, 11/16/56, New York.(129,841) 1.00   1.25

1958

☐☐ UX46   3c Statue of Liberty, 8/1/58, Philadelphia, PA
     (180,610) 1.00   1.25
☐☐ UX46a Statue of Liberty "N God We Trust", 8/1/58,
     Philadelphia, PA 175.00   250.00

1961

☐☐ UX46c Statue of Liberty, precanceled, 9/15/61,
     Philadelphia, PA ....50.00   —

1962-66

☐☐ UX48   4c Abraham Lincoln, 11/19/62, Springfield, IL
     (162,939) 1.00   1.00
☐☐ UX48a Abraham Lincoln, tagged, 6/25/66, Bellevue, OH 25.00   30.00
☐☐   7/6/66, DC 1.50   2.50
☐☐   Toledo, OH 7.50   12.50
☐☐   Overlook, OH 4.50   7.50
☐☐   Columbus, OH 7.50   12.50
☐☐   Bellevue, OH 15.00   25.00
☐☐   Cleveland, OH 6.00   10.00
☐☐   Cincinnati, OH 4.50   7.50
☐☐   Dayton, OH 3.50   6.00
☐☐   Indianapolis, IN 7.501   2.50
☐☐   Louisville, KY 7.50   12.50

UX73

US Coast Guard Eagle USA 14c

UX76

Casimir Pulaski, Savannah, 1779

UX79

Lewis and Clark Expedition, 1806

UX91

UX82

Drake's Golden Hinde 1580

UX86

UX88, UY31

HOW TO USE THIS BOOK

The number in the first column is its Scott number or identifying number. Following that is the denomination of the stamp, description, date of issue, and the value.

SCOTT NUMBER	DESCRIPTION	UNCACHETED	CACHETED

1963

☐☐ UX49 **7c Map**, 8/30/63, New York, NY (148,000 est.) 1.00   1.00

1964

☐☐ UX50 **4c Flags**, Map & "Customs," 2/22/64, DC (313,275) 1.00   1.00
☐☐ UX51 **4c Social Security**, 9/26/64, DC (293,650) 1.00   1.00
☐☐   with official government printed cachet ....—   12.00
☐☐   with blue hand cancel & government cachet ....—   20.00

1965

☐☐ UX52 **4c Coast Guard Flag**, 8/4/65, Newburyport, MA
     (338,225) 1.00   1.00
☐☐ UX53 **4c Census Bureau**, 10/21/65, Philadelphia, PA
     (275,100) 1.00   1.00

1967

☐☐ UX54 **8cMap**, 12/4/67, DC(145,896) 1.00   1.00

1968

☐☐ UX55 **5c Abraham Lincoln**, 1/4/68, Hodgenville, KY
     (159,420) 1.00   1.00
☐☐ UX56 **5c Women Marines**, 7/26/68, San Francisco, CA
     (203,714) 1.00   1.00

1970

☐☐ UX57 **5c Weather Vane**, 9/1/70, Ft. Myer, VA (285,800) 1.00   1.00

1971

☐☐ UX58 **6c Paul Revere**, 5/15/71, Boston, MA (197,000 est) 1.00   1.00
☐☐ UX59 **10c Map**, 6/10/71, New York, NY (151,000 est.) 1.00   1.00
     Total for Scott UX59 and UXC11 is 297,000.
☐☐ UX60 **6c America's Hospital**s, 9/16/71, New York, NY
     (218,200) 1.00   1.00

1972

☐☐ UX61 **6c U.S. Frigate Constellation**, 6/29/72, any city 1.00   1.00
☐☐ UX62 **6c Monument Valley**, 6/29/72, any city 1.00   1.00
☐☐ UX63 **6c Gloucester**, MA 6/29/72, any city 1.00   1.00
☐☐ UX64 **6e John Hanson**, 9/1/72, Baltimore, MD (156,000) 1.00   1.00

1973

☐☐ UX65 **6c Centenary of Postal Card**, 9/1/73, DC(289,950) 1.00   1.00
☐☐ UX66 **8c Samuel Adams**, 12/16/73, Boston, MA (147,522) 1.00   1.00
☐☐ UX67 **12c Ship's Figurehead**, 1/4/73, Miami, FL (138,500) 1.00   1.00

1975

☐☐ UX68 **7c Charles Thomson**, 9/14/75, Bryn Mawr, PA
     (153,067 est.)...1.00   1.00
     Total for Scott UX68 and UY25 is 321,910.
☐☐ UX69 **9c John Witherspoon**, 11/10/75, Princeton, NJ
     (170,340 est)...1.00   1.00
     Total for Scott UX69 and UY26 is 254,239.

"Swamp Fox" Francis Marion, 1782
UX94

UX95, UY21

UX96

UX97

UX107

HOW TO USE THIS BOOK

The number in the first column is its Scott number or
identifying number. Following that is the denomination
of the stamp, description, date of issue, and the value.

1976

☐☐ UX70 9c **Caesar Rodney**, 7/1/76, Dover, DE(150,432est.) 1.00   1.00
Total for Scott UX70 and UY27 is 307,061.

1977

☐☐ UX71 9c **Federal Court House**, 7/20/77, Galveston, TX
(245,535) 1.00   1.00
☐☐ UX72 9c **Nathan Hale**, 10/14/77, Coventry, CT (204,077 est.)....1.00   1.00
Total for Scott UX72 and UY28 is 304,592.

1978

☐☐ UX73 10c **Cincinnati Music Hall**, 5/12/78, Cincinnati, OH
(300,000) 1.00   1.00
☐☐ UX74 (10c) **John Hancock**, 5/19/78, Quincy, MA (299,623) 1.00   1.00
☐☐ UX75 10c **John Hancock**, 6/20/78, Quincy, MA (187,120)..........1.00   1.00
☐☐ UX76 14c **U.S. Coast Guard Eagle**, 8/4/78, Seattle,WA(196,400).1.00   1.00
☐☐ UX77 10c **Molly Pitcher**, 9/8/78, Freehold, NJ (180,280)...........1.00   1.00

1979

☐☐ UX78 10c **George Rogers Clark**, 2/23/79, Vincennes, IN
(260, 110) 1.00   1.00
☐☐ UX79 10c **Casimir Pulaski**, 10/11/79, Savannah, GA (210,000).1.00   1.00
☐☐ UX80 10c **Olympic Games**, 9/17/79, Eugene, OR (206,000).......1.00   1.25
☐☐ UX81 10c **Iolani Palace**, 10/1/79, Honolulu, HI (242,804)..........1.00   1.00

1980

☐☐ UX82 14c **Winter Olympic Games**, 1/15/80, Atlanta, GA
(160,977) 1.00   1.25
☐☐ UX83 10c **Salt Lake Temple**, 4/5/80, Salt Lake City, UT
(325,260) 1.00   1.00
☐☐ UX84 10c **Landing of Rochambeau**, 7/11/80, Newport, RI
(180,567) 1.00   1.00
☐☐ UX85 10c **Battle of Kings Mountain**, 10/7/80, Kings Mountain,
NC (136,130)..1.00   1.00
☐☐ UX86 19c **Golden Hinde**, 11/21/80, San Rafael, CA (290,547)...1.00   1.25

1981

☐☐ UX87 10c **Battle of Cowpens**, 1/17/81, Cowpens, SC (160,000).1.00   1.00
☐☐ UX88 (12c) **Eagle**, 3/15/81, Memphis, TN...............................1.00   1.00
☐☐ UX89 12c **Isaiah Thomas**, 5/5/81, Worcester, MA (185,610)......1.00   1.00
☐☐ UX90 12c **Nathaniel Greene**, 9/8/81, Eutaw Springs, SC
(115,755) 1.00   1.00
☐☐ UX91 12c **Lewis & Clark Expedition**, 9/23/81, St. Louis, MO....1.00   1.00
☐☐ UX92 (13c) **Robert Morris**, 10/11/81, Memphis, TN 1.00   1.25
☐☐ UX93 13c **Robert Morris**, 11/10/81, Philadelphia, PA.................1.00   1.25

1982

☐☐ UX94 13c **Francis Marion**, 4/3/82, Marion, SC (141,162) 1.00   1.25
☐☐ UX95 13c **LaSalle Claims Louisiana**, 4/7/82,
New Orleans, LA (157,691) 1.00   1.25
☐☐ UX96 13c **Philadelphia Academy of Music**, 6/18/82,
Philadelphia, PA (193,089) 1.00   1.25
☐☐ UX97 13c **Old Post Office**, 10/14/82, St. Louis, MO 1.00   1.25

1983

☐☐ UX98 **13c Oglethorpe**, 2/12/83, Savannah, GA............................1.00		1.25
☐☐ UX99 **13c Old Post Office**, 4/19/83, DC (125,056) 1.00		1.25
☐☐ UX100 **13c Olympics (Yachting)**, 8/5/83, Long Beach, CA 1.00		1.25

1984

☐ UX101 **13c The Ark and the Dove**, 3/25/84,
    St. Clement's Island, MD...1.00   1.25
☐☐ UX102 **13c Olympics (Torch)**, 4/30/84, Los Angeles, CA..............1.00   1.25
☐☐ UX103 **13c Frederic Baraga**, 6/29/84, Marquette, MI...................1.00   1.25
☐☐ UX104 **13c Historic Preservation**, 9/16/84, Compton, CA............1.00   1.25

1985

☐☐ UX105 **(14c) Charles Carroll**, 2/1/85, New Carrollton, MD 1.00   1.25
☐☐ UX106 **14c Charles Carroll**, 3/6/85, Annapolis, MD 1.00   1.25
☐☐ UX107 **25c Clipper Flying Cloud**, 2/27/85, Salem, MA.................1.25   1.50
☐☐ UX108 **14c George Wythe**, 6/20/85, Williamsburg, VA.................1.00   1.25

1986

☐☐ UX109 **14c Settling of Connecticut**, 4/18/86, Hartford, CT..........1.00   1.25
☐☐ UX110 **14c Stamps**, 5/23/86, Chicago, IL....................................1.00   1.25
☐☐ UX111 **14c Francis Vigo**, 5/24/86, Vincennes, IN.........................1.00   1.25
☐☐ UX112 **14c Settling of Rhode Island**, 6/26/86, Providence, RI.....1.00   1.25
☐☐ UX113 **14c Wisconsin Territory**, 7/3/86, Mineral Point, WI.........1.00   1.25
☐ UX114 **14c National Guard Heritage**, 12/12/86, Boston, MA
    (72,316) 1.00   1.25

1987

☐☐ UX115 **14c Self-Scouting Steel Plow**, 5/22/87, Moline, IL
    (160,009) 1.00   1.25
☐☐ UX116 **14c Constitutional Convention**, 5/25/87,
    Philadelphia, PA (138,207) 1.00   1.25
☐☐ UX117 **14c Flag**, 6/14/87, Baltimore, MD...................................1.00   1.25
☐☐ UX118 **14c Take Pride in America**, 9/22/87, Jackson, WY
    (47,281) 1.00   1.25
☐ UX119 **14c Timberline Lodge**, 9/28/87, Timberline Lodge, OR
    (63,595) 1.00   1.25

1988

☐☐ UX120 **15c Bison and Prairie**, 3/28/88, Buffalo, WY (52,075) 1.00   1.25
☐☐ UX121 **15c Blair House**, 5/4/88, DC (52,188) 1.00   1.25
☐☐ UXI22 **28c Yorkshire**, Square-rigged Packet, 6/29/88,
    Mystic, CT (46,505)..1.25   1.50
☐☐ UX123 **15c Iowa Territory**, 7/2/88, Burlington, IA (45,565).........1.00   1.25
☐☐ UX124 **15c Settling of Ohio**, Northwest Territory, 7/15/88,
    Marietta, OH (28,778)...1.00   1.25
☐☐ UX125 **15c Hearst Castle**, 9/20/88, San Simeon, CA (84,786).....1.00   1.25
☐☐ UX126 **15c The Federalist Papers**, 10/27/88, New York, NY
    (37,661) 1.00   1.25

1989

☐☐ UX127 **15c Red-tailed Hawk Sonora Desert**, 1/13/89,
    Tucson, AZ (51,891) 1.00   1.25

☐☐ UX128 15c Healy Hall, Georgetown University, 1/23/89, DC
(54,897) 1.00   1.25

☐☐ UX129 15c Great Blue Heron, Marsh, 3/17/89, Waycross, GA
(58,208) 1.00   1.25

☐☐ UX130 15c Settling of Oklahoma, 4/22/89, Guthrie, OK
(68,689) 1.00   1.25

☐☐ UX131 15c Canada Geese and Mountains, 5/5/89, Denver, CO
(59,303) 1.00   1.25

☐☐ UX132 15c Seashore, 6/17/89, Cape Hatteras, NC (67,073).........1.00   1.25

☐☐ UX133 15c Deer Beside Woodland Waterfall, 8/26/89,
Cherokee, NC (67,878)....................................1.00   1.25

☐☐ UX134 15c Hull House, Chicago, 9/18/89, Chicago, IL (53,773)...1.00   1.25

☐☐ UX135 15c Independence Hall, 9/25/89, Philadelphia, PA
(61,659) 1.00   1.25

☐☐ UX136 15c Inner Harbor Baltimore, 10/7/89, Baltimore, MD
(58,745) 1.00   1.25

☐☐ UX137 15c 59th Street Bridge, 11/8/89, New York, NY (48,044) ..1.00   1.25

☐☐ UX138 15c Capitol, 11/26/89, DC 1.00   1.25

☐☐ UX139 15c Independence Hall 12/1/89, DC...........................1.00   1.25

☐☐ UX140 15c Inner Harbor Baltimore, 12/1/89, DC.....................1.00   1.25

☐☐ UX141 15c 59th Street Bridge, 12/1/89, DC 1.00   1.25

☐☐ UX142 15c Capitol, 12/1/89, DC 1.00   1.25
Scott UX135-UX138 have inscription and copyright
symbol at lower left. Scott UX139- UX142 do not.

☐☐ UX143 15c White House, 11/30/89, DC....................................1.25   1.25

☐☐ UX144 15c Jefferson Memorial, 12/2/89, DC............................1.00   1.25

1990

☐☐ UX145 15c Rittenhouse Paper Mill, 3/13/90, New York, NY
(9,866) 1.00   1.25

☐☐ UX146 15c World Literacy Year, 3/22/90, DC (11,163)................1.00   1.25

☐☐ UX147 15c Fur Traders Descending the Missouri, 5/4/90,
St. Louis, MO (13,362) 2.00   2.25

☐☐ UX148 15c Isaac Royall House, 6/16/90, Medford, MA (21,708). 1.00   1.25

☐☐ UX150 15c Quadrangle, Stanford University, 9/11/90,
Stanford, CA (28,430)......................................1.00   1.25

☐☐ UX151 15c Constitution Hall, 10/11/90, DC (33,254)..................2.00   2.25

☐☐ UX152 15c Chicago Orchestra Hall, 10/19/90, Chicago, IL
(28,546) 1.00   1.25

1991

☐☐ UX153 19c Flag, 1/24/91, DC...1.00   1.25

☐☐ UX154 19c Carnegie Hall, 4/1/91, New York, NY.......................1.00   1.25

☐☐ UX155 19c "Old Red," Univ. of Texas, 6/14/91, Galveston, TX ...1.00   1.25

☐☐ UX156 19c Bill of Rights, 9/25/91, Richmond, VA......................1.00   1.25

☐☐ UX157 19c Notre Dame, 10/15/91, Notre Dame, IN....................1.00   1.25

☐☐ UX158 30c Niagara Falls, 8/21/91, Niagara Falls, NY 1.25   2.00

1992

☐☐ UX159 19c Old Mill, Univ. of Vermont, 1/16/92, Burlington, VT .1.00   1.25

☐☐ UX160 19c Wadsworth Atheneum, 1/16/92, Hartford, CT..........1.00   1.25

☐☐ UX161 19c Cobb Hall, Univ. of Chicago, 1/23/92, Chicago, IL.....1.00   1.25

☐☐ UX162 19c Waller Hall, 2/1/92, Salem, OR 1.00   1.25

☐☐ UX163 19c America's Cup, 5/6/92, San Diego, CA 1.00   1.25

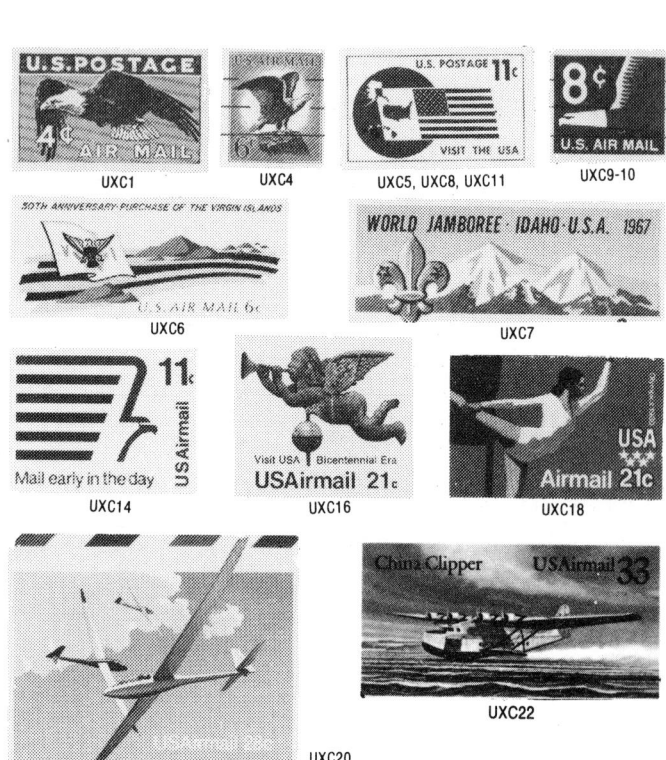

UXC1

UXC4

UXC5, UXC8, UXC11

UXC9-10

UXC6

UXC7

UXC14

UXC16

UXC18

UXC20

UXC22

HOW TO USE THIS BOOK
The number in the first column is its Scott number or
identifying number. Following that is the denomination
of the stamp, description, date of issue, and the value.

☐☐	UX164 19c **Columbia River Gorge**, 5/9/92, Stevenson, WA 1.00		1.25
☐☐	UX165 19c **Great Hall, Ellis Island**, 5/11/92, Ellis Island, NY......1.00		1.25

1993

☐☐	UX166 19c **National Cathedral**, 1/6/93, DC.................................1.00		1.25
☐☐	UX167 19c **Wren Building**, 1/6/93, Williamsburg, VA.................1.00		1.25
☐☐	UX168 19c **Holocaust Memorial**, 3/23/93, DC...........................1.00		1.25
☐☐	UX169 19c **Ft. Recovery**, 6/13/93, Fort Recovery, OH.................1.00		1.25
☐☐	UX170 19c **Playmaker's Theater**, 9/14/93, Chapel Hill, NC.........1.00		1.25
☐☐	UX171 19c **O'Kane Hall**, 9/17/93, Worcester, MA 1.00		1.25
☐☐	UX172 19c **Beecher Hall**, 10/9/93, Chicago, IL 1.00		1.25
☐☐	UX173 19c **Massachusetts Hall**, 10/14/93, Brunswick, ME 1.00		1.25

REPLY POSTAL CARDS
1892

☐☐	UY1 1c + 1c **U.S. Grant** 10/25/92, any city 350.00		—

1926

☐☐	UY12 3c + 3c **William McKinley**, 2/1/26, any city 250.00		—

1951

☐☐	UY13 2c + 2c **George Washington**, 12/29/51, DC (49,294) 1.00		2.00

1952

☐☐	UY14 2c on 1c + 2c on 1c **George Washington**, 1/1/52, any city .50.00		75.00

1956

☐☐	UY16 4c + 4c **Statue of Liberty**, 11/16/56, New York, NY (127,874) 1.00		1.25
☐☐	UY16a 4c + 4c **Statue of Liberty**, message card printed on both halves, 11/16/56, New York,NY...........................75.00		100.00
☐☐	UY16b 4c + 4c **Statue of Liberty**, reply card printed on both halves, 11/16/56, New York, NY 50.00		75.00

1958

☐☐	UY17 3c + 3c **Statue of Liberty**, 7/31/58, Boise, ID (136,768) ...1.00		1.25

1962-67

☐☐	UY18 4c + 4c **Abraham Lincoln**, 11/19/62, Springfield, IL (107,746) 1.00		1.25
☐☐	UY18a **Abraham Lincoln**, tagged, 3/7/67, Dayton, OH, earliest known use 500.00		—

1963

☐☐	UY19 7c + 7c **Map**, 8/30/63, New York, NY (122,000 est.) 1.00		1.25

1967

☐☐	UY20 8c + 8c **Map**, 12/4/67, DC (122,181)................................1.00		1.25

1968

☐☐	UY21 5c + 5c **Abraham Lincoln**, 1/4/68, Hodgenville, KY (114,580) 1.00		1.25

SCOTT NUMBER	DESCRIPTION	UNCACHETED	CACHETED

1971

☐☐ UY22 6c + 6c Paul Revere, 5/15/71, Boston, MA (143,000).......1.00 — 1.25

1972

☐☐ UY23 6c + 6c John Hanson, 9/1/72, Baltimore, MD
(105,708) .... 1.00 — 1.25

1973

☐☐ UY24 8c + 8c Samuel Adams, 12/16/73, Boston, MA (105,369) 1.00 — 1.25

1975

☐☐ UY25 7c + 7c Charles Thomson, 9/14/75, Bryn Mawr, PA
(76,533 est.)..1.00 — 1.25

☐☐ UY26 9c + 9c John Witherspoon, 11/10/75, Princeton, NJ
(83,899 est.)..1.00 — 1.25

1976

☐☐ UY27 9c + 9c Caesar Rodney, 7/1/76, Dover, DE
(100,340 est.)... 1.00 — 1.25

1977

☐☐ UY28 9c + 9c Nathan Hale, 10/14/77, Coventry, CT
(100,515 est.)...1.00 — 1.25

1978

☐☐ UY29 (10c + 10c) John Hancock, 5/19/78, Quincy, MA
(71,000 est.)...1.75 — 3.50

☐☐ UY30 10c + 10c John Hancock, 6/20/78, Quincy, MA
(61,750 est.)...1.00 — 1.25

1981

☐☐ UY31 (12c + 12c) Eagle, 3/15/81, Memphis, TN.........................1.00 — 1.25

☐☐ UY32 12c + 12c Isaiah Thomas, 5/5/81, Worcester, MA ....1.00 — 1.25

☐☐ UY32a Isaiah Thomas, Small Die ....3.00 — 5.00

☐☐ UY33 (13c + 13c) Robert Morris, 10/11/81, Memphis, TN ....1.25 — 1.25

☐☐ UY34 13c + 13c Robert Morris, 11/10/81, Philadelphia, PA ......1.25 — 1.25

1985

☐☐ UY35 (14c + 14c) Charles Carroll, 2/1/85,
New Carrollton, MD ....1.25 — 1.50

☐☐ UY36 14c + 14c Charles Carroll, 3/6/85, Annapolis, MD ....1.25 — 1.50

☐☐ UY37 14c + 14c George Wythe, 6/20/85, Williamsburg, VA.......1.25 — 1.50

1987

☐☐ UY38 14c + 14c Flag, 9/1/87, Baltimore, MD (22,314)...............1.25 — 1.50

1988

☐☐ UY39 15c + 15c Bison and Prairie, 7/1/88, Buffalo, WY
(24,338) ....1.25 — 1.50

1991

☐☐ UY40 19c + 19c Flag, 3/27/91, DC (25,562)................................1.25 — 1.50

AIR POST POSTAL CARDS
1949

☐☐ UXC1 4c Eagle in Flight, 1/10/49, DC, (236,620) 1.00   1.00

1958

☐☐ UXC2 5c Eagle in Flight, 7/31/58, Wichita, KS (156,474) 1.00   1.00

1960

☐☐ UXC3 5c Eagle in Flight, bi-colored border, 6/18/60,
           Minneapolis, MN (228,500) 1.00   1.75
☐☐   With thin dividing line at top..2.50   5.00

1963

☐☐ UXC4 6c Bald Eagle, 2/15/63, Maitland, FL (216,203) 1.00   1.50

1966

☐☐ UXC5 11c Flag & "VISIT THE USA", 5/27/66, DC (272,813) 1.00   1.00

1967

☐☐ UXC6 6c Virgin Islands, 3/31/67, Charlotte Amalie, VI,
           (346,906) 1.00   1.00
☐☐ UXC7 6c World Boy Scout Jamboree, 8/4/67,
           Farragut State Park, ID (471,585)....................................1.00   1.00
☐☐ UXC8 13c Flag & "VISIT THE USA", 9/8/67, Detroit, MI
           (178,189) 1.00   1.00

1968-69

☐☐ UXC9 8c Eagle, 3/1/68, New York, NY (179,923).......................1.00   1.00
☐☐ UXC9a Eagle, tagged, 3/19/69, DC...10.00   15.00

1971

☐☐ UXC10 9c Eagle, 5/15/71, Kitty Hawk, NC, (167,000 est.)............1.00   1.00
☐☐ UXC11 15c Flag & "VISIT THE USA", 6/10/71, New York, NY
           (146,000) 1.00   1.00

1972

☐☐ UXC12 9c Grand Canyon, 6/29/72, any city...............................1.00   1.00
☐☐ UXC13 15c Niagara Falls, 6/29/72, any city 1.00   1.00
☐☐ UXC13a Niagara Falls, address side blank ....600.00   —

1974

☐☐ UXC14 11c Stylized Eagle, 1/4/74, State College, PA,
           (160,500) 1.00   1.00
☐☐ UXC15 18c Eagle Weather Vane, 1/4/74, Miami, FL (132,114)....1.00   1.00

1975

☐☐ UXC16 21c Angel Weather Vane, 12/17/75, Kitty Hawk, NC
           (113,191) 1.00   1.25

1978

☐☐ UXC17 21c Curtiss Jenny, 9/16/78, San Diego, CA (174,886) 1.00   1.25

Subscribe To

SCOTT
Stamp Monthly

Each month it's a fascinating look at the people, places and events related to stamps. Time-saving hints, remarkable stamp discoveries and quirky amusing tales focusing on bizarre facets of the hobby, you'll find it all in Scott Stamp Monthly.

12 Issues $16.95

To subscribe call
1-800-488-5351

SCOTT NUMBER	DESCRIPTION	UNCACHETED	CACHETED

1979

☐☐ UXC18 21c Olympics (Gymnast), 12/1/79, Fort Worth, TX (150,124) 1.00   1.25

1981

☐☐ UXC19 28c First Transpacific Flight, 1/2/81, Wenatchee, WA.....1.25   1.25

1982

☐☐ UXC20 28c Gliders, 3/5/82, Houston, TX (106,932).....................1.25   1.25

1983

☐☐ UXC21 28c Olympics (Speedskating), 12/29/83, Milwaukee, WI. ..1.25   1.25

1985

☐☐ UXC22 33c China Clipper Seaplane, 2/15/85, San Francisco, CA 1.25   1.25

1986

☐☐ UXC23 33c Chicago Skyline, 2/1/86, Chicago, IL..........................1.25   1.25

1988

☐☐ UXC24 36c DC-3, 5/14/88, San Diego, CA....................................1.25   1.25

1991

☐☐ UXC25 40c Yankee Clipper, 6/28/91, Flushing, NY 1.50   2.00

OFFICIAL POSTAL CARDS
1983-91

☐☐ UZ2	13c Eagle, 1/12/83, DC..1.00		1.25
☐☐ UZ3	14c Eagle, 2/26/85, DC..1.00		1.25
☐☐ UZ4	15c Eagle, 6/10/88, DC (133,498) 1.00		1.25
☐☐ UZ5	19c Eagle, 5/24/91, Seattle, WA (23,097).........................1.00		1.50

**Cachet values in this catalogue are for an average cacheted
First Day Cover. Some FDC's, depending on the cachet, can sell
for many times the catalogue value, while others sell for less.
The Cachet Calculator lists cachetmakers, the dates
they produced FDC's and a market value multiplier.
The Calculator begins on page 40A.**

FIRST DAY CEREMONY PROGRAMS

First day ceremony programs are produced and distributed at ceremonies dedicating a new stamp. The programs normally are produced by either the U.S. Postal Service or a local sponsoring groups.

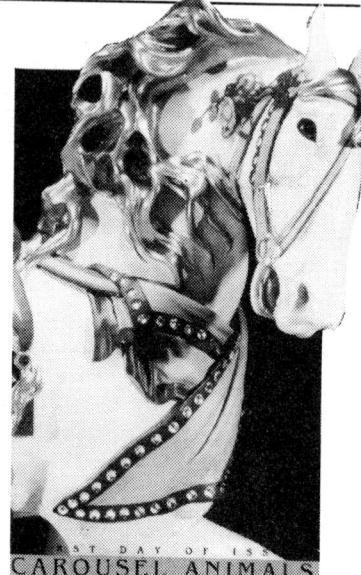

Formats of the programs vary greatly. They can be as simple as a single sheet of paper or an elaborate work of graphic art. A common element is that most programs contain the words "First Day Ceremony Program" and contain a listing of the ceremony order of events.

Collectors interested in obtaining more information regarding ceremony programs are urged to join the American Ceremony Program Society. Membership information is available from David Rosenthal, Secretary ACPS, 48 Hillary Lane, Westbury, NY 11590-1647. Send information on newly discovered programs to: Scott Pelcyger, P.O. Box 756, Butler, NJ 07405.

The following is a list of all known First Day Ceremony Programs. Values are for the most common type of programs for each issue.

Values for material from 1940-1957, unless otherwise stated, are for programs without stamps and first-day cancels. Programs containing stamps and first-day cancels usually sell for twice the stated value.

Values for material from 1958 to date, unless otherwise stated, are for programs with stamps and first-day cancels. Programs without stamps and first-day cancels usually sell for half the stated value.

1940

☐	863	10c Samuel L. Clemens, 2/13/40, Hannibal, MO	225.00
☐	873	10c Booker T. Washington, 4/7/40, Tuskegee Inst, AL	150.00
☐	875	2c Dr. Crawford W. Long, 4/8/40, Jefferson, GA	150.00
☐	886	3c Augustus Saint-Gaudens, 9/16/40, New York, NY	150.00
☐	890	2c Samuel F.B. Morse, 10/7/40, New York, NY	150.00

1945

☐	936	3c Coast Guard, 11/10/45, New York, NY	110.00
☐	937	3c Alfred E. Smith, 11/26/45, New York, NY	100.00

1946

☐	942	3c Iowa Statehood, 8/3/46, Iowa City, IA	90.00
☐	944	3c Kearny Expedition, 10/16/46, Santa Fe, NM	90.00

1947

☐	945	3c Thomas A. Edison, 2/11/47, Milan, OH	85.00
☐	946	3c Joseph Pulitzer, 4/10/47, New York, NY	85.00

| ☐ | 950 | 3c Utah, 7/24/47, Salt Lake City, UT | 75.00 |
| ☐ | 952 | 3c Everglades National Park, 12/5/47, Florida City, FL | 75.00 |

1948

☐	953	3c George Washington Carver, 1/5/48, Tuskegee Institute, AL	80.00
☐	957	3c Wisconsin Centennial, 5/29/48, Madison, WI	70.00
☐	958	5c Swedish Pioneer, 6/4/48, Chicago, IL	65.00
☐	961	3c United States-Canada Friendship, 8/2/48, Niagara Falls, NY	70.00
☐	962	3c Francis Scott Key, 8/2/48, Frederick, MD	50.00
☐	964	3c Oregon Territory, 8/14/48, Oregon City, OR	60.00
☐	966	3c Palomar Mountain Observatory, 8/30/48, Palomar Mountain, CA	75.00
☐	967	3c Clara Barton, 9/7/48, Oxford, MA	50.00
☐	968	3c Poultry Industry, 9/9/48, New Haven, CT	50.00
☐	970	3c Fort Kearny, 9/22/48, Minden, NE	45.00
☐	971	3c Volunteer Firemen, 10/4/48, Dover, DE (two types)	60.00
☐	976	3c Fort Bliss Centennial, 11/5/48, El Paso, TX	75.00
☐	978	3c Gettysburg Address, 11/19/48, Gettysburg, PA	65.00
☐	979	3c American Turners, 11/20/48, Cincinnati, OH	60.00

1949

☐	981	3c Minnesota Territory, 5/3/49, St. Paul, MN	50.00
☐	982	3c Washington & Lee University, 4/12/49, Lexington, VA	50.00
☐	984	3c Annapolis Tercentenary, 5/23/49, Annapolis, MD	50.00
☐	985	3c GAR, 8/29/49, Indianapolis, IN	45.00
☐	986	3c Edgar Allen Poe, 10/7/49, Richmond, VA	50.00

1950

☐	990	3c National Capital Sesquicentennial, 6/12/50, DC	50.00
☐	993	3c Railroad Engineers, 4/29/50, Jackson, TN	50.00
☐	994	3c Kansas City, Missouri, Centenary, 6/3/50, Kansas City, MO	40.00
☐	995	3c Boy Scouts, 6/30/50, Valley Forge, PA	45.00
☐	996	3c Indiana Territory, 7/4/50, Vincennes, IN	40.00

1951

☐	998	3c United Confederate Veterans, 5/30/51, Norfolk, VA (2 types)	40.00
☐	999	3c Nevada Centennial, 7/14/51, Genoa, NV	30.00
☐	1000	3c Landing of Cadillac, 7/24/51, Detroit, MI	35.00
☐	1001	3c Colorado Statehood, 8/1/51, Minturn, CO	30.00
☐	1002	3c American Chemical Society, 9/4/51, New York, NY	30.00
☐	1003	3c Battle of Brooklyn, 12/10/51, Brooklyn, NY	35.00

1952

☐	1004	3c Betsy Ross, 1/2/52, Philadelphia, PA	30.00
☐	1005	3c 4-H Clubs, 1/15/52, Springfield, OH	20.00
☐	1006	3c B. & O. Railroad, 2/28/52, Baltimore, MD	35.00
☐	1007	3c A.A.A., 3/04/52, Chicago, IL	30.00
☐	1009	3c Grand Coulee Dam, 5/15/52, Grand Coulee, WA	30.00
☐	1010	3c Lafayette, 6/13/52, Georgetown, SC	30.00
☐	1011	3c Mt. Rushmore Memorial, 8/11/52, Keystone, SD	30.00
☐	1012	3c Engineering Centennial, 9/6/52, Chicago, IL	30.00
☐	1014	3c Gutenberg Bible, 9/30/52, DC	35.00
☐	1015	3c Newspaper Boys, 10/4/52, Philadelphia, PA	25.00

1953

- [ ] 1017 3c National Guard, 2/23/53, DC 30.00
- [ ] 1018 3c Ohio Statehood, 3/2/53, Chillicothe, OH 25.00
- [ ] 1019 3c Washington Territory, 3/2/53, Olympia, WA 40.00
- [ ] 1020 3c Louisiana Purchase, 4/30/53, St. Louis, MO.....................30.00
- [ ] 1021 5c Opening of Japan Centennial, 7/14/53, DC 30.00
- [ ] 1022 3c American Bar Association, 8/24/53, Boston, MA................25.00
- [ ] 1023 3c Sagamore Hill, 9/14/53, Oyster Bay, NY............................30.00
- [ ] 1024 3c Future Farmers, 10/13/53, Kansas City, MO 25.00
- [ ] 1025 3c Trucking Industry, 10/27/53, Los Angeles, CA..................25.00
- [ ] 1026 3c General Patton, 11/11/53, Fort Knox, KY 75.00
- [ ] 1027 3c New York City, 11/20/53, New York, NY 25.00
- [ ] 1028 3c Gadsden Purchase, 12/30/53, Tucson, AZ............................25.00

1954

- [ ] 1029 3c Columbia University, 1/4/54, New York, NY 35.00

1954-64

- [ ] 1030 1/2c Benjamin Franklin, 10/20/55, DC 30.00
- [ ] 1031 1c George Washington, 8/26/54, Chicago, IL 30.00
- [ ] 1031A 1 1/4c Palace of the Governors, 6/17/60, Santa Fe, NM, with stamp & cancel..15.00
- [ ] 1032 1 1/2c Mount Vernon, 2/22/56, Mount Vernon, VA 40.00
- [ ] 1033 2c Thomas Jefferson, 9/15/54, San Francisco, CA..................30.00
- [ ] 1034 2 1/2c Bunker Hill Monument, 6/17/59, Boston, MA, w/stamp & cancel...20.00
- [ ] 1035 3c Statue of Liberty, 6/24/54, Albany, NY..............................35.00
- [ ] 1036 4c Abraham Lincoln, 11/19/54, New York, NY (2 types) 35.00
- [ ] 1037 4 1/2c The Hermitage, 3/16/59, Hermitage, TN 35.00
- [ ] 1038 5c James Monroe, 12/2/54, Fredericksburg, VA......................25.00
- [ ] 1039 6c Theodore Roosevelt, 11/18/55, New York, NY (2 types) 25.00
- [ ] 1040 7c Woodrow Wilson, 1/10/56, Staunton, VA............................20.00
- [ ] 1041 8c Statue of Liberty, 4/9/54, DC...20.00
- [ ] 1042 8c Statue of Liberty, 3/22/58, Cleveland, OH (3 types).........15.00
- [ ] 1042A 8c John J. Pershing, 11 / 17/61, New York, NY 15.00
- [ ] 1043 9c The Alamo, 6/14/56, San Antonio, TX 50.00
- [ ] 1044 10c Independence Hall, 7/4/56, Philadelphia, PA 25.00
- [ ] 1044A 11c Statue of Liberty, 6/15/61, Washington, DC...................22.00
- [ ] 1045 12c Benjamin Harrison, 6/6/59, Oxford, OH 12.00
- [ ] 1047 20c Monticello, 4/13/56, Charlottesville, VA...........................25.00
- [ ] 1048 25c Paul Revere, 4/18/58, Boston, MA....................................40.00
- [ ] 1049 30c Robert E. Lee, 9/21/55, Norfolk, VA 30.00
- [ ] 1050 40c John Marshall, 9/24/55, Richmond, VA 55.00
- [ ] 1051 50c Susan B. Anthony, 8/25/55, Louisville, KY 45.00
- [ ] 1052 $1 Patrick Henry, 10/7/55, Joplin, MO...................................70.00

1954-60

- [ ] 1054 1c George Washington, coil, 10/8/54, Baltimore, MD 25.00
- [ ] 1054A 1 1/4c Palace of the Governors, coil, 6/17/60, Santa Fe, NM..............15.00
- [ ] 1055 2c Thomas Jefferson, coil, 10/22/54, St. Louis, MO................30.00
- [ ] 1056 2 1/2c Bunker Hill, coil, 9/9/59, Los Angeles, CA 35.00

1954-73

- [ ] 1060 3c Nebraska Territory, 5/7/54, Nebraska City, NE 25.00

☐	1061	3c **Kansas Territory**, 5/31/54, Ft. Leavenworth, KS	25.00
☐	1062	3c **George Eastman**, 7/12/54, Rochester, NY	30.00
☐	1063	3c **Lewis & Clark Expedition**, 7/28/54, Sioux City, IA	25.00

1955

☐	1064	3c **Pennsylvania Academy of the Fine Arts**, 1/15/55, Philadelphia, PA	20.00
☐	1065	3c **Land Grant Colleges**, 2/12/55, East Lansing, MI	15.00
☐	1066	8c **Rotary International**, 2/23/55, Chicago, IL	40.00
☐	1067	3c **Armed Forces Reserve**, 5/21/55, DC	20.00
☐	1068	3c **New Hampshire**, 6/21/55, Franconia, NH	18.00
☐	1069	3c **Sop Locks**, 6/28/55, Sault Sainte Marie, MI	45.00
☐	1071	3c **Fort Ticonderoga**, 9/18/55, Ft. Ticonderoga, NY	20.00
☐	1072	3c **Andrew W. Mellon**, 12/20/55, DC	18.00

1956

☐	1073	3c **Benjamin Franklin**, 1/17/56, Philadelphia, PA	30.00
☐	1074	3c **Booker T. Washington**, 4/5/56, BTW Birthplace, VA	35.00
☐	1075	3c & 8c **FIPEX**, souvenir sheet, 4/28/56, New York, NY	35.00
☐	1076	3c **FIPEX**, 4/30/56, New York, NY	35.00
☐	1077	3c **Wildlife Conservation (Wild Turkey)**, 5/5/56, Fond du Lac, WI	25.00
☐	1078	3c **Wildlife Conservation (Antelope)**, 6/22/56, Gunnison, CO	25.00
☐	1079	3c **Wildlife Conservation (Salmon)**, 11/9/56, Seattle, WA	25.00
☐	1080	3c **Pure Food & Drug Laws**, 6/27/56, DC	18.00
☐	1081	3c **Wheatland**, 8/5/56, Lancaster, PA	18.00
☐	1082	3c **Labor Day**, 9/3/56, Camden, NJ	25.00
☐	1083	3c **Nassau Hall**, 9/22/56, Princeton, NJ	22.00
☐	1084	3c **Devils Tower**, 9/24/56, Devils Tower, WY	30.00
☐	1085	3c**Children**, 12/15/56, DC	22.00

1957

☐	1087	3c **Polio**, 1/15/57, DC (without stamp)	20.00
☐	1088	3c **Coast & Geodetic Survey**, 2/11/57, Seattle, WA	15.00
☐	1089	3c **Architects**, 2/23/57, New York, NY	15.00
☐	1090	3c **Steel Industry**, 5/22/57, New York, NY	30.00
☐	1091	3c **International Naval Review**, 6/10/57, Norfolk, VA	15.00
☐	1092	3c **Oklahoma Statehood**, 6/14/57, Oklahoma City, OK	18.00
☐	1093	3c **School Teachers**, 7/1/57, Philadelphia, PA	30.00
☐	1095	3c **Shipbuilding**, 8/15/57, Bath, ME	10.00
☐	1096	8c **Ramon Magsaysay**, 8/31/57, DC (w/stamp & w/cancel)	20.00
☐	1097	3c **Lafayette Bicentenary**, 9/6/57, Easton, PA (3 types)	25.00
☐	1098	3c **Wildlife Conservation (Whooping Cranes)**, 11/22/57, New Orleans, LA, or New York, NY (3 types)	20.00
☐	1099	3c **Religious Freedom**, 12/27/57 Flushing, NY	12.00

1958

☐	1100	3c **Gardening-Horticulture**, 3/15/58, Ithaca, NY	25.00
☐	1104	3c **Brussels Exhibition**, 4/17/58, Detroit, MI	22.00
☐	1105	3c **James Monroe**, 4/28/58, Montross, VA	20.00
☐	1106	3c **Minnesota Statehood**, 5/11/58, St. Paul, MN	25.00
☐	1107	3c **Geophysical Year**, 5/31/58, Chicago, IL	18.00
☐	1109	3c **Mackinac Bridge**, 6/25/58, Mackinac Bridge, MI	45.00
☐	1110-1111	4c & 8c **Simon Bolivar**, 7/24/58, DC	25.00
☐	1112	4c **Atlantic Cable Centennial**, 8/15/58, New York, NY	25.00

1958-59

☐ 1113 1c Lincoln Sesquicentennial, 2/12/59, Hodgenville, KY 20.00
☐ 1114 3c Lincoln Sesquicentennial, 2/12/59, New York, NY 20.00
☐ 1115 4c Lincoln-Douglas Debates, 8/27/58, Freeport, IL...........................20.00
☐ 1116 4c Lincoln Sesquicentennial, 5/30/59, DC 20.00

1958

☐ 1117-1118 4c & 8c Lajos Kossuth, 9/19/58, DC
       (w/stamp without cancel). 22.00
☐ 1119 4c Freedom of Press, 9/22/58, Columbia, MO (2 types) 25.00
☐ 1120 4c Overland Mail, 10/10/58, San Francisco, CA............................40.00
☐ 1121 4c Noah Webster, 10/16/58, West Hartford, CT 30.00
☐ 1122 4c Forest Conservation, 10/27/58, Tucson, AZ (2 types) 30.00
☐ 1123 3c Fort Duquesne, 11/25/58, Pittsburgh, PA 60.00

1959

☐ 1124 4c Oregon Statehood, 2/14/59, Astoria, OR 20.00
☐ 1125-1126 4c & 8c Jose de San Martin, 2/25/59, DC..............................22.00
☐ 1127 4c NATO, 4/1/59, DC 20.00
☐ 1128 4c Arctic Exploration, 4/6/59, Cresson, PA.................................25.00
☐ 1130 4c Silver Centennial, 6/8/59, Virginia City, NV............................50.00
☐ 1131 4c St. Lawrence Seaway, 6/26/59 2nd day, Massena, NY...................38.00
☐ 1132 4c 49 Star Flag, 7/4/59 Auburn, NY 35.00
☐ 1133 4c Soil Conservation, 8/26/59, Rapid City, SD 25.00
☐ 1134 4c Petroleum Industry, 8/27/59, Titusville, PA (2 types) 25.00
☐ 1135 4c Dental Health, 9/14/59, New York, NY....................................25.00
☐ 1136-1137 4c & 8c Ernst Reuter, 9/29/59, DC.....................................20.00
☐ 1138 4c Dr. Ephraim McDowell, 2/3/59, Danville, KY 35.00

1960-61 Credo

☐ 1139 4c George Washington, 1/20/60, Mr. Vernon, VA............................20.00
☐ 1140 4c Benjamin Franklin, 3/31/59, Philadelphia, PA 12.00
☐ 1141 4c Thomas Jefferson, 5/18/60, Charlottesville, VA 15.00
☐ 1142 4c Francis Scott Key, 9/14/60, Baltimore, MD (4 types) 15.00
☐ 1143 4c Abraham Lincoln, 11/19/60, New York, NY (3 types) 15.00
☐ 1144 4c Patrick Henry, 1/11/61, Richmond, VA (3 types)........................15.00

1960

☐ 1145 4c Boy Scout Jubilee, 2/8/60, DC 85.00
☐ 1147-1148 4c & 8c Thomas G. Masaryk, 3/7/60, DC................................15.00
☐ 1149 4c World Refugee Year, 4/7/60, DC..20.00
☐ 1150 4c Water Conservation, 4/18/60, DC...25.00
☐ 1151 4c SEATO, 5/31/6o, DC..20.00
☐ 1152 4c American Woman, 6/2/60, DC...45.00
☐ 1153 4c 50-Star Flag, 7/4/60, Honolulu, HI 20.00
☐ 1154 4c Pony Express Centennial, 7/19/60, Sacramento, CA 35.00
☐ 1155 4c Employ the Handicapped, 8/28/60, New York, NY 15.00
☐ 1156 4c World Forestry Congress, 8/29/60, Seattle, WA.........................35.00
☐ 1157 4c Mexican Independence, 9/16/60, Los Angeles, CA........................35.00
☐ 1158 4c U.S.-Japan Treaty, 9/28/60, DC 20.00
☐ 1159-1160 4c & 8c Ignacy Jan Paderewski, 10/8/60, DC..........................15.00
☐ 1161 4c Robert A. Taft, 10/10/60, Cincinnati, OH (2 types)....................25.00
☐ 1162 4c Wheels of Freedom, 10/15/60, Detroit, MI................................18.00
☐ 1163 4c Boys' Clubs of America, 10/18/60, New York, NY........................20.00

☐	1164	**4c Automated Post Office**, 10/20/60, Providence, RI 12.00
☐	1165-1166	**4c & 8c Baron Gustaf Emil Mannerheim**, 10/26/60, DC..............15.00
☐	1167	**4c Camp Fire Girls**, 11/1/60, New York, NY.......................................45.00
☐	1168-1169	**4c & 8c Giuseppe Garibaldi**, 11/2/60, DC.....................................15.00
☐	1170	**4c Senator Walter F. George**, 11/5/60, New York, NY 12.00
☐	1171	**4c Andrew Carnegie**, 11/25/60, New York, NY..................................25.00
☐	1172	**4c John Foster Dulles**, 12/6/60, DC...15.00
☐	1173	**4c Echo I**, 12/15/60, DC 25.00

1961

☐	1174-1175	**4c & 8c Mahatma Gandhi**, 1/26/61, DC..15.00
☐	1176	**4c Range Conservation**, 2/2/61, Salt Lake City, UT.........................30.00
☐	1177	**4c Horace Greeley**, 2/3/61, Chappaqua, NY......................................20.00

1961-65 Civil War Centennial

☐	1178	**4c Fort Sumter**, 4/12/61, Charleston, SC..25.00
☐	1179	**4c Battle of Shiloh**, 4/7/62, Shiloh, TN..20.00
☐	1180	**5c Battle of Gettysburg**, 7/1/63, Gettysburg, PA.................................20.00
☐	1181	**5c Battle of Wilderness**, 5/5/64, Fredericksburg, VA..........................20.00
☐	1182	**5c Appomattox**, 4/9/65, Appomattox, VA (3 types) 20.00

1961

☐	1183	**4c Kansas Statehood**, 5/10/61, Council Grove, KS..............................15.00
☐	1184	**4c Senator George W. Norris**, 7/11/61, DC..15.00
☐	1185	**4c Naval Aviation**, 8/20/61, San Diego, CA..30.00
☐	1186	**4c Workmen's Compensation**, 9/4/61, Milwaukee, WI (2 types)...........15.00
☐	1187	**4c Frederic Remington**, 10/4/61, DC...15.00
☐	1188	**4c Republic of China**, 10/10/61, DC 18.00
☐	1189	**4c Naismith-Basketball**, 11/6/61, DC...18.00
☐	1190	**4c Nursing** 12/28/61, DC...15.00

1962

☐	1191	**4c New Mexico Statehood**, 1/6/62, Santa Fe, NM................................15.00
☐	1192	**4c Arizona Statehood**, 2/14/62, Phoenix, AZ 15.00
☐	1194	**4c Malaria Eradication**, 3/30/62, DC...15.00
☐	1195	**4c Charles Evans Hughes**, 4/11/62, DC...15.00
☐	1196	**4c Seattle World's Fair**, 4/25/62, Seattle, WA 15.00
☐	1197	**4c Louisiana Statehood**, 4/30/62, New Orleans, LA............................18.00
☐	1198	**4c Homestead Act**, 5/20/62, Beatrice, NE..15.00
☐	1199	**4c Girl Scout Jubilee**, 7/24/62, Burlington, VT 22.00
☐	1200	**4c Sen. Brien McMahon**, 7/28/62, Norwalk, CT (2 types) 18.00
☐	1201	**4c Apprenticeship**, 8/31/62, DC..15.00
☐	1202	**4c Sam Rayburn**, 9/16/62, Bonham, TX...15.00
☐	1203	**4c Dag Hammarskjold**, 10/23/62, New York, NY.................................18.00
☐	1205	**4c Christmas**, 11/1/62, Pittsburgh, PA...20.00
☐	1206	**4c Higher Education**, 11/14/62, DC..15.00
☐	1207	**4c Winslow Homer**, 12/15/62, Gloucester, MA 18.00

1963

☐	1208	**5c Flag**, 1/9/63, DC.. 12.00

1962-63

☐	1209	**1c Andrew Jackson**, 3/22/63, New York, NY...15.00
☐	1213	**5c George Washington**, 11/23/62, New York, NY.................................15.00
☐	1225	**1c Andrew Jackson**, coil, 5/31/63, Chicago, IL (2 papers)...................15.00

1963

☐	1230	5c Carolina Charter, 4/6/63, Edenton, NC (2 types)............................15.00
☐	1231	5c Food for Peace, 6/4/63, DC..15.00
☐	1232	5c West Virginia Statehood, 6/20/63, Wheeling WV.........................20.00
☐	1233	5c Emancipation Proclamation, 8/16/63, Chicago, IL 15.00
☐	1234	5c Alliance for Progress, 8/17/63, DC..15.00
☐	1235	5c Cordell Hull, 10/5/63, Carthage, TN...15.00
☐	1236	5c Eleanor Roosevelt, 10/11/63, DC..15.00
☐	1237	5c Science, 10/14/63, DC 18.00
☐	1238	5c City Mall Delivery, 10/26/63, DC 22.00
☐	1239	5c Red Cross Centenary, 10/29/63, DC 15.00
☐	1240	5c Christmas, 11/1/63, Santa Claus, IN (2 papers)..........................20.00
☐	1241	5c John James Audubon, 12/7/63, Henderson, KY............................15.00

1964

☐	1242	5c Sam Houston, 1/10/64, Houston, TX 20.00
☐	1243	5c Charles M. Russell, 3/19/64, Great Falls, MT...............................40.00
☐	1244	& U546 5c New York World's Fair, 4/22/64, World's Fair, NY
		(2 types)..18.00
☐	1245	5c John Muir, 4/29/64, Martinez, CA 15.00
☐	1246	5c Kennedy Memorial, 5/29/64, Boston, MA....................................18.00
☐	1247	5c New Jersey Tercentenary, 6/15/64, Elizabeth, NJ (2 papers)..........15.00
☐	1248	5c Nevada Statehood, 7/22/64, Carson City, NV 15.00
☐	1249	5c Register & Vote, 8/1/64, DC...15.00
☐	1250	5c Shakespeare, 8/14/64, Stratford, CT 50.00
☐	1251	5c Doctors Mayo, 9/11/64, Rochester, MN.......................................25.00
☐	1252	5c American Music, 10/15/64, New York, NY 15.00
☐	1253	5c Homemakers, 10/26/64, Honolulu, HI 15.00
☐	1254-1257	5c Christmas, 11/9/64, Bethlehem, PA.......................................80.00
☐	1258	5c Verrazano-Narrows Bridge, 11/21/64, Staten Island, NY (2 types).15.00
☐	1259	5c Fine Arts, 12/2/64, DC 20.00
☐	1260	5c Amateur Radio, 12/15/64, Anchorage, AK 28.00

1965

☐	1261	5c Battle of New Orleans, 1/8/65, New Orleans, LA...........................25.00
☐	1262	5c Physical Fitness-Sokol, 2/15/65, DC..10.00
☐	1263	5c Crusade against Cancer, 4/1/65, DC..20.00
☐	1264	5c Churchill Memorial, 5/13/65, Fulton, MO 12.00
☐	1265	5c Magna Carta, 6/15/65, Jamestown, VA 40.00
☐	1266	5c International Cooperation Year, 6/26/65, San Francisco, CA 35.00
☐	1267	5c Salvation Army, 7/2/65, New York, NY 15.00
☐	1268	5c Dante Alighieri, 7/17/65, San Francisco, CA................................15.00
☐	1269	5c Herbert Hoover, 8/10/65, West Branch, IA (2 papers)....................15.00
☐	1270	5c Robert Fulton, 8/19/65, Clermont, NY...15.00
☐	1271	5c Settlement of Florida, 8/28/65, St. Augustine, FL.........................15.00
☐	1273	5c John Singleton Copley, 9/17/65, DC 15.00
☐	1274	11c International Telecommunications Union, 10/6/65, DC.................20.00
☐	1275	5c Adlai E. Stevenson, 10/23/65, Bloomington, IL............................15.00
☐	1276	5c Christmas, 11/2/65, Silver Bell, AZ (2 types)................................25.00

1965-71 Prominent Americans

☐	1278	1c Thomas Jefferson, 1/12/68, Jeffersonville, IN...............................25.00
☐	1278a	Thomas Jefferson, booklet pane of 8, 1/12/68 Jeffersonville, IN.........25.00
☐	1279	1 1/4c Albert Gallatin, 1/30/67, Gallatin, MO 20.00

☐	1280	2c Frank Lloyd Wright, 6/8/66, Spring Green, WI	18.00
☐	1280a	Frank Lloyd Wright, booklet pane of 5, 1/8/68, Buffalo, NY	20.00
☐	1280c	Frank Lloyd Wright, booklet pane of 6, 5/7/71, Spokane, WA	50.00
☐	1281	3c Francis Parkman, 9/16/67, Boston, MA	15.00
☐	1282	4c Abraham Lincoln, 11/19/65, New York, NY (2types)	15.00
☐	1283	5c George Washington, 2/22/66, DC	50.00
☐	1283B	5c George Washington, redrawn, 11/17/67, New York, NY (2 types)	15.00
☐	1284	6c Franklin D. Roosevelt, 1/29/66, Hyde Park, NY	15.00
☐	1285	8c Albert Einstein, 3/14/66, Princeton, NJ	20.00
☐	1286	10c Andrew Jackson, 3/15/67, Hermitage, TN	20.00
☐	1286A	12c Henry Ford, 7/30/68, Greenfield Village, MI	22.00
☐	1287	13c John F. Kennedy, 5/29/67, Brookline, MA	28.00
☐	1288	15c Oliver Wendell Holmes, 3/8/68, DC	28.00
☐	1289	20c George C. Marshall, 10/24/67, Lexington, VA	25.00
☐	1290	25c Frederick Douglass, 2/14/67, DC	32.00
☐	1291	30c John Dewey, 10/21/68, Burlington, VT	35.00
☐	1292	40c Thomas Paine, 1/29/68, Philadelphia, PA	40.00
☐	1293	50c Lucy Stone, 8/13/68, Dorchester, MA	45.00
☐	1294	$1 Eugene O'Neill, 10/16/67, New London, CT	50.00
☐	1295	$5 John Bassett Moore, 12/3/66, Smyrna, DE	75.00

1966-75

☐	1297	3c Francis Parkman, coil, 11/4/75, Pendleton, OR	15.00
☐	1299	1c Thomas Jefferson, coil, 1/12/68, Jeffersonville, IN	25.00
☐	1303	4c Abraham Lincoln, coil, 5/28/66, Springfield, IL	25.00
☐	1304	5c George Washington, coil, 9/8/66, Cincinnati, OH	15.00
☐	1305C	$1 Eugene O'Neill, coil, 1/12/73, Hempstead, NY	50.00

1966

☐	1306	5c Migratory Bird Treaty, 3/16/66, Pittsburgh, PA	18.00
☐	1307	5c Humane Treatment of Animals, 4/9/66, New York, NY (2 types)	12.00
☐	1308	5c Indiana Statehood, 4/16/66, Corydon, IN	15.00
☐	1309	5c American Circus, 5/2/66, Delavan, WI (2 types)	22.00
☐	1310	5c SIPEX, 5/21/66, DC	20.00
☐	1311	5c SIPEX, souvenir sheet, 5/23/66, DC	25.00
☐	1312	5c Bill of Rights, 7/1/66, Miami Beach, FL	25.00
☐	1313	5c Polish Millennium, 7/30/66, DC	15.00
☐	1314	5c National Park Service, 8/25/66, Yellowstone National Park, WY (2 types)	15.00
☐	1315	5c Marine Corps Reserve, 8/29/66, DC	18.00
☐	1316	5c General Federation of Women's Clubs, 9/12/66, New York, NY (2 types)	20.00
☐	1317	5c Johnny Appleseed, 9/24/66, Leominster, MA	20.00
☐	1318	5c Beautification of America, 10/5/66, DC	25.00
☐	1319	5c Great River Road, 10/21/66, Baton Rouge, LA	20.00
☐	1320	5c Savings Bonds-Servicemen, 10/26/66, Sioux City, IA	15.00
☐	1321	5c Christmas, 11/1/66, Christmas, MI	25.00
☐	1322	5c Mary Cassatt, 11/17/66, DC	22.00

1967

☐	1323	5c National Grange, 4/17/67, DC	25.00
☐	1324	5c Canada Centenary, 5/25/67, Montreal, Canada	18.00
☐	1325	5c Erie Canal 7/4/67, Rome, NY	18.00
☐	1326	5c Peace - Lions, 7/5/67, Chicago, IL	15.00

☐	1327	5c Henry David Thoreau, 7/12/67, Concord, MA	15.00
☐	1328	5c Nebraska Statehood, 7/29/67, Lincoln, NE	15.00
☐	1329	5c Voice of America, 8/1/67, DC	20.00
☐	1330	5c Davy Crockett, 8/17/67, San Antonio, TX	18.00
☐	1331-1332	5c Space Accomplishments, 9/29/67, Kennedy Space Center, FL	20.00
☐	1333	5c Urban Planning, 10/2/67, DC	20.00
☐	1334	5c Finnish Independence, 10/6/67, Finland, MN	18.00
☐	1335	5c Thomas Eakins, 11/2/67, DC	18.00
☐	1336	5c Christmas, 11/6/67, Bethlehem, GA	20.00
☐	1337	5c Mississippi Statehood, 12/11/67, Natchez, MS	18.00

1968-71

☐	1338	6c Flag and White House, 1/24/68, DC	15.00
☐	1338A	6c Flag and White House, coil, 5/30/69, Chicago, IL	15.00

1968

☐	1339	6c Illinois Statehood, 2/12/68, Shawneetown, IL	18.00
☐	1340	6c Hemis Fair '68, 3/30/68, San Antonio, TX	18.00
☐	1341	$1 Airlift, 4/4/68, Seattle, WA	70.00
☐	1342	6c Youth-Elks, 5/1/68, Chicago, IL	15.00
☐	1343	6c Law and Order, 5/17/68, DC	20.00
☐	1344	6c Register and Vote, 6/27/68, DC	20.00
☐	1345-1354	6c Historic Flags, 7/4/68, Pittsburgh, PA	30.00
☐	1355	6c Walt Disney, 9/11/68, Marceline, MO	45.00
☐	1356	6c Father Marquette, 9/20/68, Sault Ste. Marie, MI	15.00
☐	1357	6c Daniel Boone, 9/26/68, Frankfort, KY	15.00
☐	1358	6c Arkansas River Navigation, 10/1/68, Little Rock, AR	50.00
☐	1359	6c Leif Erikson, 10/9/68, Seattle, WA	30.00
☐	1360	6c Cherokee Strip, 10/15/68, Ponca, OK	18.00
☐	1361	6c John Trumbull, 10/18/68, New Haven, CT	20.00
☐	1362	6c Waterfowl Conservation, 10/24/68, Cleveland, OH	25.00
☐	1363	6c Christmas, 11/1/68, DC	25.00
☐	1364	6c American Indian, 11/4/68, DC	20.00

1969

☐	1365-1368	6c Beautification of America, 1/16/69, DC	25.00
☐	1369	6c American Legion, 3/15/69, DC	15.00
☐	1370	6c Grandma Moses, 5/1/69, DC	20.00
☐	1371	6c Apollo 8, 5/5/69, Houston, TX	25.00
☐	1372	6c W.C. Handy, 5/17/69, Memphis, TN	16.00
☐	1373	6c California Settlement, 7/16/69, San Diego, CA	25.00
☐	1374	6c John Wesley Powell, 8/1/69, Page, AZ	18.00
☐	1375	6c Alabama Statehood, 8/2/69, Huntsville, AL	18.00
☐	1376-1379	6c Botanical Congress, 8/23/69, Seattle, WA	30.00
☐	1380	6c Dartmouth College Case, 9/22/69, Hanover, NH	10.00
☐	1381	6c Professional Baseball, 9/24/69, Cincinnati, OH	70.00
☐	1382	6c Intercollegiate Football, 9/26/69, New Brunswick, NJ	50.00
☐	1383	6c Dwight D. Eisenhower, 10/14/69, Abilene, KS	15.00
☐	1384	6c Christmas, 11/3/69, Christmas, FL	25.00
☐	1385	6c Hope For Crippled, 11/20/69, Columbus, OH	15.00
☐	1386	6c William M. Harnett, 12/3/69, Boston, MA	18.00

1970

☐	1387-1390	6c Natural History, 5/6/70, New York, NY	20.00
☐	1391	6c Maine Statehood, 7/9/70, Portland, ME	20.00

☐   1392   6c Wildlife Conservation, 7/20/70, Custer, SD 15.00

1970-74

☐   1393   6c Dwight D. Eisenhower, 8/6/70, DC...15.00
☐   1393D 7c Benjamin Franklin, 10/20/72, Philadelphia, PA.............................18.00
☐   1395c 8c Dwight D. Eisenhower, booklet pane of 4, 1/28/72,
          Casa Grande, AZ...32.00
☐   1395d 8c Dwight D. Eisenhower, booklet pane of 7, 1/28/72,
          Casa Grande, AZ...50.00
☐   1396   8c USPS Emblem, 7/1/71, DC 10.00
☐   1397   14c Fiorello H. LaGuardia, 4/24/72, New York, NY 18.00
☐   1398   16c Ernest T. Pyle, 5/7/71, DC...10.00
☐   1399   18c Elizabeth Blackwell, 1/23/74, Geneva, NY.............................10.00
☐   1400   21c Amadeo Giannini, 6/27/73, San Mateo, CA 12.00

1970

☐   1405   6c Edgar Lee Masters, 8/22/70, Petersburg, IL 22.00
☐   1405   6c Edgar Lee Masters, 2nd Day, 8/23/70, Garnett, KS 38.00
☐   1406   6c Woman Suffrage, 8/26/70, Adams, MA 25.00
☐   1407   6c South Carolina, 9/12/70, Charleston, SC 20.00
☐   1408   6c Stone Mountain Memorial, 9/19/70, Stone Mountain, GA 10.00
☐   1409   6c Fort Snelling, 10/17/70, Fort Snelling, MN................................12.00
☐   1410-1413 6c Anti-Pollution, 10/28/70, San Clemente, CA 30.00
☐   1414-1418 6c Christmas Toys, 11/5/70, DC (without insert) (2 types).............20.00
☐   1414a-1418a Christmas Toys, Precancel, 11/5/70, DC 50.00
☐   1419   6c United Nations, 11/20/70, New York, NY 12.00
☐   1420   6c Landing of the Pilgrims, 11/21/70, Plymouth, MA........................15.00
☐   1421   6c Disabled Veterans, 11/24/70, Cincinnati, OH 15.00
☐   1422   6c U.S. Serviceman, 11/24/70, Montgomery, AL 12.00

1971

☐   1423   6c American Wool Industry, 1/19/71, Las Vegas, NV 18.00
☐   1424   6c Douglas MacArthur, 1/26/71, Norfolk, VA 15.00
☐   1425   6c Blood Donor, 3/12/71, New York, NY 18.00
☐   1426   8c Missouri Sesquicentennial, 5/8/71, Independence, MO 18.00
☐   1427-1430 8c Wildlife Conservation, 6/12/71, Avery Island, LA 25.00
☐   1431   8c Antarctic Treaty, 6/23/71, DC 12.00
☐   1433   8c John Sloan 8/2/71, Lock Haven, PA 12.00
☐   1434-1435 8c Space Achievement Decade, 8/2/71, Huntsville, AL (3 papers).35.00
☐   1436   8c Emily Dickinson, 8/28/71, Amherst, MA 12.00
☐   1437   8c San Juan, 9/12/71, San Juan, PR..18.00
☐   1438   8c Prevent Drug Abuse, 10/4/71, Dallas, TX 15.00
☐   1439   8c CARE, 10/27/71, New York, NY...18.00
☐   1440-1443 8c Historic Preservation, 10/29/71, San Diego, CA 50.00
☐   1444-1445 8c Christmas, 11/10/71, DC (without insert)...................................10.00

1972

☐   1446   8c Sidney Lanier, 2/3/72, Macon, GA 12.00
☐   1447   8c Peace Corps, 2/11/72, DC..12.00
☐   1448-1451 2c National Parks Centennial, 4/5/72, Hatteras, NC
          (without insert)..15.00
☐   1452   6c National Parks Centennial, 6/26/72, Vienna, VA 35.00
☐   1453   8c National Parks Centennial, 3/1/72, DC 25.00
☐   1453   8c National Parks Centennial, 3/1/72, Yellowstone National Park,
          WY...30.00

	1454	15c National Parks Centennial, 7/28/72, McKinley Park, AK	35.00
	1455	8c Family Planning, 3/18/72, New York, NY	15.00
	1456-1459	8c Colonial American Craftsmen, 7/4/72, Williamsburg, VA	15.00
	1460-1462,	C85 6c-15c Olympic Games, 8/17/72, Washington, DC (2 types)	10.00
	1463	8c Parent Teacher Association, 9/15/72, San Francisco, CA	10.00
	1464-1467	8c Wildlife Conservation, 9/20/72, Warm Springs, OR	12.00
	1468	8c Mail Order, 9/27/72, Chicago, IL	30.00
	1469	8c Osteopathic Medicine, 10/9/72, Miami, FL	10.00
	1470	8c Tom Sawyer, 10/13/72, Hannibal, MO	20.00
	1471-1472	8c Christmas, 11/9/72, DC (without insert)	12.00
	1473	8c Pharmacy, 11/10/72, Cincinnati, OH	10.00
	1474	8c Stamp Collecting, 11/17/72, New York, NY	12.00

1973

	1475	8c Love, 1/26/73, Philadelphia, PA	12.00
	1476	8c Colonial Communications (Pamphleteer), 2/16/73, Portland, OR	12.00
	1477	8c Colonial Communications (Broadside), 4/13/73, Atlantic City, NJ	12.00
	1478	8c Colonial Communications (Post Rider), 6/22/73, Rochester, NY	12.00
	1479	8c Colonial Communications (Drummer), 9/28/73, New Orleans, LA	12.00
	1480-1483	8c Boston Tea Party, 7/4/73, Boston, MA	25.00
	1484	8c George Gershwin, 2/28/73, Beverly Hills, CA	45.00
	1485	8c Robinson Jeffers, 8/13/73, Carmel, CA	12.00
	1486	8c Henry O. Tanner, 9/10/73, Pittsburgh, PA	12.00
	1487	8c Willa Cather, 9/20/73, Red Cloud, NE	8.00
	1488	8c Copernicus, 4/23/73, DC	10.00
	1489-1498	8c Postal Service Employees, 4/30/73, DC (3 cities)	15.00
	1499	8c Harry S. Truman, 5/8/73, Independence, MO	15.00
	1500-1502	6c-15c Electronics, 7/10/73, New York, NY	30.00
	1503	8c Lyndon B. Johnson, 8/27/73, Austin, TX	15.00

1973-74 Rural America

	1504	8c Angus & Longhorn Cattle, 10/5/73, St. Joseph, MO	15.00
	1505	10c Chautauqua, 8/6/74, Chautauqua, NY	15.00
	1506	10c Wheat, 8/16/74, Hillsboro, KS	15.00

1973

	1507-1508	8c Christmas, 11/7/73, DC (without insert)	15.00

1973-74

	1509	10c Crossed Flags, 12/8/73, San Francisco, CA	18.00
	1510d	10c Jefferson Memorial, booklet pane of 6, 8/5/74, Oakland, CA	25.00
	1518	6.3c Liberty Bell, coil, 10/1/74, DC	10.00

1974

	1525	10c Veterans of Foreign Wars, 3/11/74, DC	15.00
	1526	10c Robert Frost, 3/26/74, Derry, NH	12.00
	1527	10c EXPO '74, 4/18/74, Spokane, WA	15.00
	1528	10c Horse Racing, 5/4/74, Louisville, KY (with insert)	22.00
	1529	10c Skylab, 5/14/74, Houston, TX	20.00
	1530-1537	10c Centenary of UPU, 6/6/74, DC	20.00
	1538-1541	10c Mineral Heritage, 6/13/74, Lincoln, NE	22.00
	1542	10c Kentucky Settlement, 6/16/74, Harrodsville, KY	10.00
	1543-1546	10c First Continental Congress, 7/4/74, Philadelphia, PA	20.00
	1547	10c Energy Conservation, 9/23/74, Detroit, MI	10.00

□	1548	10c **Legend of Sleepy Hollow**, 10/10/74, North Tarrytown, NY	20.00
□	1549	10c **Retarded Children**, 10/1/74, Arlington, TX	20.00
□	1550-1551	10c **Christmas**, 10/23/74, New York, NY	25.00
□	1550-1552	10c **Christmas**, 10/23/74, New York, NY (less than 10 known)	100.00

1552 was added to the 1550-1551 program.

1975

□	1553	10c **Benjamin West**, 2/10/75, Swarthmore, PA	20.00
□	1554	10c **Paul Laurence Dunbar**, 5/1/75, Dayton, OH	12.00
□	1555	10c **D.W. Griffith**, 5/17/75, Beverly Hills, CA	12.00
□	1556	10c **Pioneer-Jupiter**, 2/28/75, Mountain View, CA	20.00
□	1557	10c **Mariner 10**, 4/4/75, Pasadena, CA	20.00
□	1558	10c **Collective Bargaining**, 3/13/75, DC	15.00
□	1559	8c **Sybil Ludington**, 3/25/75, Carmel, NY	12.00
□	1560	10c **Salem Poor**, 3/25/75, Cambridge, MA	15.00
□	1561	10c **Haym Salomon**, 3/25/75, Chicago, IL	18.00
□	1562	18c **Peter Francisco**, 3/25/75, Greensboro, NC	15.00
□	1563	10c **Lexington-Concord Battle**, 4/19/75, Concord, MA	15.00
□	1563	10c **Lexington-Concord Battle**, 4/19/75, Lexington, MA	15.00
□	1564	10c **Battle of Bunker Hill**, 6/17/75, Charlestown, MA (2 types)	15.00
□	1565-1568	10c **Military Uniforms**, 7/4/75, DC	18.00
□	1571	10c **International Women's Year**, 8/26/75, Seneca Falls, NY	18.00
□	1572-1575	10c **Postal Service Bicentennial**, 9/3/75, Philadelphia, PA	18.00
□	1577-1578	10c **Banking & Commerce**, 10/6/75, New York, NY	12.00
□	1579-1580	10c **Christmas**, 10/14/75, DC (with insert) (2 types)	20.00

1975-81

□	1581-1585	1c-4c **Americana Series**, 12/8/77, St. Louis, MO	12.00
□	1592	10c **Contemplation of Justice**, 11/17/77, New York, NY	10.00
□	1593	11c **Early American Printing Press**, 11/13/75, Philadelphia, PA	12.00
□	1594	& 1816 12c **Liberty's Torch**, sheet & coil, 4/8/81, Dallas, TX	12.00
□	1595a-1595c	13c **Liberty Bell**, booklet panes, 10/31/75, Cleveland, OH	20.00
□	1595d	13c **Liberty Bell**, booklet pane of S, 4/2/76, Liberty, MO	15.00
□	1596	13c **Eagle & Shield**, 12/1/75, Juneau, AK	12.00
□	1597	15c **Ft. McHenry Flag**, 6/30/78, Baltimore, MD	12.00
□	1598a	**Ft. McHenry Flag**, booklet pane of 8, 6/30/78, Baltimore, MD	50.00
□	1603	24c **Old North Church**, 11/14/75, Boston, MA	12.00
□	1604	28c **Fort Nisqually**, 8/11/78, Tacoma, WA	10.00
□	1605	29c **Sandy Hook Lighthouse**, 4/14/78, Atlantic City, NJ	12.00
□	1606	30c **Morris Township School No. 2**, 8/27/79, Devils Lake, ND	15.00
□	1608	50c **Iron "Betty" Lamp**, 9/11/79, San Juan, PR	22.00
□	1611	$2 **Kerosene Table Lamp**, 11/16/78, New York, NY	18.00
□	1612	$5 **Railroad Lantern**, 8/23/79, Boston, MA	30.00
□	1614	7.7c **Saxhorns**, 11/20/76, New York, NY	12.00
□	1615	7.9c **Drum**, 4/23/76, Miami, FL	12.00
□	1615C	8.4c **Grand Piano**, 6/13/78, Interlochen, MI	35.00
□	1616	9c **Dome of the Capitol**, 3/5/76, Milwaukee, WI	15.00
□	1617	10c **Contemplation of Justice**, 11/4/77, Tampa, FL	12.00
□	1618	13c **Liberty Bell**, 11/25/75, Allentown, PA	12.00
□	1618C	15c **Fort McHenry Flag**, 6/30/78, Baltimore, MD	50.00
□	1622	13c **Flag over Independence Hall**, 11/15/75, Philadelphia, PA	12.00

1975-77

| □ | 1623c | 13c **Flag over Capitol + 9c Capitol**, booklet pane of 8, perf. 10, 3/11/77, New York, NY | 20.00 |

☐ 1623c-1623d 13c Flag over Capitol & 9c Capitol, booklet pane of 8 with perf.
10 1/2x11 stamps added, 3/11/77, New York, NY.............................70.00
☐ 1625 13c Flag Over Independence Hall, coil, 11/15/75, Philadelphia, PA 50.00

1976

☐ 1632 13c Interphil, 1/17/76, Philadelphia, PA...............................15.00
☐ 1633-1682 13c State Flags, 2/23/76 (4 cities).................................45.00
☐ 1683 13c Telephone Centenary, 3/10/76, Boston, MA.....................15.00
☐ 1684 13c Commercial Aviation, 3/19/76, Chicago, IL......................15.00
☐ 1685 13c Chemistry, 4/6/76, New York, NY 15.00
☐ 1686-1689 13c-31c Bicentennial Souvenir Sheets, 5/29/76, Philadelphia, PA
(any single stamp) (2 types) 25.00
☐ 1690 13c Benjamin Franklin, 6/1/76, Philadelphia, PA....................15.00
☐ 1691-1694 13c Declaration of Independence, 7/4/76, Philadelphia, PA.........40.00
☐ 1695-1698 13c Olympic Games, 7/16/76, Lake Placid, NY 20.00
☐ 1699 13c Clara Maass, 8/18/76, Belleville, NJ 15.00
☐ 1701-1702 13c Christmas (Copley & Currier), 10/27/76, Boston, MA 20.00
☐ 1703 13c Christmas (Currier), Photogravure, 10/27/76, Boston, MA............25.00

1977

☐ 1704 13c Washington at Princeton, 1/3/77, Princeton, NJ...........................18.00
☐ 1705 15c Sound Recording, 3/23/77, DC 18.00
☐ 1706-1709 13c Pueblo Pottery, 4/13/77, Santa Fe, NM......................12.00
☐ 1710 13c Lindbergh Flight, 5/20/77, Roosevelt Sta., NY 25.00
☐ 1711 13c Colorado Statehood, 5/12/77, Denver, CO 12.00
☐ 1712-1715 13c Butterflies, 6/6/77, Indianapolis, IN 18.00
☐ 1716 13c Lafayette, 6/13/77, Charleston, SC 15.00
☐ 1717-1720 13c Skilled Hands for Independence, 7/4/77, Cincinnati, OH........18.00
☐ 1721 13c Peace Bridge, 8/4/77, Buffalo, NY 15.00
☐ 1722 13c Battle of Oriskany, 8/6/77, Utica, NY 22.00
☐ 1725 13c Alta California, 9/9/77, San Jose, CA 10.00
☐ 1726 13c Articles of Confederation, 9/30/77, York, PA 16.00
☐ 1727 13c Talking Pictures, 10/6/77, Hollywood, CA 25.00
☐ 1728 13c Surrender at Saratoga, 10/7/77, Schuylerville, NY..................15.00
☐ 1729 13c Christmas (Washington at Valley Forge), 10/21/77,
Valley Forge, PA 25.00
☐ 1730 13c Christmas (mailbox), 10/21/77, Omaha, NE 20.00

1978

☐ 1731 13c Carl Sandburg, 1/6/78, Galesburg, IL..............................15.00
☐ 1732-1733 13c Captain Cook, 1/20/78, Anchorage, AK, or Honolulu, HI.........18.00

1978-80

☐ 1734 13c Indian Head Penny, 1/11/78, Kansas City, MO 15.00
☐ 1737a 15c Roses, booklet pane of 8, 7/11/78, Shreveport, LA.....................20.00
☐ 1742a 15c Windmills, booklet pane of 10, 2/7/80, Lubbock, TX....................48.00

1978

☐ 1744 13c Harriet Tubman, 2/1/78, DC......................................25.00
☐ 1745-1748 13c American Quilts, 3/8/78, Charleston, WV 20.00
☐ 1749-1752 13c American Dance, 4/26/78, New York, NY 10.00
☐ 1753 13c French Alliance, 5/4/78, York, PA 12.00
☐ 1754 13c Early Cancer Detection, 5/18/78, DC 25.00
☐ 1755 13c Jimmie Rodgers, 5/24/78, Meridian, MS 20.00
☐ 1756 15c George M. Cohan, 7/3/78, Providence, RI..........................18.00

	1758	15c Photography, 6/26/78, Las Vegas, NV	15.00
	1759	15c Viking Missions to Mars, 7/20/78, Hampton, VA	25.00
	1760-1763	15c American Owls, 8/26/78, Fairbanks, AK	18.00
	1764-1767	15c American Trees, 10/9/78, Hot Springs National Park, AR	18.00
	1768	15c Christmas (Madonna), 10/18/78, DC	12.00
	1769	15c Christmas (Hobby Horse), 10/18/78, Holly, MI	20.00

1979

	1770	15c Robert F. Kennedy, 1/12/79, DC	30.00
	1771	15c Martin Luther King, Jr., 1/13/79, Atlanta, GA	30.00
	1772	15c International Year of the Child, 2/15/79, Philadelphia, PA	10.00
	1773	15c John Steinbeck, 2/27/79, Salinas, CA	15.00
	1774	15c Albert Einstein, 3/4/79, Princeton, NJ	18.00
	1775-1778	15c Pennsylvania Toleware, 4/19/79, Lancaster, PA	12.00
	1779-1782	15c American Architecture, 6/4/79, Kansas City, MO	20.00
	1783-1786	15c Endangered Flora, 6/7/79, Milwaukee, WI	15.00
	1787	15c Seeing Eye Dogs, 6/15/79, Morristown, NJ	25.00
	1788	15c Special Olympics, 8/9/79, Brockport, NY	18.00
	1789	15c John Paul Jones, 9/23/79, Annapolis, MD	15.00

1979-80

	1790	10c Olympic Games, 9/5/79, Olympia, WA	15.00
	1791-1794	15c Olympic Games, 9/28/79, Los Angeles, CA	15.00
	1795-1798	15c Winter Olympic Games, 2/1/80, Lake Placid, NY	15.00

1979

	1799	15c Christmas (Virgin and Child), 10/18/79, DC	12.00
	1800	15c Christmas (Santa Claus), 10/18/79, North Pole, AK	15.00
	1801	15c Will Rogers, 11/4/79, Claremore, OK	20.00
	1802	15c Vietnam Veterans, 11/11/79, DC	25.00

1980

	1803	15c W.C. Fields, 1/29/80, Beverly Hills, CA	25.00
	1804	15c Benjamin Banneker, 2/15/80, Annapolis, MD	25.00
	1805-1810	15c National Letter Writing Week, 2/25/80, DC	12.00
	1821	15c Frances Perkins, 4/10/80, DC	10.00
	1822	15c Dolley Madison, 5/10/80, DC	10.00
	1823	15c Emily Bissell, 5/31/80, Wilmington, DE	8.00
	1824	15c Helen Keller, 6/27/80, Tuscumbia, AL	18.00
	1825	15c Veterans Administration, 7/21/80, DC	10.00
	1826	15c Bernardo de Galvez, 7/23/80, New Orleans, LA	10.00
	1827-1830	15c Coral Reefs, 8/26/80, Charlotte Amalie, VI	25.00
	1832	15c Edith Wharton, 9/5/80, New Haven, CT	12.00
	1833	15c Education, 9/12/80, DC	10.00
	1834-1837	15c Pacific Northwest Indian Masks, 9/25/80, Spokane, WA	20.00
	1838-1841	15c American Architecture, 10/9/80, New York, NY	10.00
	1842	15c Christmas (Madonna & Child), 10/31/80, DC	14.00
	1843	15c Christmas (Wreath & Toys), 10/31/80, Christmas, MI	20.00

1980-85 Great Americans

	1844	1c Dorothea Dix, 9/23/83, Hampden, ME	8.00
	1845	2c Igor Stravinsky, 11/18/82, New York, NY	6.00
	1846	3c Henry Clay, 7/13/83, DC	8.00
	1847	4c Carl Schurz, 6/3/83, Watertown, WI	8.00
	1848	5c Pearl Buck, 6/25/83, Hillsboro, WV	15.00

☐	1849	6c Walter Lippmann, 9/19/85, Minneapolis, MN....................8.00
☐	1850	7c Abraham Baldwin, 1/25/85, Athens, GA 8.00
☐	1851	8c Henry Knox, 7/25/85, Thomaston, ME 8.00
☐	1852	9c Sylvanus Thayer, 6/7/85, Braintree, MA 8.00
☐	1853	10c Richard Russell, 5/31/84, Winder, GA...........................8.00
☐	1854	11c Alden Partridge, 2/12/85, Norwich Univ., VT...............8.00
☐	1855	13c Crazy Horse, 1/15/82, Crazy Horse, SD 28.00
☐	1856	14c Sinclair Lewis, 3/21/85, Sauk Centre, MN.....................8.00
☐	1857	17c Rachel Carson, 5/28/81, Springdale, PA........................16.00
☐	1858	18c George Mason, 5/7/81, Gunston Hall, VA 8.00
☐	1859	19c Sequoyah, 12/27/80, Tahlequah, OK..............................14.00
☐	1860	20c Ralph Bunche, 1/12/82, New York, NY..........................8.00
☐	1861	20c Thomas Gallaudet, 6/10/83, West Hartford, CT..............12.00
☐	1862	20c Harry S Truman, 1/26/84, DC..8.00
☐	1863	22c John J. Audubon, 4/23/85, New York, NY......................6.00
☐	1864	30c Frank Laubach, 9/2/84, Benton, PA 8.00
☐	1865	35c Charles Drew, 6/3/81, DC...16.00
☐	1866	37c Robert Millikan, 1/26/82, Pasadena, CA 10.00
☐	1867	39c Grenville Clark, 3/20/85, Hanover, NH.........................10.00
☐	1868	40c Lillian Gilbreth, 2/24/84, Montclair, NJ.......................10.00
☐	1869	50c Chester W. Nimitz, 2/22/85, Fredericksburg TX 15.00

1981-83

☐	1874	15c Everett Dirksen, 1/4/81, Pekin, IL................................18.00
☐	1875	15c Whitney Moore Young, 1/30/81, New York, NY 12.00
☐	1876-1879 18c Flowers, 4/23/81, Ft. Valley, GA...................................18.00
☐	1889a 18c Wildlife, booklet pane of 10, 5/14/81, Boise, ID 18.00
☐	1890-1893a 18c Flag, sheet, coil, booklet pane of 8, 4/24/81, Portland, ME....20.00
☐	1896b 20c Flag, booklet pane of 10, 11/17/83, DC.............................10.00

1981-83 Transportation Coils

☐	1897	1c Omnibus, 8/19/83, Arlington, VA..................................12.00
☐	1897A 2c Locomotive, 5/20/82, Chicago, IL..................................15.00
☐	1898	3c Handcar, 3/25/83, Rochester, NY..................................15.00
☐	1898A 4c Stagecoach, 8/19/82, Milwaukee, WI.............................15.00
☐	1899	5c Motorcycle, 10/10/83, San Francisco, CA......................20.00
☐	1904	10.9c Hansom Cab, 3/26/82, Chattanooga, TN...................20.00
☐	1907	18c Surrey, 5/18/81, Notch, MO 18.00

1981

☐	1910	18c American Red Cross, 5/1/81, DC...................................10.00
☐	1911	18c Savings & Loan Sesquicentennial, 5/8/81, Chicago, IL 10.00
☐	1912-1919 18c Space Achievement, 5/21/81, Kennedy Space Center, FL........22.00
☐	1920	18c Professional Management, 6/18/81, Philadelphia, PA....8.00
☐	1921-1924 18c Preservation of Wildlife Habitats, 6/26/81, Reno, NV...........10.00
☐	1925	18c International Year of the Disabled, 6/29/81, Milford, MI.....8.00
☐	1926	18c Edna St. Vincent Millay, 7/10/81, Austerlitz, NY 10.00
☐	1927	18c Alcoholism, 8/19/81, DC..8.00
☐	1928-1931 18c American Architecture, 8/28/81, DC 8.00
☐	1932-1933 18c Babe Zaharias & Bobby Jones, 9/22/81, Pinehurst, NC........15.00
☐	1934	18c Frederic Remington, 10/9/81, Oklahoma City, OK 12.00
☐	1935-1936 18c & 20c James Hoban, 10/31/81, DC...................................25.00
☐	1937-1938 18c Battles of Yorktown & Virginia Capes, 10/16/81, Yorktown,VA..12.00
☐	1939	20c Christmas (Botticelli), 10/28/81, Chicago, IL 12.00

	1940	20c Christmas (Bear & Sleigh), 10/28/81, Christmas Valley, OR	18.00
1941	20c John Hanson, 11/5/81, Frederick, MD	10.00
1942-1945	20c Desert Plants, 12/1 1/81, Tucson, AZ (2 types)	18.00

1982

	1949a	20c Bighorn Sheep, booklet pane of 10, 1/8/82, Bighorn, MT	18.00
1950	20c Franklin D. Roosevelt, 1/30/82, Hyde Park, NY	12.00
1951	20c Love, 2/1/82, Boston, MA	10.00
1952	20c George Washington, 2/22/82, Mt. Vernon, VA (2 types)	10.00
1953-2002	20c State Birds & Flowers, 4/14/82, DC (any Block of 4)	12.00
2003	20c U.S.-Netherlands Recognition, 4/20/82, DC	22.00
2004	20c Library of Congress, 4/21/82, DC	8.00
2005	20c Consumer Education, 4/27/82, DC	8.00
2006-2009	20c Knoxville World's Fair, 4/29/82, Knoxville, TN	10.00
2010	20c Horatio Alger, 4/30/82, Willow Grove, PA	12.00
2011	20c Aging Together, 5/21/82, Sun City, AZ	10.00
2012	20c The Barrymores, 6/8/82, New York, NY	6.00
2013	20c Dr. Mary E. Walker, 6/10/82, Oswego, NY	10.00
2014	20c International Peace Garden, 6/30/82, Dunseith, ND	10.00
2015	20c America's Libraries, 7/13/82, Philadelphia, PA	8.00
2016	20c Jackie Robinson, 8/2/82, Cooperstown, NY	35.00
2017	20c Touro Synagogue, 8/22/82, Newport, RI	10.00
2018	20c Wolf Trap Farm Park, 9/1/82, Vienna, VA	8.00
2019-2022	20c American Architecture, 9/30/82, DC	8.00
2023	20c St. Francis of Assisi, 10/7/82, San Francisco, CA	18.00
2024	20c Ponce de Leon, 10/12/82, San Juan, PR	10.00
2025	13c Christmas (Kitten & Puppy), 11/3/82, Danvers, MA	20.00
2026	20c Christmas (Madonna), 10/28/82, DC	10.00
2027-2030	20c Christmas (Children), 10/28/82, Snow, OK	18.00

1983

	2031	20c Science & Industry, 1/19/83, Chicago, IL	10.00
2032-2035	20c Balloons, 3/31/83, Albuquerque, NM	18.00
2036	20c U.S.-Sweden, 3/24/83, Philadelphia, PA	14.00
2037	20c Civilian Conservation Corps, 4/5/83, Luray, VA	8.00
2038	20c Joseph Priestley, 4/13/83, Northumberland, PA	8.00
2039	20c Voluntarism, 4/20/83, DC	8.00
2040	20c U.S.-Germany, 4/29/83, Germantown, PA	15.00
2041	20c Brooklyn Bridge, 5/17/83, Brooklyn, NY	6.00
2042	20c Tennessee Valley Authority, 5/18/83, Knoxville, TN	8.00
2043	20c Physical Fitness, 5/14/83, Houston, TX	10.00
2044	20c Scott Joplin, 6/9/83, Sedalia, MO (2 types)	28.00
2045	20c Medal of Honor, 6/7/83, DC (2 types)	14.00
2046	20c Babe Ruth 7/6/83, Chicago, IL	35.00
2047	20c Nathaniel Hawthorne, 7/8/83, Salem, MA	10.00
2048-2051	13c 1984 Los Angeles Olympics, 7/28/83, South Bend, IN	12.00
2052	20c Signing of Treaty of Paris, 9/2/83, DC	10.00
2053	20c Civil Service, 9/9/83, DC	8.00
2054	20c Metropolitan Opera, 9/14/83, New York, NY	6.00
2055-2058	20c American Inventors, 9/21/83, DC	8.00
2059-2062	20c Streetcars, 10/8/83, Kennebunkport, ME	12.00
2063	20c Christmas (Madonna), 10/28/83, DC	10.00
2064	20c Christmas (Santa Claus), 10/28/83, Santa Claus, IN	10.00
2065	20c Martin Luther, 11/11/83, DC	10.00

1984

☐	2066	20c Alaska Statehood, 1/3/84, Fairbanks, AK 8.00
☐	2067-2070 20c Winter Olympic Games, 1/6/84, Lake Placid, NY....................12.00
☐	2071	20c Federal Deposit Insurance Corporation, 1/12/84, DC 8.00
☐	2072	20c Love, 1/31/84, DC 8.00
☐	2073	20c Carter Woodson, 2/1/84, DC 10.00
☐	2074	20c Soil & Water Conservation, 2/6/84, Denver, CO...........................8.00
☐	2075	20c Credit Union Act, 2/10/84, Salem, MA 8.00
☐	2076-2079 20c Orchids, 3/5/84, Miami, FL..14.00
☐	2080	20c Hawaii Statehood, 3/12/84, Honolulu, HI...................................8.00
☐	2081	20c National Archives, 4/16/84, DC 8.00
☐	2082-2085 20c 1984 Los Angeles Olympics, 5/4/84, Los Angeles, CA 12.00
☐	2086	20c New Orleans World Exposition, 5/11/84, New Orleans, LA...........8.00
☐	2087	20c Health Research, 5/17/84, New York, NY 6.00
☐	2088	20c Douglas Fairbanks, 5/23/84, Denver, CO....................................8.00
☐	2089	20c Jim Thorpe, 5/24/84, Shawnee, OK...25.00
☐	2089	Jim Thorpe (2nd Day), 5/25/84, Yale, OK 35.00
☐	2090	20c John McCormack, 6/6/84, Boston, MA 10.00
☐	2091	20c St. Lawrence Seaway, 6/26/84, Massena, NY 10.00
☐	2092	20c Waterfowl Preservation Act, 7/2/84, Des Moines, IA.................12.00
☐	2093	20c Roanoke Voyages, 7/31/84, Manteo, NC...................................25.00
☐	2094	20c Herman Melville, 8/1/84, New Bedford, MA..............................12.00
☐	2095	20c Horace A. Moses, 8/6/84, Bloomington, IN................................8.00
☐	2096	20c Smokey The Bear, 8/13/84, Capitan, NM.................................15.00
☐	2097	20c Roberto Clemente, 8/17/84, Carolina, PR.................................30.00
☐	2098-2101 20c Dogs, 9/7/84, New York, NY 10.00
☐	2102	20c Crime Prevention, 9/26/84, DC..8.00
☐	2103	20c Hispanic Americans, 10/31/84, DC...10.00
☐	2104	20c Family Unity, 10/1/84, Shaker Heights, OH................................8.00
☐	2105	20c Eleanor Roosevelt, 10/11/84, Hyde Park, NY 8.00
☐	2106	20c Nation of Readers, 10/16/84, DC..8.00
☐	2107	20c Christmas (Madonna), 10/30/84, DC...10.00
☐	2108	20c Christmas (Santa Clans) 10/30/84, Jamaica, NY........................10.00
☐	2109	20c Vietnam Veterans Memorial, 11/10/84, DC 18.00

1985

☐	2110	22c Jerome Kern, 1/23/85, New York, NY 6.00
☐	2114-2115 22c Flag, sheet and coil, 3/29/85, DC...10.00
☐	2115b 22c Flag Over Capitol, test coil, 5/23/87, Secaucus, NJ...................8.00
☐	2121a 22c Seashells, booklet pane of 10, 4/4/85, Boston, MA......................15.00

1985-87 Transportation Coils

☐	2123	3.4c School Bus, 6/8/85, Arlington, VA..12.00
☐	2125	& 2128 4.9c Buckboard & 8.3c Ambulance, 6/21/85, Reno, NV.........20.00
☐	2126	5.5c Star Route Truck, 11/1/86, Fort Worth, TX 12.00
☐	2127	7.1c Tractor, 2/6/87, Sarasota, FL...12.00
☐	2127a 7.1c Tractor, ZIP + 4 precancel, 5/26/89, Rosemont, IL 8.00
☐	2129	8.5c Tow Truck, 1/24/87, Tucson, AZ..12.00
☐	2130	11 c Stutz Super Bearcat, 6/11/85, Baton Rouge, LA.......................12.00
☐	2131	12c Stanley Steamer, 4/2/85, Kingfield, ME 12.00
☐	2134	14c Iceboat, 3/23/85, Rochester, NY..12.00
☐	2135	17c Dog Sled, 8/20/86, Anchorage, AK..12.00
☐	2136	25c Bread Wagon, 11/22/86, Virginia Beach, VA.............................12.00

1985

- 2137   22c Mary McLeod Bethune, 3/5/85, DC 8.00
- 2138-2141 22c Duck Decoys, 3/22/85, Shelburne, VT 14.00
- 2142   22c Winter Special Olympics, 3/25/85, Park City, UT.........................10.00
- 2143   22c Love, 4/17/85, Hollywood, CA 10.00
- 2144   22c Rural Electrification Administration, 5/11/85, Madison, SD.........10.00
- 2145   22c Ameripex '86, 5/25/85, Rosemont, IL 10.00
- 2146   22c Abigail Adams, 6/14/85, Quincy, MA 10.00
- 2147   22c Frederic Auguste Bartholdi, 7/18/85, New York, NY..................12.00
- 2149   18c Washington Monument, coil, 11/6/85, DC.............................12.00
- 2150   21.1c Sealed Envelopes, coil, 10/22/85, DC 12.00
- 2152   22c Korean War Veterans, 7/26/85, DC.......................................12.00
- 2153   22c Social Security Act, 8/14/85, Baltimore, MD..........................15.00
- 2154   22c World War I Vets, 8/26/85, Milwaukee, WI 10.00
- 2155-2158 22c Horses, 9/25/85, Lexington, KY 14.00
- 2159   22c Public Education in America, 10/1/85, Boston, MA....................6.00
- 2160-2163 22c International Youth Year, 10/7/85, Chicago, IL.......................8.00
- 2164   22c Help End Hunger, 10/15/85, DC 8.00
- 2165   22c Christmas (Madonna & Child), 10/31/85, Detroit, MI..................10.00
- 2166   22c Christmas (Poinsettia), 10/30/85, Nazareth, MI 10.00

1986

- 2167   22c Arkansas Statehood, 1/3/86, Little Rock, AR 8.00

1986-90 Great Americans

- 2168   1c Margaret Mitchell, 6/30/86, Atlanta, GA...8.00
- 2169   2c Mary Lyon, 2/28/87, South Hadley, MA 12.00
- 2170   3c Dr. Paul Dudley White, 9/15/86, DC...8.00
- 2171   4c Father Flanagan, 7/14/86, Boys Town, NE...8.00
- 2172   5c Hugo Black, 2/27/86, DC..8.00
- 2173   5c Luis Munoz Marin, 2/18/90, San Juan, PR 6.00
- 2176   10c Red Cloud, 8/15/87, Red Cloud, NE 10.00
- 2177   14c Julia Ward Howe, 2/12/87, Boston, MA...8.00
- 2178   15c Buffalo Bill Cody, 6/6/88, Cody, WY 18.00
- 2179   17c Belva Ann Lockwood, 6/18/86, Middleport, NY 6.00
- 2180   21c Chester Carlson, 10/21/88, Rochester, NY....................................20.00
- 2182   23c Mary Cassatt, 11/4/88, Philadelphia, PA 10.00
- 2183   25c Jack London, 1/11/86, Glen Ellen, CA 8.00
- 2184   28c Sitting Bull, 9/14/89, Rapid City, SD 8.00
- 2186   40c Claire Chennault, 9/6/90, Monroe, LA 6.00
- 2188   45c Dr. Harvey Cushing, 6/17/88, Cleveland, OH.............................10.00
- 2191   56c John Harvard, 9/3/86, Boston, MA 10.00
- 2192   65c General Hap Arnold, 11/5/88, Gladwyne, PA 10.00
- 2194 $1 Bernard Revel, 9/23/86, New York, NY 8.00
- 2194A $1 Johns Hopkins, 6/7/89, Baltimore, MD 15.00
- 2195 $2 William Jennings Bryan, 3/19/86, Salem, IL 15.00
- 2196 $5 Bret Harte, 8/25/87, Twain Harte, CA..20.00

1986

- 2201a 22c Stamp Collecting, booklet pane of 4, 1/23/86,
  State College, PA 12.00
- 2202   22c Love, 1/30/86, New York, NY 12.00
- 2203   22c Sojourner Truth, 2/4/86, New Paltz, NY......................................6.00
- 2204   22c Republic of Texas, 3/2/86, San Antonio, TX, or Washington on
  the Brazos, TX 10.00

☐	2209a	22c Fish, booklet pane of 5, 3/21/86, Seattle, WA	12.00
☐	2210	22c Public Hospitals, 4/11/86, New York, NY	6.00
☐	2211	22c Duke Ellington, 4/29/86, New York, NY	8.00
☐	2216-2219	22c Presidents Souvenir Sheets, 5/22/86, Chicago, IL (Scott 2216 only)	15.00
☐	2220-2223	22c Polar Explorers, 5/28/86, North Pole, AK	8.00
☐	2224	22c Statue of Liberty, 7/4/86, Liberty Island, NY	40.00
☐	2226	2c Locomotive, coil, re-engraved, 3/6/87, Milwaukee, WI	12.00
☐	2235-2238	22c Navajo Art, 9/4/86, Window Rock, AZ	10.00
☐	2239	22c T.S. Eliot, 9/26/86, St. Louis, MO	8.00
☐	2240-2243	22c Woodcarved Figurines, 10/1/86, DC	12.00
☐	2244	22c Christmas (Madonna), 10/24/86, DC	12.00
☐	2245	22c Christmas (Winter Village), 10/24/86, Snow Hill, MD	12.00

1987

☐	2246	22c Michigan Statehood, 1/26/87, Lansing, MI	8.00
☐	2247	22c Pan American Games, 1/29/87, Indianapolis, IN	8.00
☐	2248	22c Love, 1/30/87, San Francisco, CA	8.00
☐	2249	22c Jean Baptiste Pointe du Sable, 2/20/87, Chicago, IL	10.00
☐	2250	22c Enrico Caruso, 2/27/87, New York, NY	6.00
☐	2251	22c Girl Scouts of America, 3/12/87, DC	10.00

1987-88 Transportation Coils

☐	2252	3c Conestoga Wagon, 2/29/88, Conestoga, PA	12.00
☐	2253	& 2262 5c Milk Wagon & 17.5c Marmon Wasp, 9/25/87, Indianapolis, IN	12.00
☐	2254	5.3c Elevator, 9/16/88, New York, NY	10.00
☐	2255	7.6c Carreta, 8/30/88, San Jose, CA	12.00
☐	2256	8.4c Wheelchair, 8/12/88, Tucson, AZ	12.00
☐	2257	10c Canal Boat, 4/11/87, Buffalo, NY	10.00
☐	2258	13c Police Patrol Wagon, 2 types, 10/29/88, Anaheim, CA	10.00
☐	2259	13.2c Railroad Coal Car, 7/19/88, Pittsburgh, PA	12.00
☐	2260	15c Tugboat, 7/12/88, Long Beach, CA	12.00
☐	2261	16.7c Popcorn Wagon, 7/7/88, Chicago, IL	14.00
☐	2263	20c Cable Car, 10/28/88, San Francisco, CA	12.00
☐	2264	20.5c Fire Engine, 9/28/88, San Angelo, TX	12.00
☐	2265	21c Railroad Mail Car, 8/16/88, Santa Fe, NM	12.00
☐	2266	24.1c Tandem Bicycle, 10/26/88, Redmond, WA	12.00

1987-88

☐	2274a	22c Special Occasions, booklet pane of 10, 4/20/87, Atlanta, GA	15.00
☐	2275	22c United Way, 4/28/87, DC (2 types)	8.00
☐	2276	22c Flag & Fireworks, 5/9/87, Denver, CO	8.00
☐	2278	25c Flag with Clouds, 5/6/88, Boxborough, MA	10.00
☐	2280	25c Flag over Yosemite, coil, 5/20/88, Yosemite, CA	10.00
☐	2281	25c Honeybee, coil, 9/2/88, Omaha, NE	12.00
☐	2283a	25c Pheasant, booklet pane of 10, 4/29/88, Rapid City, SD	15.00
☐	2285b	25c Owl & Grosbeak, booklet pane of 10, 5/28/88, Arlington, VA	10.00
☐	2286-2335	22c American Wildlife, 6/13/87, Toronto, Canada	30.00

1987-89 Ratification of the Constitution

☐	2336	22c Delaware, 7/4/87, Dover, DE	12.00
☐	2337	22c Pennsylvania, 8/26/87, Harrisburg, PA	12.00
☐	2338	22c New Jersey, 9/11/87, Trenton, NJ	12.00
☐	2339	22c Georgia, 1/6/88, Atlanta, GA	12.00

	2340	22c Connecticut, 1/9/88, Hartford, CT	12.00
	2341	22c Massachusetts, 2/6/88, Boston, MA	12.00
	2342	22c Maryland, 2/15/88, Annapolis, MD	12.00
	2343	22c South Carolina, 5/23/88, Columbia, SC	12.00
	2344	22c New Hampshire, 6/21/88, Concord, NH	12.00
	2345	22c Virginia, 6/25/88, Williamsburg, VA	12.00
	2346	25c New York, 7/26/88, Albany, NY	12.00
	2347	25c North Carolina, 8/22/89, Fayettesville, NC	10.00
	2347	North Carolina (2nd day), 8/23/89, Durham, NC	18.00
	2347	North Carolina (2nd day), 8/23/89, Eden, NC	6.00
	2347	North Carolina (2nd day), 8/23/89, Edenton, NC	18.00
	2347	North Carolina (2nd day), 8/23/89, Greensboro, NC	18.00
	2347	North Carolina (2nd day), 8/23/89, High Point, NC	25.00
	2347	North Carolina (2nd day), 8/23/89, Hillsborough, NC	20.00
	2347	North Carolina (2nd day), 8/23/89, New Bern, NC	6.00
	2347	North Carolina (2nd day), 8/23/89, Raleigh, NC	6.00
	2347	North Carolina (2nd day), 8/23/89, Ridgeway, NC	6.00
	2347	North Carolina (2nd day), 8/23/89, Winston-Salem, NC	6.00
	2348	25c Rhode Island, 5/29/90, Pawtucket, RI	10.00

1987

	2349	22c US-Morocco Diplomatic Relations, 7/17/87, DC	10.00
	2350	22c William Faulkner, 8/3/87, Oxford, MS	8.00
	2351-2354	22c Lacemaking, 8/14/87, Ypsilanti, MI	8.00
	2359a	22c Drafting of the Constitution Bicentennial, booklet pane of 5, 8/28/87, DC	10.00
	2366a	22c Locomotives, booklet pane of 5, 10/1/87, Baltimore, MD	15.00
	2367	22c Christmas (Madonna & Child), 10/23/87, DC	8.00
	2368	22c Christmas (Ornaments), 10/23/87, Holiday, CA	16.00
	2369	22c 1988 Winter Olympics, 1/10/88, Anchorage, AK	10.00

1988

	2370	22c Australia Bicentennial, 1/26/88, DC	10.00
	2371	22c James Johnson, 2/2/88, Nashville, TN	10.00
	2371	James Johnson (not 1st day), 2/3/88, Jacksonville, FL	28.00
	2371	James Johnson (not 1st day), 2/11/88, Baltimore, MD	28.00
	2372-2375	22c Cats, 2/5/88, New York, NY	12.00
	2376	22c Knute Rockne, 3/9/88, Notre Dame, IN	15.00
	2377	25c Francis Ouimet, 6/13/88, Brookline, MA	10.00
	2379	45c Love, 8/8/88, Shreveport, LA	10.00
	2380	25c 1988 Summer Olympics, 8/19/88, Colorado Springs, CO	10.00
	2385a	25c Classic Cars, booklet pane of S, 8/25/88, Detroit, MI	12.00
	2386-2389	25c Antarctic Explorers, 9/14/88, DC	10.00
	2390-2393	25c Carousel Animals, 10/1/88, Sandusky, OH	30.00
	2394	$8.75 Express Mail, 10/6/88, Terre Haute, IN	35.00
	2396a, 2398a	25c Special Occasions, booklet pane orb, 10/22/88, King of Prussia, PA	15.00
	2399	25c Christmas (Madonna), 10/20/88, DC	10.00
	2400	25c Christmas (Sleigh & Village), 10/20/88, Berlin, NH	10.00

1989

	2401	25c Montana Statehood, 1/15/89, Helena, MT	8.00
	2402	25c A. Phillip Randolph, 2/3/89, New York, NY	6.00
	2403	25c North Dakota Statehood, 2/21/89, Bismarck, ND	6.00
	2404	25c Washington Statehood, 2/22/89, Olympia, WA	6.00

	2409a	25¢ **Steamboats**, booklet pane of 5, 3/3/89, New Orleans, LA 10.00
	2410	25¢ **World Stamp Expo**, 3/16/89, New York, NY 6.00
	2411	25¢ **Artuno Toscanini**, 3/25/89, New York, NY 6.00

1989-90 Constitution Bicentennial

	2412	25¢ **House of Representatives**, 4/4/89, DC................................6.00
	2413	25¢ **U.S. Senate**, 4/6/89, DC 100.00
	2414	25¢ **Executive Branch**, 4/16/89, Mr. Vernon, VA 6.00
	2415	25¢ **U.S. Supreme Court**, 2/2/90, DC 6.00

1989

	2416	25¢ **South Dakota Statehood**, 5/3/89, Pierre, SD 6.00
	2417	25¢ **Lou Gehrig**, 6/10/89, Cooperstown, NY 15.00
	2418	25¢ **Ernest Hemingway**, 7/17/89, Key West, FL 8.00
	2419	25¢ **Moon Landing**, 7/20/89, DC (USPS souvenir only)............8.00
		(with NASA program)..50.00
	2420	25¢ **Letter Carriers**, 8/30/89, Milwaukee, WI ....—
	2421	& UX135 25¢ **Bill of Rights & 15¢ Philadelphia Cityscape**
		postal card, 9/25/89, Philadelphia, PA 6.00
	2422-2425	25¢ **Dinosaurs**, 10/1/89, Lake Buena Vista, FL 15.00
	2422-2425	**Dinosaurs** (2nd day), 10/2/89, Amarillo, TX.................8.00
	2422-2425	**Dinosaurs** (not 1st day), 10/2/89, Ann Arbor, MI 10.00
	2422-2425	**Dinosaurs** (not 1st day), 10/2/89, Beverly Hills, CA 6.00
	2422-2425	**Dinosaurs** (not 1st day), 10/24/89, Chicago, IL..............10.00
	2422-2425	**Dinosaurs** (not 1st day), 10/2/89, Grand Junction, CO....6.00
	2422-2425	**Dinosaurs** (not 1st day), 10/2/89, Lubbock, TX...............8.00
	2422-2425	**Dinosaurs** (not 1st day), 10/2/89, Memphis, TN..............14.00
	2422-2425	**Dinosaurs** (not 1st day), 10/2/89, New York, NY............10.00
	2422-2425	**Dinosaurs** (not 1st day), 10/2/89, Oklahoma City, OK 8.00
	2422-2425	**Dinosaurs** (not 1st day), 10/2/89, San Antonio, TX........18.00
	2422-2425	**Dinosaurs** (not 1st day), 10/3/89, St. Paul, MN............10.00
	2427, 2427a	25¢ **Traditional Christmas**, sheet stamp & booklet pane,
		10/19/89, DC..8.00
	2428, 2429a	25¢ **Contemporary Christmas**, sheet stamp & booklet pane,
		10/19/89, Westport, CT...8.00
	2431	25¢ **Eagle & Shield**, self-adhesive stamp, 11/10/89,
		Virginia Beach, VA..6.00
	2433	**World Stamp Expo '89**, souvenir sheet, 11/17/89, DC 10.00
	2434-2437	25¢ **Traditional Mail Delivery**, 11 / 19/90, DC.............10.00
	2438	**Traditional Mail Delivery**, souvenir sheet, 11/28/89, DC..........10.00

1990

	2439	25¢ **Idaho Statehood**, 1/6/90, Boise, ID 6.00
	2440, 2441a	25¢ **Love**, sheet stamp & booklet pane, 1/18/90, Romance, AR....6.00
	2442	25¢ **Ida B. Wells**, 2/1/90, Chicago, IL.................................6.00
	2443a	25¢ **Beach Umbrella**, booklet pane, 2/3/90, Sarasota, FL............6.00
	2444	25¢ **Wyoming Statehood**, 2/23/90, Cheyenne, WY 6.00
	2445-2446	25¢ **Classic Films**, 3/23/90, Hollywood, CA 10.00
	2449	25¢ **Marianne Moore**, 4/18/90, Brooklyn, NY......................6.00

1990 Transportation Coils

| | 2452 | 5¢ **Circus Wagon**, 8/31/90, Syracuse, NY (2 types).................8.00 |
| | 2468 | $1 **Seaplane**, 4/20/90, Phoenix, AZ..................................10.00 |

1990

- 2474a 25c **Lighthouse**, booklet pane of 5, 4/26/90, DC.................................10.00
- 2475 25c **Flag**, plastic self-adhesive ATM stamp, 5/18/90, Seattle, WA..........6.00
- 2476 **$2 Bobcat**, 6/1/90, Arlington, VA...10.00
- 2496-2500 25c **Olympians**, 7/6/90, Minneapolis, MN.................................10.00
- 2505a 25c **Indian Headresses**, booklet pane of 5, 8/17/90, Cody, WY..............6.00
- 2506 & 2507 25c **Federated States of Micronesia & Marshall Islands**, 9/28/90, DC...8.00
- 2508-2511 25c **Sea Creatures**, 10/3/90, Baltimore, MD, Grand Rapids, MI 10.00
- 2512 & C127 25c & 45c **Pre-Columbian Customs**, 10/12/90, Grand Canyon, AZ..6.00
- 2513 25c **Dwight D. Eisenhower**, 10/13/90, Abilene, KS...........................8.00
- 2514 & 2514a 25c **Traditional Christmas**, sheet stamp & booklet pane, 10/18/90, DC 8.00
  - Error program (2514 only) 12.00
- 2515 & 2516 25c **Contemporary Christmas**, sheet stamp & booklet pane, 10/18/90, Evergreen, CO 8.00
  - Error program (2515 only) 12.00

1991

- 2524 & 2527 29c **Flower**, sheet and booklet, 4/5/91, Rochester, NY 10.00
- 2528 29c **Flag with Olympic Rings** (not 1st day), 4/22/91, Austin, TX.........15.00
- 2528 29c **Flag with Olympic Rings** (not 1st day), 4/22/91, Bismarck, ND (set of 7) 12.00
- 2528 29c **Flag with Olympic Rings** (not 1st day), 4/22/91, Frankfort, KY....15.00
- 2528 29c **Flag with Olympic Rings** (not 1st day), 4/22/91, Indianapolis, IN 15.00
- 2528 29c **Flag with Olympic Rings** (not 1st day), 4/22/91, Jackson, MS 15.00
- 2528 29c **Flag with Olympic Rings** (not 1st day), 4/22/91, Juneau, AK 8.00
- 2528 29c **Flag with Olympic Rings** (not 1st day), 4/22/91, Lincoln, NE 10.00
- 2528 29c **Flag with Olympic Rings** (not 1st day), 4/22/91, Oklahoma City, OK 10.00
- 2528 29c **Flag with Olympic Rings** (not 1st day), 4/22/91, Pierre, SD..........15.00
- 2528 29c **Flag with Olympic Rings** (not 1st day), 4/22/91, Providence, RI...15.00
- 2528 29c **Flag with Olympic Rings** (not 1st day), 4/22/91, Raleigh, NC 15.00
- 2528 29c **Flag with Olympic Rings** (not 1st day), 4/22/91, Richmond, VA ...15.00
- 2528 29c **Flag with Olympic Rings** (not 1st day), 4/22/91, St. Paul, MN 15.00
- 2528 29c **Flag with Olympic Rings** (not 1st day), 4/22/91, Tallahassee, FL...6.00
- 2528 29c **Flag with Olympic Rings** (not 1st day), 4/22/91, Trenton, NJ 6.00
- 2530, C129, UC63, UC63a 19c **Balloon**, 40c **William Piper**, 45c **Eagle aerograms**, 5/17/91, Denver CO 12.00
- 2531 29c **Flag** (2 types), 5/30/91, Waterloo, NY..6.00
- 2532 50c **Switzerland**, 2/22/91, DC..6.00
- 2533 29c **Vermont**, 3/1/91, Bennington, VT 6.00
- 2534 29c **Savings Bonds**, 4/30/91, DC...6.00
- 2534 **Savings Bonds** (not 1st day), 5/1/91, Milwaukee, WI 6.00
- 2534 **Savings Bonds** (not 1st day), 5/1/91, New York, NY.............................10.00
- 2535-2537, U621 29c **Love stamps and envelope**, 5/9/91, Honolulu, HI 6.00
- 2538 29c **William Saroyan**, 5/22/91, Fresno, CA (2 types).............................6.00

1991-93

- 2539 $1 **USPS-Olympics**, 9/29/91, Orlando, FL..6.00
- 2540 $2.90 **Eagle & Olympic Rings**, 7/7/91, San Diego, CA 8.00
- 2541 $9.95 **Eagle & Olympic Rings**, 6/16/91, Sacramento, CA 18.00
- 2543 $2.90 **Futuistic Space Shuttle**, 6/3/93, Kennedy Space Center, FL.........8.00

1991

☐	2549a	29c Fishing Flies, booklet pane of 5, 5/31/91, Cuddebackville, NY 8.00
☐	2550	29c Cole Porter, 6/8/91, Peru, IN 6.00
☐	2551	29c Desert Storm, 7/2/91, DC...10.00
☐	2551	Desert Storm (not 1st day), 7/3/91, Charlotte, NC....................................18.00
☐	2551	Desert Storm (not 1st day), 7/3/91, Greensboro, NC................................18.00
☐	2551	Desert Storm (not 1st day), 7/3/91, Raleigh, NC 18.00
☐	2551, 2552	29c Desert Storm, 7/2/91, DC...35.00
☐	2553-2557	29c Summer Olympics, 7/12/91, Los Angeles, CA 8.00
☐	2558	29c Numismatics, 8/13/91, Chicago, IL...6.00
☐	2559	29c World War II, souvenir sheet of 10, 9/3/91, Phoenix, AZ..............10.00
☐	2560	29c Basketball, 8/28/91, Springfield, MA...10.00
☐	2560	29c Basketball (not 1st day), 8/28/91, Richfield, OH................................12.00
☐	2561	29c District of Columbia, 9/7/91, DC 6.00
☐	2561	District of Columbia (not 1st day city), 9/7/91, Houston, TX.............12.00
☐	2566a	29c Comedians, booklet stamps, 8/29/91, Hollywood, CA.....................8.00
☐	2567	29c Jan Matzeliger, 9/15/91, Lynn, MA 8.00
☐	2577a	29c Space Exploration, 10/1/91, Pasadena, CA 8.00
☐	2577a	Space Exploration (not 1st day), 10/18/91, Langley, VA 18.00
☐	2577a	Space Exploration (not 1st day), 10/18/91, Wallops Island, VA 18.00
☐	2578	29c Traditional Christmas, 10/17/91, Houston, TX 6.00
☐	2579, 2980-2985	29c Contemporary Christmas, 10/17/91, Santa, ID...............6.00

1992-93

☐	2594	29c Pledge of Allegiance (black), 9/8/92, Rome, NY 6.00
☐	2595-2597	29c Eagle & Shield, 9/25/92, Dayton, OH 10.00
☐	2605-2606	(10c) Eagle & Shield, coils, 5/29/93, Secaucus, NJ.......................10.00

1992

☐	2616	29c World Columbian Stamp Expo, 1/24/92, Rosemont, IL.................10.00
☐	2617	29c W.E.B. Dubois, 1/31/92, Atlanta, GA...10.00
☐	2617	W.E.B. Dubois (not 1st day), 2/1/92, Los Angeles, CA.............................6.00
☐	2617	W.E.B. Dubois (not 1st day), 2/12/92, Sacramento, CA.............................6.00
☐	2618	29c Love, 2/6/92, Loveland, CO...10.00
☐	2620-2623	29c Voyages of Columbus, 4/24/92, Christiansted, VI 6.00
☐	2624-2629	Columbian Souvenir Sheets, 5/22/92, Chicago, IL.......................40.00
☐	2630	29c New York Stock Exchange, 5/17/92, New York, NY 6.00
☐	2631-2634	29c Space Accomplishements, 5/29/92, Chicago, IL 6.00
☐	2635	29c Alaska Highway, 5/30/92, Fairbanks, AK 6.00
☐	2636	29c Kentucky, 6/1/92, Danville, KY 6.00
☐	2642a	29c Hummingbirds, booklet pane of 5, 6/15/92, DC.............................22.00
☐	2647-2696	29c Wildflowers, 7/24/92, Columbus, OH 8.00
☐	2697	29c World War II, souvenir sheet of 10, 8/17/92, Indianapolis, IN......10.00
☐	2698	29c Dorothy Parker, 8/22/92, West End, NJ 6.00
☐	2700-2703	29c Minerals, 9/17/92, DC..10.00
☐	2704	29c Juan Rodriguez Cabrillo, 9/28/92, San Diego, CA 6.00
☐	2705-2709	29c Wild Animals, booklet pane of 5, 10/1/92, New Orleans, LA.....6.00
☐	2705-2709	Wild Animals (not 1st day), booklet pane of 5, 10/2/92, Newark, NJ...6.00
☐	2710	29c Traditional Christmas, 10/22/92, DC..6.00
☐	2714-2718	29c Contemporary Christmas, 10/22/92, Kansas City, MO.............6.00
☐	2719	29c Christmas, self-adhesive, 10/28/92, New York, NY 6.00
☐	2720	29c Chinese New Year, 12/30/92, San Francisco, CA 6.00

1993

AIR POST STAMPS

☐	C30	30c Twin-motored Transport, 9/25/41, Kansas City, MO	70.00
☐	C32	5c Skymaster, 9/25/46, DC	70.00
☐	C34	10c Pan American Union Building, 8/30/47, DC	45.00
☐	C35	15c New York Skyline, 8/20/47, New York, NY	40.00
☐	C40	6c Alexandria Bicentennial, 5/11/49, Alexandria, VA	40.00
☐	C42	10c UPU, 11/18/49, New Orleans, LA	40.00
☐	C43	15c UPU, 10/7/49, Chicago, IL	40.00
☐	C44	25c UPU, 11/30/49, Seattle, WA	40.00
☐	C45	6c Wright Brothers, 12/17/49, Kitty Hawk, NC	50.00
☐	C46	80c Diamond Head, 3/6/52, Honolulu, HI	60.00
☐	C47	6c Powered Flight, 5/29/53, Dayton, OH	35.00
☐	C48	4c Eagle in Flight, 9/3/54, Philadelphia, PA	45.00
☐	C51	7c Blue Jet, 7/31/58, Philadelphia, PA	30.00
☐	C52	Blue Jet, coil, 7/31/58, Miami, FL	25.00
☐	C53	7c Alaska Statehood, 1/3/59, Philadelphia, PA	20.00
☐	C54	7c Balloon Jupiter, 8/17/59, Lafayette, IN	40.00
☐	C55	7c Hawaii Statehood, 8/21/59, Honolulu, HI	30.00
☐	C56	10c Pan American Games, 8/27/59, Chicago, IL (2 types)	20.00
☐	C57	10c Liberty Bell, 6/10/60, Miami, FL (2 types), uncanceled	20.00
☐	C58	15c Statue of Liberty, 11/20/59, New York, NY	25.00
☐	C59	25c Abraham Lincoln, 4/22/60, San Francisco, CA	30.00
☐	C60	7c Red Jet, 8/12/60, Arlington, VA	20.00
☐	C60a	Red Jet, booklet pane of 6, 8/19/60, St. Louis, MO	20.00
☐	C61	7c Red Jet, coil, 10/22/60, Atlantic City, NJ	30.00
☐	C62	13c Liberty Bell, 6/28/61, New York, NY	18.00
☐	C63	15c Statue of Liberty, 1/13/61, Buffalo, NY	25.00
☐	C64	8c Jet Airliner over Capitol, 12/5/62, DC (2 types)	30.00
☐	C66	15c Montgomery Blair, 5/3/63, Silver Springs, MD	12.00
☐	C67	6c Bald Eagle, 7/12/63, Boston, MA	14.00
☐	C68	8c Amelia Earhart, 7/24/63, Atchison, KS	18.00
☐	C69	8c Robert H. Goddard, 10/5/64, Roswell, NM	10.00
☐	C70	8c Alaska Purchase, 3/30/67, Sitka, AK	15.00
☐	C71	20c John James Audubon, 4/26/67, Audubon, NY (2 types)	12.00
☐	C72	10c 50-Star Runway, 1/5/68, San Francisco, CA	14.00
☐	C74	10c Airmail Service, 5/15/68, DC (3 types)	12.00
☐	C74	Airmail Service (not 1st day city), 5/15/68, Detroit, MI	25.00
☐	C75	20c "USA" & Jet, 11/22/68, New York, NY	14.00
☐	C76	10c Moon Landing, 9/9/69, DC (2 types)	22.00
☐	C76	Moon Landing, 9/10/69 (2nd day), Apollo, PA	40.00
☐	C77	& UXC10 9c Delta Wing Plane, 5/15/71, Kitty Hawk, NC (2 types)	18.00
☐	C78	11c Jet Airliner, 5/7/71, Spokane, WA	25.00
☐	C78a	Jet Airliner, booklet pane of 4 + 2 labels, 5/7/71, Spokane, WA	45.00
☐	C79	13c Winged Airmail Envelope, 11/16/73, New York, NY	10.00
☐	C79a	& C83 Winter Airmail Envelope, booklet pane of 5 + label & coil, 12/27/73, Chicago, IL	30.00
☐	C80	17c Statue of Liberty, 7/13/71, Lakehurst, NJ	20.00
☐	C81	21c "USA" & Jet, 5/21/71, DC (2 types)	18.00
☐	C82	11c Jet Airliner, coil, 5/7/71, Spokane, WA	35.00
☐	C84	11c National Parks Centennial, 5/3/72, Honaunau, HI	35.00
☐	C86	11c Electronics Progress, 7/10/73, New York, NY	30.00
☐	C87	18c Statue of Liberty, 1/11/74, Hempstead, NY	20.00
☐	C89-C90	25c & 31c Plane & Globe, 1/2/76, Honolulu, HI	25.00
☐	C91-C92	31c Wright Brothers, 9/23/78, Dayton, OH	14.00
☐	C93-C94	21c Octave Chanute, 3/29/79, Chanute, KS	14.00

☐	C95-C96	25c Wiley Post, 11/20/79, Oklahoma City, OK 14.00
☐	C97	31c Olympic Games, 11/1/79, Colorado Springs, CO............................14.00
☐	C98	40c Philip Mazzei, 10/13/80, DC...8.00
☐	C99-C100	28c Blanche Stuart Scott & 35c Glenn Curtiss, 12/30/80, Hammondsport, NY...15.00
☐	C101-C104	28c 1984 Olympic Games, 6/17/83, San Antonio, TX...................15.00
☐	C105-C108	40c 1984 Olympic Games, 4/8/83, Los Angeles, CA 18.00
☐	C109-C112	35c 1984 Olympic Games, 11/4/83, Colorado Springs, CO 18.00
☐	C113-C114	33c Alfred V. Verville & 39c Lawrence & Elmer Sperry, 2/13/85, Garden City, NY...8.00
☐	C115	& UXC22 44c Transpacific Airmail, 2/15/85, San Francisco, CA 8.00
☐	C116	44c Junipero Serra, 8/22/85, San Diego, CA......................................8.00
☐	C117	44c Settling of New Sweden, 3/29/88, Wilmington, DE......................14.00
☐	C117	Settling of New Sweden, 3/30/88 (2nd day), Gibbstown, NJ.............28.00
☐	C117	Settling of New Sweden, 3/30/88 (2nd day), Philadelphia, PA 22.00
☐	C118	& UXC24 45c Samuel P. Langley & 36c DC-3, 5/14/88, San Diego, CA..12.00
☐	C119	36c Igor Sikorsky, 6/23/88, Stratford, CT 12.00
☐	C120	45c French Revolution Bicentennial, 7/14/89, DC 8.00
☐	C122-C125	45c Futuristic Mail Delivery, 11/28/89, DC 10.00
☐	C126	Futuristic Mail Delivery, souvenir sheet, 11/24/89, DC 10.00
☐	C130	50c Antarctic Treaty, 6/21/91, DC 6.00
☐	C131	50c America, 10/12/91, Anchorage, AK 6.00

SPECIAL DELIVERY STAMPS

☐	E20	20c Special Delivery Letter, 10/13/54, Boston, MA 35.00
☐	E21	30c Special Delivery Letter, 9/3/57, Indianapolis, IN 30.00
☐	E22	45c Arrows, 11/21/69, New York, NY (2 types) 20.00
☐	E23	60c Arrows, 5/10/71, Phoenix, AZ...20.00

POSTAGE DUE STAMPS

☐	J89-J1011/2c-$5 Postage Due, 6/19/59, New York, NY (without due stamps) ..35.00

OFFICIAL STAMPS

☐	O138A & O141 15c & 25c Great Seal, coil, 6/11/88, Corpus Christi, TX............8.00

HUNTING PERMIT STAMPS

☐	RW54	$10 Redheads, 7/1/87, DC (without stamp) 15.00
☐	RW55	$10 Snow Goose, 7/1/88, DC (without stamp) 20.00
☐	RW55	Snow Goose, 7/1/88, DC (with stamp)......................................40.00
☐	RW55	Snow Goose, 7/1/88, Eden Prairie, MN (with any stamp canceled) 40.00
☐	RW56	$12.50 Lesser Scaup, 6/30/89, DC (without stamp) 10.00
☐	RW56	$12.50 Lesser Scaup, 6/30/89, DC (with stamp)..........................25.00
☐	RW56	$12.50 Lesser Scaup (not 1st day), 7/1/89, Lincoln, NE (with any stamp) 10.00
☐	RW56	$12.50 Lesser Scaup (not 1st day), 7/1/89, Lincoln, NE (with duck stamp) 35.00
☐	RW57	$12.50 Whistling Ducks (not 1st day), 7/1/90, Bloomington, MN (with any stamp) 10.00
☐	RW57	$12.50 Whistling Ducks (not 1st day), 7/1/90, Bloomington, MN (with duck stamp) 35.00
☐	RW58	$15 King Eiders, 6/30/91, DC (with any stamp)...................................10.00
☐	RW58	$15 King Eiders, 6/30/91, DC (with duck stamp)................................30.00
☐	RW58	$15 King Eiders (not 1st day), 7/1/91, East Dorset, VT (with any stamp) 10.00

☐	RW58	$15 King Eiders (not 1st day), 7/1/91, East Dorset, VT (with duck stamp) 35.00
☐	RW59	$15 Spectacled Eider, 6/30/92, DC (with any stamp)............................10.00
☐	RW59	$15 Spectacled Eider, 6/30/92, DC (with duck stamp)........................30.00
☐	RW59	$15 Spectacled Eider (not 1st day), 7/1/92, Jackson, NJ (with any stamp) 10.00
☐	RW59	$15 Spectacled Eider (not 1st day), 7/1/92, Jackson, NJ (with duck stamp) 35.00

STAMPED ENVELOPES

☐	U541	1 1/4c Benjamin Franklin, 6/25/60, Birmingham, AL 25.00
☐	U542	2 1/2c George Washington, 5/28/60, Chicago, IL................................30.00
☐	U543	4c Pony Express Centennial, 7/19/60, St. Joseph, MO 30.00
☐	U544	& UX48 5c Abraham Lincoln, 11/19/62, Springfield, IL....................15.00
☐	U547	& U549 1 1/4c Liberty Bell & Old Ironsides, 1/6/65, DC....................18.00
☐	U548	1 4/10c Liberty Bell, 3/26/68, Springfield, MA 18.00
☐	U550	5c Eagle, 1/5/65, Williamsburg, PA 18.00
☐	U551	6c Statue of Liberty, 1/4/68, New York, NY 15.00
☐	U554	6c Herman Melville, 3/7/70, New Bedford, MA..................................12.00
☐	U555	6c Youth Conference, 2/24/71, DC 25.00
☐	U557	& UC43 8c Eagle & 11c Jet Plane, 5/6/71, Williamsburg, PA 20.00
☐	U563	8c Bowling, 8/21/71, Milwaukee, WI 18.00
☐	U564	8c Aging Conference, 11/15/71, DC 25.00
☐	U565	8c International Transportation Exhibition, 5/2/72, DC....................18.00
☐	U567	10c Liberty Bell, 12/5/73, Philadelphia, PA......................................25.00
☐	U568	1 8/10c "Volunteer Yourself," 8/23/74, Cincinnati, OH 12.00
☐	U571	10c Seafaring Tradition, 10/13/75, Minneapolis, MN........................12.00
☐	U572	13c American Homemaker, 2/2/76, Biloxi, MS 12.00
☐	U573	13c American Farmer, 3/15/76, New Orleans, LA..............................15.00
☐	U574	13c American Doctor, 6/30/76, Dallas, TX 12.00
☐	U575	13c American Craftsman, 8/6/76, Hancock, MA................................12.00
☐	U576	13c Liberty Tree, 11/8/75, Memphis, TN 12.00
☐	U577	2c Star & Pinwheel, 9/10/76, Hempstead, NY 10.00
☐	U578	2.1c (numerals), 6/3/77, Houston, TX 10.00
☐	U582	13c Bicentennial, 10/15/76, Los Angeles, CA....................................12.00
☐	U587	15c Auto Racing, 9/2/78, Ontario, CA 14.00
☐	U589	3.1c "authorized nonprofit organization," 5/18/79, Denver, CO........10.00
☐	U595	15c Veterinary Medicine, 7/24/79, Seattle, WA 10.00
☐	U597	15c Highwheeler Bicycle, 5/16/80, Baltimore, MD............................10.00
☐	U598	15c America's Cup, 9/15/80, Newport, RI 15.00
☐	U599	15c Italian Honeybee & Orange Blossoms, 10/10/80, Paris, IL 18.00
☐	U600	18c Hand & Braille, 8/13/81, Arlington, VA..8.00
☐	U602	20c Great Seal of the United States, 6/15/82, DC 10.00
☐	U603	20c Purple Heart, 8/6/82, DC 10.00
☐	U605	20c "Remember Our Paralyzed Veterans," 8/3/83, Portland, OR..........6.00
☐	U606	20c Small Business, 5/7/84, DC..8.00
☐	U609	6c U.S.S. Constitution, 5/3/85, Boston, MA 8.00
☐	U614	25c "USA" & Circle of Stars, 3/10/89, Cleveland, OH..........................8.00
☐	U616	25c Love, 9/22/89, McLean, VA (2 types) 6.00
☐	U617	25c Shuttle & Space Station, hologram, 12/3/89, DC 10.00
☐	U620	11.1c Birds Nonprofit, 5/3/91, Boxborough, MA................................10.00
☐	U622	29c Magazine Industry, 10/7/914, Naples, FL 6.00
☐	U627	29c Environment, 4/22/92, Chicago, IL 22.00
☐	U629	29c Americans with Disabilities, 7/22/92, DC 6.00
☐	U630	29c Kitten, 10/2/93, King of Prussia, PA 10.00

AIR POST STAMPED ENVELOPES

UC18	6c DC-4 Skymaster, 9/22/50, Philadelphia, PA	30.00
UC33	7c Blue Jet, 11/21/58, New York, NY	35.00
UC34	7c Red Jet, 8/18/60, Portland, OR	30.00
UC35	11c Jet Airliner & Globe, 6/16/61, Johnstown, PA	35.00
UC37	8c Jet Airliner, 1/7/65, Chicago, IL	25.00
UC38	11c John F. Kennedy, 5/29/65, Boston, MA	15.00
UC39	13c John F. Kennedy, 5/29/67, Chicago, IL	20.00
UC40	10c Jet Liner, 1/8/68, Chicago, IL	15.00
UC42	13c Human Rights Year, 12/3/68, DC	18.00
UC44	15c Birds in Flight, 5/28/71, Chicago, IL	18.00
UC46	15c Hot Air Ballooning Championships, 2/19/73, Albuquerque, NM	15.00
UC47	13c Bird in Flight, 12/1/73, Memphis, TN	15.00
UC50	22c "USA," 1/16/76, Tempe, AZ	10.00
UC51	22c "USA," 11/3/78, St. Petersburg, FL	10.00
UC53	30c "USA," 12/29/80, San Francisco, CA	15.00
UC54	30c "USA," 9/21/81, Honolulu, HI	18.00
UC55	30c "USA" & Globe, 9/16/82, Seattle, WA	14.00
UC56	30c World Communications Year, 1/7/83, Anaheim, CA	14.00
UC57	30c 1984 Olympics, 10/14/83, Los Angeles, CA	12.00
UC58	36c Weather Satellites, 2/14/85, Goddard Flight Center, MD	8.00
UC60	36c Mark Twain & Halley's Comet, 12/4/85, Hannibal, MO	10.00
UC62	39c Montgomery Blair, 11/20/89, DC or Silver Spring, MD	10.00

OFFICIAL POSTAL STATIONERY

U079	& U080 45c & 65c red & blue, 3/17/90, Springfield, VA	6.00

POSTAL CARDS

UX45	& UY16 4c Statue of Liberty + 4c Statue of Liberty paid reply postal card, 6/28/71, DC	60.00
UX49	7c Map of Continental United States, 8/30/63, New York, NY	18.00
UX50	4c Flags & Map of United States, 2/22/64, DC	20.00
UX51	4c Americans "Moving Forward,", 9/26/64, DC	20.00
UX52	4c Coast Guard Flag, 8/4/65, Newburyport, MA	20.00
UX53	4c Crowd & Census Bureau Punch Card, 10/21/65, Philadelphia, PA	30.00
UX54	8c Map of Continental United States, 12/4/67, DC	15.00
UX55	5c Abraham Lincoln, 1/4/68, Hodgenville, KY	20.00
UX56	5c Woman Marine, 7/26/68, San Francisco, CA	20.00
UX57	5c Weather Vane, 9/1/70, Fort Myer, VA	15.00
UX58	6c Paul Revere, 5/15/71, Boston, MA	12.00
UX59	& UXC11 10c Map of Continental United States & 11c Emblem of Commerce Department's Travel Service, 6/10/71, New York, NY	15.00
UX60	6c New York Hospital, 9/16/71, New York, NY	22.00
UX64	6c John Hanson, 9/1/72, Baltimore, MD	12.00
UX65	6c Liberty, 9/14/73, DC	20.00
UX66	8c Samuel Adams, 12/16/73, Boston, MA	12.00
UX67	& UXC15 12c Ship's Figurehead & 18c Eagle Weather Vane, 1/4/74, Miami, FL	15.00
UX68	7c Charles Thomson, 9/14/75, Bryn Mawr, PA	10.00
UX69	9c John Witherspoon, 11/10/75, Princeton, NJ	10.00
UX70	9c Cesaer Rodney, 7/1/76, Dover, DE	10.00
UX71	9c Federal Court House, Galveston, TX, 7/20/77, Galveston, TX	20.00
UX72	9c Nathan Hale, 10/14/77, Coventry, CT	10.00
UX73	10c Cincinnati Music Hall, 5/12/78, Cincinnati, OH	15.00
UX74	(10c) John Hancock, 5/19/78, Quincy, MA	12.00

- [ ] UX76 **14c Coast Guard Cutter Eagle**, 8/4/78, Quincy, MA......................10.00
- [ ] UX77 **10c Molly Pitcher Firing Cannon**, 9/8/78, Freehold, NJ.....................12.00
- [ ] UX78 **10c George Rogers Clark & Frontiersmen**, 2/23/79, Vincennes, IN....12.00
- [ ] UX79 **10c Casimir Pulaski**, 10/11/79, Savannah, GA.......................................18.00
- [ ] UX80 **10c Olympic Games**, 9/17/79, Eugene, OR...12.00
- [ ] UX81 **10c Iolani Palace**, 10/1/79, Honolulu, HI..20.00
- [ ] UX82 **14c 13th Winter Olympic Games**, 1/15/80, Atlanta, GA....................15.00
- [ ] UX83 **10c Salt Lake Temple**, 4/5/80, Salt Lake City, UT..............................15.00
- [ ] UX84 **10c Rochambeau's Fleet**, 7/11/80, Newport, RI....................................18.00
- [ ] UX85 **10c Whig Infantryman**, 10/7/80, Kings Mountain, NC.......................14.00
- [ ] UX86 **19c Golden Hinde**, 11/21/80, San Rafael, CA..15.00
- [ ] UX87 **10c Cols. Washington & Tarleton**, 1 / 17/81, Cowpens, SC.................18.00
- [ ] UX89 **12c Isaiah Thomas**, 5/5/81, Worcester, MA...8.00
- [ ] UX90 **12c Nathanael Greene**, 9/8/81, Eutaw Springs, SC..............................14.00
- [ ] UX91 **12c Lewis & Clark Expedition**, 9/23/81, St. Louis, MO......................10.00
- [ ] UX93 **13c Robert Morris**, 11/10/81, Philadelphia, PA....................................10.00
- [ ] UX94 **13c Francis Marion**, 4/3/82, Marion, SC..12.00
- [ ] UX95 **13c Rene Robert Cavelier**, Sieur de la Salle, 4/7/82, New Orleans, LA10.00
- [ ] UX96 **13c Philadelphia Academy of Music**, 6/18/82, Philadelphia, PA.........10.00
- [ ] UX97 **13c Old Post Office**, St. Louis, 10/14/82, St. Louis, MO......................12.00
- [ ] UX98 **13c Gen. Oglethorpe Meeting Chief Temo-Chi-Chi**, 2/12/83, Savannah, GA..12.00
- [ ] UX99 **13c Old Post Office**, Washington, D.C., 4/19/83, DC..............................8.00
- [ ] UX100 **13c Olympics 84**, Yachting, 8/5/83, Long Beach,CA............................10.00
- [ ] UX101 **13c Ark & Dove**, 3/25/84, St. Clement's Is., MD....................................8.00
- [ ] UX102 **13c Runner Carrying Olympic Torch**, 4/30/84, Los Angeles, CA.........10.00
- [ ] UX103 **13c Frederic Baraga & Indian Guide**, 6/29/84, Marquette, MI.............8.00
- [ ] UX104 **13c Dominquez Adobe at Rancho San Pedro**, 9/16/84, Compton, CA..6.00
- [ ] UX106 **14c Charles Carroll**, 3/6/85, Annapolis, MD..6.00
- [ ] UX107 **25c Clipper Flying Cloud**, 2/27/85, Salem, MA......................................6.00
- [ ] UX108 **14c George Wythe**, 6/20/85, Williamsburg, VA......................................6.00
- [ ] UX109 **14c Thomas Hooker & Hartford Congregation**, 4/18/86, Hartford, CT..6.00
- [ ] UX110 **14c Stamp Collecting**, 5/23/86, Chicago, IL..8.00
- [ ] UX111 **14c Francis Vigo**, 5/24/86, Vincennes, IN...6.00
- [ ] UX112 **14c Roger Williams**, 6/26/86, Providence, RI..6.00
- [ ] UX113 **14c Miners**, 7/3/86, Mineral Point, WI..6.00
- [ ] UX114 **14c The First Muster**, 12/12/86, Boston, MA...6.00
- [ ] UX115 **14c Self-Scouring Steel Plow**, 5/22/87, Moline, IL.................................8.00
- [ ] UX116 **14c Convening of the Constitutional Convention**, 5/25/87, Philadelphia, PA..6.00
- [ ] UX117 **14c Flag**, 6/14/87, Baltimore, MD...6.00
- [ ] UX118 **14c Take Pride in America**, 9/22/87, Jackson, WY.................................8.00
- [ ] UX119 **14c Timberline Lodge**, 9/28/87, Timberline Lodge, OR..........................8.00
- [ ] UX121 **15c Blair House**, 5/4/88, DC...10.00
- [ ] UX122 **28c Yorkshire**, 6/29/88, Mystic, CT...12.00
- [ ] UX123 **15c Harvesting Corn Fields**, 7/2/88, Burlington, IA..............................12.00
- [ ] UX124 **15c Flatboat Ferry**, 7/15/88, Marietta, OH..12.00
- [ ] UX125 **15c Hearst Castle**, 9/20/88, Sun Simeon, CA.......................................10.00
- [ ] UX126 **15c Pressman**, 10/27/88, New York, NY...10.00
- [ ] UX127 **15c Red-Tailed Hawk & Sonora Desert**, 1/13/89, Tucson, AZ.............6.00
- [ ] UX128 **15c Healy Hall**, 1/23/89, DC..6.00
- [ ] UX129 **15c Great Blue Heron**, 3/17/89, Waycross, GA..6.00
- [ ] UX131 **21c Canada Geese & Mountains**, 5/5/89, Denver, CO..............................6.00
- [ ] UX132 **15c Seashore**, 6/19/89, Cape Hatteras, NC..6.00

☐ UX133 15c The Woodlands, 8/26/89, Cherokee, NC 6.00
☐ UX134 15c Hull House, 9/16/89, Chicago, IL 6.00
☐ UX138 15c Washington Cityscape, 11/26/89, DC 10.00
☐ UX139-UX142 15c Cityscapes, block of 4, 12/1/89, DC 12.00
☐ UX143 15c White House, 11/30/89, DC 10.00
☐ UX144 15c Jefferson Memorial, 12/2/89, DC 10.00
☐ UX145 15c American Papermaking, 3/13/90, New York, NY (2 types) 12.00
☐ UX146 15c Literacy, 3/22/90, DC 6.00
☐ UX147 15c George Caleb Bingham, 5/4/90, St. Louis, MO 6.00
☐ UX148 15c Isaac Royal House, 6/16/90, Medford, MA 6.00
☐ UX150 15c Stanford University, 9/30/90, Stanford, CA (2 types) 6.00
☐ UX151 15c Constitution Hall, 10/11/90, DC 6.00
☐ UX152 15c Chicago Orchestra Hall, 10/19/90, Chicago, IL 6.00
☐ UX154 19c Carnegie Hall, 4/1/91, New York, NY 6.00
☐ UX155 19c Old Red, 6/14/91, Galveston, TX 6.00
☐ UX156 19c Bill of Rights, 9/25/91, Richmond, VA 6.00
☐ UX157 19c Notre Dame, 10/15/91, Notre Dame, IN 6.00
☐ UX159 19c Old Mill, 10/29/91, Burlington, VT 6.00
☐ UX160 19c Wadsworth AtheneumLi, 1/16/92, Hartford, CT 6.00
☐ UX161 19c Cobb Hall, 1/23/92, Chicago, IL 6.00
☐ UX162 19c Waller Hall, 2/1/92, Salem, OR 6.00
☐ UX164 19c Columbia River Gorge, 5/9/92, Stevenson, WA 6.00
☐ UX165 19c Ellis Island, 5/11/92, Ellis Island, NY 6.00
☐ UX167 19c Wren Building, 2/8/93, Williamsburg, VA 6.00
☐ UX168 19c Holocaust Memorial, 3/23/93, DC 6.00
☐ UX169 19c Fort Recovery, 6/13/93, Fort Recovery, OH 6.00
☐ UX170 19c Playmakers Theater, 9/14/93, Chapel Hill, NC 6.00
☐ UX172 19c Beecher Hall, 10/9/93, Jacksonville, IL 6.00
☐ UX173 19c Massachusetts Hall, 10/14/93, Brunswick, ME 6.00

AIR POST POSTAL CARDS

☐ UXC2 5c Eagle in Flight, 7/31/58, Wichita, KS 35.00
☐ UXC3 5c Eagle in Flight, 6/18/60, Minneapolis, MN 25.00
☐ UXC4 6c Bald Eagle, 2/15/63, Maitland, FL 20.00
☐ UXC5 11c Emblem of Commerce Department's Travel Service,
         5/27/66, DC...20.00
☐ UXC6 6c Virgin Islands & Territorial Flag, 3/31/67, Charlotte Amalie, VI 20.00
☐ UXC7 6c Borah Peak, Lost River Range, 8/4/67, Farragut State Park, ID 35.00
☐ UXC8 13c Emblem of Commerce Department's Travel Service, 9/8/67,
         Detroit, MI (2 types) 15.00
☐ UXC9 8c Eagle, 3/1/68, New York, NY 15.00
☐ UXC14 11c Eagle, 1/4/74, State College, PA 10.00
☐ UXC16 21c Angel Gabriel Weather Vane, 12/17/75, Kitty Hawk, NC 15.00
☐ UXC17 21c Curtiss Jenny, 9/16/78, San Diego, CA 10.00
☐ UXC18 21c Gymnast, 12/1/79, Fort Worth, TX 10.00
☐ UXC19 28c Clyde Pangborn & Hugh Herndon, Jr., 1/2/81,
         Wenatchee, WA 10.00
☐ UXC20 28c Gliders, 3/5/82, Houston, TX 8.00
☐ UXC21 28c Speedskater, 12/28/83, Milwaukee, WI 6.00
☐ UXC23 33c Chicago Skyline, 2/1/86, Chicago, IL 6.00
☐ UXC24 36c DC3, 5/14/88, San Diego, CA 6.00
☐ UXC25 40c Yankee Clipper, 6/28/91, Flushing, NY 6.00

PLATE NUMBER COIL FDC

Since early 1981, nearly all coil stamps issued by the United States have plate numbers printed on the stamps at regular intervals. The tiny digits printed in the stamps' bottom margins have given rise to the fastest growing area of modern United States stamp collecting — plate number coils (PNC).

Not all plate numbers exist on FDC's — only the Ones that are printed before the stamp is issued or very shortly after the first day, during the grace period for submitting covers to be canceled.

Because some PNC first-day covers are scarce and expensive, and some forgeries have already appeared on the philatelic market, collectors are advised to have costly FDC's expertized.

SCOTT NUMBER	DESCRIPTION	PLATE NO.	SINGLE VALUE	STRIP OF 3 VALUE
☐ 1891	18c Flag, 4/24/81	1	75.00	150.00
☐		2	225.00	425.00
☐		3	325.00	525.00
☐		4	200.00	350.00
☐		5	150.00	—
☐ 1895	20c Flag over Supreme Court, 12/17/81	1	20.00	40.00
☐		2	100.00	200.00
☐		3	200.00	400.00
☐ 1897	1c Omnibus, 8/19/83	1	9.00	13.00
☐		2	9.00	13.00
☐ 1897A	2c Locomotive, 5/20/82	3	12.00	20.00
☐		4	12.00	20.00
☐ 1898	3c Handcar, 3/25/83	1	10.00	20.00
☐		2	10.00	20.00
☐		3	10.00	20.00
☐		4	10.00	20.00
☐ 1898A	4c Stagecoach, 8/19/82	1	10.00	18.50
☐		2	10.00	18.50
☐		3	10.00	18.50
☐		4	10.00	18.50
☐ 1899	5c Motorcycle, 10/10/83	1	10.00	15.00
☐		2	10.00	15.00

SCOTT NUMBER	DESCRIPTION	PLATE NO.	SINGLE VALUE	STRIP OF 3 VALUE
		3		2000.
		4	1200.	1800.
1900	5.2c Sleigh, 3/21/83	1	15.00	30.00
		2	15.00	30.00
1900a	Sleigh, untagged (Bureau precanceled), 3/21/83	1	800.	800.
		2	800.	800.
1901	5.9c Bicycle, 2/17/82	3	15.00	25.00
		4	15.00	25.00
1901a	Bicycle, untagged (Bureau precanceled), 2/17/82	3	2000.	2000.
		4	2000.	2000.
1902	7.4c Baby Buggy, 4/7/84	2	10.00	20.00
1902a	Baby Buggy, untagged (Bureau precanceled), 4/7/84	2	2000.	2000.
1903	9.3c Mail Wagon, 12/15/81	1	20.00	40.00
		2	20.00	40.00
		3	1000.	2000.
		4	1000.	2000.
1903a	Mail Wagon, untagged Bureau precanceled), 12/15/81	1		2500.
		2		2500.
		3	2000.	2000.
		4	2000.	2000.
1904	10.9c Hansom Cab, 3/26/82	1	17.50	35.00
		2	17.50	35.00
1904a	Hansom Cab, untagged (Bureau precanceled), 3/26/82	1	2000.	2000.
		2	2000.	2000.
1905	11c Caboose, 2/3/84	1	15.00	35.00
1906	17c Electric Auto, 6/25/82	1	17.50	30.00
		2	17.50	30.00
1907	18c Surrey, 5/18/81	1	20.00	45.00
		2	30.00	45.00
		3	700.00	1500.
		4	700.00	1500.
		5	100.00	200.00
		6	100.00	200.00
		7	400.00	800.00
		8	100.00	200.00
		9	450.00	900.00
		10	450.00	900.00
1908	20c Fire Pumper, 12/10/81	1	75.00	150.00
		2	150.00	300.00
		3	15.00	40.00
		4	15.00	40.00
		5	100.00	175.00
		6	100.00	175.00
		7	1000.	—
		8	1000.	—
		10	2500.	—
2005	20c Consumer Education, 4/27/82	1	25.00	40.00
		2	25.00	40.00
		3	25.00	40.00

SCOTT NUMBER	DESCRIPTION	PLATE NO.	SINGLE VALUE	STRIP OF 3 VALUE
		4................25.00		40.00
☐ 2112	(22c)"D"&Eagle, 2/1/85	1................10.00		17.50
☐		2................10.00		17.50
☐ 2115	22c Flag over Capitol Dome, 3/29/85	1................35.00		65.00
☐		2................15.00		25.00
☐		5................		2500.
☐ 2115b	22c Flag over Capitol Dome, inscribed "T" at bottom, 5/23/87	1................15.00		
☐ 2123	3.4c School Bus, 6/8/85	1................6.50		12.50
☐		2................6.50		12.50
☐ 2124	4.9c Buckboard, 6/21/85	3................7.50		13.50
☐		4................7.50		13.50
☐ 2124a	Buckboard, untagged (Bureau precanceled), 6/21/85	3................2000.		2000.
☐		4................2000.		2000.
☐ 2125	5.5c Star Route Truck, 11/1/86	1................7.50		12.50
☐ 2125a	Star Route Truck, untagged (Bureau precanceled), 11/1/86	1................		40.00
☐ 2126	6c Tricycle, 5/6/85	1................6.50		10.00
☐ 2126a	Tricycle, untagged (Bureau precanceled), 5/6/85	1................—		—
	FDC's of the 6c Tricycle untagged are not believed to be legitimate, but are listed here for reference.			
☐ 2127	7.1c Tractor, 2/6/87	1................		12.50
☐ 2127a	Tractor, untagged (Bureau precancel "Nonprofit Org."in black), 2/6/87	1................		30.00
☐ 2127a	Tractor, untagged (Bureau precancel), "Nonprofit 5-Digit Zip + 4" in black), 5/26/89	1................—		10.00
☐ 2128	8.3c Ambulance, 6/21/86	1................7.50		12.50
☐		2................7.50		12.50
☐ 2128a	Ambulance, untagged (Bureau precanceled), 6/21/86	1................2000.		—
☐		2................2000.		—
☐ 2129	8.5c Tow Truck, 1/24/87	1................—		10.00
☐ 2129a	Tow Truck, untagged (Bureau precanceled), 1/24/87	1................		15.00
☐ 2130	10.1c Oil Wagon, 4/18/85	1................7.50		10.00
☐ 2130a	Oil Wagon, untagged (red Bureau precancel), 6/27/88	2................		8.50
☐ 2131	11c Stutz Bearcat, 6/11/85	3................12.50		17.50
☐		4................12.50		17.50
☐ 2132	12c Stanley Steamer, 4/2/85	1................7.50		12.50
☐		2................7.50		12.50
☐ 2132a	Stanley Steamer, untagged (Bureau precanceled), 4/2/85	1................2500.		—
☐ 2132a	Stanley Steamer, B Press, untagged (Bureau precanceled)	1................2000.		2000.
	There was no official first day of issue for the B Press version of this stamp.Cacheted covers exist canceled September 3, 1987, the date the stamp was placed on sale at the Philatelic Sales Unit in Washington, DC, currently the earliest known postmark. The stamp actually was placed on sale prior to that date at other locations, so there is a possibility of even earlier covers.			
☐ 2133	12.5c Pushcart, 4/18/85	1................7.50		12.50
☐ 2134	14c Iceboat, 3/23/85	1................15.00		20.00

SCOTT NUMBER	DESCRIPTION	PLATE NO.	SINGLE VALUE	STRIP OF 3 VALUE
☐		2	15.00	20.00
☐		3	—	2500.
☐		4	—	2500.
☐	2134b Iceboat, B Press, 9/30/86	2		2000.
	There was no official first day of issue for the B Press version of this stamp. The earliest known use was September 30, 1986, but no cacheted covers are known.			
☐	2135 17c Dog Sled, 8/20/86	2	—	10.00
☐	2136 25c Bread Wagon, 11/22/86	1	—	12.50
☐	2149 18c George Washington, 11/6/85	1112	20.00	35.00
☐		3333	20.00	35.00
☐	2149a George Washington, untagged			
	(Bureau precanceled), 11/6/85	11121	45.00	75.00
☐		33333	45.00	75.00
☐	2150 21.1c Letters, 10/22/85	111111	15.00	25.00
☐	2150a 21.1c Letters, untagged			
	(Bureau precanceled), 10/22/85	111111	35.00	65.00
☐	2225 1c Omnibus, re-engraved, 11/26/86	1	7.50	12.50
☐	2226 2c Locomotive, re-engraved, 3/6/87	1		8.50
☐	2228 4c Stagecoach, re-engraved, 8/15/86	1		350.00
	There was no official first day of issue for Scott 2228, but cacheted covers exist canceled August 15, 1986, the earliest known use.			
☐	2231 8.3c Ambulance, B Press, untagged			
	(Bureau precanceled), 8/29/86	1		1000.
	There was no official first day of issue for the B Press version of this stamp, but cacheted covers exist canceled August 29, 1986, the earliest known use.			
☐	2252 3c Conestoga Wagon, 2/29/88	1		7.50
☐	2253 5c Milk Wagon, 9/25/87	1		7.50
☐	2254 5.3c Elevator, 9/16/88	1		7.50
☐	2255 7.6c Carreta, 8/30/88	1		7.50
☐		2		1000.
☐	2256 8.4c Wheel Chair, 8/12/88	1		7.50
☐		2		750.00
☐	2257 10c Canal Boat, 4/11/87	1		8.50
☐	2258 13c Patrol Wagon, 10/29/88	1		7.50
☐	2259 13.2c Coal Car, 7/19/88	1		7.50
☐	2260 15c Tugboat, 7/12/88	1		7.50
☐	2261 16.7c Popcorn Wagon, 7/7/88	1		7.50
☐	2262 17.5c Racing Car, 9/25/87	1		8.50
☐	2262a Racing Car, untagged			
	(Bureau precanceled), 9/25/87	1		10.00
☐	2263 20c Cable Car, 10/28/88	1		7.50
☐		2		60.00
☐	2264 20.5c Fire Engine, 9/28/88	1		7.50
☐	2265 21c Railroad Mail Car, 8/16/88	1		7.50
☐		2		1500.
☐	2266 24.1c Tandem Bicycle, 10/26/88	1		7.50
☐	2279 (25c) "E" & Earth, 3/22/88	1111		7.50
☐		1211		10.00
☐		1222		7.50
☐		2222		25.00
☐	2280 25c Flag Over Yosemite, 5/20/88	1		10.00

SCOTT NUMBER	DESCRIPTION	PLATE NO.	SINGLE VALUE	STRIP OF 3 VALUE
☐		2		10.00
☐		3		150.00
☐		4		150.00
☐	2280	25c Flag Over Yosemite, pre-phosphored paper, 2/14/89 5		20.00
☐		6		40.00
☐		7		8.50
☐		8		8.50
☐		9		60.00
☐		10		1500.
☐	2281	25c Honeybee, 9/2/88 1		10.00
☐		2		30.00
☐	2451	4c Steam Carriage, 1/25/91 1		6.50
☐	2452	5c Circus Wagon, engr., 8/31/90 1		6.50
☐	2452B	5c Circus Wagon, photo., 12/8/92 1		6.50
☐	2453	5c Canoe, engr., 5/25/91 1		6.50
☐	2454	5c Canoe, photo., 10/22/91 ....S11		6.50
☐	2457	10c Tractor Trailer, engr., 5/25/91 1		6.50
☐	2464	23c Lunch Wagon, 4/12/91 1		8.50
☐		3		7.50
☐	2468	$1 Seaplane, 4/20/90 1		10.00
☐	2518	(29c) "F", 1/22/91 1111		10.00
☐		1211		100.00
☐		1222		10.00
☐		2211		25.00
☐		2222		10.00
☐	2523	29c Flag over Mt. Rushmore, engr., 3/29/91 1		7.50
☐		2		7.50
☐		3		7.50
☐		4		7.50
☐		5		7.50
☐		6		7.50
☐		7		7.50
☐	2523A	29c Flag over Mt. Rushmore, photo., 7/4/91 11111		7.50
☐	2525	29c Flower, rouletted, 8/16/91 ......S1111		7.50
☐	2526	29c Flower, perf., 3/3/92 2222		7.50
☐	2529	19c Fishing Boat, 8/8/91 111		7.50
☐		112		15.00
☐		212		7.50
☐		424		250.00
☐	2604	(10c) Eagle & Shield, ABNC, 12/13/91 A11111		7.50
☐		.................................A11112		7.50
☐		.................................A12213		30.00
☐		.................................A21112		7.50
☐		.................................A21113		7.50
☐		.................................A22112		7.50
☐		.................................A22113		7.50
☐		.................................A32333		125.00
☐		.................................A33333		7.50
☐		.................................A33334		750.00
☐		.................................A33335		7.50
☐		.................................A34424		350.00

SCOTT NUMBER	DESCRIPTION	PLATE NO.	SINGLE VALUE	STRIP OF 3 VALUE
	............................A34426............................			350.00
	............................A43324............................			15.00
	............................A43325............................			15.00
	............................A43326............................			15.00
	............................A43334............................			15.00
	............................A43335............................			15.00
	............................A43426............................			25.00
	............................A53335............................			25.00
	............................A54444............................			50.00
	............................A54445............................			50.00
	............................A77777............................			750.00
2605	(10c) Eagle & Shield, BEP, 5/29/93 11111			6.50
2606	(10c) Eagle & Shield, Stamp Venturers, 5/29/93 ....S11111...............6.50			
2607	23c Flag Pre-sort, 9/27/91 ....A111			7.50
	............................A112............................			250.00
	............................A122............................			250.00
	............................A212............................			7.50
	............................A222............................			7.50
2608	23c Reflected Flag Pre-sort, ABNC, 7/21/92 ....A1111			7.50
	............................A2222			7.50
2608A	23c Reflected Flag Pre-sort, BEP, 10/9/92 1111......................			7.50
2608B	23c Reflected Flag Pre-sort, Stamp Venturers, 5/14/93 ....S111			7.50
2609	29c Flag over White House, 4/23/92 ....1............................			7.50
	............................2............................			7.50
	............................3............................			7.50
	............................4............................			7.50
	............................5............................			7.50
	............................6............................			7.50
	............................7............................			7.50

OFFICIAL STAMPS

O135	20c Great Seal, 1/12/83 ....1...................30.00			75.00
O139	(22c) Great Seal, 2/4/85 ....1...................35.00			80.00

COMPUTER VENDED POSTAGE

31	29c ECA GARD, 8/20/92 ....1............................			7.50

RESIGNATION, AND
DEATH-IN-OFFICE COVERS

All values given are for cacheted covers postmarked on the date of the presidents' inauguration, resignation or death-in-office. Uncacheted covers sell for about one-half of the catalogue value. Values for covers after 1945 are for unaddressed cacheted covers. Addressed covers after 1949 sell for about one-half of the catalogue value.

- [ ] **McKinley** Mar. 4, 1901 ....—
- [ ] **T. Roosevelt** Mar. 4, 1905 ....—
- [ ] **Taft** Mar. 4, 1909 ....—
- [ ] **Wilson** Mar. 4, 1913 ....—
- [ ] **Wilson** Mar. 5, 1917 ....—
- [ ] **Harding** Mar. 4, 1921 ....—
- [ ] **Harding** Aug. 2, 1923 ....—
- [ ] **Coolidge** Mar. 4, 1925 ....—
- [ ] **Coolidge** Aug. 3, 1923 ....—
- [ ] **McKinley** Sept. 14, 1901, Assassination cover Death in Office ....1500.
- [ ] **Hoover** Mar. 4, 1929 ....150.00
- [ ] **F.D. Roosevelt** 1st Term, Mar. 4, 1933 ....50.00
- [ ] **F.D. Roosevelt** 2rid Term, Jan. 20, 1937 ....200.00
- [ ] **F.D. Roosevelt** 3rd Term, Jan. 20, 1941 ....150.00
- [ ] **F.D. Roosevelt** 4th Term, Jan. 20, 1945 ....100.00
- [ ] **F.D. Roosevelt** Date of Death, Apr. 12, 1945, canceled at Roosevelt, NY 50.00
- [ ] **Truman** 1st Term, Apr. 12, 1945 ....125.00
- [ ] **Truman** 2nd Term, Jan. 20, 1949 ....50.00
- [ ] **Eisenhower** 1st Term, Jan. 20, 1953 ....15.00
- [ ] **Eisenhower** 2nd Term, Jan. 21, 1957 ....10.00
    Note: 1/20/57 was a Sunday. However, some Artcraft and Fluegel cacheted covers do have the 1/20/57 cancel.
- [ ]   With Artcraft cachet 35.00
- [ ]   With Fluegel cachet 75.00
- [ ] **Kennedy** Jan. 20, 1961 ....15.00
- [ ]   With Fluegel cachet 25.00
- [ ] **Kennedy** Assassination cover, Nov. 22, 1963 ....25.00
- [ ] **Kennedy** Assassination cover, Nov. 22, 1963, with FDC of
    Scott 1246 on May 29, 1964 ....20.00
- [ ] **L.B. Johnson** Jan. 20, 1965 ....5.00
- [ ]   With Fluegel cachet 25.00
- [ ] **Nixon** 1st Term, Jan. 20, 1969 ....8.00
- [ ] **Nixon** 2nd Term, Jan. 20, 1973 ....5.00
- [ ] **Nixon** Announces resignation, canceled Aug 8, 1974 on same cover
    canceled Jan. 20, 1973 ....20.00
- [ ] **Nixon** Resigns to Congress, Aug. 9, 1974 ....3.00
- [ ] **Nixon** Resigns to Congress, canceled Aug. 9, 1974 on same cover
    canceled Jan. 20, 1973 ....10.00
- [ ] **Ford**, V.P. Dec. 6, 1973 ....5.00
- [ ] **Ford** Aug. 9, 1974 ....4.00
- [ ] **Carter** Jan. 20, 1977 ....3.00
- [ ] **Reagan** Jan. 20, 1981 ....3.00
- [ ] **Reagan** Jan. 21, 1985 ....3.00
- [ ] **Bush** Jan. 20, 1989 ....3.00
- [ ] **Clinton** Jan. 20, 1993 ....3.00

PATRIOTIC COVERS OF WW II

Listed below are significant World War II patriotic dates. Values are for related, printed-cacheted covers, canceled on the appropriate date. The listed values reflect the work of the following cachet makers: Crosby, Fidelity, Fleetwood/Knapp, Fleetwood/Staehle, Fluegel, Richardson/Knapp, Smartcraft, and Teixeria.

In addition, Minkus and several other cachet makers made a group of general purpose patriotic covers such as "Win the War" and "Sink the Japs". These covers generally have a value of $3.00 each, while uncanceled covers have a value of 75c each.

WWII COVERS DESCRIPTION	CACHETED SINGLE
☐ Pearl Harbor, 12/7/41	100.00
☐ U.S. Declares War on Japan, 12/8/41	20.00
☐ Germany and Italy Declare War on U.S., 12/11/41	20.00
☐ Churchill arrives at the White House, 12/22/41	20.00
☐ Manila and Cavite Fall, 1/2/42	25.00
☐ Singapore Surrenders, 2/15/42	20.00
☐ Japan takes Java, 3/10/42	20.00
☐ Marshall Arrives in London, 4/8/42	20.00
☐ Air Raid on Tokyo by Doolittle, 4/18/42	25.00
☐ Fort Mills Corregidor Island Surrenders, 5/6/42	20.00
☐ Madagascar Occupied by U.S., 5/9/42	20.00
☐ Bombing of Cologne, 6/6/42	20.00
☐ Japan Bombs Dutch Harbor, AK, 6/6/42	20.00
☐ Six German Spies Sentenced to Death, 8/7/42	20.00
☐ Brazil at War, 8/22/42	20.00
☐ Battle of El Alamein, 10/23/42	30.00
☐ Invasion of North Africa (Operation Torch), 11/8/42	25.00
☐ Gas rationing is Nationwide, 12/1/42	20.00
☐ The Casablanca Conference, 1/22/43	30.00
☐ The Quebec Conference, 8/14/43	30.00
☐ Battle of the Bismarck Sea, 3/13/43	30.00
☐ Invasion of Attu, 5/11/43	30.00
☐ Italy Surrenders, 9/8/43	20.00
☐ Mussolini Escapes, 9/18/43	20.00
☐ U.S. Drives Germans out of Naples, 10/2/43	20.00
☐ Italy Declares War on Germany, 10/13/43	20.00
☐ Hull Eden Stalin Conference, 10/25/43	20.00
☐ U.S. Government Takes over Coal Mines, 11/3/43	20.00
☐ The Cairo Meeting, 11/25/43	30.00
☐ The Teheran Meeting, 11/28/43	30.00
☐ Soviets Reach Polish Border, 1/4/44	20.00
☐ U.S. Captures Cassino, 3/15/44	20.00
☐ D-Day Single Face Eisenhower, 6/6/44	100.00
☐ Invasion of Normandy D-Day, 6/6/44	20.00
☐ U.S. Bombs Philippines, 8/10/44	20.00
☐ Liberation of Paris, 8/23/44	30.00
☐ Liberation of Brussels, 9/4/44	25.00
☐ Liberation of Luxembourg, 9/10/44	25.00
☐ Liberation of Athens, 10/14/44	25.00
☐ Liberation of Belgrade, 10/16/44	25.00
☐ Invasion of the Philippines, 10/20/44	25.00
☐ The Pied Piper of Leyte-Philippine Invasion, 10/21/44	35.00

	Description	Price
☐	Liberation of Tirana, 11/18/44	25.00
☐	100,000 Yanks Land on Luzon, 1/10/45	25.00
☐	Liberation of Warsaw, 1/17/45	30.00
☐	Liberation of Manila, 2/4/45	25.00
☐	Yalta Conference, 2/12/45	25.00
☐	Budapest Liberated, 2/13/45	25.00
☐	Corregidor is Ours, 2/17/45	25.00
☐	Cologne is Taken, 3/6/45	20.00
☐	Historical Rhine Crossing, 3/8/45	20.00
☐	Bombing of Tokyo, 3/10/45	20.00
☐	Capture of Iowa Jima, 3/14/45	20.00
☐	Battle of the Inland Sea, 3/20/45	20.00
☐	Crossing of the Rhine, 3/24/45	20.00
☐	Okinawa Invaded, 4/1/45	20.00
☐	Japanese Cabinet Resigns, 4/7/45	20.00
☐	Liberation of Vienna, 4/10/45	20.00
☐	Death of Roosevelt-Truman becomes President, 4/12/45	65.00
☐	Patton Invades Czechoslovakia, 4/18/45	20.00
☐	Berlin Invaded, 4/21/45	20.00
☐	Berlin is Encircled, 4/25/45	20.00
☐	GI Joe and Ivan Meet at Torgau-Germany, 4/26/45	20.00
☐	Liberation of Italy, 5/2/45	20.00
☐	Berlin Falls, 5/2/45	20.00
☐	Liberation of Rangoon, 5/3/45	20.00
☐	5th and 7th Armies Meet at the Brenner Pass, 5/4/45	20.00
☐	Liberation of Copenhagen, 5/5/45	20.00
☐	Liberation of Amsterdam, 5/5/45	20.00
☐	Liberation of Oslo, 5/8/45	20.00
☐	Liberation of Prague, 5/8/45	20.00
☐	V-E Day, 5/8/45	35.00
☐	Invasion of Borneo, 6/11/45	20.00
☐	Okinawa Captured, 6/21/45	20.00
☐	United Nations Conference, 6/25/45	25.00
☐	American Flag Raised Over Berlin, 7/4/45	25.00
☐	Big Three Meet at Potsdam, 8/1/45	25.00
☐	Atomic Bomb, 8/6/45	65.00
☐	Russia Declares War on Japan, 8/8/45	20.00
☐	Japan Capitulates, 8/14/45	20.00
☐	Liberation of China, 9/2/45	20.00
☐	V-J Day, 9/2/45	35.00
☐	Liberation of Korea, 9/2/45	20.00
☐	Flag Raising over Tokyo-MacArthur takes over, 9/8/45	20.00
☐	Gen. Wainwright Rescued from the Japanese, 9/10/45	20.00
☐	Nimitz Post Office, 9/10/45	20.00
☐	Operation Crossroads, 6/3/46	100.00
☐	Bikini Atomic Bomb Test, 7/1/46	100.00
☐	Independence of the Philippines, 7/4/46	25.00
☐	Moscow Peace Conference, 3/10/47	20.00

☐☐ _____
☐☐ _____
☐☐ _____
☐☐ _____
☐☐ _____
☐☐ _____
☐☐ _____
☐☐ _____
☐☐ _____
☐☐ _____
☐☐ _____
☐☐ _____
☐☐ _____
☐☐ _____
☐☐ _____
☐☐ _____
☐☐ _____
☐☐ _____
☐☐ _____
☐☐ _____
☐☐ _____
☐☐ _____
☐☐ _____
☐☐ _____
☐☐ _____
☐☐ _____
☐☐ _____
☐☐ _____
☐☐ _____
☐☐ _____
☐☐ _____
☐☐ _____
☐☐ _____
☐☐ _____
☐☐ _____

☐☐ _____
☐☐ _____
☐☐ _____
☐☐ _____
☐☐ _____
☐☐ _____
☐☐ _____
☐☐ _____
☐☐ _____
☐☐ _____
☐☐ _____
☐☐ _____
☐☐ _____
☐☐ _____
☐☐ _____
☐☐ _____
☐☐ _____
☐☐ _____
☐☐ _____
☐☐ _____
☐☐ _____
☐☐ _____
☐☐ _____
☐☐ _____
☐☐ _____
☐☐ _____
☐☐ _____
☐☐ _____
☐☐ _____
☐☐ _____
☐☐ _____
☐☐ _____
☐☐ _____
☐☐ _____
☐☐ _____
☐☐ _____
☐☐ _____

☐☐ _____
☐☐ _____
☐☐ _____
☐☐ _____
☐☐ _____
☐☐ _____
☐☐ _____
☐☐ _____
☐☐ _____
☐☐ _____
☐☐ _____
☐☐ _____
☐☐ _____
☐☐ _____
☐☐ _____
☐☐ _____
☐☐ _____
☐☐ _____
☐☐ _____
☐☐ _____
☐☐ _____
☐☐ _____
☐☐ _____
☐☐ _____
☐☐ _____
☐☐ _____
☐☐ _____
☐☐ _____
☐☐ _____
☐☐ _____
☐☐ _____
☐☐ _____
☐☐ _____
☐☐ _____
☐☐ _____
☐☐ _____

INDEX TO ADVERTISERS